Gregory's

PACIFIC TRAVEL FACT FILE

30th edition 2006

PUBLISHED BY: BRAYNART PUBLISHING
(a division of Universal Publishers Pty Ltd)
PO Box 1530 Macquarie Centre
NSW Australia 2113
1 Waterloo Road
Macquarie Park NSW Australia 2113

WITHIN AUSTRALIA
Phone: (02) 9857 3730
Fax: (02) 9878 3016
Email: pacifictravel@universalpublishers.com.au

OUTSIDE AUSTRALIA
Phone: (612) 9857 3730
Fax: (612) 9878 3016
Email: pacifictravel@universalpublishers.com.au

PUBLISHING MANAGER: Glynne Keelan
Email: gkeelan@universalpublishers.com.au

INTERNATIONAL ACCOUNT CO-ORDINATOR: William Richardson
Email: wrichardson@universalpublishers.com.au

EDITOR: Jill Innamorati-Varley
Email: jvarley@universalpublishers.com.au

PRODUCTION MANAGER: Dominik Mohila
Email: pacifictravel@universalpublishers.com.au
Production Co-ordinator: Leeanne Yap
Email: lyap@universalpublishers.com.au

SALES CO-ORDINATOR: Tracey Tattersall
Email: ttattersall@universalpublishers.com.au

PRINTING: Sing Cheong Printing Co. Ltd, Hong Kong

National Library of Australia
Cataloguing-in-Publication Data
ISBN: 0 7319 1751 0

MAIN COVER PHOTO: Mooloolaba beach, Mooloolaba
Courtesy Tourism Queensland

Braynart PUBLISHING

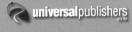

A DIVISION OF **universal**publishers

CW00357914

Ocean

UNITED STATES

● SAN FRANCISCO

● LOS ANGELES

MEXICO

● HONOLULU

HAWAIIAN
ISLANDS

HAWAII

KIRIBATI

TARAWA

FRENCH POLYNESIA

BORA BORA

● MANIHI

TAHAA

RANGIROA

RAIATEA

TETIAROA

SAMOA

APIA

MOOREA

PAGO PAGO

PAPEETE

TAHITI

TUVALU

AMERICAN
SAMOA

WALLIS

FUTUNA

FIJI ISLANDS

SAVUSAVU

VANUA
LEVU

VAVA'U

COOK ISLANDS

PORT
VILA

NADI

SUVA

AITUTAKI

ALOFI

A'TIU

VITI
LEVU

AVARUA

NIUE

VANUATU

NUKU'ALOFA

RAROTONGA

KINGDOM
of TONGA

EASTER
ISLAND

AUCKLAND

N
NW   NE

W   E

WELLINGTON

SW   SE

NEW
EALAND

S

International Dateline

surrender**taste**indulge...

...the **coolest** resort in fiji

The Pearl South Pacific offers guests the islands' ... lifestyle and ...
with styling, design, concept and service ... indulgence and personal ...
The Pearl South Pacific is allied to both The Greens South Pacific ... and ...
where living is ... and seasonal ...

...so come play.

www.thepearlsouthpacific.com
www.thegreenssouthpacific.com
info@thepearlsouthpacific.com

THE PEARL

SOUTH PACIFIC
FIJI ISLANDS

PACIFIC TRAVEL FACT FILE

WELCOME to our fresh, new look at the islands and facilities of the South Pacific

As you leaf through this, the 30th Edition of Gregoryís Pacific Travel Fact File, you will find a wealth of hotels, resorts, services and tour operators at your fingertips and a ready-to-go guide of to the South Pacific Islands.

Gregory's Pacific Travel Fact File throughout its 30 year history continues to be the 'bible' most utilised by travellers and operators throughout this beautiful region – a how-to of where to stay, where to play, what to do and how to get there.

Our new team piloted by William Richardson has taken the Guide forward, travelling extensively, increasing the coverage of countries and islands to 26 and expanding its reach and distribution to the four corners of the globe. In it you will find a new look, new design, new easy to read maps and an on line booking and enquiry service www.pacifictravel.com.au or www.pacifictravelfactfile.com – that puts you just a click away from paradise.

Where else in the world would you want to be?

We wish you sunny days, balmy evenings and happy travelling.

Jill Innamorati-Varley
Editor

**To order or subscribe to
Gregory's Pacific Travel Fact File
please contact Braynart Publishing.
Email: ttattersall@universalpublishers.com.au
or complete the subscription form on last page.**

VIRGIN BLUE SERVICE. EVERYWHERE.

26 DESTINATIONS • AUSTRALIA-WIDE
NEW ZEALAND • SOUTH PACIFIC

PHOTO: COURTESY TOURISM QUEENSLAND

AUSTRALIA

THERE'S much to learn about Australia. For instance, this island continent of some 20 million people has a coastline of 36,735 kilometres; endless miles of unspoilt beaches, tropical rainforest, mountain ranges and vast tracts of desert, making Australia a country of contrast.

The longest stretch of straight railway track in the world crosses the Nullarbor Plain that runs from Nurina in Western Australia to near Watson in South Australia – a track that is dead straight for 478 kilometres. Western Australia also has the longest stretch of straight road in Australia – 148 kilometres on the Eyre Highway at Caiguna. Crossing the southern edge of the Nullarbor Plain, it is the only sealed road from Perth to Adelaide, a 2700 kilometre drive.

It is home to the world's longest continuous fence known as the 'dingo fence', which runs through central Queensland for 5,531 kilometres. It is 1.8 metres high and is designed to keep sheep safe from Australia's native dog. On the subject of sheep, Australia's 140 million sheep (mostly merinos) are found on around 53,000 Australian properties, and produce more than 70 per cent of the world's wool. It is also the world's largest exporter of beef with 24 million head of cattle.

It's a country with over 7,000 beaches – more than any other nation and flourishing flora with at least 25,000 species of plants, while Europe only supports 17,500.

Spending Christmas at the beach or skiing in August may seem strange but Australia's seasons are the opposite of the northern hemisphere – summer officially starts in December and winter in June. But even in winter you'll enjoy blue skies and warm, bright days.

Australia's climate and the fact that it is the driest continent on earth makes it a fabulous holiday destination all year round, whatever you're planning to do. In the Australian winter you can ski in the southern states one day and be diving in the balmy waters of the Great Barrier Reef in Queensland the next. Such temperate conditions make al fresco dining, sublime days on the beach or the water, outdoor barbeques, and a huge variety of sports a way of life here. No wonder Aussies believe life is for living!

One of the country's most easily recognised mammals, the kangaroo is unique to Australia. There are more kangaroos in Australia now than when Australia was first settled, estimated to be around 40 million.

AUSTRALIA AT A GLANCE

TOURISM AUSTRALIA
Post: GPO Box 2721, Sydney NSW 2001
Ph (612) 9360 1111 Fax (612) 9331 6469
Email: corpaffairs@tourism.australia.com
Website: www.tourism.australia.com

GEOGRAPHIC LOCATION

Australia is the sixth largest country in the world. It's about the same size as the 48 mainland states of the USA and 50 per cent larger than Europe, but has the lowest population density in the world - only two people per square kilometre.

AIRLINES

Airlines offering competitive fares fly to Australia on a regular basis, whether from the US and Canada or from the UK, Europe and Asia. You can fly direct or island hop across the Pacific to a number of international gateways on the eastern seaboard including Sydney, Melbourne, Brisbane, Cairns and Hobart. Around-the-world tickets to Australia are often a great deal as they offer airline flexibility and a number of stops. And circle-Pacific tickets are a cost-effective option for travellers from the US, Asia and New Zealand.

ARRIVAL/DEPARTURE INFORMATION

A valid passport or similar acceptable travel document is required of all people wishing to travel to and enter Australia. Everyone, except holders of Australian and New Zealand passports, requires a visa to enter Australia. New Zealand passport holders apply for a visa upon arrival in Australia. All other passport holders must hold a visa before travelling to Australia.

Customs - There are strict laws prohibiting or restricting the entry of drugs, steroids, weapons, firearms, protected wildlife and associated products.

Australia's environment is unique. Food, plant and animal products from overseas could introduce destructive pests and diseases to the country. Quarantine items include fresh or packaged food, fruit, eggs, meat, vegetables, seeds, skins, feathers, wood and plants. Failure to declare food, plant and animal material could result in serious fines.

Each traveller over 18 years of age can bring 2250ml of alcoholic liquor and 250 cigarettes or 250 grams of tobacco products duty/tax free. There is a duty free allowance for goods, including those intended as gifts (a tax-free allowance) of $A900 per person or $A450 per person under 18.

CURRENCY

Australian currency ($A) is decimal with the dollar as the basic unit (100 cents equals one dollar). Notes come in $100, $50, $20, $10, and $5 denominations.

CLIMATE

Australia's seasons are the reverse of those in the northern hemisphere. From Christmas on the beach to midwinter in July, Australia's climate is typically mild in comparison with the extremes that exist in both Europe and North America. The Australian landmass is relatively arid with 80 per cent of the country having a median rainfall of less than 600 millimetres per year and 20 per cent having less than 300 millimetres (the average is 450 millimetres). Temperature ranges can also be substantial with highs recorded over 50 degrees Celsius and lows well below zero. Minimum temperatures, however, are typically not as low as those recorded in other continents. This is mainly because of Australia's relatively low latitude and lack of high mountains.

ELECTRICITY

The electrical current in Australia is 220-240 volts, AC 50Hz.

HANDICRAFTS

There is an enormous variety of authentic Aboriginal art for sale from traditional dot and bark paintings, modern 'earth pigment' screen prints, decorated jewellery and wood carvings, to boomerangs, didgeridoos, weapons, ceramics and scarves.

POPULATION

In April 2005 the resident population of Australia was in excess of 20 million.

LANGUAGE

English is the official and common language but Australia also has a unique colloquial language that can confuse visitors when they first hear it. From 'fair dinkum' to 'cobber', our colloquial language is common throughout the land.

Map not to scale © Copyright Universal Publishers 2005

LOCAL CONSIDERATIONS

Medicare is Australia's public health care system. Eligibility is generally restricted to permanent residents of Australia. Australia has Reciprocal Health Care Agreements with Finland, Italy, Malta, the Netherlands, New Zealand, Sweden, the United Kingdom and the Republic of Ireland. Minimise your exposure to the sun. Wear a broad-brimmed hat, cover up and apply water-resistant sunscreen frequently.

Always swim or surf at patrolled beaches between the red and yellow flags, which mark the safest area for swimming. Religion - Australia is a Christian country but nearly every other religion is represented including members of the Jewish, Moslem, Buddhist and Hindu faiths.

Tipping - Tipping is not obligatory in Australia. You are not obliged to give your tour guide a tip.

TELECOMMUNICATIONS

Australia offers modern and reliable telecommunication services. Telephone, post, email and Internet services are all readily available to visitors.

TIME ZONE

There are three time zones in Australia, running east to west. Eastern Standard Time (EST) operates in New South Wales, Australian Capital Territory, Victoria, Tasmania and Queensland. Central Standard Time (CST) in South Australia and Northern Territory. Western Standard Time (WST) in Western Australia. CST is half an hour behind EST, while WST is two hours behind EST.

TRANSPORT

Australia is a vast continent full of amazing sights. If you're here on a short trip, you may prefer to travel by air. Australia's domestic airlines provide extensive coverage allowing you to hop quickly between cities and sights. Or if you prefer a more leisurely pace, travel by rail or road. Australia has a vast network of well-maintained roads and highways with some of the most beautiful road touring in the world. Vehicle hire is simple. And all cities, except Hobart, are linked by a rail network.

BRISBANE

BEAUTIFUL weather and the busiest and largest retail precinct between Sydney and Singapore – that's Brisbane! Mixed in with over 2000 retail outlets in the Downtown city area alone, there is ready access to specialty shops, fine restaurants and eateries. Everything is within easy reach and the live, free entertainment in the famous Queen Street Mall which meanders for half a kilometre, often includes international acts and chart toppers.

The city of Brisbane nestles alongside the serpentine Brisbane River and along the strip at Eagle Street Pier, CBD side, you'll find many superb award-winning restaurants and eateries. Whether you are in the mood for al fresco or desire something more sophisticated and formal you'll find it here and of course the plethora of Asian eateries is testament to Australian's ongoing love affair with Asian cuisine. Aficionados of café culture are not forgotten either with many varied theme cafés throughout Brisbane that have become as much a part of the everyday life of the city as any in Europe. Brisbane has even become internationally recognised for such and don't be surprised if you find many top acts performing live in the bars, clubs and restaurants throughout town. They are as much at home in these gigs as they are performing in the stunning internationally-acclaimed Arts Centre.

No longer the large country town, Brisbane is as cosmopolitan and modern a city as you'd expect to find anywhere, with the added advantage that the glorious climate has helped to foster an ambience of relaxed quiet informality that you seldom find anywhere else. It is a character that is definitely and characteristically Australian.

There are many 'adventures' to suit a wide variety of tastes within short travelling distances around Brisbane. From the adrenalin rush of swimming with sharks or tobogganing down the world's largest coastal sand dunes to 'ghost busting' in a notorious decommissioned jail and inner city cemeteries – there's something for everyone. For outdoors pleasure seekers there is every diversion imaginable from snorkelling, diving, mustering cattle and those who simply want to get out amongst nature will find the pristine rainforests listed in the world heritage a joy to trek and explore!

In every sense, Brisbane is a 'new world city' and a traveller's delight – chances are, you'll want to come back again and again!

THE KOORALBYN HOTEL RESORT

LOCATION
Routley Drive, Kooralbyn,
Queensland 4285

EMAIL
golf@kooralbynresort.com.au

PHONE/FAX
Ph 1800 073 108
Fax (617) 5544 6260

FACILITIES
18 hole championship
golf course, 4-star
accommodation, conference
facilties, cinema, spa
and gymnasium,
swimming pool.

ATTRACTIONS
Golf, Aussie muster –
sheep shearing, whip
cracking, boomerang
throwing, kangaroo
spotting, horse riding,
4WD training facility, sky
diving, bowls, volley ball.

CREDIT CARDS
Amex, Diners,
MasterCard & Visa.

Kooralbyn Hotel Resort is a 4 Star Country Resort, Championship Golf Course and Conference Centre nestled in Queensland's Gold Coast Hinterland, just over 1 hours drive from Brisbane and the Gold Coast. The Resort is far enough off the beaten track to offer visitors a real "country" experience – but close enough to the main Centres to keep travel costs and time to a minimum. The Kooralbyn Golf Course has earned the respect and admiration of thousands of golfers since it opened over 20years ago – and it is still regarded as outstanding because of the natural environment and abundant wildlife. It was the original Resort Course in Australia, and it's rich history is the envy of many of the newer "designer" courses in Australia. During 2005 – substantial improvements will be undertaken to the Course – including the installation of state of the art watering systems, modifications to some holes, and a top class Club House/Pro Shop Facility. The improvements are aimed at returning Kooralbyn to it's rightful place in the top 20 layouts in Australia. The Resort offers many other attractions including the famous "Aussie Muster" – the only true outback experience in Queensland consisting of sheep shearing demonstrations, horse riding, whip cracking, boomerang throwing, and other activities. For the adventurous – there is sky diving and 4WD Training, whilst the less adventurous can choose from Mini Golf, Bowls or Volley Ball.

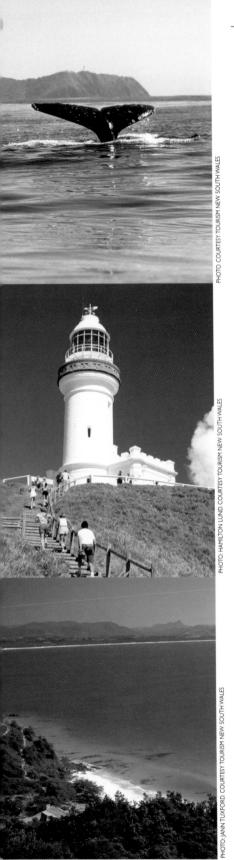

PHOTO COURTESY TOURISM NEW SOUTH WALES

PHOTO: HAMILTON LUND. COURTESY TOURISM NEW SOUTH WALES

PHOTO: JANN TUXFORD. COURTESY TOURISM NEW SOUTH WALES

BYRON BAY

FROM humble beginnings, Byron Bay has undergone many transitions from dairy farming to major meat exporter, followed by sand mining and whaling. However, in the last 40 years Byron Bay has been transformed into a popular tourist, alternate lifestyle and sea change destination.

It is located on the New South Wales north coast where the Cape Byron Lighthouse dominates Australia's most easterly point - 53° 39´ east, a popular place to visit for its spectacular views. Just off the Pacific Highway, 800 kilometres north of Sydney, 175 kilometres south of Brisbane, the Byron Shire has a population of close to 30,000, while the town of Byron Bay has a population of around 9000. Airports are located in Ballina (30 minutes south) or Coolangatta (60 minutes north) while buses and trains arrive regularly.

It is a destination renowned for its surfing beaches and beautiful rainforests where adventure sports, fine dining, live entertainment and alternative spiritual and health therapies are also available.

Idyllic summer temperatures range from an average of 21C - 28C and average winter temperatures of 15C - 21C, thus allowing both locals and visitors to enjoy plenty of outdoor activities including the many festivals throughout the year.

BYRON BAY ABORIGINAL CULTURE AND HERITAGE

Aboriginal people have lived and visited the area for at least 22,000 years and Byron Bay was known as a place of plenty - a point of land that was called Walgun, which means The Shoulder. It gave views, shelter and sandy beaches, seafood, wildlife, rainforest fruits and always clean spring water. Walgun was also a place for many Dreamtime stories.

Then about 6,000 years ago, sea levels rose and drowned eight kilometres of land around Cape Byron, leaving it exposed as a coastal promontory and submerging many ancient aboriginal sites. In the Cape's Palm Valley a surviving midden and open campsite is over 1,000 years old and quite possibly the only and definitely the oldest of its type in the region. The sites, which remain, are testament to a vibrant culture and an abundant environment.

The NSW north coast is the traditional territory of the Bunjalung people. Two sub-groups (or clans) included the Byron Bay area in their territory. The Arkwal were in the south; the Minjunbal had the north. It is estimated that 200 years ago, about 500 Aboriginals lived here.

BAY ROYAL APARTMENTS

LOCATION
Byron Bay, Australia

EMAIL
bayroyal@nor.com.au

PHONE/FAX
Ph (612) 6680 9187
Fax (612) 6680 9205

ADDRESS
24-28 Bay Street, Byron Bay, NSW, 2481

FACILITIES
Salt water swimming pool, full size tennis court, BBQ area, undercover key entry parking.

CREDIT CARDS
Bankcard, MasterCard, Visa.

The best beach in Australia now has the best accommodation! Lose yourself in the luxury and style of Byron Bay's premier self contained apartments nestled in the relaxed surrounds of Byron Bay's beautiful beachscape.

Located directly across from Byron's Main Beach and only a short stroll to all of Byron's restaurants and shopping facilities makes Bay Royal Apartments one of Byron's most sought after locations.

Guests can enjoy a game of tennis on the full size court exclusive to Bay Royal Apartments. Then relax by the secluded saltwater pool and large outdoor entertainment/barbeque area.

Each apartment has been elegantly decorated with attention to detail and finishing touches throughout. The living areas are spacious and comfortable ... perfect for entertaining or relaxing. All apartments have private balconies with ocean facing views.

ATTRACTIONS
Cape Byron Headland, the most easterly point of Australia, six fantastic beaches to choose from, whale watching - June & Sept/Oct, local markets in the area every Sunday, art galleries, abundance of eateries and fine dining restaurants, live music at most hotels each night.

BAYVIEW LODGE APARTMENTS

LOCATION
Byron Bay, Australia

EMAIL
baysand@linknet.com.au

PHONE/FAX
Ph (612) 6685 7073
Fax (612) 6685 8599

ADDRESS
22 Bay Street, Byron Bay, NSW 2481

CREDIT CARDS
American Express, Bankcard, Diners Club, MasterCard and Visa.

Located right opposite main beach, these fully self-contained apartments are set in lush tropical gardens and only 2 minutes walk to town centre. 21 units in block.

➤ Outdoor BBQ area
➤ Fully equipped kitchens
➤ All linen provided
➤ Internal laundry
➤ Private balconies

PHOTO COURTESY TOURISM NEW SOUTH WALES

CHUUK

DELICATE ECOSYSTEM

ONE of the four Federated States of Micronesia, Chuuk (formerly known of Truk) is composed of 15 large volcanic-based islands and 270 outer atoll islets. The main island, Weno (formerly Moen) is the capital and commercial centre, accommodating approximately 60 per cent of Chuuk's 65,000 residents. Part of the Caroline Islands, it stands in the heart of Micronesia, 480 kilometres north of the Equator and east of the Prime Meridian. Neighbouring countries include Guam (885 kilometres to the northwest), Japan (3200 kilometres to the north) and Hawaii (4500 kilometres to the east).

One of the world's most glorious diving destinations, it also draws visitors fascinated by its unspoiled beaches, unique ecosystems and cultural and historical attractions.

The central lagoon that is the focus of Chuuk is one of the largest in the world, measuring 85 kilometres at its widest point and enclosing an area of 2130 square kilometres. The entire lagoon has been declared a national monument.

BELOW THE WAVES

The islands within Chuuk lagoon include Dublon, Eton Fefan, the Faichuk islands and the Picnic Islands. Outside the lagoon, Chuuk's islands includes the Mortlock Islands, Hall Islands and Western Islands.

During World War II, Chuuk served as the naval headquarters of the Imperial Japanese Navy's North Pacific Fleet. As the American forces were island-hopping across the central Pacific, military strategists employed Operation Hailstorm, an aerial bombardment of the Japanese fleet that left much of the fleet on the bottom of Chuuk Lagoon.

It remains to this day, presenting a most unusual dive location that also serves as a dramatic reminder of the incredible conflict that was the war in the Pacific.

CHUUK VISITORS BUREAU
PO Box 1142, Weno, Chuuk 96942
Tel: (691) 330 4133 Fax: (691) 330 4194
Email: mfritz@mail.fm
Website: www.visit-fsm.org

Arrival/departure information

Visas are not required for tourist visits up to 30 days. Your 30 days start afresh each time you move to a different island group. US citizens can extend their permit for up to a year.

There is a US$10 departure tax from Chuuk.

CURRENCY

US dollars are the official currency. There are no commercial banks on Chuuk so make sure you've got enough cash to get by before you visit these areas.

CLIMATE

Water temperatures are 29° Celsius and incredibly calm between December and May. Average temperature above water is 30° Celsius.

ELECTRICITY

110/120V, 60Hz

HANDICRAFTS

Craftsmen carve Chuukese lovesticks – slender, dagger-shaped wooden rods carved on each side, which are sold in handfuls to tourists with an eye for exotic souvenirs. Traditional Mortlockese masks of hibiscus wood, once worn by men during battle and to ward off evil spirits, they are also carved for Chuuk's tourist trade.

POPULATION

Chuuk's total population is 53,319.

GEOGRAPHIC LOCATION

Chuuk State, with the famous 'Truk Lagoon' is located about 590 southeast of Guam and 3372 miles southwest of Hawaii. It consists of 11 mangrove-fringed islands in the Chuuk lagoon, and a series of 14 outlying atolls and low islands surrounding the lagoon. This lagoon is one of the world's largest enclosed lagoons. Enclosed by a 225 kilometre long barrier reef, the lagoon covers an area of 2128 square kilometres.

AIRLINES

Airline connections from Guam to Chuuk Lagoon are available through Continental Air Micronesia.

There are flights from Weno to Ulul, the main island; a couple of field trip ships also visit Ulul irregularly.

LANGUAGE

English is the official and common language while most indigenous languages fall within the Austronesian language family.

LOCAL CONSIDERATIONS

Light and casual clothing for Chuuk's tropical climate. Cotton dresses, shorts and sneakers or sandals are appropriate for women. For men, lightweight summer slacks or shorts, sport shirts or T-shirts and comfortable shoes or sandals. Sunglasses and light plastic raincoats are advisable. When visiting traditional areas, respect local customs and note that mini skirts and short shorts are frowned upon by the locals.

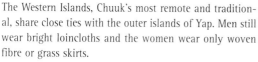

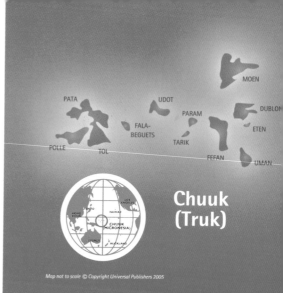

Map not to scale © Copyright Universal Publishers 2005

Chuuk (Truk)

The Western Islands, Chuuk's most remote and traditional, share close ties with the outer islands of Yap. Men still wear bright loincloths and the women wear only woven fibre or grass skirts.

There are no guesthouses on any of the islands, but the governor's office on Weno can sometimes help with accommodation arrangements.

The hospital on Weno is adequate to take care of all normal needs. Non-prescription medicines and toilet articles are available from general stores. Prescription medicines must be obtained from pharmacies or hospitals. Visitors are advised to bring enough prescription medicine to cover the period of their visit. Also, all over-the-counter medicines and toiletries may not be identical to items from their home city.

Typhoid, paratyphoid and tetanus shots are strongly recommended.

Despite the American influence, tipping is not really done. Religion – Christian.

TELECOMMUNICATIONS

The FSM Telecommunications Center provides international telephone, telex, and facsimile service, as does the Truk Stop Hotel's business centre.

TIME ZONE

GMT/UTC plus 10 hours.

TRANSPORT

Weno Island (Chuuk) has an efficient share taxi system and an extensive weekday system of commuter boats between its islands, and private speedboats do short runs throughout the country.

UNDERWATER GHOST TOWN

PRESERVED FOREVER

WITH dive gear firmly in place, the visitor enters the glorious blue of the Chuuk Lagoon. Almost immediately, an entirely different and quite alien world is encountered. Bright tropical fish and other marine life swarm the crystal clear waters but farther down are where the real mysteries lie.

Frozen in time, like an insect caught in amber, is a Japanese naval graveyard of some 60 ships. Some are scattered in pieces across the lagoon floor, others remain largely intact. The largest is the 163-metre passenger ship, the Heian Maru. As with most of the wrecks, divers can spends days exploring the dramatic aftermath of Operation Hailstorm.

The history of Chuuk had many such moments of conflict. Renowned as a savage and unconquerable people, the ancient Chuuk people were left largely alone by European explorers. The original settlers came to the area from points unknown 1500 years ago. While much of the Pacific was opened up by Spanish explorers, Chuuk was the last of the Micronesias to be converted to Christianity.

Today's Chuukese have maintained their rich cultural attributes of days gone by, with a deep respect for family lineage and customs. The culture is richly expressed in the intricate traditional arts – dances and chants, weavings, carvings and in the outer islands open ocean navigation and canoe building.

MICRONESIA'S GEM

Chuuk is easy to access by way of Continental Airlines services to Pohnpei and Guam. It is 10 hours ahead of Greenwich Mean Time with the local currency being the US dollar. Temperatures range around 27° Celsius throughout the year. English is widely spoken.

Chuuk's district centre on Weno, the second-largest island, is where visitors can experience a taste of island life by visiting the local stores jammed with everything from kerosene stoves to ladies wear and handicrafts.

Throughout the islands, the close value that Chuukese place on traditional values are readily apparent. There are few Pacific Islanders who are as close to nature as those on Chuuk and a visit to local villages and into the hinterland provides invaluable insights.

CULTURE AND COLOUR

THE pace of life slows right down outside Weno. The wide range of flora and fauna are an eco-tourist's delight with rare birds and wild orchids ready to tantalise the imagination at every turn. One enjoyable way of traversing the lagoon and visiting some of the many uninhabited islands and islets is by sea kayak. Modern sportscraft are also available and the sight of the tradewinds-filled sailcraft and windsurfers crossing the emerald waters is a sight beyond measure.

The outer reefs, filled almost to overflowing with tropical fish and colourful coral, provide another way to pass the lazy days.

Tonaachau Mountain is, at 229 metres, the loftiest peak on Weno. The mountain is the legendary home of the God Souwoniras and his divine son. Situated by the Wichon River and Falls, the Wichon Men's Meeting House is the spot where Weno chiefs are reputed to have met with Poomey, eldest of the six brothers who were the first chiefs of Chuuk. The shallow pool at the base of the Falls is still used for bathing and sport, just as it was in historic times. The site of Poomey's dwelling on a mountaintop may be seen from the peak and his gardens are nearby. Numerous petroglyphs are etched in the exposed basalt above the falls.

One souvenir of a visit to Chuuk will be the traditional lovesticks. In times past, slender wooden rods were individually carved by Chuuk men; each different from the other. A courting warrior would show his intended the design so she would know his brand and at night it would be passed through the woman's thatched hut in order to make an assignation. Legend has it that the lovestick would be intertwined in the woman's hair, silently awakening her and drawing her outside without rousing her family.

COOK
ISLANDS

AT the very centre of the Polynesian triangle, the Cook Islands group consists of 15 islands scattered across 2 million square kilometres of the Pacific Ocean. It is bordered to the west by Tokelau, the Samoas and Niue and to the east by Tahiti and the islands of French Polynesia. The islands, north to south, are Penrhyn, Rakahanga, Manihiki, Pukapuka, Nassau, Suwarrow, Palmerston, Aitutaki, Manuae, Mitiaro, Takutea, Atiu, Mauke, Rarotonga and Mangaia.

With a land area of just 240 square kilometres, the islands range from low coral atolls to the mountainous majesty of Rarotonga, the largest island of the group and home to the capital, Avarua.

AWAY FROM IT ALL

The Cook Islands' magical tranquillity is only matched by the people themselves. A smiling face greets the visitor at every turn in the road, the hospitality is warm and spontaneous, their dancing exuberant, their mood relaxed.

Here is to be found a wonderfully rewarding holiday experience, unmatched elsewhere; a special kind of unspoilt and unhurried pleasure and a rich contentment that will leave the visitor refreshed in body and mind, and in spirit, too.

The great Polynesian migration that peopled so many of the Pacific Islands was responsible for the traditional make-up of the Cook Islands.

With no snakes, wild animals or poisonous insects, the Cook Islands are safe and whatever isolated trail or beachside ramble the visitor takes, nature can be enjoyed in all its glory.

PICTURE: SOUTH PACIFIC TOURISM ORGANISATION

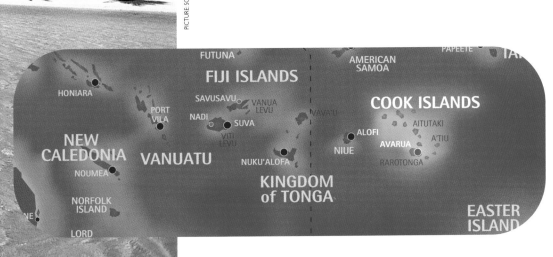

COOK ISLANDS
AT A GLANCE

COOK ISLANDS TOURISM CORPORATION
PO Box 14, Rarotonga, Cook Islands
Tel: (682) 29 435   Fax: (682) 21 435
Email: headoffice@cook-islands.com
Website: www.cook-islands.com

PICTURE: SOUTH PACIFIC TOURISM ORGANISATION

value of NZ$250 - no duty. Goods in excess of NZ$250 are liable for duty. All visitors must have a current passport. A bona fide visitor does not require an entry permit provided he/she possesses an onward passage (booked and paid for) and does not intend staying for more than 31 days. Vaccinations are not necessary unless arriving from an infected area. The Cook Islands are free of serious diseases and pests of plants and animals.
Departure Tax: Adult: NZ$25.00. Children 2-11 years: NZ$10.00. Infants under 2 years are exempt.

CURRENCY
The unit of currency is the New Zealand dollar, supplemented by coinage minted for local use, which is not negotiable outside the Cook Islands.

CLIMATE
Summer temperatures range between 29° Celsius and 23° Celsius. In July-September, the temperature ranges between 25.3° Celsius and 18.6° Celsius. Severe weather is rare and infrequent.

ELECTRICITY
Voltage is 240 volts 50 cycles, the same as New Zealand and Australia. Some hotels and motels have provision for 110 volt AC electric shavers.

HANDICRAFTS
Local crafts and souvenirs can be found at such places as Tarani's Crafts & Pearl and the Punanganui Marketplace.

LANGUAGE
Cook Islands Maori is the local language but everyone speaks English.

POPULATION
18,021 people (2001 Census).

GEOGRAPHICAL LOCATION
The Cook Islands are located on the Tropic of Capricorn, latitude 9 to 22 degrees south.

AIRLINES
International: Air New Zealand operates regular scheduled flights from New Zealand, Tahiti and Fiji. There are also connecting Air New Zealand flights from Australia, North America, Asia and Europe. Pacific Blue has a once a week service via Christchurch.
Domestic: Air Rarotonga flies regular services daily to most outer islands except on Sundays although there is one flight on Sunday evening to/from Aitutaki. For more information on Air Rarotonga visit www.airraro.com. Air New Zealand: www.airnewzealand.com.au and Pacific Blue www.virginblue.com.au

ARRIVAL/DEPARTURE INFORMATION
Rarotonga International Airport is two kilometres from Avarua. Visitors may bring in 200 cigarettes or 250 grams of tobacco or up to 50 cigars or the equivalent, two litres of spirits or wine or 4.5 litres of beer. Goods up to the

PICTURE: SOUTH PACIFIC TOURISM ORGANISATION

PICTURE: SOUTH PACIFIC TOURISM ORGANISATION

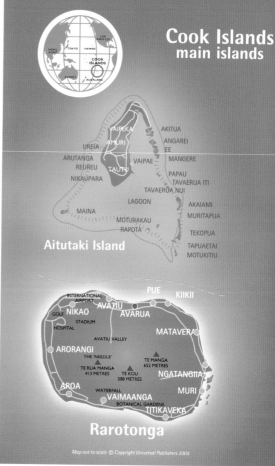

Cook Islands main islands

Aitutaki Island

Rarotonga

Map not to scale © Copyright Universal Publishers 2005

LOCAL CONSIDERATIONS

- Dress code is informal, however brief attire should not be worn when visiting towns, villages or churches. Nude or topless sunbathing will cause offence.
- Medical and dental services are available 24 hours a day.
- There are no poisonous animals or insects.
- Religion: Christian.
- Tipping is not customary.

TELECOMMUNICATIONS

All southern islands and some northern islands have a modern communications system providing telephones and on some islands, faxes.

Internet and email services are available on most islands. Cybercafes are located around Rarotonga.

Digital network for mobile phones on Rarotonga only.

TIME ZONE

The Cook Islands is 10 hours behind Greenwich Mean Time.

TRANSPORT

Cook Island Buses operate Monday-Saturday every half hour around Rarotonga. On Sunday one bus operates during the day in a clockwise direction only. Bus stops are situated around the island but a simple wave will ensure you are picked up and set down wherever you like.

Rental cars, motor scooters and bicycles are available for hire at some shops and hotels.

Driving is on the left hand side of the road.

Drivers are required to have a current Cook Islands Driver's Licence available from the Police Station in Avarua on presentation of own licence. The cost is NZ$10.00 with a compulsory practical test, NZ$5.00 for a motor scooter.

PICTURE: SOUTH PACIFIC TOURISM ORGANISATION

PICTURE: SOUTH PACIFIC TOURISM ORGANISATION

PICTURE: COOK ISLANDS TOURISM

PICTURE: NOEL BARTLEY

A WORLD TO EXPLORE

THE Cook Islanders love their sport and its an enthusiasm often shared by visitors as well. Although the lures of a Pacific Island destination often turn towards the less active pursuits, it's always entertaining to watch a game of rugby, soccer or league. The locals also take a healthy interest in such team sports as cricket and boxing.

Visitors to the Cook Islands during the Constitution Festival, held in August, will not only witness a range of cultural events but also some spectacular sporting tournaments.

The Cook Islands are renowned for their diving opportunities and these cater for any level of expertise. Canyons, caves and such varieties of coral as plate, shelving, mushroom and brain, make this underwater world an unusual terrain. Visibility is generally superb throughout the islands, ranging anywhere up to 60 metres.

ALL LEVELS OF EXPERTISE

Adventurers can dive on the wreck of the SS Maitai, which was wrecked just off shore from Avarua in December 1916. With no lives lost, the 3393-ton vessel, owned by the Union Steam Ship Company, had traded between the Cook Islands and Tahiti.

Dedicated snorkellers will also not be left out with some great sites, especially around Rarotonga and on the outlying islands. The reef surrounding Rarotonga has some special places, including the Muri Lagoon and the Titikaveka Lagoon.

Bushwalkers will enjoy the cross-country trail that begins at Avatiu Harbour and skirts the western side of Maungatea, emerging on the southern coast near Vaimaanga. Wigmore's Waterfall is one of the more spectacular sights along the way.

Other activities on the Cook Islands include deepsea fishing, saltwater fly and light tackle sportfishing, whalewatching, wind-surfing, sailing and golf.

There's no shortage of activities available, even if it's just lazing away the brilliant sunny days on the beach.

ARTS & CRAFT

Visitors to the Cook Islands will be pleasantly surprised at the variety of unique items of handicraft, jewellery, art and clothing available for sale. There is an excellent choice of retail outlets, all offering a friendly welcome and a word of local expertise when it comes to selecting that special item to take home.

One of the finest examples of local handicraft is the rito hat. Intricately woven and in many appealing styles, they are a vital part of every Cook Islands woman's dress. Another item of clothing is the Pareu. This two-metre-long length of cloth is a practical garment for the hot climate and the colourful fabric is often tie-dyed in an infinite variety of colours and patterns.

Among the most popular items of choice are wooden carvings, the most renowned being of the phallic demi-god 'Tangaroa'. Other pieces in demand are clubs, spears, canoes and slit drums (pate), from the northern islands.

Authentic handicrafts often come from islands that specialise in a particular item. For instance, ornate shell and seed hatbands and ei (lei) come from Mangaia, whilst finely woven pandanus mats are a souvenir of Pukapuka. Tapa decorated with traditional cultural patterns is made on Atiu.

The women of the Cook Islands are well known for their needlework, particularly the hand-stitched quilts known as tivaevae. Each quilter has her own distinctive colourful patterns and one piece may take several months to make, which is reflected in the cost.

The most romantic souvenir, of course, is the cultured black pearl. The northern island of Manihiki and Penryhn are world famous for producing this jewel of lustrous and sensual beauty. Reputable dealers belonging to the Pearl Guild of the Cook Islands can advise you on how best to make your choice from either loose pearls or jewellery.

PICTURE: SOUTH PACIFIC TOURISM ORGANISATION

PICTURE: COOK ISLANDS TOURISM

PICTURE: COOK ISLAND TOURISM

PICTURE: SOUTH PACIFIC TOURISM ORGANISATION

PICTURE SOUTH PACIFIC TOURISM ORGANISATION

PICTURE COOK ISLANDS TOURISM

PICTURE COOK ISLANDS TOURISM

RAROTONGA

PARADISE REGAINED

THERE'S something for everybody in Rarotonga, the main island and central focus of the Cook Islands group. Covering 67 square kilometres, Rarotonga commands a large part of the Cook's total land area but there are many regular visitors who wouldn't want it any other way.

It has a certain rakish appeal, especially in the capital of Avarua, that reminds many of the legendary South Pacific of Somerset Maugham and James A Michener.

Certainly, the busy little port at Avatiu Harbour, a short walk west of central Avarua on the north coast of Rarotonga, with a constant stream of activity with private yachts calling in from points of the globe, fishing boats, diving charters and inter-island shipping, points to this.

In Avarua proper, there's no way to describe the laidback yet subliminally electric ambience without recalling the town's raucous early days. Before the advent of television, mobile telephones and the Internet, the way around the world was a slow-going concern and a spinnaker filled with an ocean breeze made arriving at a place like Rarotonga a red letter day. Celebrations were called for and the social side of such a town sometimes verged on the wild.

Today, little has changed. Cook Islanders are ebullient people and mixed with a constantly changing population of tourists and itinerant yachties, there's always the chance for a long chat and an even longer evening recalling past triumphs and future glories. In this way, a visit to the privately-owned Rarotonga Brewery is worth considering.

QUIETER PURSUITS

Visitors in search of tradition and culture aren't starved for choices, either. The Cook Islands Library and Museum is a worthy place to start, followed by a visit to the National Cultural Centre.

The Marae Arai-Te-Tonga, located between Avarua and Matavera on the north-west side of the island, is considered the most sacred site on the island. The stone structures were vitally important in the social life of the Koutu, the royal court of the reigning Ariki or High Chief.

It was a special place where all offerings to the ancient gods were first assembled prior to being conveyed to and placed upon the Marae or meeting place. Investitures, annual tribal feasts and the presentation of the 'first fruits' were held there.

Although a well-maintained road circles the island, a far more interesting piece of Cook Islands history can be found a little farther inland. The Ara Metua is also known as the Great Road of Toi. Chief Toi is said to have arrived in the Cook Islands during the original Polynesian migration in the 7th and 8th centuries.

Toi presided over the creation of a grand road, built of paving stones, laid through the inland swamps. This all-weather road is still in existence, despite being almost 1000 years old.

When the early explorers arrived on Rarotonga, they were staggered to find the Great Road of Toi and while there's much in the way of legends to explain its presence, the original reason for its construction remains shrouded in mystery.

PICTURE: SOUTH PACIFIC TOURISM ORGANISATION

PICTURE: NOEL BARTLEY

PICTURE: SOUTH PACIFIC TOURISM ORGANISATION

THE EDGEWATER RESORT

www.edgewater.co.ck

LOCATION
Rarotonga Cook Island

EMAIL
stay@edgewater.co.ck

PHONE/FAX
Ph (682) 25 435
Fax (682) 25 475

ADDRESS
PO Box 121 Rarotonga
Cook Islands

FACILITIES
Air-cond. rooms with private balconies, car & bike hire, fresh water swimming pool, Health Spa, Hair Salon, Fitness Centre, 2 restaurants/bar, Tours Desk, close to golfclub and airport, floodlit tennis courts.

ATTRACTIONS
Beachfront location, beach/sunset weddings, snorkelling, swimming, dive trips, waterfront restaurant & bar, activities, tennis, golf

CREDIT CARDS
All major credit cards accepted

ACCOMMODATION
244 guestrooms, including 69 Deluxe Suites. All rooms are air conditioned and feature ceiling fan, colour TV with satellite channels, refrigerator, private balcony or patio, IDD phone, tea/coffee making facilities and daily maid service. The Beachfront and VIP Deluxe Suites also include a romantic spa bath, hairdryer, iron/ironing board, nightly turn-down service and superb lagoon and ocean views. All room rates include Daily Tropical Breakfast.

FEATURES
An idyllic Beachfront setting with spectacular sunsets. The resort is also set amongst 6 acres of tranquil, tropical gardens and offers 2 restaurants/bars, Tour desk, Internet/games room, Budget rent-a-car, souvenir shops, Black Pearl shop, Health Spa, Hair Salon, Fitness Centre, Guest Laundry, Romantic wedding options and an air-conditioned conference centre for up to 120 people.

ACTIVITIES
With the clear blue lagoon at your doorstep try out the swimming and snorkelling amongst the amazing colourful fish or perhaps reef walking. On site we also have a swimming pool, 2 tennis courts and a complimentary daily activities programme which may include water volleyball, Polynesian dance & drum lessons, Cook Island dancing, head/neck lei making. We are able to book other tours/activities also such as golf, fishing/dive excursions, 4WD safari trips, lagoon cruises etc etc.

FOR FURTHER INFORMATION
See website for rates. Prices quoted in NZD.

PACIFIC RESORT RAROTONGA

www.pacificresort.com

LOCATION
Muri Beach, Rarotonga
Cook Islands

EMAIL
rarotonga@pacificresort.
co.ck

PHONE/FAX
Ph (682) 20 427
Fax (682) 21 427

ADDRESS
PO Box 790
Rarotonga, Cook Islands

CONTACT
Thomas Koteka

FACILITIES
Fans, air conditioning,
self-contained, fridges,
IDD phones, tea/coffee
making, private balcony,
restaurants, bar, laundry,
boutique, safety deposit
facilities, babysitting
services, tour desk,
childrens club

ATTRACTIONS
Beachfront location, safe
swimming at all tides,
diving, snorkelling, kayaks,
row boats, game fishing,
island style weddings,
glass bottom boat cruises

CREDIT CARDS
American Express, Diners,
MasterCard & Visa.

ACCOMMODATION
64 one and two-bedroom self-contained apartments and villas, either beachfront or garden setting. All accommodations have fans and air conditioning, kitchen and in-room dining facilities, private patio, IDD telephone, daily housekeeping services. The two-bedroom villas are very spacious and each has two bathrooms, private laundry facilities. The Villas and Beachfront Units have TV's and CD Stereo's

FEATURES
24-hour Reception desk, Fully licensed Restaurant and Bar, Rental cars and bikes. Email and Internet access, Free laundry facilities. Coin operated clothes dryer, Tour desk, Giftshop, South Pacific Designer Shop, Wedding co-ordinator, Beach Hut and activities, Babysitting, Safety deposit facilities.

Relax by our pool or swim in the lagoon and sunbathe on magnificent Muri Beach.

ACTIVITIES
Rarotonga's best spot for watersports. snorkelling gear and kayaks are complimentary to houseguests. Glass Bottom Lagoon Cruiser offering a snorkelling Cruise with lunch provided.

On-site booking facilities for big game fishing, scuba diving, reef fishing, golf, tennis, lawn bowling, squash, sailing, windsurfing, local tours, outer island excursions, island-style weddings and island picnics.

FOR FURTHER INFORMATION
Please see our website for full booking details and current rates.

THE RAROTONGAN
BEACH RESORT & SPA

www.therarotongan.com

The Rarotongan
Beach Resort & Spa

LOCATION
Aro'a Beach, Rarotonga
EMAIL
info@rarotongan.co.ck
PHONE/FAX
Ph (682) 25 800
Fax (682) 25 799
ADDRESS
PO Box 103, Rarotonga
Cook Islands
FACILITIES
New Honeymoon Bungalow with private pool, new Beachside Junior Suites, Captain Andy's Beach Bar & Grill, TE VAKA Restaurant, Treetops Verandah Room, thatched Wedding/Dining Gazebo, personal wedding planner, wedding groups, SpaPolynesia, Salon VIVO, gift boutiques, art gallery, pool, activities hut, 24 hour internet booths, 24 hour reception, guest laundry, kids club, babysitting, tour/vehicle hire desk.

ATTRACTIONS
On Rarotonga's best beach – secluded, white sandy beach with all-day sun, crystal clear blue lagoon, superb off-beach snorkelling, all-tide swimming, fish feeding, spectacular sunsets, sunset cocktails, beachfront dining, fine Pacific cuisine, top island shows with authentic umu (fire pit) feast, Manager's Sunset Cocktail Party, beach weddings.
CREDIT CARDS
All major credit cards.

ACCOMMODATION
Superbly located directly on a white sand beach lapped by Aro'a Lagoon (the Lagoon of Love) with all-day sun and stunning sunsets. All guest accommodations offer verandah, air-conditioning, super king bed, satellite TV/DVD, in room movies, CD player/radio, safe, filtered tap water, room service. Whirlpool spa bath, open air shower in Deluxe Beachfront Junior Suites and Deluxe Beachside Junior Suites, full kitchen in Two Bedroom Beachside Suites and Grand Beachfront Suites. Incurable romantics enjoy the gorgeous Honeymoon Bungalow set in its own garden with private pool, open air shower and outdoor spa bath.

FEATURES
The Cook Islands have been described by USA's Conde Nast Traveler as having a "scenic brilliance". Here on delicious Rarotonga (the capital isle), The Rarotongan Beach Resort & Spa is nestled between the majestic lush mountains and the natural coral reef. Recognised as "the most Rarotongan of Rarotonga's resorts", this independent resort is renowned for its warm island hospitality and convivial South Seas atmosphere. For the perfect romantic escape stay at The Rarotongan Beach Resort & Spa before flying off together to The Aitutaki Lagoon Resort & Spa – simply sublime.

ACTIVITIES
The Rarotongan offers the perfect balance between seclusion and exciting diversions including complimentary snorkelling lessons, fish feeding, night snorkelling, kayaks, beach volleyball, tennis, guided village walks, coconut tree climbing and husking show, lessons in island dancing, flower garland (lei) making, pareu (sarong) tying, ukulele and log drum playing, palm-frond weaving, and island cooking. All island adventures are nearby including game-fishing, nature treks, 4WD mountain safari tour, lagoon cruise. Perfect for a complete tropical escape, relaxing yet re-invigorating.

FOR FURTHER INFORMATION
Email us for information on the latest-available special offers

SEA CHANGE VILLAS

www.sea-change-rarotonga.com

LOCATION
Titikaveka

EMAIL
info@sea-change-rarotonga.com

PHONE/FAX
Ph: (682) 22532
Fax: (682) 22730

ADDRESS
PO Box 937 Avarua
Rarotonga

FACILITIES
Swimming pool to each villa. Canoes, snorkelling gear, sun lounges

ATTRACTIONS
Deep sea fishing, lagoon tours, tramping, flying, tennis, golf

CREDIT CARDS
Visa, MasterCard, Amex.

Sea Change Villas has three absolute Beachfront villas which are two steps from the sweeping white sand lagoon and three Plantation Villas which are set amongst luxuriant tropical gardens featuring, banana, paw paw, coconut and mango trees. Plantation Villas are approximately seventy paces to the beach and all get lagoon views.

All villas have fully equipped designer kitchens, home theatre systems with complimentary DVD's and CD's provided.

Bedrooms have four-poster super king beds adorned with sheer netting and extra large ensuite bathrooms.

A unique aspect is that each villa has its own private fresh water swimming pool, which is designed so that you can sit and enjoy a refreshing cool drink while having a soak. Also relax by taking in the spectacular Beachfront Villas' lagoon views and Plantation Villas' lagoon and mountain views.

Come and enjoy the Cook Island experience while staying at our exclusive luxury villas.

CROWN BEACH RESORT

www.crownbeach.com

LOCATION
Rarotonga Cook Islands

EMAIL
info@crownbeach.com

PHONE/FAX
Ph (682) 23 953
Fax (682) 23 951

ADDRESS
PO Box 47
Rarotonga, Cook Islands

FACILITIES
Two Bars, Crystal clear swimming pool, Volleyball, Snorkelling, Close to Mini-market and bottle shop.

ATTRACTIONS
Spa and Massage Complex, Two Onsite Restaurants, Onsite Dive Centre, Full Concierge and Tour Desk, Sunset Weddings, Scooter and car rental and Beachfront location.

CREDIT CARDS
MasterCard and Visa card welcome (Amex accepted)

ACCOMMODATION
Our 21 private, individual and spacious villas are situated amongst 4.5 acres of tropical gardens. All villas have separate bedroom, bathroom and living room with a fully self-contained kitchen. Villas are fully air conditioned with ceiling fans, screen doors, TV/VCR, CD player, IDD telephone and outdoor deck with loungeing furniture. All guests receive a complimentary fruit basket on arrival, tropical buffet breakfast and complimentary snorkelling equipment and the use of our traditional canoes.

FEATURES
We are located on the sunset side of the island, which is ideal for romantic sunset wedding ceremonies and once in a lifetime escapes. We offer full concierge service, tour desk and orientation, laundry, room service and pool and beach service.

The Crown Beachside Restaurant offers relaxed, sunset dining right on our white sand beach with excellent food. The Windjammer Restaurant offers fine dining and is rated one of the best on the island.

Our Motto "Royal Pampering Island Style".

LAGOON LODGES

www.lagoonlodges.com

LOCATION
Lagoon Lodges is located on the sheltered South Western side of the island just 400 metres from the Rarotongan Beach Resort & 12 kilometres from the main township.

EMAIL
des@lagoon.co.ck

PHONE/FAX
Ph (682) 22 020
Fax (682) 22 021

ADDRESS
Box 45 Rarotonga
Cook Islands

FACILITIES
All villas complete with modern kitchens, insect screened windows. Indoor/outdoor terrace cafe offers complimentary daily tropical breakfasts & Sunday BBQ's while a TV lounge and bar are also available

ACCOMMODATION
Villas and Bungalows are individual, fully self-contained with dining and lounge areas, and outdoor terraces. Daily service, beach towels, hair dryers, IDD phones, in room safes.

Muri Beach Villa 3 Brm with own pool located at Muri lagoon – sleep 7, 2 bathrooms/laundry.
3 Brm Villa (private location) with Own pool – sleeps up to 7, 2 bathrooms/laundry.
2 Brm Villa Delux Polynesian Style each bedroom with ensuite – sleeps 6
2 Brm Villa Std Large units ideal for families
1 Brm Bung Modern spacious units – sleeps 4
Studio Unit Roomy with kitchen – sleeps 3
Rates from NZ$195 to NZ$715 per night inclusive of taxes.

FEATURES
Freshwater swimming (and children's) pool, children's play area, volley ball, 24-hour guests laundry, tour desk, regular bus services at the gate, rental bikes and cars. Easy access to white sand beach, snorkelling equipment and kayaks provided. Personal airport meet-and-greet service available.

MURI BEACH VILLA

www.lagoonlodges.com

LOCATION
Beachfront
Rarotonga

EMAIL
des@lagoon.co.ck

PHONE/FAX
Ph (682) 22 020
Fax (682) 22 021

ADDRESS
PO Box 45
Rarotonga, Cook Islands

FACILITIES
Self-contained, private house, pool, Gazebo, TV/Video/CD

CREDIT CARDS
All major cards accepted

A stunning waters-edge location on Muri Lagoon, close to the Pacific Resort and 10km from Lagoon Lodges. This 3Brm. (2 bathroom) Villa has fully equipped kitchen with oven, microwave, fridge/freezer and dishwasher. The open plan dining/lounge area with TV/Video/CD Stereo leads to an extensive covered terrace, with outdoor dining and large timber deck area. A Kikau Gazebo complements the private fresh water pool that overlooks the white sand beach. A fully equipped laundry, BBQ area, Kayaks and Snorkelling gear are provided. Bedding is Split Kings. Servicing is undertaken three times weekly and maximum occupancy is seven persons.
See our website for full details.
Rates from $715.

PUAIKURA REEF LODGES

www.puaikura.co.ck

LOCATION
Arorangi, South West side of the island

EMAIL
accommodation @puaikura.co.ck

PHONE/FAX
Ph (682) 23 537
Fax (682) 21 537

ADDRESS
PO box 397, Rarotonga, Cook Islands

HOSTS
Barry and Judy Warner

FACILITIES
12 Spacious, airy self-contained units with cooking, fridge/ freezers, one bedroom and studio units, all units have IDD phones and private balconies, 64 paces to a white sand beach and snorkelling lagoon.

CREDIT CARDS
Visa, MasterCard

ATTRACTIONS
Puaikura Reef Lodges is a small property with a welcoming atmosphere, friendly and relaxed providing opportunity to meet others or to relax in privacy on your own verandah which overlooks the lagoon and pool. Ideally situated with a store and a takeaway restaurant next door a and large resort within walking distance with onsite bicycle and moped hire with buses passing every 1/2 hour. Close to sporting amenities ie golf, dive centre, tennis.

Facilities include a swimming pool (13 meters), guest barbeque, honesty bar, library, e-mail station, onsite moped and bicycle hire plus free use of snorkelling gear.

CLUB RARO RESORT

www.clubraro.co.ck

LOCATION
Northern side of Rarotonga

EMAIL
holiday@clubraro.co.ck

PHONE/FAX
Ph (682) 22 415
Fax (682) 24 415

ADDRESS
PO Box 483
Rarotonga Cook Islands

ATTRACTIONS
A convenient 2km from town, complimentary tropical breakfast daily, Swim-up pool Bar, Free pool introductory scuba sessions twice weekly.

FACILITIES
Air-conditioned rooms, fesh water pool/poolbar, restaurants/bar, tennis court, games room, internet booth, tour desk, guest laundry.

CREDIT CARDS
All major credit cards accepted

ACCOMMODATION
This small intimate Resort offers 55 guestrooms in 3 categories - Premium Beachfront, Poolside and Garden. All rooms are air-conditioned and feature ceiling fans, IDD phone, satellite TV, Radio/alarm clocks, refrigerator, tea/coffee making facilities, ensuite bathroom, and private patio with outdoor furniture.

Club Raro has the only swim up pool bar on Rarotonga, and features three amazing sundecks with thatched umbrellas that overlook the sparkling lagoon and reef.

A broad range of eating options are available from either our Ocean View or Palms Restaurant serving breakfast, lunch and dinner daily. Happy Hour is a must between 5 - 7 and all day Saturday along with our Sunday pool BBQ. Scooter and pushbike hire are also provided.

White Wedding package and traditional Function Hall are available. Honeymooners receive a complementary room upgrade (subject to availability), a bottle of sparkling wine and a tropical fruit basket on arrival.

MURI BEACH HIDEAWAY

www.muribeachhideaway.com

LOCATION
Muri Beach Rarotonga
Cook Islands

EMAIL
mbhaway@oyster.net.ck

PHONE/FAX
Ph (682) 29 005
Fax (682) 29 005

ADDRESS
PO Box 3092
Rarotonga Cook Islands

HOSTS
Pauline & Theresa

ATTRACTIONS
located on Muri Beach lagoon. Restaurants & aqua sports centre & stores all with in easy walking distance

CREDIT CARDS
Visa, Mastercard

ACCOMMODATION
Beachfront location, 5 individually styled bungalows (Polynesian style) set amongst personally landscaped gardens.

Each bungalows with private balcony and natural inviting decor.

FACILITIES
Fully self-contained kitchen includes gas hob, fridge/freezer, microwave, blender, toasted sandwich maker, tea and coffee facilities, ceiling fans, irons, ironing boards, colour TV, radio clocks, hairdryers.

Phones available in each unit with their own number for friends and family to keep in touch.

Laundry facility, barbeque available, kayaks, snorkelling gear, hammocks.

ARRIVAL
Airport transfers (by arrangement), complimentary fresh fruit basket, milk, bottled water on arrival.

MANUIA BEACH BOUTIQUE HOTEL

www.manuia.co.ck

LOCATION
Beachfront Rarotonga,
Cook Islands

EMAIL
rooms@manuia.co.ck

PHONE/FAX
Ph (682) 22 461
Fax (682) 22 464

ADDRESS
PO Box 700
Rarotonga, Cook Islands

FACILITIES
Air conditioned, fans, tea/coffee
facilities, fridge, in room safe, IDD
phones, hairdryers, private balcony,
licensed restaurant, bar, pool

ATTRACTIONS
Situated on a white sand beach
amid tropical gardens on the
sheltered western sunset coast

CREDIT CARDS
All major cards accepted

ACCOMMODATION
24 Polynesian-styled thatched duplex bungalows with
large private verandahs, all have air conditioning, ceiling
fans, tea/coffee making facilities, refrigerator, IDD phone
and are all insect screened. Beachfront rooms have full
lagoon views. Garden rooms are set amidst lush tropical
gardens. Bonus: Welcome bottle of champenoise and
fruit juice, tropical breakfast daily, afternoon tea daily
with fresh baked goods, rooms serviced twice daily with
nightly turndown service with pillow gift. Free to view
DVD movies 3 x a week. No children under 12 years of
age please.

FEATURES
"The Right on the Beach" restaurant and bar offers a
wonderful dining experience. Island Night every Saturday
night. Beach BBQ every Wednesday night. Private dining
options are available. Fresh water swimming pool with
complimentary use of beach towels.
Free use of snorkelling gear. Hammocks and sun lounges
on the beach, Laundry service 7 days. Activities such as
diving, tours, car and scooter hire plus much more can be
arranged. Small weddings are a specialty. Spectacular
sunsets.
The hotel offers a perfect setting for a tranquil and
romantic getaway for the discerning holidaymaker.

THE RAROTONGAN SUNSET

www.rarotongansunset.com

LOCATION
Rarotonga, Cook Islands

EMAIL
welcome@rarosunset.co.ck

PHONE/FAX
Ph (682) 28 028
Fax (682) 28 026

ADDRESS
PO Box 377
Rarotonga, Cook Islands

MANAGER
Nicholas St Leger Reeves

FACILITIES
Air conditioned, full
kitchens, private
bathroom, colour TV, IDD
phone, alarm/radio,
ceiling fan, refrigerator

CREDIT CARDS
All major credit cards are
accepted

ACCOMMODATION
19 spacious self-contained apartments,
8 absolute beachfront with a further 11 set
among lush tropical gardens. All apartments are
fully air conditioned, have full kitchens,
microwaves, private bathroom, colour TV, IDD
phone, king size beds, alarm/radio, ceiling fan,
refrigerator, interconnecting rooms available on
request. All rooms are serviced daily except Sundays. Maximum pax in apartments is 3 adults.

FEATURES & AMENITIES
Cocktail bar overlooks the freshwater pool. Onsite
laundry, motor scooters, ice, bananas and
masks/snorkels, 1km to golf course 9 holes, tour
desk, meet/greet and airport transfers available in
private coach. There are 7 restaurants within
walking distance of the resort.

AROA BEACHSIDE INN
www.aroabeach.com

LOCATION:
Sunset Side Rarotonga
13 miles of white sand beach
EMAIL:
aroa@cookislands.co.ck
PHONE/FAX
Ph (682) 22 166
Fax (682) 22 169
ADDRESS:
PO Box 2160, Arorangi,
Rarotonga, Cook Islands
ROOM FACILITIES:
Fully self contained, lagoon
view from every deck,
ceiling fans and screened.
ATTRACTIONS:
Beachfront, good
Swimming/Snorkelling/
Kayaking, Shipwreck Hut-
guest bar with light snacks,
weekly BBQ with
entertainment

ACCOMMODATION
Studios all with ocean views, screened with ceiling fans, fully equipped kitchens with fridge/freezer & microwave, colour TV, radio/alarm CD player, DVD and VCR players available on request. Private bathroom and deck. Complimentary starter pack, fruit basket and tropical breakfast. All rooms are serviced daily.

FACILITIES
Beachfront, good swimming, snorkelling and kayaking. 'Shipwreck Hut' – guest beach bar with light snacks, weekly sunset BBQ with entertainment, 2 shops and cafes within 5 min walk and on bus-line.

SUNHAVEN BEACH BUNGALOWS
www.ck/sunhaven

LOCATION
Rarotonga, Cook Islands
EMAIL
sunhaven@
beachbungalows.co.ck
PHONE/FAX
Ph (682) 28 465
Fax (682) 28 464
ADDRESS
PO Box 100
Rarotonga, Cook Islands
HOSTS
Dennis & Patti Hogan
FACILITIES
Café, self contained, TV,
insect screened, pool
ATTRACTIONS
Beachfront kayaks,
snorkelling
CREDIT CARDS
Visa & MasterCard

The perfect hideaway located on the western side of Rarotonga nestled amongst tropical palms and sits at the edge of the lagoon.

Comprising – one-bedroom Bungalows and Suites, Studio Suite, Deluxe Studio and Standard Studio. 8 x beachfront/1 x garden. Our modern self-contained fully serviced rooms are superbly equipped. Our no children policy ensures peace and quiet.

FEATURES
Fully equipped kitchen, microwave, fridge/freezer, TV, IDD telephone, pedestal fans, over-bed ceiling fan, insect screens, large private covered verandah. A/C in some rooms.

AMENITIES
On site café, grocery store and laundry, BBQ, freshwater swimming pool, kayaks, beach loungers and hammocks, complimentary snorkelling gear. See website for rates.

WHITESANDS BEACH VILLAS
www.whitesands.co.ck

LOCATION
Beachfront
Rarotonga

EMAIL
whitesands@whitesands.co.ck

PHONE/FAX
Ph (682) 22 919
Fax (682) 22 918

ADDRESS
PO Box 1022
Rarotonga Cook Islands

FACILITIES
TV, CD, DVD, self contained,
white sandy beach

Whitesands Beach Villas is right on the beach in Titikaveka. One of the best places for snorkelling and swimming on the island. Each Villa features a mezzanine floor, full amenities, personal laundry, TV, DVD, CD Stereo and a large 6x3m deck overlooking the crystal-clear lagoon and white sandy beach. Daily housemaiding is provided for each villa. Each villa can sleep up to 5. Our rates are NZ$275 per night for 2 persons, and NZ$25 per extra person. We cater for honeymooners, couples, families and large groups of people. Children are welcome, special conditions apply. Visit us today, you won't be disappointed!

RAROTONGA BACKPACKERS
www.rarotongabackpackers.com

LOCATION
Rarotonga, Cook Islands
(sunset side of the island)
EMAIL
stay@rarotongabackpackers.
com
PHONE/FAX
Ph (682) 21 590
Fax (682) 21 590
ADDRESS
PO Box 3103, Avarua,
Rarotonga, Cook Islands
FACILITIES
double, twin, dorm, single or
self contained rooms,
swimming pool, internet,
laundry, fully equipped
kitchen, hot water, free
airport pickup (international
only)snorkelling island nights
CREDIT CARDS
Visa, MasterCard

Rarotonga Backpackers is a family run multi-level complex situated on the west side of the island. We are located in a secluded spot perched on a hill, 300 metres from the popular Raemaru track yet still only 400 metres from the beach and coconut rat race. We can offer dorm, double, twin/single rooms and self contained bungalow accommodation as well as beachfront houses for rent.

Watch out for our new complex right on the beach, opening September 2005.

Double rooms with ensuites, beach huts, self contained bungalows etc.

We hope to see you there!

Kia Manuia Paul and Rebecca Brown

MURI BEACHCOMBER

www.beachcomber.co.uk

LOCATION
Rarotonga, Cook Islands

EMAIL
muri@beachcomber.co.ck

PHONE/FAX
Ph 21022
Fax 21323

ADDRESS
PO Box 379
Rarotonga

GUEST FACILITIES
Tour-desk, wedding-packages, snorkelling-equipment, hairdryer, swimming-pool, guest-laundry, BBQs, Petanque, Kayaks. Guest-lounge with TV/DVD. Rental-motorbikes onsite. 5 restaurants close-by, 2 adjacent grocery stores.

CREDIT CARDS
Amex, MasterCard and Visa

ACCOMMODATION
Situated on beautiful Muri Lagoon, Muri Beachcomber has 16 Seaview, 2 Garden, a two-bedroom Family-Garden Unit plus 3 Watergarden Villas. Units/villas are self-contained with separate air-conditioned bedrooms and well-equipped kitchen. Children welcome in Family/Garden Units.
Villas offer seclusion and a little more luxury, a short stroll to the beach. Featuring TV/DVD/telephone/individual BBQs. Honeymooners retreat.

COMPLIMENTARY
Fruit-basket, welcome breakfast-pack, milk, juice on arrival. International transfers. Tea/coffee/sugar. Honeymooners: Bottle of Bubbly-upgrade from Seaview Unit to Watergarden Villa (conditions apply).

PALM GROVE

www.palmgrove.net

LOCATION
Rarotonga, Cook Islands

EMAIL
beach@palmgrove.co.ck

PHONE/FAX
Ph (682) 20 002
Fax (682) 21 998

ADDRESS
PO Box 23
Rarotonga, Cook Islands

FACILITIES
All bungalows have full kitchens with fridge/freezer, microwave, fans, hairdryer, IDD phones.

CREDIT CARDS
All major cards accepted

Beachfront bungalows command a magnificent panoramic view of the white sandy beach and waters of the Titikaveka lagoon, complemented by 13 bungalows in the landscaped garden area. All bungalows are self-contained with kitchen, dining area, private bathroom and patio.
Freshwater swimming pool, 2 BBQ areas, laundry, library, TV lounge, Yellow Hibiscus Restaurant and Bar. Airport meet and greet service, motor scooter for hire on-site, tour desk.

COMPLIMENTARY
Daily tropical breakfast, snorkelling equipment and canoes.

PARADISE INN

www.paradiseinnrarotonga.com

LOCATION
Rarotonga, Cook Islands

EMAIL
paradise@oyster.net.ck

PHONE/FAX
Ph (682) 20 544
Fax (682) 22 544

ADDRESS
PO Box 674
Rarotonga, Cook Is

FACILITIES
Self contained, central location, bar.

Paradise Inn offers a unique alternative to motel accommodation in the most casual and laidback atmosphere in Rarotonga. Just a few minutes walk to the museum/library, Cook Islands Christian Church, the post office, cafes and many fine restaurants and shops, the Paradise Inn is best suited to adults and children over 12. The self-contained, fully furnished accommodation with skylights and ceiling fans has a split-level living area and a spiral staircase leading to a sleeping loft. In the beautifully appointed recreation and bar area with its outdoor terrace and elevated sundeck you can relax and enjoy your favourite drink and enjoy the most commanding view of the blue Pacific. Our friendly staff will serve you in true Polynesian style - from housekeeping and laundry service to booking activities; it's all possible in Paradise.
Very reasonable rates.
See our website for further details.

SUNRISE BEACH BUNGALOWS

www.sunrise.co.ck

LOCATION
Beachfront
Muri Beach

EMAIL
motel@sunrise.co.ck

PHONE/FAX
Ph (682) 20 417
Fax (682) 24 417

ADDRESS
PO Box 251
Rarotonga, Cook Islands

FACILITIES
Self contained, pool, guest laundry, BBQ.

4 Waterfront & 2 garden bungalows & 2 adjoining units situated only 2 minutes from Muri beach. This property is designed for the "get awayers". Take advantage of the dozens of sporting, cultural or sightseeing adventures. Your cool individual bungalow is located amongst tropical foliage, flowers and palms. The Sunrise is a very private resort situated 200m off the main road and only 20m from the sea. All units are self catering with colour TV's and private facilities. Each unit has a Queen and Single bed, sunny covered patio. Facilities offered are: guest laundry, swimming pool, gas BBQ, snorkelling equipment. TVs. A grocery shop is situated on the main road. There is a regular bus service which passes by 5 minutes pas the hour. We are situated on a white sandy swimming beach. Come to the Sunrise Beach Bungalows & experience true relaxation and comfort!

FISHING

RECREATIONAL diving is firmly established in the Cook Islands with the longest running operator having set up more than thirty years ago. Crystal-clear water and moderate temperatures make this a diver's delight, both for already qualified divers or those simply wishing to give it a go. Full SCUBA Training is available from introductory level right up to Instructor ratings and, of course, a good selection of specialty courses. Being a volcanic Island, the outer reef offers a diverse variety of sites with most dives being in the 12- to 30-metre range. There are several wrecks to explore but the main attractions are natural rather than man-made. Photographic opportunities abound, with canyons, caves, walls, drop offs and varieties of coral including plate, mushroom and brain in the thirty- to sixty-metre visibility water, all this in an ocean that teems with colourful fish of all shapes and sizes. With Rarotonga being a circular island, there is always a calm side to dive. All diving is shore-based boat diving with the major operators using RIBs (rigid Inflatable boats) and most operators trailer their boats to ensure the shortest trip possible to the various dive sites. Water temperatures vary between 23 and 30 degrees Celsius and wetsuits are provided in the cooler months. Although no shore diving is available there are single and "Two tank" dives offered with both morning and afternoon departures plus regular night diving. Whilst there are no guaranteed performers such as the rays of Caymans or the Mantas of Yap, anything is possible and the real thrill is not knowing what is around the next corner.

SEASHELLS

www.seashells.co.ck

LOCATION
Avarua Rarotonga,
Cook Islands

EMAIL
trish@seashells.co.ck

PHONE/FAX
Ph (682) 24 317
Fax (682) 24 318
Mobile (682) 55 102

ADDRESS
PO Box 814
Avarua Rarotonga,
Cook Islands

FACILITIES
Self contained, TV/video,
fans, hairdryer

Four deluxe fully self-contained spacious 2-bedroom apartments in a garden setting only 50 metres from the beach and no road to cross.
All units have colour TV, video and CD system, DVD, phone, fans, flyscreens, hairdryer. Microwave, full kitchens, super kingsized beds. Internet/email available conditions apply, individual BBQ, large decks with views of the mountains. On site laundry.
Children are most welcome.
Units are serviced every 2nd day.
Close to many restaurants, bars, shops – hire cars, tours and attractions, the beach and sunsets.

SOKALA VILLAS

www.sokalavillas.com

LOCATION
Rarotonga Cook Islands

EMAIL
villas@sokala.co.ck

PHONE/FAX
Ph (682) 29 200
Fax (682) 21 222

ADDRESS
PO Box 82
Rarotonga Cook Islands

FACILITIES
King size beds, bedrooms are
air conditioned, self-
contained, fans, airport
transfers.

ATTRACTIONS
Beachfront location, safe
swimming all high tides,
close to sailing club,
island weddings.

ACCOMMODATION
Sokala has seven spacious villas, five of which have their own swimming pool in the centre of a large wooden deck. No children under 12. Lagoon view villas (with upstairs bedroom). Each has hand-hewn four poster kingsize bed, slate floors, pine interior walls, kitchenettes, and overhead fans. Rates from NZ$480. Located in a secluded corner of Muri Lagoon with views across to palm-lined islets. Guests receive private airport transfers and complimentary sparkling wine and fruit bowl on arrival. Within walking distance is the Rarotonga Sailing Club and many restaurants. Sokala is an ideal hideaway for honeymooners and those looking for a relaxing, romantic holiday.
FOR FURTHER INFORMATION
See our website for full booking details and current rates.

PICTURE: SOUTH PACIFIC TOURISM ORGANISATION

PICTURE: COOK ISLANDS TOURISM

AITUTAKI

EXPERIENCE THE DIFFERENCE

IT doesn't seem too long ago that the expansive Aitutaki Lagoon saw the stirring sight of massive flying boats coming in to land on the turquoise waters. The lagoon served as a refuelling stop for TEAL (now Air New Zealand) flying boats servicing the famous Coral Route between North America and the South Pacific.

Those days are long gone and the largest plane now coming in to Aitutaki is the small Air Rarotonga plane bringing tourists on a one-hour flight from the capital. The lagoon, extending some 45 kilometres around, is peaceful.

Many islets and motus or small islands dotting the lagoon, including Moturakau, provide nesting places for birds while visitors can swim and snorkel in such delightful places as the evocative Honeymoon Island.

It's said that a visit to the Cook Islands isn't complete without a trip to the beautiful island of Aitutaki. The second-most visited of the Cook Islands after Rarotonga, it lies 220 kilometres north of the capital. It measures just 20 square kilometres and is partly volcanic in origin.

PICTURE: SOUTH PACIFIC TOURISM ORGANISATION

PICTURE: SOUTH PACIFIC TOURISM ORGANISATION

HERITAGE SIGNIFICANCE

Legend has it that Aitutaki's highest point, the 124-metre Maungapu, is the top of Rarotonga's Raemaru Peak, stolen away by local warriors. Aitutaki was the first island in the Cook group to embrace Christianity when the Reverend John Williams of the London Missionary Society arrived in 1821.

Travelling with Williams was a young missionary, Papeiha, from the Society Islands, who stayed on when Williams continued his travels and dedicated the rest of his life to his task. The CICC Church, construction of which started in 1828, is the oldest church in the Cook Islands and has a memorial to John Williams and Papeiha.

Captain William Bligh of HMS Bounty fame is credited with being the first European to sight the island in 1789, just weeks before the infamous mutiny. A favourite stop for whalers in the 1850s, the British flag was raised in 1888 at which time Aitutaki and Rarotonga were included in the boundaries of New Zealand.

PICTURE: SOUTH PACIFIC TOURISM ORGANISATION

PICTURE: NOEL BARTLEY

THE AITUTAKI LAGOON RESORT & SPA

www.aitutakilagoonresort.com

LOCATION
Akitua Island, Aitutaki, Cook Islands

EMAIL
info@aitutakilagoonresort.co.ck
or info@rarotongan.co.ck

PHONE/FAX
Ph (682) 31 203
Fax: (682) 31 202

ADDRESS
PO Box 99 Aitutaki, Cook Islands

FACILITIES
SpaPolynesia spa therapy centre, Flying Boat Beach Bar & Grill, Bounty Restaurant, gift boutique, swimming pool, activities beach hut, guest lounge with TV / video, tour desk, laundry service. All bungalows feature airconditioning, overhead fan, spacious private verandah with sunlounges, king bed, refrigerator, coffee/tea making facilities, TV/DVD, CD player/radio, IDD phone, bathrobes, hairdryer, iron/ironing board, daily housemaid service, turndown service, room service.

ATTRACTIONS
Aitutaki's best location, prime beachfront, private island, unsurpassed lagoon views, all-tide swimming, the Cook Islands' only overwater bungalows, top island dinner/shows, Aitutaki's only spa, perfect romantic retreat.

CREDIT CARDS
All major credit cards accepted

ACCOMMODATION
Conde Nast Traveler wrote: "Aitutaki is an exquisite atoll" with "the most vivid lagoon colors anyone has ever seen." The Aitutaki Lagoon Resort & Spa was showcased on Conde Nast's cover which described it as: "The Aitutaki Lagoon is *the* resort on *the* beach ... nowhere could be more idyllic." The Aitutaki Lagoon Resort & Spa is the only resort set directly on breathtakingly-beautiful Aitutaki Lagoon and rests on its own secluded private island, once the landfall of Captain William Bligh and the HMS Bounty. Encircled by expansive beaches the colour of champagne, the Resort enjoys commanding views across the vast, surreal-aqua lagoon to the motu (small isles) beyond. The Aitutaki Lagoon Resort & Spa features the only Overwater Bungalows in the Cook Islands, a quintessentially Polynesian experience complete with thatched roof, pandanus-lined walls, spacious bathroom with double vanity, beautiful appointments and a delightful open-air shower with direct access to the inviting lagoon waters. The Resort's 37 spacious bungalows also include Deluxe Beachfront, Beachfront and Garden Bungalows, and offer a distinctively Cook Islands experience with thatched roofs and tropical furniture.

FEATURES
For a truly memorable experience enjoy a soothing massage at SpaPolynesia, then relax with a long, cool sunset cocktail at the enchanting Flying Boat Beach Bar & Grill and gaze out together across the magnificent grandeur of the lagoon as the moon and stars come out for the evening. Aitutaki's most superb location and the ultimate romantic hideaway in the heart of the South Pacific. Absolute Aitutaki.

ACTIVITIES
Travellers come to Aitutaki not so much to 'do' as to 'be'. This is the place to loll on the beach, laze in a hammock, take a languid dip in the luminous lagoon, to deeply relax into one another's company, and to re-discover the best in you. For when the mood takes you there is a range of complimentary diversions available, including snorkelling, fish feeding, crab hunting, kayaks, pedal boats, beach volleyball, guided walks, bicycles, and coconut climbing and husking show. Lagoon cruises, bonefishing, gamefishing and tours of Aitutaki Island are all nearby.

FOR FURTHER INFORMATION
Email or fax us for the latest available offers.

PACIFIC RESORT AITUTAKI

www.pacificresort.com

LOCATION
Aitutaki Cook Islands

EMAIL
aitutaki@
pacificresort.co.ck

PHONE/FAX
Ph (682) 31 720
Fax (682) 31 719

ADDRESS
PO Box 90
Aitutaki, Cook Islands

CONTACT
Thomas Koteka

FACILITIES
Fresh water horizon pool,
air conditioning,
overhead fans, TVs, piped
DVD movies, IDD phones,
in-room safe, tea and
coffee facilities, fridge,
restaurant and bar,
poolside cafe,
in-room dining

ATTRACTIONS
Beachfront location with
great snorkelling,
wedding packages, daily
orientations, tour desk,
cyber room, fantastic
views, private health spa,
Aitutaki Lagoon

CREDIT CARDS
All major cards accepted

ACCOMMODATION
"Pacific Resort Aitutaki with 28 rooms is the Cook Islands' only luxury resort. Guests can choose their own style of Polynesian hideaway. a Beachfront Bungalow, Beachfront Suite or Beachfront Villa. All individual hideaways are beautifully appointed in an eclectic blend of timber furnishings enhanced by panoramic views of Aitutaki's world famous lagoon. All accommodations are airconditioned, are spacious with kingsize beds, have thatched roofs, expansive cool decks and tropical outdoor showers."

FEATURES
The Rapae Bay Restaurant is the perfect platform to view an amazing Pacific Sunset, while feasting on the real hidden treasures of the Pacific. After spending the morning exploring the Aitutaki Lagoon by snorkel, kayak, pedal boat or lagoon tour...The Black Rock Café and Bar located on the Pool deck is the perfect spot to lounge under an umbrella and enjoy a lunch or a light snack. Guests can also take the opportunity to indulge in an array of soothing Spa Treatments designed to harmonise, mind, bodyand spirit. Pacific Resort Aitutaki is a member of Small Luxury Hotels of the World.

ACTIVITIES
By day you can appreciate the tropical beauty as you meander through the gardens under a canopy of palms and majestic mahogany trees. Lie by the fresh water pool or the crystal-clear lagoon only a few steps away, go snorkelling in the crystal clear lagoon. Snorkel gear, kayaks and canoes are complimentary. Hire a vehicle for sightseeing or enjoy a variety of tour options on spectacular Aitutaki Lagoon. Sailing, windsurfing, scuba diving and big game fishing are also available.

FOR FURTHER INFORMATION
See our website for full booking details and current rates.

OLD TIMES

MANGAIA, the southernmost of the Cook Islands group, is said to be the oldest island in the Pacific with limestone and volcanic samples having been dated 18 million years. Located 180 kilometres south of Rarotonga and with an area of 52 square kilometres, the island is surrounded by a fortress-like barrier of makatea or raised coral that reaches 60 metres above sea level.

Countless limestone caves, some containing ancient skeletons, prove worthy of exploration. The Te Rua Rere or Flying Cave is a large space crowded with dramatic stalactite formations. The interior of Mangaia has several swamps and a small lake.

The easternmost of the Cook Islands, Mauke has a close coastal reef that reveals shallow swimming spots. There are numerous caves throughout the island and some of the best to visit include Vai Tango, near the village of Ngatiarua, and Motuanga Cave which is riddled with small chambers containing pools ideal for swimming.

An interesting attraction is the Oliveta Church at Kamiangatau. A conflict between competing villages during the construction of the church is evident in that it has two very different interior designs contained within its walls. The pulpit railing is inlaid with Chilean dollars.

ARE MANUIRI

www.adc.co.ck

LOCATION
Atiu Cook Islands

EMAIL
adc@adc.co.ck

PHONE/FAX
Ph (682) 33 031
Fax (682) 33 032

ADDRESS
PO Box 13 Atiu
Cook Islands

FACILITIES
Fans, library, airport
transfers, bicycles, car hire

CREDIT CARDS
MasterCard & Visa

Two 2-bedroom and one family bedroom, communal bathroom/toilet facilities and fully equipped kitchen, fans and screened windows. Lounge/dining room. A multi-lingual selection of books. Guided tours. A visit to the local coffee plantation is well worthwhile. Tours include a tasting session at the Atiu Fibre Arts Studio Gallery which is producing high quality fibre crafts with a distinctive South Pacific Touch. Using local plant material (tapa cloth) cotton or silk, each artwork is designed locally and carries the unique design that the Atiu Fibre Arts Studio is now famous for. Many creations have found their way into private and public collections worldwide.

ATIU VILLAS, ATIU ISLAND

www.atiuvillas.co.ck

LOCATION
Edge of central plateau,
Atiu Island

EMAIL
atiu@ihug.co.nz

ON-LINE BOOKINGS
www.atiuvillas.co.ck

PHONE/FAX
Ph (682) 33 777
Fax (682) 33 775

ADDRESS
Box 7, Atiu Island,
Cook Islands

FACILITIES
Licensed restaurant,
tennis court, rental vehicles,
solar hot water

CREDIT CARDS
Visa, MasterCard

Situated on the scenic adventure island of Atiu, these delightful villas are set in tropical gardens and surrounded by pineapple fields and forest.
Each villa is fully self-contained and each includes a well stocked pantry and mini-bar. These island style villas take from 1 to 5 people and are made entirely of colourful local timbers. The tour desk offers cave, island, historical, burial, fishing, sightseeing, coffee, bird and eco-tours.
Also available is a visit to an authentic tumunu gathering to hear the stories, discuss events and partake in Atiu's powerful bush beer.
Saturday is Atiu Villas island night, featuring the ura Atiu. On Sunday the bakers bake, the tours operate, the tumunu are open, the secluded beaches are there to enjoy and you can go to church. For more information about Atiu visit www.atiu.info

PARADISE COVE

www.paradisecove.co.ck

LOCATION
Aitutaki Cook Islands

EMAIL
paradisecove@aitutaki.net.ck

PHONE/FAX
Ph (682) 31 218 or
Ph (682) 31 589
Fax (682) 31 456

ADDRESS
PO Box 64
Aitutaki, Cook Islands

FACILITIES
Self contained units,
beachfront, TV,
lagoon tours,
snorkelling island nights

ACCOMMODATION
Self-contained polynesian style Beachfront Bungalows with thatched roofing, sunset views and located right on the beach. Contains bathroom and some kitchen facilities with bar fridge and either king size or 2 twin beds, fans, insect screened.

Rates for Beachfront Bungalows: $160. Complimentary bus transfers from airport with complimentary Tropical Breakfast served at your bungalow each morning.

PICTURE: NOEL BARTLEY

PICTURE: NOEL BARTLEY

OUTER ISLANDS

DIVERSE & EXCITING

SPREADING over some two million square kilometres of ocean, there's a diverse range of islands comprising the Cook group. A number are easily accessible by air from Rarotonga and provide a very special experience, a step back in time to encounter life pretty much the way it was before the arrival of Europeans.

Atiu is the third largest of the Cook Islands and is a fascinating destination, riddled with caves and surrounded by makatea or raised coral, cliffs and white sand beaches. Orovaru Beach is where Captain James Cook landed in 1777. The barrier reef lies close to shore and the four main villages – Areora, Tengatangi, Mapumai and Teenui – are grouped together on a central plateau some 71 metres above sea level. A road, extending 20 kilometres around the island, is the best means by which to explore.

The Anatakitaki Cave is the most visited and the nesting place for the swift-like Kopeka birds, which are seen only at dusk. Another bird to look out for is the Moo (pronounced Maw-aw) a family member of the New Zealand Notornis or Pukeko. The inhabitants take great delight in presenting visitors with a local delicacy, itiki or eels, caught in Lake Te Roto.

Another local custom to take part in is trying bush beer, a potentially explosive brew made from imported yeast, sugar, hops and malt.

Itiki is also a popular dish on the small flat island of Mitiaro. Renowned as one of the friendliest islands, village life revolves around the Cook Islands Christian Church Betela – where visitors can experience the rousing hymns at the Sunday service.

Walks along the reef at low tide, a visit to the subterranean caves for swimming, and exploring the swampy Rotonui and Potoiti lakes, home of Itiki's celebrated eels, all provide enduring memories.

BLACK GOLD

MANIHIKI is one of the two Cook Islands given over to cultured pearl production. Measuring just 5.4 kilometres long and with a four-kilometre-wide lagoon, it is regarded for its outstanding natural beauty. The black pearls of Manihiki are justifiably famous.

Penrhyn Island, also known as Tongareva, is another renowned for cultured pearl production. The northernmost of the Cook Islands, it boasts a beautiful lagoon measuring 280 square kilometres and was a base for US forces during World War II. The black-lipped oyster, Pentad Margaritifera, is utilised for the production of black pearls.

Other outlying islands of the Cook Group include Suwarrow – the Cook Island's only national park, and Nassau, which has no airstrip and is serviced only an inter-island ship that takes three days to make the journey from Rarotonga.

PICTURES: SOUTH PACIFIC TOURISM ORGANISATION

THE COOK ISLANDS FACT SHEET
ACCREDITED BUSINESSES

RAROTONGA

TRAVEL AGENTS

TRAVEL AGENTS	Box	Fax	Phone	Email
Cook Islands Holidays.com	947	21530	21530	askunclejeff @cookislandsholidays .co.ck
Hugh Henry Travel & Tours Ltd	440	25420	25350	helen@hughhenry.co.ck
Island Hopper Vacations	240	23027	22026	vacation @islandhopper.co.ck
Jetsave Travel	40	28807	27707	jetsave@cooks.co.ck
Tipani Tours	4	23266	25266	tours@tipani.co.ck

TRANSPORT

TRANSPORT	Box	Fax	Phone	Email
Cooks Buses	613	25513	25512	kcook@oyster.net.ck
Raro Tours Ltd	440	25326	25325	coaches @rarotours.co.ck
Tiare Transport	516	29627	55217	tiaretransport @oyster.net.ck

TOURS & ACTIVITIES

TOURS & ACTIVITIES	Box	Fax	Phone	Email
Adventure Flights	787	25315	55311 25317	tonygus @oyster.net.ck
Akura Charters Fishing Tours	378		54355	fish@akura.co.ck
Capt. Tama's Cruizes & Watersports	3017	23810	27350	weddings @tamascruizes.co.ck
Cook Islands Cultural Village	320	25557	21314	viltours@oyster.net.ck
Cook Island Divers	201	22484	22483	gwilson@ci-divers.co.ck
Captain Ina's Fishing Tours	613	25513	25512	kcook@oyster.net.ck
Dive Rarotonga	38	21878	21873	info@diverarotonga.co.ck
Highland Paradise	3227		28924	highland@oyster.net.ck
Kids In Action	2142	25240	25018	tinairo@oyster.net.ck
Nautica Sail School	3060	27106	27349	dine@sailsrestaurant.co.ck
Pacific Expeditions	3063	23513	52400	graham @pacific-expeditions.com
Pacific Marine Charters	770	25237	21237	pacmarine @cookislands.co.ck
Pa's Trek	666	21079	21079	jillian @pasbungalows.co.ck
Paradise Sailing Tours	394		55225	albertobachmann @yahoo.com
Raro Eco Tours	39	21143	21043	raro-ecotours @oyster.net.ck
Raro Ocean Adventures	3191	23777	23777	info @oceanadventures.co.ck
Raro Safari Tours	380	23629	23629	sambo @rarosafaritours.co.ck
Reef Sub	2075		25837	reefsub@oyster.net.ck
Reef to See	395	25353	22212	reef2see@oyster.net.ck
Takitumu Conservation Area	3036	29906	29906	kakerori@tca.co.ck
The Dive Centre	142	20238	20238	scuba@thedivecentre-rarotonga.com

RENTAL COMPANIES

RENTAL COMPANIES	Box	Fax	Phone	Email
Avis Rent a Car	317	21702	22833	rentacar@avis.co.ck
Budget	607	20888	20895	rentals@budget.co.ck
Fun Rentals	598	22436	22426	funcars @funrentals.co.ck
Island Car & Bike Hire	2083	23632	22632	vinsen@islandcarhire.co.ck
Rarotonga Rentals	679	27236	22326	cutejag@oyster.net.ck

EATING OUT/BARS

EATING OUT/BARS	Phone	Description
Blue Note Café	23236	Breakfast & Lunch daily.
Café Salsa	22215	Breakfast, Lunch & Dinner daily.
Café Hideaway	22345	Breakfast & Lunch. Mon-Sat mornings.
Da Carlo – Italian Restaurant	23743	Dinner only. Wed-Sun 'Real Italian' Cuisine.
Flame Tree Restaurant	25123	Dinner only every night. Asian & European.
Hopsing's Restaurant	20367	Dinner only. Closed Sun. Chinese.
Kikau Hut	26860	Dinner Mon-Sat. European
Outrigger Restaurant	27632	Sun-Fri Dinner only from 6pm. International Cuisine
Pawpaw Patch	27189	Breakfast & Dinner nightly. (Moana Sands Hotel)
Sails Restaurant	27349	Lunch & Dinner daily. European menu & island flavours.
Saltwater Café	20020	Mon-Fri 8am-4pm/Sun 10-4. Dinner Wednesday nights.
Staircase Restaurant & Bar	21254	Dinner only Wed-Sat. Island Nights Thursday & Friday.
Tamarind House Restaurant	26487	Fine Pacific Cuisine. Open Tues-Sat 8:30am – 11pm.
The Hangar Café	25317	Lunch only Mon-Sat.
Trader Jack's/Jack in the Box	26464	Seafood Specialist. Lunch & Dinner. Mon-Sun.
Tumunu Restaurant	20501	Dinner only every night. European & Seafood.
Vaima Restaurant	26123	Dinner only. Closed Wednesdays.
Windjammer Restaurant	23950	Dinner only. Closed Tuesdays.

RETAIL/SERVICES

RETAIL/SERVICES	Phone	Description
Beachcomber Ltd.	21939	Jewellery, black pearls, glass blowing, art gallery.
BELT Hair Therapy	24122	Weddings, hairstyles & makeup.
Bergman & Sons	21902	Black pearls & jewellery.
Eagle Eye Design	28030	Web site design & photography.
Farm Direct Pearls	20635	Loose pearls & pearl jewellery.
Fishers Black Pearls	23358	Loose & set black pearls.
Foodland Supermarket	23378	Groceries, fruits and vegies.
Fruits of Rarotonga	21509	Café & locally produced preserves.
Fuji Image Centre	26238	Developing & Processing Images.
Goldmine	24823	Jewellery & gifts.
Island Craft	22009	Art gallery & picture framing.
Island Weddings	27023	Wedding & celebration planners.
Kenwall Gallery	25526	Art gallery & souvenirs.
Moana Gems	22312	Black pearl jewellery.
My Beauty & Spa	23933	Full service spa & gel nails.
Pacific Arts	20200	Handicrafts & pearls.
Pacific Brides Inc	20532	Mobile hair and makeup service..
Pacific Gifts & Souvenirs	23458	Black pearls, jewellery & handicrafts.
Perfumes of Rarotonga	25238	Perfumes, essential oils, soap.
Raina Trading	23601	Handicrafts & pearls.
Tarani's Craft & Pearls	21139	Art work & hand-painted clothing.
The Art Studio	27768	Handicrafts, black pearls & jewellery.
Tokerau Jim Pearl Designs	24304	Pearl shell designs & jewellery.
Treasure Chest	22325	Clothing & handicrafts.

TAXIS

TAXIS	Phone
Areiti Taxis	23012
Kia Orana Taxis	20203
MLT Taxis	21397
Parekura Taxis	26490
See Plus Taxis	23870

COOK ISLANDS TOURISM CORPORATION
Head Office, P.O. Box 14, Rarotonga, Cook Islands. Phone: (682) 29 435, Fax: (682) 21 435
Email: headoffice@cook-islands.com, Website: www.cook-islands.com

COOK ISLANDS
TOURISM CORPORATION

HEAD OFFICE
PO Box 14 Rarotonga, Cook Islands
Tel: (682) 29 435 Fax: (682) 21 435
Email: headoffice@cook-islands.com
Web: www.cook-islands.com

NEW ZEALAND OFFICE
Albert Numanga, Talei Wong
PO Box 37391 Auckland, New Zealand
Tel: (649) 366 1106 Fax: (64 9) 309 1876
Email: nzmanager@cook-islands.com

AUSTRALIA OFFICE
Mereana Taruia, Mata Wichman
PO Box 20 Guildford, NSW 2161
Tel: (612) 9955 0446 Fax: (612) 9955 0447
Email: ausmanager@cook-islands.com

EUROPE
Karin Zwiers, Frank Hoffmann, Janina Gunther
Petersburger Strasse 94, 10247 Berlin, Germany
Tel: (49 30) 4225 6027 Fax: (49 30) 4225 6286
Email: europemanager@cook-islands.com

ASIA
Eckard Kremer
C/o Pacific Leisure Group, 8/F Maneeya Center
518/5 Ploenchit Road Bangkok 10330, Thailand
Tel: (66 2) 652 0507 Fax: (66 2) 652 0509
Email: asiamanager@cook-islands.com

UNITED KINGDOM
Kevin Harris, Sarah Brooks, Alex Bergin
Nottcut House, 36 Southwark Bridge Road
London. SE1 9EU, England
Tel: (44 0 20) 7202 6369 Fax: (44 0 20) 7928 0722
Email: ukmanager@cook-islands.com

USA
Mike Smith, Asher Senyk
17880 Skypark Circle, Suite 250
Irvine, California 92614
Tel: (949) 476 4086 Fax: (949) 476 4088
Email: usamanager@cook-islands.com

CANADA
Rick Buecking, Marilyn Scott
1133-160A Street White Rock,
British Columbia V4A 7G9, Canada
Tel: (604) 541 9877 Fax: (604) 541 9812
Email: canadamanager@cook-islands.com

PICTURE: FIJI VISITORS BBUREAU

FIJI
ISLANDS

ONE of the South Pacific's most enduring and popular tourist destinations, Fiji has something for everybody and for every budget. Most of Fiji's hotels are right beside the ocean, offering their guests the romance and indulgence of the tropical Pacific at very reasonable prices.

Easy to get around and with much to see and do, Fiji's greatest attribute is the warmth and generosity of its people. The indigenous Fijians are intensely proud of their nation and for good reason. The destination is further buoyed by a multicultural society that also mingles Indian, European and Chinese lifestyles and influences.

It's an amazingly beautiful place, of tall mountains and pristine rainforests, of lively towns and villages where visitors are treated as part of the extended family, of spectacular snorkelling and diving locations and white sand beaches perfect for lazing away the tropical days. It is a landscape tailormade for the perfect vacation.

VACATION THRILLS

FIJI comprises about 300 islands dotted across 518,000 square kilometres and is located 5100 kilometres south-west of Hawaii and 3170 kilometres north-east of Sydney.

Only about one-third of the islands are inhabited. The main island groups include the Mamanuca Group, home to Viti Levu, Fiji's biggest island at 10,390 square kilometres. The Yasawa Group lies to the north-west of Viti Levu, Vanua Levu and Taveuni to the north, the Lomaiviti and Lau groups to the east and the Kadavu Group to the south.

The stress of modern-day life evaporates upon arrival in Fiji. The genuine smiles and shy greetings of the Fijian people will provide memories that last forever. And draw visitors back time after time.

FIJI VISITORS BUREAU
PO Box 9217 Nadi Airport, Fiji Islands
Tel: (679) 672 2433 Fax: (679) 672 0141
Email: infodesk@fijifvb.gov.fj
Website: www.BulaFiji.com

PICTURE FIJI VISITORS BUREAU

GEOGRAPHICAL LOCATION

Fiji, an island group in the South Pacific Ocean, about two-thirds of the way from Hawaii to New Zealand comprises some 300 islands dotted across 518,000 square kilometres. It is slightly smaller in size than New Jersey.

AIR/SEA PORTS

Nadi Airport is the main international gateway and Nausori near Suva is also used as another international airport. There are several domestic airports throughout the country. Travel between the two main islands, Viti Levu and Vanua Levu, is by air and sea. The major ports are Suva, Lautoka, Levuka and Malau (off Vanua Levu). Suva is the largest. Lautoka is the main port for Western Viti Levu.

ARRIVALS/DEPARTURES INFORMATION

Fiji has two International airports - Nadi, on the western side and Nausori on the east coast of Viti Levu near Suva both of which provide air connections to all of the world's major cities, with direct flights to the USA, Canada, Australia, New Zealand, Japan, and Korea, serviced by eight international carriers. Fiji's national airline, Air Pacific, provides many of those flights with a fleet that includes Boeing 747s and 767s. Most places in Fiji are served by an airport or airstrip. A valid passport is required for at least three months beyond the intended period of stay and a ticket for return or onward travel. Entry visas are granted on arrival for a stay of four months or less for nationals of Commonwealth countries. Nationals of other countries require pre-arranged visas which can be appllied for at the nearest Fiji High Commission in their respective country. Visas on application to the Department of Immigration in Suva, Lautoka or Nadi may be extended for up to six months. An onward or return ticket and sufficient funds is also necessary. If you wish to stay more than six months, consult the Department of Immigration. Visitors may bring in two litres of alcohol liquor, or four litres of wine, or four litres of beer, 500 cigarettes or 500 grams of tobacco, cigars, etc. Goods up to the value of $F400 per passenger attract no duty. You can bring in a combination of any of these goods (cigarettes) provided it does not exceed the equivalent quantity under any one item. Fiji prohibits the importation of vegetable matter, seeds, or any animal product without a permit from the Ministry of Agriculture, Fisheries and Forests. Only yellow fever and cholera vaccinations are required for those arriving from infected areas.

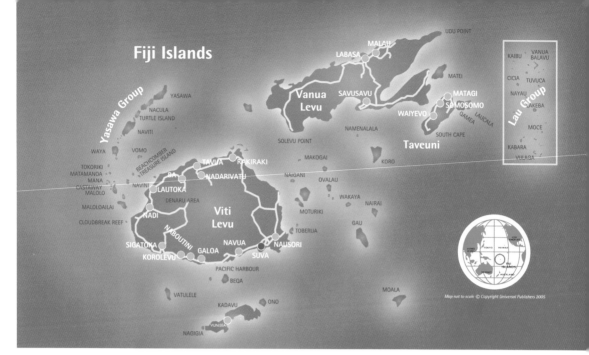

DEPARTURE TAX
Visitors are required to pay F$20.00 departure tax in Fijian currency following check-in. Children under 12 are exempt.

CURRENCY
The Fijian dollar is the basic unit of currency. At the time of this publication, $F1 was equivalent to: USA: 0.6070; UK(GBP): 0.3205; Australia: 0.7740; New Zealand: 0.8453; Japan YEN: 64.01, Hong Kong: 4.734. Major credit cards are welcomed in most places.

CLIMATE
Fiji enjoys an ideal South Sea tropical climate. Maximum summer temperatures average 31° Celsius (88°F) with the mean minimum 22° Celsius (72° F), winter average maximum is 29° Celsius (84°F) and mean minimum 19° Celsius (66°F). The interior of the large islands is much cooler.

ELECTRICITY
The electrical current is 240 volts AC 50 Hz. Fiji has three-pin power outlets identical to Australia and New Zealand. Leading hotels and resorts offer universal outlets for 240v or 110v shavers, hair dryers, etc.

LANGUAGE
Fiji is an English-speaking country although the two major races – Fijians and Indians have their own language.

POPULATION
The population of approximately 832,494 is multi-racial, composed of indigenous Fijians, Indians, Europeans, part Europeans and Chinese. Of these, 52.8 per cent are Fijian and 40.3 per cent are Indian, others 6.9 per cent.

LOCAL CONSIDERATIONS
Religion. Fijians are mainly Christian, Indians are Hindu, and there is a Muslim minority.

Tipping is not generally encouraged in Fiji.

Both men and women should be careful to respect local feelings. Wearing bikinis and ultra-brief swimming costumes is fine at resorts but not when visiting villages or shopping in town.

Hospitals are located in major centres and there are health centres in rural areas.

TELECOMMUNICATIONS
Most hotels have direct dialling facilities. The international country IDD code for Fiji is 679. There are no area codes. Services include domestic direct dialling and facsimile, Internet and email.

Telecom Fiji offers paging and voice mail. Vodafone Fiji provides a GSM digital mobile communication service. Card phones are also available in urban centres and can be bought from post offices, service situations and outer islands.

TIME ZONES
9am in Fiji is 9pm in London previous day, 4pm New York previous day, 1pm Los Angeles previous day, 6am Tokyo same day, 9am Auckland same day, 7am Sydney same day.

TRANSPORT
Fiji has bus services, taxi, ferry services, seaplane and helicopter services, rental car companies, two domestic airlines (Sun Air and Air Fiji) which provide efficient services and make getting around Fiji a breeze. The open air buses are a unique way to travel - providing a chance to observe Fiji up close.

PICTURE: FIJI VISITORS BUREAU

FRIENDLIEST FACES OF FIJI VITI LEVU

FOR many visitors, the primary focus of Fiji will be Viti Levu (Great Land). Covering 10,390 square kilometres, it is Fiji's biggest island and home to the capital, Suva. Located on the eastern side of the island, Suva is a bustling city although the first sight of Fiji for arrivals will be Nadi International Airport, nine kilometres from the town of Nadi on the western coast.

Nadi and Fiji are linked by two highways; the Queens Road hugs the southern coastline, while the Kings Road, which passes through Latoka, the second largest city after Suva, and an almost endless procession of sugar canefields along the northern coast.

A north-south mountain range peaks at Tomanivi or Mt Victoria, at 1323 metres the highest point in Fiji. Other mountains on Viti Levu Koroba (1076 metres), Tuvutau or Mt Gordon (933 metres) and Monavatu (913 metres).

TRADITIONAL OR MODERN

THE Viti Levu highlands gets visitors far away from the resort atmosphere. Here are small villages that have withstood the encroaching pull of civilisation. The Koroyanitu National Park near Lautoka is dominated by Mt Koroyanitu or Mt Evans and provides a great number of scenic attractions. Navala on the banks of the Ba River brings visitors up close to a traditional Fijian village. The Namosi highlands, on the south coast west of Suva have deep river canyons and pretty waterfalls.

Close to Viti Levu are a number of islands that host upmarket tourist resorts. The easiest to access is Denarau, connected to the mainland by a bridge, while a number of smaller islands notably in the Mamamuca group to the west and on the picturesque Beqa Lagoon can be accessed by boat and range between exclusive, family and mid-priced resorts.

Whether it's on Viti Levu with its multitude of sights or the relative isolation of the smaller islands, the resort experience provides a complete vacation package.

PICTURE: FIJI VISITORS BUREAU

CALENDAR OF EVENTS

PICTURE: FIJI VISITORS BUREAU

PICTURE: FIJI VISITORS BUREAU

FIJI is noted for its festivals, all colourful and filled with fun. The following is a selection of the more popular that you may not be familiar with. Of course, holidays such as Easter and Christmas are of great importance to this nation. Sugar Festival – Fiji's Sugar Festival, Lautoka comes alive with its annual Sugar Festival held in September. Bula Festival – Nadi Town also has its annual Bula (welcome) Festival in July. Prophet Mohammed's Birthday – This is a Muslim festival which is celebrated in June or November. Diwali Festival – A very pretty sight which occurs every year throughout Fiji is the Hindu Festival of lights, commonly called the Diwali Festival, when Hindu homes are decorated, often elaborately with lights. The festival is held each year on the first half of the Hindu month of Kartika (October – November).

The Hibiscus Festival – Fiji's carnival of the year is held in Suva during the month of August. The festival coincides with the 1st or 2nd week of the school holidays.

CERE

CERE is a traditional ceremony of welcome accorded to new ships, canoes, vehicles etc. This involves a lot of pomp, ceremonial jubilation and fun/gaiety as women with bales of cloth, mats and tapa come to welcome the new ship or vehicle. Usually women hold expensive gifts like whales teeth and men chase after the women with gifts. Whoever 'catches' the women with the tabua etc take them as trophies/spoils of the ceremony.

MEKE

THE Fijian meke features men and women in a programme of traditonal song and dance. The various provinces in Fiji have different dance routines. The meke usually depicts a story. The performances are colourful and participants wear traditional island costumes of printed bark cloth (tapa) and accessories woven from flowers and leaves. Musical accompaniment is provided Lali (drum carved from the bark of a tree) and a hollow bamboo pole beaten rhythmically on the ground.

FIREWALKING

ONE of the more spectacular sights in Fiji is the Fijian and Indian firewalking. The Fijians perform this at hotels on Viti Levu, or on the Island of Beqa where they were first given this gift according to legend. The Indians perform the firewalking as a Hindu religious observance. Check with the Fiji Visitors Bureau or your hotel tour desk for details of where the firewalking will be performed.

LOVO

THE lovo is a traditional Fijian feast in which food is wrapped in banana leaves and cooked slowly in an earth oven over smouldering stones, providing a distinctive faintly smokey flavour. Vegetables, fish and meats are placed in the oven and many of the dishes are prepared in coconut milk. The centrepiece of the lovo is often a whole pig.

Our Service...*going that extra mile!*

Meet & Greet was very enthusiastic and a great start to my Fiji trip. *Lauren Camillari - Australia*

Excellent Concept and made a difference in my holiday bargain hunting. R & B Cauerly - Australia

Great staff on the ground...Outstanding and made us feel at home in Fiji. *J. Watson - California USA*

"We focus on doing that little extra for all our clients. Our team in Fiji know that the difference between ordinary and extraordinary service is that little extra."

Damend Gounder, CEO. ADVENTURE & ENDLESS HOLIDAYS

We were transferred on time by courteous and considerate drivers. *Ken Kirk - VIP Discovery Channel "Eco Challenge 2002"*

Paradise Lounge was amazing & Incredible service. Staff was wonderful & friendly. Above Expectation. *Ten Grassi - USA*

 Adventure & Endless Holidays (Fiji) Ltd.

Nakula 3, Votualevu, Nadi
P.O. Box 9241, Nadi Airport, Fiji Islands
Contact: Damend Gounder Tel: (679) 672 0066 Fax: (679) 672 0072
Email: adven@connect.com.fj
Website: www.adventurefiji.com

Achieving Excellence In Tourism Services

GET THE FIJI HOLIDAY FEELING, THE MOMENT YOU STEP ABOARD

With Air Pacific your holiday starts early. And with destinations all over the Pacific (Australia, New Zealand, Los Angeles, Japan, Hawaii, Vanuatu, Samoa, Tonga, Solomon Islands and Canada) you can enjoy the relaxed service, warmth and South Pacific tradition of caring we are famous for.

So step aboard Your Island In The Sky and get that Fiji holiday feeling!

AIR PACIFIC
FIJI'S INTERNATIONAL AIRLINE

Say 'Bula Vinaka' with Vodafone

Bula Vinaka is the friendly greeting in Fiji and Vodafone Fiji will help keep you in touch.

Roaming...

If you have arranged roaming with your service provider before leaving home. Vodafone will give you an excellent coverage in most locations in Fiji. If you have roaming and want to call within Fiji just dial the local number. To call internationally, dial 00, country code, area code & telephone number.

Voicemail...

Even though you're here in Fiji, you can still retrieve your voicemails. You don't have to worry about those

calls that you've missed out. It does not matter which part of the world the calls are from, if you miss them... you can still retrieve them.

Customer Care...

If you have any questions or need help, call our customer care on 123. We are available 24 hours a day to be of service to you. Customer care will give you all the information about Vodafone services in Fiji, tariff information, connect you through to local numbers, provide local directory assistance and wakeup calls.

Let everyone know what a great time you're having.

• Suva: 331 2000 • Nadi: 670 3666 • Lautoka: 666 8000 • Labasa: 881 7817 • Website: www.vodafone.com.fj

Avis Fiji.

- Great range of current model cars!
- 8 offices across the Fiji Islands:
  Nadi Airport, Sheraton Fiji Resort,
  Sheraton Royal Denarau Resort,
  Shangri-La's Fijian Resort, Korotogo,
  Korolevu, Nausori Airport, Suva.

For details and reservations:

Fiji
Phone (679) 6722233 Fax (679) 6720482
Email: aviscarsfj@connect.com.fj
Website: www.avis.com.fj

Australia
136 333

New Zealand
Toll Free 0800 655 111

CT2340

explore fiji with hertz

HER 050SCA

To make a reservation just phone
Hertz Fiji on (679) 338 0981, your
local travel agent or visit hertz.com

Go with the world's #1

NADI
& BEYOND

THE gateway to the Fiji Islands, Nadi could be dismissed as simply the entry and exit point for visitors on their way to Nadi International Airport. But curious travellers will want to spend some time in this city which gathers around the scenic charms of Nadi Bay.

Fiji's third largest city, Nadi grew almost by accident. During World War II, a small airstrip had been extended for use by military aircraft and in the late 1940s was further developed to Civil Aviation standards. It became the first international airport in Fiji and as tourist numbers grew, so did this small town set amidst canefields and with a spectacular aspect across Nadi Bay.

In the colonial period, the people of Levuka, Fiji's first capital (it was moved from Ovalau Island to Suva on Viti Levu in 1882), sniffed at Nadi which had something of a "Wild West" atmosphere. Nowadays, a program of beautification is making Nadi quite a showpony of a city, its streets bustling with tourists drawn to the duty-free stores, restaurants, bars and handicraft outlets. The markets, especially, on a Saturday provide some special shopping opportunities.

Nadi has a large Indian population and visitors should seek out some of the magnificent temples and mosques, including the Sri Siva Subramaniya Swami Temple, a masterful tribute to Hinduism.

Accessible from Nadi are the Mamanuca and Yasawa island groups. They are located in what is virtually a huge lagoon dotted with islands and islets of all sizes. The waters teem with colourful marine life and wherever the visitors chooses to make land, there's plenty to do. Snorkelling, diving, swimming and all sorts of watersports are readily available.

Nadi is where you'll find the most visitor's facilities in Fiji and, of course, the greatest number of souvenir shops, but check around first. Nadi is the ideal place to pick up those last moment things you might want to purchase for your friends at home before departing.

TOKATOKA RESORT

LOCATION
Nadi, Fiji

EMAIL
tokatokaresort
@connect.com.fj

PHONE/FAX
Ph (679) 672 0222
Fax (679) 672 0400

ADDRESS
PO Box 9305
Nadi Airport, Fiji

FACILITIES
Air conditioning, fans,
cable TV, self-contained
units, disabled rooms,
boutique, licensed
restaurant

ATTRACTIONS
Giant waterslide, courtesy
transfers to and from
airport, free golf fees at
Nadi Airport, golf course

CREDIT CARDS
All major credit
cards accepted.

The Tokatoka Resort Hotel is located directly opposite Nadi International Airport.

FEATURES
A choice of either hotel rooms or villas. Deluxe villas and suites offer cooking facilities. Eight villas are specifically designed for the physically impaired with wheelchair access, telephone, showers and other special features for the disabled.

The swimming pool is surrounded by lush tropical gardens and is popular with guests of all ages. The pool is complete with four 25 metre swim lanes, an exciting waterslide, children's paddle pool, water caves, waterfalls, swim-up bar and a large canopy covering most of the pool providing shade from the tropical sun. The bedrooms are air conditioned with an option of ceiling fans.

A MEMORABLE SELECTION OF FOOD
It is a place to unwind and enjoy an island cocktail and a cultural feast of Fijian, Indian curries or international fare.

Dine in the evening, under the stars to the soft sounds of live Fijian music as you enjoy your favourite wine to compliment your meal.

... AND THERE IS MORE
Shop at Jack's, one of Fiji's better stores, visit our beauty clinic for a mind relaxing massage, or enjoy the ministrations of our top class hair dressers in our salon. Internet is available at our Internet café.

MINI-CENTRES FOR FUNCTIONS
There is also two mini-conference centres, one for up to 100 and the other to seat 60.

FOR FURTHER INFORMATION
See website for rates and booking details.

AQUARIUS RESORT

www.aquarius.com.fj

LOCATION
Wailoaloa Beach, Nadi

PHONE/FAX
Ph (679) 672 6000
Fax 679) 672 6001

EMAIL
reservations@
aquarius.com.fj

ADDRESS
17 Wailoaloa Road, Nadi

FACILITIES
Free Airport Pickup,
Linens & Towels, Guest
Luggage Storage,
Telecards, Cable TV
Lounge, ISDN High
Speed Internet, Bar &
Restaurant, Laundry,
Large Designer
swimming pool,
full time tour desk.

CREDIT CARDS
Major Cards

Opened in February 2003, this new 40-bed resort - Aquarius Fiji came about when Terry Buckley and his Fiji-born wife Louise decided to convert the two condominiums into something of a phenomenon for backpackers. It has been so successful with backpackers and bargain-holiday hunters that they are hoping to do the same on a property they have their eye on in both Samoa and the Cook Islands.

You'll instantly fall in love with the place once you set your eyes on Aquarius Fiji. In fact, Aquarius has had it's share of great reviews here and abroad with nzoom.com travel news stating that "For budget holidays in the South Pacific, this could be, - to borrow from a hit song from the 1960's musical Hair- the dawning of the Age of Aquarius". Imagine from F$25.00 for dorms to $89 for deluxe beachfront rooms, you can actually live your dream at Aquarius Fiji, enjoying the sun, breathtaking views, beachfront location, serenity and bliss! Your stay at Aquarius Fiji will be quiet and peaceful in lush green surroundings and a great swimming pool that leads right up to the ocean. With a promise that Head Chef will make nothing less than the most mouth watering meals from a limited but excellent menu and continental breakfast. There's no excuse, so get there now, you can afford it, you need the break, so take it!

ROOM RATES
6 & 12 Bed Dorms - $25.00 per person,
2 Bed Dorms - $28.00 per person,
Ocean View Doubles - $89.00 per room for 2 pax (extra person $ 25.00),
Standard Doubles - $79.00 per room for 2 pax (extra person $25.00).
All rooms have ensuite, and the 6 & 12 bed dorms are air-conditioned, while the others have ceiling fans.

RAFFLES GATEWAY MOTEL

LOCATION
Nadi, Fiji

EMAIL
gateway.reservation@
rafflesgroup.com.fj

PHONE/FAX
Ph (679) 672 2444
Fax (679) 672 0620

ADDRESS
PO Box 9891
Nadi Airport, Fiji

FACILITIES
Air conditioned,
tea/coffee-making,
hairdryer, licensed
restaurant, pool, tour
desk, gift shop, IDD
phones, Internet café and
pool table.

ATTRACTIONS
Gigantic waterslide,
conference centre,
floodlit tennis, courtesy
airport coach.

CREDIT CARDS
Amex, Diners, MasterCard
& Visa

ACCOMMODATION
5 suites, 67 deluxe and 22 standard rooms. All rooms are air conditioned with refrigerator, tea and coffee-making facilities, radio, ISD telephone, colour television and movies are free through channels 3, 4, 5 on the TV, hairdryer in every room. Room service is available 24 hours.

FEATURES
The most convenient hotel to Nadi Airport with Hotel Courtesy Bus transport available. 18-hour bar service/coffee shop, laundry, babysitting service, function room seating 100.

ACTIVITIES
Wonderful pool complex with gigantic slide, spa pool and tennis court on the property. Gift shop and tour desk in lobby area, 10 minutes from Nadi town for shopping. Inexpensive meals at the cafe restaurant and a la carte dining in the air-conditioned restaurant.

FOR FURTHER INFORMATION
See our website for full booking details and current rates.

NADI BAY RESORT HOTEL

LOCATION
Nadi Fiji

EMAIL
nadibay@connect.com.fj

PHONE/FAX
Ph (679) 672 3599
Fax (679) 672 0092

ADDRESS
Wailoaloa Road, Nadi NAP
0359, Nadi Airport

FACILITIES
Internet services,
airport bus, luggage
storage, library, laundry,
2 swimming pools,
2 bars, happy hour,
2 restaurants, SKY TV,
beauty salon, boutique.

CREDIT CARDS
All major cards accepted.

The gateway hotel for backpackers, where guests become friends!

Your introduction to Fiji is the new Nadi Bay Resort Hotel, where our friendly tour desk staff are happy to assist with travel plans for your Fiji experience.

The Nadi Bay Resort Hotel offers attractive rates for travellers who are planning to spend time in Nadi before or after their visits to the Yasawas or other exciting island backpacker resorts. Our resort is the perfect budget facility for travellers who want comfort and a sense of friendship while they explore Fiji.

The Nadi Bay Resort Hotel is located just a few minutes by road from the airport and seaplane base, and offers a variety of air-conditioned accommodation including dorms, standard rooms and apartments.

With a happy hour every night, a luxurious swimming pool, live music and smiles all around, guests are assured of a great time at the Nadi Bay Resort Hotel, one of Fiji's finest budget accommodation facilities.

TANOA ⛱ HOTELS
TANOA INTERNATIONAL

LOCATION
Nadi, Fiji

EMAIL
tanoahotels@
connect.com.fj

PHONE/FAX
Ph (679) 672 0277
Fax (679) 672 0191

ADDRESS
Voualevu Road
PO Box 9203
Nadi Airport, Fiji

CREDIT CARDS
All major cards
accepted

A business-style hotel with resort ambience... set amongst 14 acres of lush tropical gardens and conveniently located 5 minutes from Nadi International Airport. With 135 tastefully appointed air-conditioned rooms and suites complemented by thoughtful amenities facilities and services provides the perfect combination of comfort and functionality.

Rooms and Suites provide IDD phones, modem access, clock radio, hairdryer, cable television, refrigerator, in room safes, electronic key card access, iron & ironing board, complimentary tea and coffee-making facilities, private balconies.

Al fresco Dining in the 24-Hour All Day Garden Court Restaurant and Adjacent Air-Conditioned Gallery Restaurant, 24-Hour In-Room Dining, Guest Laundries, Poolside Bar and Lounge, Live Entertainment. Theme Nights, 24-Hour Reception, ATM & Currency Exchange, 5 Purpose-Built Meeting and Conference Venues, Free Air-Conditioned Airport Shuttle Bus, Tour and Sightseeing Desk, Three Retail Outlets, Swimming and Spa Pool, Sauna, Floodlit Tennis Courts, Fitness Centre, Therapeutic Massage.

TANOA ⛱ HOTELS
TANOA APARTMENTS

LOCATION
Nadi, Fiji

EMAIL
tanoaapartments@
tanoahotels.com.fj

PHONE/FAX
Ph (679) 672 3685
Fax (679) 672 1193

ADDRESS
Votualevu Road
PO Box 9211
Nadi Airport, Fiji

FACILITIES
Kitchenette with fridge,
microwave, 2-burner
stove, toaster, cooking
utensils and crockery
and cutlery.
Bedroom and lounge
with phone and TV.

Self contained . . . fully air conditioned and serviced apartments located a minute from the Tanoa International – units are either Deluxe, Penthouse or 2-bedroom... perched on a hilltop with sweeping views of the Nadi Airport and surrounding rural areas. Ideal for long term stayers or families wanting to base themselves in Nadi.

Reception, pool, sauna, spa, tennis, laundromat, barbecue, children's play area, free parking. Free airport shuttle transfers. Guest can also avail the services and facilities at the Tanoa International.

FIJI MOCAMBO HOTEL

LOCATION
Nadi Fiji

EMAIL
mocambo@connect.com.fj

PHONE/FAX
Ph (679) 672 2000
Fax (679) 672 0324
Australia Toll-free:1800 222 448
New Zealand Toll-free
0800 442 179
USA & Canada Toll-free
1800 942 5050
Tokyo: 81 3 3263 7068
London: 44 20 8747 8485

ADDRESS
PO Box 9195, Nadi Airport, Fiji

FACILITIES
Air-conditioned rooms, swimming pool, restaurants & bars, 9-hole golf course, tennis courts, games room, conference facilities and business centre.

CREDIT CARDS
American Express, Diners Club, JCB, MasterCard & Visa

ACCOMMODATION
128 fully air-conditioned rooms with private balconies, television, in-room video, IDD telephones, tea/coffee making facilities, refrigerator and 24-hour service.

FEATURES
Fiji Mocambo Hotel is set on 42 acres of tropical gardens overlooking the picturesque Sleeping Giant mountains, is just 5mins from the Nadi International Airport and 15mins from Nadi's main shopping area. For the vacationer, the hotel offers a wide range of leisure activities such as golf, tennis and island tours. Complementing Fiji Mocambo's recreational facilities are two restaurants including a 24-hour coffee shop, cultural dinner and show, bar and nightclub, shopping arcade and a tour desk, making it an ideal base for discovering Fiji's beautiful beaches and fascinating culture.

BONUS
Complimentary airport shuttle, two children under 18 stay free (room only) when sharing with 2 adults utilising existing bedding.

FOR FURTHER INFORMATION
Visit our website for full booking details and current rates.

GRAND MELANESIAN HOTEL
www.hexagonfiji.com

LOCATION
Nadi, Fiji

EMAIL
melnesianhotl@connect.com.fj

PHONE/FAX
Ph (679) 672 2438
Fax (679) 672 0425

ADDRESS
P.O. Box 10410, Nadi Airport, Fiji Islands.

FACILITIES
Two pools, restaurant, bar, rooms have air conditioning or fans, deluxe and standard rooms have phones, Sky TV in deluxe rooms. TV in standard rooms.

CREDIT CARDS
All major cards accepted.

Suitable for long or short stays for businesspersons, tourists and families. Rooms are available as doubles, twins or connecting rooms. Deluxe rooms have a fridge, TV, phone, radio and bathtub. 2 Filtered swimming pools, one with a slide and sunken bar. Restaurant and bar opens from 6.30am to 10.00pm.

24 hour reception and porterage. Ample off street parking.

See website for rates and booking details.
www.hexagonfiji.com.fj

GRAND WEST'S VILLAS
www.hexagonfiji.com

LOCATION
Nadi, Fiji

EMAIL
grandwestvillas
@connect.com.fj

PHONE/FAX
Ph (679) 672 4833
Fax (679) 672 5015

ADDRESS
P.O. Box 266, Nadi, Fiji Islands.

FACILITIES
2 bedroom self-contained villas, 1 bedroom apartments and studio units. pool with waterslide, tennis courts, restaurant & bar, grocery and gift shop, walking distance to golf course and Wailoaloa public beach, ample off street parking.

CREDIT CARDS
All major cards accepted.

FEATURES
20 fully self-contained two-storey units, 10 one bedroom apartments, 10 studios and 2 executive suites. Two storey units have 2 upstairs bedrooms each with ensuites. Fully equipped kitchen and fully furnished lounge area downstairs. 1bedroom apartments have a lounge area with one double bed and two single beds. Studio rooms have a single double bed. The resort is suitable for tourists, families or businesspersons. Pool with slide. Tennis courts. 24 hour reception. Restaurant and bar. 24-hour security. Grocery and gift shop. Ample off street parking.
See website for rates and bookings details.
www.hexagonfiji.com.fj

CAPRICORN INTERNATIONAL HOTEL
www.capricornfiji.com

LOCATION
Nadi Fiji
EMAIL
capricorn@connect.com.fj
PHONE/FAX
Ph (679) 672 0088
Fax (679) 672 0522
ADDRESS
PO Box 9043
Nadi Airport Fiji
FACILITIES
Spa, 10 channel satelite TV, beauty & massage salon, kids water slide and play area, multipurpose bure, 17 bed dormitory
ATTRACTIONS
Centrally located 7 min drive from Nadi International Airport. Ideal Location to start your Fijian holiday
CREDIT CARDS
Amex, Diners Card, MasterCard & Visa

ACCOMMODATION
68 air-conditioned rooms with tea and coffee-making facilities, IDD telephone, television, refrigerator, radio, laundry, car park, pool table and 24 hour reception. Room rates includes light continental breakfast and 24 hour courtesy transfers. Rates from $F85 to $F160 per night. All rates are inclusive of 12.50% value added tax.

FEATURES
5 minutes from Nadi Airport. 24-hour reception, spa/swimming pool in tropical gardens, cocktail bar, restaurant serving food from the best of European, Indian, Fijian and Asian influences. Gift shop, tour desk and car rental desk. Conference facilities available for up to 60 people. Foreign currency exchange, house doctor, laundry.

SANDALWOOD LODGE
www.bulafiji.com

LOCATION
Nadi Fiji

EMAIL
sandalwood@connect.com.fj

PHONE/FAX
Ph (679) 672 2044
Fax (679) 672 0103

OWNER/MANAGERS
Ana & John Birch

ADDRESS
Box 9454, Nadi Airport
Fiji Islands

FACILITIES
Private facilities, kitchenette air conditioned, Sky TV

CREDIT CARDS
Amex, Diners,
MasterCard & Visa

33 units with private facilities, air conditioned, kitchenette, balcony/ patio. ISD phone, Sky TV.

Orchid Wing units are more spacious with queen size bed, ensuite ironing facilities. Garden Wing slightly smaller. Rates from $F66 + 12.5% VAT.

Freeform swimming pool, garden setting, guest laundry, tour desk.

Conveniently situated between Nadi Airport (5km) and Nadi Town (3km).

Courtesy airport transfers for all flights. 24-hour reception.

See website for full booking details and current rates.

CLUB FIJI RESORT

www.clubfiji-resort.com

LOCATION
Nadi Fiji

EMAIL
reservation@
clubfiji-resort.com

PHONE/FAX
Ph (679) 670 2189
Fax (679) 672 0350

ADDRESS
PO Box 9619
Nadi Airport

FACILITIES
Fridges, coffee/tea-making, boutique, pool, licensed restaurant, Internet access, PADI diving, windsurfing, beachfront location.

CREDIT CARDS
Amex, MasterCard & Visa

Traditional Fijian-style resort. Bures have fridges, ensuite bathroom, coffee and tea. Private verandahs. Villas have twin vanities and hairdryers. Writing desks, music.

Coffee shop/boutique with Internet facilities. Token-operated laundry, ISD phone. Specialising in traditional and European foods. A la carte menu or buffet nights, taco night, Fijian Lovo night, beach BBQ, Mongolian BBQ and Japanese Teppanyaki Grill. Fun lively bar where you will meet many nationalities. PADI diving and many trips and tours, sailing Laser boats, windsurfing and paddleboards. 5 and 7-night Adventure Holidays available.

See our website for full booking details and current rates.

WEST'S MOTOR INN

www.hexagonfiji.com

LOCATION
Nadi, Fiji

EMAIL
westsmotorinn
@connect.com.fj

PHONE/FAX
Ph (679) 672 0044
Fax: (679) 672 0071

ADDRESS
P.O. Box 10097, Nadi Airport, Fiji Islands.

FACILITIES
Two swimming pools, Deluxe room are air-conditioned and have TV, fridge, tea/coffee making facilities and IDD phones, conference rooms, restaurant and bar.

CREDIT CARDS
All major cards accepted.

FEATURES
Two swimming pools. Restaurant and bar. Suitable for long or short stays for businesspersons, tourists and families. Rooms are available as doubles, twin rooms and triples. Deluxe and standard rooms have air condition and IDD phones. Sky TV in deluxe rooms only. 2 conference rooms. 24 hour reception and security. Ample off street parking.

See website for rates and booking details.
www.hexagonfiji.com.fj

FIRST LANDING RESORT

www.firstlandingfiji.com

LOCATION
Vuda Point, Fiji

EMAIL
firstlanding@connect.com.fj

PHONE/FAX
Ph (679) 666 6171
Fax (679) 666 8882

ADDRESS
PO Box 348
Lautoka, Fiji

FACILITIES
Private balcony, air conditioning, fridge, fan, tea/coffee making facilities, spa bath, beach, pool, boutique, restaurant, bar, IDD phones.

ATTRACTIONS
Beachfront location, beautiful gardens & setting, award-winning seafood restaurant, 15 minutes from airport.

CREDIT CARDS
All major cards accepted.

ACCOMMODATION
32 plantation-style timber bures with garden or beachfront setting, polished timber floors, private verandah, ensuite bathroom (spa bath in beachfront bures), air conditioning, fans, hairdryer, ISD phone, tea/coffee making facilities. 2 bedroom villas also available. Rates from F$225.00 per bure per night including Buffet Breakfast.

FEATURES
Boutique-style resort situated 13km by road from Nadi airport, next to Vuda Yacht Marina. Stunning setting with tropical gardens, massive raintrees and towering palms. The only white sand beach in Nadi area. Award-winning beachfront restaurant features seafood, wood-fired cooking, local specialties and much more. Sunset Dinner Cruise from Denarau.

ACTIVITIES
PADI dive facility, snorkelling, canoes, reef walking, trekking, diving and fishing trips, island hopping, village visits, sightseeing tours, car hire, shopping trips, tour desk.

PRICES
See our website for full booking details and current rates and specials.

Winner 2002 Fiji Excellence in Tourism Award for Quality Accommodation.

HORIZON BEACH BACKPACKERS RESORT

www.horizonbeachfiji.com

LOCATION
Nadi Bay, Fiji

EMAIL
horizon@connect.com.fj

PHONE/FAX
Ph (679) 6722 832/
6724 578
Fax (679) 6720 662

ADDRESS
Nadi Bay Beach, PO Box
1401
Nadi, Fiji

FACILITIES
Air-conditioned rooms,
swimming pool, restaurant,
laundry, TV lounge, family
rooms, email, phone and fax.

CREDIT CARDS
Visa, MasterCard, Amex

ACCOMMODATION & FEATURES

Cool, clean and spacious rooms priced to suit any budget – Standard, Air-Con or Ocean View with sunset balconies. All rooms have private ensuite facilities. Backpacker dormitory specials. Horizon has a comfortable, friendly atmosphere where travellers feel at home. Centrally located, next to the beach at Nadi Bay and only 10 minutes from both the International Airport and Nadi Town, Horizon Backpackers Resort is an excellent base while exploring Fiji's tropical island paradise. Free breakfast, free luggage storage and free 24-hour airport meet and pick up.

ACTIVITIES

Booking agents for outer island accommodation, day tours, cruises, packages. Activities with cost: Horse-riding, golf, diving, game fishing, PADI dive instruction.

NOMADS SKYLODGE

www.nomadsskylodge.com.fj

LOCATION
Queens Road, Near Nadi
Airport, Fiji

EMAIL
bookings
@nomadsskylodge.com.fj

PHONE/FAX
Ph (679) 672 2200
Fax (679) 672 4330

ADDRESS
PO Box 9222
Nadi Airport Fiji

FACILITIES
Meeting rooms with
secretariat services, Tour Desk,
24 hour Reception Desk, Gift
Shop, Free parking, Free
Lugguage Storage, Self
operated Laundromat, Foreign
currency exchange.

CREDIT CARDS
Amex, Diners, Visa, Mastercard

ACCOMMODATION

A broad range of clean and spacious air-conditioned rooms available from double bed ensuites with TV, phone, fridge and tea/coffee facilities, to self contained cooking units and 4 &6 bed ensuites dormitory style rooms. Nomads Skylodge is surrounded by 11 acres of lush tropical gardens and is only 3 min drive from the Nadi International Airport.

WE OFFER:

free shuttle from the airport, pool, spa, great bar with lounge and large screen, SKY TV, Internet, games room with pool table, dart boards, beach volleyball, indoor basketball & soccer, a restaurant offering awesome local cuisine as well as your home favourites. Access to public transport. For more detailed information visit our website:
www.nomadsskylodge.com.fj

ANCHORAGE BEACH RESORT

www.anchoragefiji.com

LOCATION
Vuda Point, Lautoka,
Fiji Islands.

EMAIL
anchorage@connect.com.fj

PHONE/FAX
Phone: (679) 666 2099
Fax: (679) 666 5571

ADDRESS
PO Box 10314, Nadi
Airport, Fiji Islands.

Panoramic views of the magnificent Nadi Bay and the picturesque garden of the Sleeping Giant mountain!!

Anchorage is a small tranquil resort at Vuda point only 15 minutes from the Nadi International Airport and 2 minutes from the Historical Viseisei Village with famous Fijian hospitality and a relaxing environment. All rooms are situated on or just back from the palm fringed ocean or set amongst our lush tropical gardens offering spectacular Ocean and fabulous garden views. All rooms offer all modern facilities.

WAILOALOA BEACH RESORT

www.nadi-hotel-beach-resort-fiji.com

LOCATION
Nadi, Fiji

EMAIL
wailoaloabeachresort
@yahoo.com.au

PHONE/FAX
Ph (679) 672 6633
Fax (679) 672 1800

ADDRESS
PO Box 1476 Nadi Fiji Islands

FACILITIES
Restaurant, bar, room service,
tea and coffee making, fans
in room. tour desk.

ATTRACTIONS
Horse riding, volley ball,
basket ball and big jogging
area and the beach and
stunning views.

CREDIT CARDS
MasterCard, Visa.

ACCOMMODATION

Wailoaloa Beach Resort is the cheapest and the newest resort in Fiji. We area situated at Wailoaloa Road close to Nadi Bay Beach. Consider staying with us on your next visit to Fiji!

LOCATION

Approximately 3 kilometres from the Nadi city centre, and about halfway between Nadi and the International Airport.

ACCOMMODATION

Choose between fan-cooled or air-conditioned rooms. Suitable for singles, doubles or families. We also offer dormitory accommodation for backpackers.

RATES

Backpackers F$20 including breakfast.
Families from F$45.

VITI LEVU
ITS SURROUNDS
& BEYOND

LAUTOKA

THE city of Lautoka is only a twenty-minute ride by bus from Nadi and offers a more typical town area. There are several good restaurants, hotels, an arts and craft gallery located at the Waterfront Hotel and a thriving market. It is also the departure point for many tours and cruises to the offshore islands.

RAKIRAKI

RAKIRAKI, a quaint old Colonial town, located north of Fiji's main island. Viti Levu is situated along miles of beautiful coastline and spectacular terrain. The area is also enhanced by some of the best weather in the Fiji Islands year around.

Rakiraki is also the getaway to the northern outer island resorts such as Nananu-I-ra. The Rakiraki Hotel is a well-known landmark here and is a popular stopover for travellers this side of Viti Levu.

TAVUA/BA

TAVUA, between Ba and Rakiraki, is known for its gold mine which is owned by Emperor Gold Mines. The discovery of the metal led to the creation of the Vatukoula town. (Vatukoula means gold stone).

LOMAIVITI

THIS group of islands to the east of Viti Levu includes Ovalau, Motoriki, Batiki, Nairai and the private island of Wakaya, famous in Fiji for its wild deer. There is very little visitor traffic in these islands, with the exception of Ovalau, although there are airfields on Koro and Gau, with a private landing strip on Wakaya.

OVALAU

LOCATED off the eastern side of Viti Levu, the island is the home of the old capital of Fiji, Levuka. This was the sight of the deed of cession in 1874. The waterfront of the old capital looks much like it did a century earlier. There are small guest houses, a hotel, a dive operation, a port, and the centre of Fiji's fishing industry complete with fish-canning factory.

NAIGANI ISLAND RESORT

www.naiganiresort.com

LOCATION:
Naigani Island, Fiji

EMAIL
naigani@connect.com.fj

PHONE/FAX
Ph (679) 331 2069
or (679) 330 2057
Fax (679) 330 2058

ADDRESS
PO Box 12539, Suva, Fiji

FACILITIES
Private balconies, fans, tea/coffee making facilities, beach, pool, boutique, restaurant, bar.

ATTRACTIONS
Beachfront location, beautiful gardens/setting, great snorkelling/scuba diving, beach massage, par 27 golf course.

CREDIT CARDS
All major credit cards accepted.

ACCOMMODATION
17 bures in beachfront or garden settings, a combination of spacious double plantation rooms and two bedroom bures which lay in a bay on a beautiful tropical island with white sandy beaches and crystal clear lagoons. All rooms are fan cooled and offer fridges & tea/coffee making facilities.

FEATURES
Located off the northeast coast of Viti Levu, one and half hours from Suva close to Wakaya Island. A well appointed beachfront resort offering, privacy and unobtrusive personalised service in true Fijian hospitality. Set off the beaten track, the plantation style setting affords visitors a quaint old world charm of the South Seas that are some of the simple pleasures in life that a fortunate few adventures will discover at Naigani Island Resort.

ACTIVITIES
There is as little or as much as you wish to do ranging from beach massages to interesting walks and visits to traditional and historical locations on the island or trips to nearby former Capital Levuka town. There is world class scuba diving, great snorkelling and excellent light tackle fishing, canoes, windsurfing, a beachfront swimming pool and a fun par 27 golf course.

Visit our website for enquiries and bookings.

TANOA ⚓ HOTELS
TANOA WATERFRONT
www.tanoahotels.com

LOCATION
Lautoka, Fiji

EMAIL
waterfront@connect.com.fj

PHONE/FAX
Ph (679) 666 4777
Fax (679) 666 5870

ADDRESS
Marine Drive, PO Box 4653, Lautoka, Fiji

FACILITIES
Air conditioned, private balcony, satellite TV, IDD phone, fridge, hairdryer, tea/coffee facilities, clock/radio

CREDIT CARDS
All major cards accepted

Corporate style . . . Lautoka's premier accommodation, located on the foreshore with only a minutes walk into the city and easy access to Lautoka Wharf, departure point for day trips and cruises to island resorts.

Air conditioned Fin's restaurant with indoor and outdoor dining, Sunset Bar, pool, in-house laundry, gym, business centre with Internet access. Conference and function facilities.

46 rooms categorised as Superior and Executive Rooms with city or harbour views.

TANOA ⚓ HOTELS
TANOA RAKIRAKI
www.tanoahotels.com

LOCATION
Rakiraki, Fiji

EMAIL
rakirakihotel@
tanoahotels.com.fj

PHONE/FAX
Ph (679) 669 4101
Fax (679) 669 4545

ADDRESS
Kings Highway
PO Box 31
Rakiraki, Fiji

FACILITIES
Air conditioned, phone, fridge, tea/coffee facilities, radio, TV, hairdryer.

Your home away from home . . . in colonial-style setting with warm, genuine hospitality, a relaxed pace and some home-style cooking are just part of what this property offers. Your best choice for that well-deserved rest and relaxation getaway.

Located halfway between Suva and Nadi on the Kings Highway.

36 rooms surrounded by well manicured gardens. Pool, recreation bure, bowling green, tennis, cocktail/lounge bar, restaurant, laundry facilities.

YASAWA

THE Yasawa Group, made up of some 20 islands of volcanic origin, lies in a chain north-west of Viti Levu. The islands commence about 40km north-west of Lautoka and stretch for 80km. Some of the larger islands are: Yasawa, Waya, Nacula, Naviti, Yaqeta and Matacawalevu. Nanuya Levu better known as Turtle Island is the base for one of Fiji's most exclusive resorts and is also the site of filming of the movie Blue Lagoon, starring Brooke Shields in 1979. The islands have white sandy beaches and crystalline waters, lush tropical rainforests and soaring volcanic peaks that attract the refreshing tropical rain. The Yasawas The western most islands in Fiji, are magnificent in their mountain scenery, isolated beaches, and limestone formations, the most famous being the limestone caves at Sawa-I-Lau with its ancient wall writings.

BLUE LAGOON CRUISES
Boutique Small Ship Cruising

Imagine waking every morning to a new paradise. Days of turquoise seas, palm fringed islands, and the intimate tranquillity of boutique small ship cruising. While we're spoiling you, we'll cruise to unspoilt islands, visit remote Fijian villages, swim and snorkel in some of the most beautiful waters in the world. In the relaxed ambience of a Blue Lagoon Cruise you will be taken on a magical voyage. Departing from the crowds, and sailing past the Mamanuca Islands, you will be spirited towards the exquisitely remote Yasawa Islands. Only a few

hours each day is spent underway, with the rest spent at anchor in a sheltered lagoon and ashore, so you can go exploring, play water sports, enjoy cultural activities or simply do nothing at all. With a maximum of 72 passengers on any one of our five boutique cruise ships, and six unique itineraries, we offer you the luxury of choice – when you'd like to depart on your voyage, how long you'd like to spend in a remote paradise, and the style of ship that will allow you to relax.

Cruise Options – All cruises depart Lautoka (25 minutes from Nadi International Airport)

- **4 Day/3 night Gold Club Cruise** – Departs Mondays & Thursdays 3:00 pm, returning Day 4 at 12 noon
- **7 Day/6 night Gold Club Cruise** – Departs on Monday at 3pm returning on Day 7 at 12 noon.
- **4 Day/3 night Club Cruise** – Departs Monday & Thursdays 3:00 pm, returning Day 4 at 12 noon
- **3 Day/2 night Club Cruise** – Departs Saturdays 10:00 am,

returning Day 3 at 4:00 pm
- **Cruise in Luxury Dive in Paradise** -7 Day/6 night Gold Club Adventure Dive cruise, Departs first Monday of each month (see www.cruiseinluxurydiveinparadise.com)
- **Historical and Cultural Cruise** - 7 Day/6 night Gold Club journey through Melanesian, Micronesian and Polynesian cultures

Packages

- Wedding – The ultimate island wedding on our own private island
- Honeymoon – Pampered with a Picnic in Paradise or Bubbly Breakfast in bed
- Anniversary – Reaffirmation of Vows
- Families - Special two cabin family rates

- Barefoot Conferences, Meetings & Incentives a speciality
- Island Pickups from Castaway, Matamanoa, Malolo,Tokoriki & Mana on Gold Club Cruises only.
- Scuba Diving – Available on every cruise
- Group packages and Private Charters available

Gold Club Cruise Vessels

MV Mystique Princess
As the fleet's flagship, this 56 metre mini cruiser is more like a private yacht than a cruise ship. She has 36 deluxe air-conditioned staterooms, a luxurious air conditioned 120 seat dining saloon, air-conditioned forward lounge suitable for conferencing, three sundecks, Sky Deck cocktail bar, Lagoon Spa, and laundry.

MV Fiji Princess
The 60 metre Fiji Princess is the only catamaran and newest addition to the Blue Lagoon Fleet. She has 34 deluxe air-conditioned cabins and provides excellent on-board amenities including a dining saloon, spacious upper deck lounge bar, sun deck bar, foyer, boutique, Lagoon Spa, swimming pool, laundry, four sundecks and on-board non-motorised water toys.

Club Cruise Vessels

MV Yasawa Princess
54 metre ship has 33 air-conditioned cabins – 66 person capacity, 100 seat dining saloon, air-conditioned forward lounge suitable for conferencing, two sundecks, cocktails bar and laundry.

MV Nanuya Princess
49 metre ship has 26 air-conditioned cabins – 52 person

capacity, 75 seat dining saloon, air-conditioned forward lounge, two sundecks, cocktail bar and laundry.

MV Lycianda
39 metre ship with 21 air-conditioned cabins – 42 person capacity, 60 seat dining saloon, sundeck and cocktail bar.

Reservations
Contact your travel agent or Blue Lagoon Cruises, 183 Vitogo Parade, Lautoka
PO Box 130 Lautoka Fiji Islands • (679) 666 1622 or (679) 666 1268 • Fax (679) 666 4098
Email: reservations@connect.com.fj • Web: www.bluelagooncruises.com

PLANTATION RESORT

www.plantationisland.com

ACCOMMODATION
18 deluxe beachfront bures, 20 large 2-bedroom garden bures, 54 studio (1 room) garden bures, 41 air-conditioned hotel rooms. Ceiling fans in bures and rooms, refrigerator, tea/coffee-making facilities in all rooms/bures, IDD phones.

FEATURES
100 hectares nestled in the beautiful blue lagoon of the large island of Malololailai in the Mamanuca Group. Transfers are by 'Malalo Cat' 3 times daily from Denarau Marina or a 10-minute flight from Nadi Airport. Plantation is gifted with 7 kilometres of pristine white sandy beaches, Plantation Island Resort has much to offer to everyone – singles, couples, families and honeymooners. They are wedding specialists. Choice of restaurants and bars plus a snack bar and mini supermarket on the resort. Games room, video room, large swimming pool and children's pool with slide. Children have access to Creche and playcentre with full-time activities director. Conference facilities to seat max. 50 persons.

ACTIVITIES
Par-32, 9-hole golf course, mini golf, lawn bowls, volleyball, rugby and netball fields, tennis, table tennis, pool table, daily free snorkelling, handline fishing and snorkelling trips. Off-shore excursions and surfing at nearby Namotu and Wilkes. WATERSPORTS: Most non-motorised are free including paddle boats, windsurfing and snorkelling gear.

CHARGEABLE WATERSPORTS: Available are scuba and scuba diving, water-skiing, knee boarding, para-flying, big banana, coral viewing in the semi-submersible and catamarans.

FOR FURTHER INFORMATION
See our website for full booking details and current rates.

MALOLO ISLAND RESORT

www.maloloisland.com

LOCATION
Mamanuca Islands, Fiji

EMAIL
reservations@
maloloadmin.com.fj

PHONE/FAX
Resort
Ph (679) 666 9192
Fax (679) 666 9197
Mainland Admin Office
Ph Accounts (679) 672 4275
Ph Reservations
(679) 672 0978 (Direct line)
Fax
Accounts/reservations
(679) 672 4299

ADDRESS
PO Box 10044
Nadi Airport, Fiji

FACILITIES
Air conditioned, fridge, tea &
coffee-making, separate
bathrooms, lounge area,
restaurants, bars, babysitting,
conference facilities, fresh
water pool, safety deposit,
beauty & body therapy spa,
kids club

ATTRACTIONS
Coral sand beach, safe
swimming, diving,
snorkelling, windsurfing,
deepsea fishing, Hobiecats,
all watersports, bushwalking,
Fijian cultural activities

CREDIT CARDS
All major cards accepted

ACCOMMODATION
Air-conditioned accommodation comprising 30 Oceanview Bures, 18 Deluxe Oceanview Bures and 1 Family Bure. All feature air conditioning, fridge, tea and coffee facilities, separate bathrooms, lounge area, overhead fans and spacious verandahs.

FEATURES
Pristine white coral sand beaches, panoramic views and Fiji's only lagoon and sandy beach fresh water swimming pools. A superb choice of menus created by our internationally-trained Chef.

Several transfer options – One-hour cruise aboard Catamaran; 10-minute seaplane.

ACTIVITIES
(complimentary) Snorkelling, windsurfing, coral viewing, Hobiecats, games room, bush-walking trails, Kids Club, Fijian cultural activities, board games, ocean kayaks, volleyball, inter-Island trekking.

(chargeable) PADI scuba diving, sports and deepsea fishing, water skiing, banana boat rides, local village trips, island hopping, seaplane tours, secluded island trips, Leilani's Beauty Spa. Small conferences, meetings or incentives. Perfect venue for weddings and the ultimate romantic destination for honeymoons.

FOR FURTHER INFORMATION
For full booking details current rates etc please see our website.

VOMO ISLAND RESORT, MANAGED BY SOFITEL

www.sofitel.com.fj

LOCATION
Private Island Fiji

EMAIL
res@vomo.com.fj
Phone/Fax
Ph (679) 666 9755
Fax (679) 666 7997

WEBSITE
www.vomofiji.com
www.sofitel.com.fj

RESERVATIONS
Toll free accor res
numbers in Australia:
1300 65 65 65 Local
call cost, Toll free
NZ 0 800 44 4422 and
Toll free USA/Canada
1800 221 4542

ADDRESS
PO Box 5650, Lautoka Fiji

ATTRACTIONS
Private island, villa
accommodation, safe
swimming all tides, off
the shore snorkelling,
private picnics, scuba
diving, deepsea fishing

CREDIT CARDS
Amex, Diners, JCB,
MasterCard & Visa

ACCOMMODATION
29 deluxe villas of rich simplicity, located on the beachfront and the hillside overlooking the azure ocean and distant islands. Each villa generous in space at 60sq metres in size has been tailored to fit perfectly with its natural environment and provides a serene escape for the discerning traveler. Each villa boasts a separate living area, separate dressing area, spa baths and separate shower, extended sundeck with lounge chairs and al fresco dining, Air conditioning and ceiling fans, bathrobes and slippers, comprehensive mini bar selection, CD player, direct dial internet access and tea/coffee making facilities.

FEATURES
Located 30 km West of Nadi International airport, a 15-20 minute scenic flight either by seaplane or helicopter will get you there. The Resort features 2 restaurants and 2 bars overlooking the beach and distant islands, serving cooked breakfast, light island style lunches, gourmet dinners, cocktails and wines from our International wine list. A fresh water swimming pool, Beauty spa and boutique deliver experiences with attention to detail and a smile.

ACTIVITIES
Private picnics on the island of Vomo Lai Lai. Snorkelling among Fiji's best coral reefs. Over three kilometres of unspoiled beaches. Windsurfing, sailing, scuba diving, deepsea game fishing, beach activities centre, tennis, badminton, volleyball, 9-hole par-3 golf course, croquet, adventure trekking and bushwalking, Fijian ceremonial bure, offshore village excursions, scenic helicopter flights.

MANA ISLAND RESORT

LOCATION
Mamanuca Islands Fiji

EMAIL
info@manafiji.com

PHONE/FAX
Ph (679) 666 1333
Island (679) 666 1455
Fax (679) 666 2713
Island (679) 665 0788

ADDRESS
PO Box 610
Lautoka Fiji

FACILITIES
Air conditioned,
hairdryers,
tea/coffee-making,
phones, wedding chapel,
licensed restaurants,
pools, boutique,
games room

ATTRACTIONS
Beachfront location,
safe swimming all tides,
scuba diving, paraflying,
jet ski, snorkelling,
floodlit tennis

CREDIT CARDS
Amex, Diners, JCB,
MasterCard & Visa

ACCOMMODATION
Honeymoon bure, beachfront bures, executive bures and deluxe ocean view bures feature ceiling fan, mini-bar, patio and ensuite bathroom with separate toilet. All bures are air conditioned and have telephones in the room. Rates from $F400 include full American breakfast and free use of all non-motorised water sports.

FEATURES
Three restaurants (including a fine dining restaurant), beach bar, pool, lounge bar providing entertainment nightly – 3 live floorshows weekly. Special children's program, baby sitting, full-time nurse. The largest gem in The String Of Jewel Resort that make up The Mamanuca Group. Located on a 300-acre island, the resort prides itself in its surround of open and secluded pristine beaches and submerged reefs, with clear waters teeming with almost every type of tropical fish imaginable. A 12-minute airplane or chopper hop from Nadi supplements the seaplane and cruise ship modes of transport.

ACTIVITIES
Complimentary on Mana Island: windsurfers, Hobiecats, canoes, spy boards, snorkels and masks, fins, tennis (including equipment), volleyball and table tennis – cultural activities.

Other watersports available: Paraflying, big banana ride, jet ski, semi-submersible, hand-line or big game fishing, island hopping, sunset cruise, water-ski, knee board, uninhabited island day cruise, snorkelling safari. PADI 5-star scuba diving, scuba.

FOR FURTHER INFORMATION
See our website for booking details and current rates.

EFFORTLESS ADVENTURE

NAI'A

Dive Fiji and Beyond
Nai'a Fiji
www.naia.com.fj
explore@naia.com.fj
US Toll Free
1 866 776 5572
Fiji Telephone
+679 345 0382
Fiji Fax
+679 345 0566

Big 5 Expeditions

1. Fiji's Finest Coral Reefs
Unrivalled variety and diversity: deep-ocean seamounts, barrier reefs, current-flushed channels, shallow coral gardens and fringing mangrove in protected lagoons. According to veteran diver and filmmaker, Stan Waterman, *"Magnificent wide-angle colour and lots of bizarre macro – absolutely terrific!"*

2. Humpback Whales, Tonga
Swim eye to eye with giant singing whales during their winter migration to mate and give birth in Tonga's Ha'apai Islands. Assist field scientists against a backdrop of ancient volcanoes and remote atolls.

3. Discovery & Exploration
Extended adventure expeditions in Fiji and beyond. Survey and save the wild Phoenix Archipelago in Kiribati, Vanuatu's mysterious reefs and wrecks or New Caledonia's unique biodiversity.

4. Science & Conservation
Join on-board study projects or special research journeys. Learn from the experts' presentations, knowledgeable local guides and international guest scientists like Dr Gerald Allen.

5. Film, Video & Photo
Shoot with pros like IMAX* and High-Def Video producers, Howard & Michele Hall. Capture fish behaviour with Paul Humann and Ned Deloach. Expose exquisite detail with Roger Steene.

TREASURE ISLAND RESORT

www.fiji-treasure.com

LOCATION
Mamanuca Islands, Fiji
EMAIL
treasureisland
@connect.com.fj
PHONE/FAX
Ph (679) 666 6999
Fax (679) 666 6955
ADDRESS
PO Box 2210
Lautoka, Fiji
FACILITIES
Grand Bure Elevuka
Restaurant, free kids club,
free non-motorised water
sports, fishing, subsurface
5 star Gold Palm PADI dive
centre, tennis, Senikai Spa
& Gym, speed boat
transfers, wedding chapel.
ATTRACTIONS
Snorkelling, diving,
weddings, village visits,
fishing, island hopping.
CREDIT CARDS
All major cards accepted.

Treasure Island Resort, Fiji. One of life's simple pleasures. This intimate 15 acre island resort is just 16 kilometres off the west Coast of Viti Levu, just 20 minutes by fast boat transfer.

With a natural marine reserve surrounding the island, Treasure boasts some of the most picturesque underwater landscapes in Fiji. Leave the water to enjoy your deluxe ocean view Bure in air-conditioned comfort. All of Treasure's 67 Bures lie just within the rim of white sand that surrounds the island.

The new Senikai Spa and Gym is offers a full range of facilities to pamper your clients into relaxation and the all new 5 star PADI dive centre will drive them off the deep end.

Rediscover Treasure, so much or so little to do, your choice...

One of life's simple pleasures.

AUSTRALIAN REPRESENTATIVE
Paul Cutler Ph (612) 9997 1515
Email: paul@treasure.com.fj

BOUNTY ISLAND RESORT

www.fiji-bounty.com

LOCATION
Mamanuca Islands, Fiji
EMAIL
bounty@treasure.com.fj
PHONE/FAX
Ph (679) 6666 999
Fax (679) 6666 955
ADDRESS
PO Box 2210
Lautoka, Fiji
FACILITIES
Free non-motorised
watersports, bare foot bar,
games area, lounge with
satellite TV, DVD. Speed
boat Transfers, diving,
snorkeling, babysitting
ATTRACTIONS
snorkeling, diving, village
visits, fishing, island
hopping.
CREDIT CARDS
All major cards accepted.

No valet parking or bell boys here. This is an opportunity to truly get back to nature and enjoy a warm, friendly, personalized and affordable tropical island experience. The closest island to the mainland in the Mamanuca group, Bounty Island, one of Fijis newest resorts is less than 15 minutes by boat from Nadi, making it an ideal getaway from the mainland. The island's 48 acres are surrounded by golden sandy beaches, clear pristine waters and a marine reserve that provides spectacular snorkeling. The resorts comfortable and affordable accommodation includes 20 ensuite beach front bures with queen beds, a large conditioned dormitory and eight private rooms. The Fat Grouper restaurant and the bare-foot Beach Bar are great places to enjoy a sunset cocktail and make new friends. The complex also has a small general store stocking essentials like sunscreen, toiletries, snacks and books. A wide range of activities include bush trekking, turtle feeding, kayaking, catamaran sailing, snorkeling, snooker table at the bar, cycling and beach volleyball. There is also an activities room with Stereo, DVD, Satellite TV and lounge area.

AUSTRALIAN REPRESENTATIVE
Paul Cutler Ph (612) 9997 1515
Email: paul@treasure.com.fj

DENARAU ISLAND

SITUATED just west of Viti Levu, largest of the 332 Fijian islands, Denarau Island lies across a small causeway separating the island from the mainland.

One of the leading integrated tourism destinations in the South Pacific, Denarau Island is located a convenient 20 minutes from Nadi International Airport and 7 minutes from Nadi town and is home to three luxurious Sheraton Resorts and the world-class Denarau Golf & Racquet Club.

Apart from offering a sophisticated hotel and recreational experience, Port Denarau with its shops and a growing marina has become a major transit hub for Fiji tourism. With many of the smaller islands in the archipelago accessible only by boat, it is now the main transfer point for the resorts off the coast of Nadi in the Mamanuca and Yasawa groups. Port Denarau is also the principal point of departure for soft adventure cruises on traditional tall ships, island day trips, brigantines offering day and dinner cruises and jetboat rides, making Denarau Island an ideal first stop on any Fijian holiday.

Sport is big on Denarau with the Denarau Golf & Racquet Club offering a spectacular 18-hole par-72 championship golf course. The 7135-yard course has been designed around the island's extensive waterways. An impressive clubhouse comprising a restaurant, bar and pro-shop overlooks the 9th, 10th and 18th holes. A 300-yard plus driving range and an adjacent complex with 10 courts complement the club's facilities.

GOLF TERRACE APARTMENTS

www.golfterraces.com.fj

LOCATION
Denarau Island, Fiji

EMAIL
sales@golfterraces.com.fj

PHONE/FAX
Ph (679) 675 0557
Fax (679) 675 0899

ADDRESS
PO Box 9520,
Nadi Airport, Fiji

FACILITIES
Two BBQ's for guest use.
Air-conditioned guest lounge
serving continental breakfast.
UV Protected Children's play
area adjacent to resort

ATTRACTIONS
Boasting "Denarau's small
resort that's big on service",
next to Port Denarau Marina
and Cardo's Restaurant with
easy access to other resorts
and many diverse restaurants
on Denarau Island.

ACCOMMODATION
The forty 1, 2 and 3 bedroom self-contained, air-conditioned, beautifully appointed apartments have fully equipped kitchens with dishwasher, cook-top, fridge & microwave and laundry facilities with washing machine & dryer. Tastefully furnished dining and living areas open onto decks or patios with stunning views over the championship golf course to the majestic Nausori Highlands.

FEATURES
All the benefits of apartment living in a resort setting, Golf Terraces is located on Denarau Island 20 minutes from Nadi International Airport, 7 minutes from Nadi town and an easy stroll to Port Denarau. The complex has a 25-metre lap pool set within landscaped gardens with poolside BBQ area & putting green. Brand new, 5 mins from Port Denarau, Golf Terraces will appeal to all markets particularly families who desire the convenience and comfort of a fully furnished apartment at an affordable rate.

ACTIVITIES
Diverse range of activities which Denarau offers including golf and tennis and many tours offered by tour operators. The Denarau shuttle (complimentary) passes the door regularly allowing easy access to the many other resorts on the island and array of facilities, shops, restaurants, coffee shop and Yees Deli.

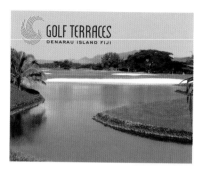

THE CORAL COAST

TOURISM WONDERLAND

IT was once a best-kept-secret where Fiji's expatriate community built their holiday homes. Now, it's promoted as one of Fiji's most sophisticated tourism precincts. The Coral Coast is located along the southern shoreline of Viti Levu, extending from Natadola Beach (considered by many to be Fiji's finest beach) in the west to Pacific Harbour in the east. It is easily accessed from Nadi and Suva by way of the scenic Queens Road.

The centre of the Coral Coast is considered to be Sigatoka, located on the banks of the Sigatoka River, Fiji's longest. The nearby Sigatoka Sand Dunes National Park was the first national park established in the nation and has remnants of Fiji's earliest history. Archeological digs have revealed relics and human remains dating back 3000 years. An interpretive centre is located on the Queen's Road.

PACIFIC HARBOUR

Pacific Harbour is a relatively new tourism development, dating from the early 1970s. At the eastern end of the Coral Coast, Pacific Harbour is the gateway to the beautiful Beqa lagoon. Measuring some 360 square kilometres, it is dominated by the 36-square-metre volcanic Beqa Island. Renowned for its sportsfishing and wide selection of beaches, the lagoon contains a number of upmarket resorts.

Pacific Harbour is 45 minutes from Suva and offers a choice of good hotels and restaurants. Home to many expatriates, the area has one of the finest beaches this side of the island. Visitors come here mostly to visit the Cultural Centre and Marketplace of Fiji and to see a theatrical display of Fijian people in pre-European times. No conventional stage here. History is retold in theatre and dances. The area is also known for its fine golf course.

See also page 94.

SHANGRI-LA'S FIJIAN RESORT

www.shangri-la.com

LOCATION
Coral Coast Fiji

EMAIL
fij@shangri-la.com

PHONE/FAX
Ph (679) 652 0155
Fax (679) 650 0402
Individual Reservations
Australia Toll Free
1800 222 448
New Zealand Toll Free
0800 442 179
USA & Canada Toll Free
1800 942 5050
Tokyo: 81 3 3263 7068
London: 44 20 8747 8485

ADDRESS
Private Mail Bag (NAP
0353), Nadi International
Airport, Fiji

FACILITIES
Air conditioned, private
balconies, refrigerators,
IDD telephones, televisions,
4 restaurants, 6 bars, 24-
hour room service, in-room
safes, shopping arcade,
tour desk, car rental, guest
laundry, beauty spa,
business centre and
conference centre.

CREDIT CARDS
American Express, Diners
Club, JCB, MasterCard &
Visa

Shangri-La's Fijian Resort, situated on its own private
109-acre Yanuca Island and conveniently connected to
the main island by a causeway, offers pure white sandy
beaches and blue lagoons evocative of Fiji. Inspired by
a traditional Fijian village, the layout and atmosphere
of the resort is complemented by the friendly and professional service of the local staff.

ACCOMMODATION
The resort has 436 rooms each with its own private balcony overlooking the lagoon or ocean. For those seeking a little more luxury there are 12 Executive Suites
and four secluded Beach Bures right on the waterfront.

All rooms feature air conditioning, IDD telephone,
in-room safe, fridge, tea and coffee-making facilities,
toiletries, hairdryer, bath robes, iron and board
and televisions.

CHILD POLICY
Up to two children per room aged 12 years and under
can eat for free and two children 18 years and under
stay for free when sharing with 2 adults.

ACTIVITIES
The resort offers a wealth of choices for the entire family including complimentary use of non-motorised
water sports, deepsea fishing, diving including PADI
diving courses, only resort with white sandy beach on
mainland, 3 swimming pools including an adults only
pool, 9-hole golf course, 4 tennis courts, gymnasium,
beauty spa, beach massage and complimentary kids
club for kids under 12.

ATTRACTIONS
Private island location, weekly Firewalking, Lovo and
Meke show, Seaside Wedding Chapel, 5-Star PADI dive
centre, Blackwatch Game Fishing Boat, nightly Live
entertainment.

TARIFF
Visit our website for full booking details and
current rates.

THE NAVITI RESORT

LOCATION
Coral Coast Fiji

EMAIL
res@navitiresort.com.fj

PHONE/FAX
Ph (679) 653 0444
Fax (679) 653 0099

ADDRESS
PO Box 29
Korolevu Fiji

FACILITIES
Air conditioned,
tea/coffee-making,
licensed restaurants,
day/night tennis, golf,
boutique

ATTRACTIONS
Beachfront location,
beach massage,
watersports, scuba diving,
bar, gym, jacuzzi

CREDIT CARDS
American Express,
Diners Club, JCB,
MasterCard & Visa

ACCOMMODATION
140 air-conditioned rooms with private balcony or patio. Tea/coffee-making, mini-bar, IDD phones, hairdryers. Rates from $F315.00.

FEATURES
Ideally located between Suva and Nadi. 4 Restaurants, 4 bars, Kids Club, 4 tennis courts, 24 hour room service, executive 9-hole golf course, playground, boutique and souvenir shop. Swimming and wading pool, shuffle board, archery, beauty centre, mini fitness centre, beach massage, tour desk, taxi service, currency exchange service, safety deposit and doctor's service.

COMPLIMENTARY
Day – tennis, basketball, netball, badminton, volleyball, snorkelling mask/flippers, sandshoes, sailing, canoeing, windsurfing (inc. lessons), guided reef and early morning walks, kayaking, Hobiecat and archery.

NOMINAL FEE
Golf green fees, coral viewing, deep-sea fishing, bicycle rides, sunset cruises, night tennis, fire-walking and scuba diving.

For further information

See our website for rates and booking details.

THE WARWICK FIJI

www.warwickfiji.com

LOCATION
Coral Coast Fiji

EMAIL
warwickstar@
warwickfiji.com.fj
warwickres@
warwickfiji.com.fj

PHONE/FAX
Ph (679) 653 0555
Fax (679) 653 0155
(679) 653 0010

ADDRESS
PO Box 100
Korolevu Fiji

FACILITIES
Air conditioned, tea & coffee-making, fridges, mini-bars, iron board, TV & hairdryers. VCRs for hire, videogames, car rentals, tour desk. Laundry, valet & secretarial services.

ATTRACTIONS
Beach location, windsurfing, canoeing, snorkelling, reef walks, par course walks, tennis, fish feeding, gym

CREDIT CARDS
Amex, Diners, JCB, MasterCard & Visa

ACCOMMODATION
250 rooms and suites with air conditioning, hot and cold water, tea/coffee-making facilities, refrigerators, mini-bars, iron/board, TV and hairdryer in all rooms, VCR's for hire.

FEATURES
Is set on brilliant white sandy beach at edge on Fiji's Famed Coral Coast. Just 90 minutes by car from Nadi International Airport.

5 Restaurants, 6 bars, fitness gym, 2 swimming pools with swim-up bar, 4 tennis courts, 2 squash courts, Kids Club, conference facilities, car rentals, taxis service, tour desk, laundry and valet service, doctors' service, hair salon, 24-hour room service, secretarial services, currency exchange services, and video games.

ACTIVITIES
Windsurfing, canoeing, snorkelling, reef walks, par course circuit, tennis, village visits, hotwater spring hikes, volleyball, bushwalks, fish feeding, shop, bay and deepsea fishing, scuba diving, jacuzzi, bicycle tours, village tours, horse-riding tours, theme nights, cultural entertainment, in-house live band.

FOR FURTHER INFORMATION
See our website for rates and booking details.

TAMBUA SANDS BEACH RESORT

LOCATION
Coral Coast, Fiji

EMAIL
tambuasands
@connect.com.fj

PHONE/FAX
Ph (679) 650 0399
Fax (679) 652 0265

ADDRESS
PO Box 177
Sigatoka, Fiji

FACILITIES
Coffee/tea makers, ceiling fans, fridges, boutique shop with internet service, licensed restaurant and bar, pool, tour desk

CREDIT CARDS
Amex, MasterCard & Visa

ACCOMMODATION
This intimate and relaxed resort on Fiji's Coral Coast sits amidst an unspoiled coconut plantation fronting a lovely white sand beach with coral reef beyond. 25 beach front and ocean view bures (cottages) are spacious, private and pervade an atmosphere of peace and tranquility. Some bures are interconnecting. All have ensuite bathrooms.

FEATURES
The Tarana Restaurant serves delectable cocktails and cuisine of an amazing standard at very reasonable prices. The restaurant is known for its seafood and local dishes. Visit out boutique shop. Bathe in the warm lagoon, laze around our fresh water pool, play a round of croquette or simply relax and soak up the sun rays. If you're feeling energetic, get busy with our recreation staff for snorkelling, kayaking, diving, hiking, reef walks and visits to Fijian villages. A tour consultant is available for booking a variety of day trips and cruises. The Tambua Serenaders entertain nightly with songs of the Pacific, followed by Island theme nights (kava ceremony, pottery and weaving demos, and traditional Fijian dancing and singing etc.). On Sunday enjoy acappella singing by our village choir. Tambua Sands, "a great value for money resort".

ROBINSON CRUSOE ISLAND BUDGET ACCOMMODATION

LOCATION
Coral Coast Fiji

EMAIL
robinsoncrusoe@
connect.com.fj

PHONE/FAX
Ph (679) 651 0100
Fax (679) 651 2900

ADDRESS
PO Box 2580
Nadi Fiji

FEATURES
Beachfront, Fijian thatched accommodation

Few miles north of Natadola Beach on Fiji's Coral Coast this 25-acre island, access is boat only including a 30-minute jungle river cruise followed by a short trip across the lagoon.
Clean and modest island-style accommodation. Fijian-style cuisine. Fishing and snorkelling trips, learn about traditional island medicine on our jungle bush walk.
Learn how to husk a coconut and catch coconut land crabs, join a traditional fish drive and cook your own catch over hot coals. Learn coconut tree climbing.
Play beach volleyball, Reefwalking with a village guide, Sunday services and village visit. Learn Polynesian/Melanesian dance then be part of the awesome island night entertainment. Beach party 'Fiji style' around an open fire under a starry sky.

VAKAVITI BACKPACKERS

LOCATION
Coral Coast
of Viti Levu

EMAIL
info@vakaviti.com

PHONE/FAX
Ph (679) 650 0526
Free call within Fiji:
0800 650 0526
Fax (679) 652 0424

ADDRESS
PO Box 5
Sigatoka
Fiji Islands

Vakaviti is situated along the beautiful Coral Coast, one hour's drive from Nadi International airport and 6 kilometres from Sigatoka town.
Set on a hillside amongst tropical gardens overlooking the beach and reef, Vakaviti offers clean, comfortable and affordable fully self-contained accommodation. Enjoy a relaxed and friendly atmosphere.

AMENITIES
Swimming pool, beach access, Internet service, mountain bike hire, BBQ, takeaway menu, library exchange, tour desk, surfing trips, mini-bus service, Laundry service available on request.

FIJI

CRUSOE'S RETREAT
www.crusoesretreat.com

LOCATION
Coral Coast
EMAIL
reservations@
crusoesretreat.com.fj
PHONE/FAX
Ph (679) 6500 185
Fx (679) 6520 666
ADDRESS
PO Box 20
Korolevu Fiji Islands
FACILITIES
Climate controlled wine room, restaurant, 2 bars, boutique / gift shop, dive operation, activities bure, volleyball court, grass tennis court, tour desk, kids climbing gym, guest library
ATTRACTIONS
Lush secluded location, full range of complimentary activities & nightly entertainment, unique location next to Namaqumaqua Village, nicest beach & swimming waters on the coral coast, family owned & operated

Crusoe's Retreat is a family owned and operated Resort. With just 28 free standing BuresCrusoe's Retreat welcomes just 60 guests at any one time. The 'Wining and Dining' experience at Crusoe's Retreat is exceptional. We have the best Wine List in Fiji! Our Climate Controlled Wine Room keeps them all at a constant temperature to ensure your ultimate enjoyment. Guests may immerse themselves in the range of complimentary activities and cultural experiences available every minute. With the Namaqumaqua Village bordering the property guests have the unique opportunity of experiencing the culture and hospitality of Fiji's beautiful people. Dive Crusoe's is our on-site PADI accredited dive operation. There are over 20 sites to suit all levels of experience. Crusoe's Retreat is an intimate and unique property that offers guests a five star experience for a three star budget. Just five minutes in this idyllic paradise and you will know you have discovered Fiji's Best Kept Secret!

THE NEW CROWS NEST RESORT
www.crowsnestfiji.com

A WHOLE NEW EXPERIENCE

LOCATION
Coral Coast, Fiji
EMAIL
crowsnest@connect.com.fj
PHONE /FAX
Ph (679) 6500230
Fax (679) 6520354
ADDRESS
PO Box 270, Sigatoka, Fiji
FACILITIES
Air conditioned, tea/coffee making, refrigerator, ceiling fan, hairdryer balconies, TV, IDD phones, restaurant, bar, pool, tour desk, boutique, conference room, Mini Mart, laundry service, babysitting, table tennis pool table etc..

This intimate resort is located in the heart of the Coral Coast, 50 minutes from the Nadi International Airport. The resort has been Upgraded and refurbished but maintains Its nautical origins. Set back 30 metres from the beach are 15 Executive Ocean View and 10 Deluxe Ocean View self-contained villas with modern amenities.
The poolside restaurant, serves local dishes, seafood and good old fashioned roasts at most affordable prices. Guests enjoy island songs by our serenades and tropical cocktails from our Quarterdeck Bar. Cultural theme nights, snorkelling, kayaking, reef walks, village visits etc.
The New Crows Nest -" A Holiday You Will Treasure At A Price You Can Afford"

PACIFIC HARBOUR

A TWO-HOUR scenic drive from Fiji's International Airport in Nadi, Pacific Harbour was developed as a complete visitor destination with its own 18-hole championship golf course, and inland waterway (where owners of luxury villas moor their pleasure craft), hotels, a shopping centre in the late 19th century style and a cultural centre. There's a long stretch of beach at Pacific Harbour and an international resort hotel – Centra Pacific Harbour - located on the beachfront. The Centra offers scuba diving by Aqua-Trek, tennis courts, and its own bars and restaurants.

You can stroll barefoot along endless beaches, go diving in world famous Beqa Lagoon, play a round of golf on the Robert Trent Jones Jr. 18-hole course or head by express bus into Suva or up the famous Coral Coast to Nadi. Alternatively, you can explore the lush interior by boating down the Navua River past waterfalls and native villages. Feeling a little adventurous? How about game fishing, river rafting, jet skiing, surfing, sailing, hiking or horseback riding? After a day of shopping and fine dining, you might catch a little Fijian singing, dancing and fire walking.

The nearby island of Beqa (pronounced Benga) is home to the legendary firewalkers and is a world-renowned diving location. The legendary tradition of firewalking is still performed on special occasions. The firewalking skill is possessed by Beqa's Sawau tribesmen living in the four villages on the windward, or southern side of the island. In special cases, however, members of the other tribes who have been adopted by the Sawau tribe have successfully performed the ceremony. The main village is known as Dakuibeqa where the chief of the tribe known as Tui Sawau lives.

For board riders Beqa has a fantastic surf break, Frigate's Passage - a world-class break with a powerful and consistent hollow left.

LAGOON RESORT

LOCATION
Pacific Harbour Fiji

EMAIL
lagoon@connect.com.fj

PHONE/FAX
Ph (679) 345 0100
Fax (679) 345 0270

ADDRESS
PO Box 11
Pacific Harbour

FACILITIES
Air conditioning, fans, cable TV, net access, self-contained units, boutique, licensed restaurant

ATTRACTIONS
Bull shark-feeding, Beqa Lagoon, golf course

CREDIT CARDS
Amex, Mastercard & Visa

FEATURES
A surreal resort set in an elegant, exotic, romantic location of 3 acres of landscaped grounds between an 18-hole golf course and the canal leading to Beqa Lagoon where our dive shop specialises in the world's best "Bull Shark-Feeding", in a marine park. Game fishing and adventures are the other features of Lagoon Resort as well as having access to the longest, safest and the best beach in Fiji. Bars, restaurants, swimming pool, gymnasium, full size billiard table, bikes, kayaks, table tennis and walking tracks are some of the activities available. Retreats and conferences often take the whole resort like the 16 Prime Minister's Leader Retreat in 2002, while "Anaconda 2" was filmed there in 2003. Hosts are Kiwi owners, Heather & Jim Sherlock.

ACCOMMODATION
6 Standard, 7 Deluxe, 4 Suites and 4 Self-Contained Units all with Italian marble bathrooms, bath, shower, large beds, air conditioner, fan, fridge, satellite TV, IDD phone/internet, tea & coffee making.

surrender**taste**indulge…

…the **coolest** resort in fiji

The Pearl South Pacific

THE
PEARL

SOUTH PACIFIC
FIJI ISLANDS

SUVA KEY TO PARADISE

ANYONE who wonders how far Fiji has come since the coup in May of 2000 need only look at the Capital, Suva. Once again this gateway to the fabulous Fijian Islands is bustling and the destination that has delighted travellers for decades is proving why it remains one of the most enduringly popular destinations on earth. With growth and refurbishment everywhere, Suva is once again the main entry point to those arriving to experience the many delights of the unique 'Fijian experience'.

There are more than 300 islands that make up the Fijian group and Suva, the capital, remains the hub of commerce and cultural life located on the Island of Viti-Levu. Suva pulsates with life with myriad diversions to entice the traveller and adventure seeker. From the plethora of duty-free stores to the local shops and special boutique shops, serious shoppers will have much to enjoy. Suva has also become renowned for its many bars, nightclubs and restaurants and is the centre for the many sightseeing tours that depart to the other islands and attractions throughout the group. For those who enjoy soaking up the ambience of an exotic location, annual festivals and carnivals such as the Hibiscus festival and Suva Christmas carnival have long enthralled visitors.

There are two main routes into Suva. Flying into the International airport Nadi one has a three-and-a-half hour journey by road into Suva itself or, alternatively, the faster option is to fly into Nausouri Airport, which is a mere 20-minute drive into Suva.

Nausouri is also the air-gateway to some of the many other islands in the Fiji group and as a growing number of international flights arrive and depart from Nausouri Airport, you may wish to discuss your options with your travel agent.

Once in Suva, getting around on foot is easy enough and it is a great way to see the many local attractions. The duty-free stores that have given Suva its reputation as a duty-free shoppers paradise abound and local souvenir shops mix in with a plethora of sophisticated boutique shops to ensure shoppers have every choice at their fingertips!

From designer merchandise to native artifacts and souvenirs, there's something for everyone and every taste and if you want to try out your bargaining skills in acquiring some inexpensive shells, native artifacts or jewellery don't miss the Handcraft Centre on Stinson Parade.

One Sunday every month, the local artisans under the banner of 'the Republic of Cappuccino' hold their open fair where visitors can purchase items, again at extremely reasonable prices. This is in addition to the many week-long shopping sales that are regularly held in Suva and it is not uncommon for streets to be closed off to cater for a large number of stalls, food outlets and carnival rides!

For those wishing to escape and get out among 'nature' the Colo-i-Suva on Princess Road makes a wonderful diversion. This nature reserve, resplendent with waterfalls, natural pools and trails among lush tropical vegetation, epitomises the unspoiled splendour that one imagines everything a tropical paradise should be. It is an ideal place to hike, picnic or just to relax and 'get away from it all'.

In a similar vein, the Thurston Gardens, located on the original site of Suva (next door to the Museum), is well worth a visit. Currently undergoing a major refurbishment that will see the gardens restored to its former glory, it contains a large collection of South Pacific flora and an avenue of 101 Royal Palms.

Those who enjoy outdoor activities will find many outlets in Suva. Divers are well served with the nearby spectacular underwater sights of Beqa Island Lagoon beckoning. Beqa is accessed from Pacific Harbour which is just 40 minutes outside Suva. For those wishing to indulge in some game fishing, Suva Yacht Club is the hub where one can organise an excursion. Surfers, too, will not be disappointed with several beaches easily accessible.

THOSE with an interest in the cultural aspects of the Fijian Islands will doubtlessly find the Fijian Museum in Suva an extremely satisfying experience. With large ranges of artifacts and historical treasures providing an amazing insight into the past as well as giving a comprehensive history of the Islands' heritage, it's a must.

With many of the major hotels and resorts providing dazzling live 'Fijian' shows nightly, visitors are guaranteed memories galore with the pulsating rhythms and excitement of the unique and colourful Fijian culture. These events are open to all (including non guests) and most feature the famous Kava ceremonies, dancers and the traditional feasts. No visit to Suva is ever complete without experiencing one of these dazzling shows.

Traditional Fijian culture encompasses the telling of legends and stories through song and dance called, the 'meke'. To see meke at its best, the visitor need only travel 40 minutes west of Suva to the Cultural Centre at Pacific Harbour, where a traditional dance troupe regularly entertains and enthralls audiences with their energetic performances. Day excursions can be easily arranged through one of the many agents in Suva.

As many visitors to Fiji in the past have noted, Suva is a city of contrasts and choices. In the midst of a natural tropical Paradise it boasts facilities that are as modern as today with raw simplicity often alongside the epitome of sophistication.

For the visitor who wants the convenience and comforts of a modern city, or the person who wants to 'escape', Suva can please both – after all, she has been doing it well for a very long time now. If a Fijian holiday is part of your agenda in the near future, do allow yourself time to experience Suva – the timing has never been better!

RAFFLES TRADEWINDS HOTEL

www.rafflestradewinds.com

LOCATION
Lami, Fiji

EMAIL
tradewindsresv
@connect.com.fj

PHONE/FAX
Ph (679) 336 2450
Fax (679) 336 2455

ADDRESS
PO Box 3377
Lami, Fiji

FACILITIES
Pool, business services, colour TV, tea/coffee facilities, IDD phones, laundry service

ATTRACTIONS
Floating restaurant, water sports, complimentary shuttle to Suva. Water's edge location

CREDIT CARDS
All major credit cards

ACCOMMODATION
Suva's only resort hotel features 108 air-conditioned rooms, ocean view with private balconies. 24-hour room service, 5 channel TV with CNN plus 3 free movie video channels.

FEATURES
10 minutes from the heart of Suva City. Ideally located right on the water's edge of the beautiful and tranquil, Bay of Islands at Lami. Fully comprehensive convention and meeting facilities able to accommodate from 10 to 500 people. Cultural and modern entertainment on request for groups. Children under 12 get 50% off food and beverage. Floating restaurant Bar and Lounge.

ACTIVITIES
All water sports available including scuba diving, swimming pool. Tennis, golf, daily excursions and tours arranged at tour desk.

FOR FURTHER INFORMATION
See our website for full booking details and current rates.

TANOA HOTELS
TANOA PLAZA

www.tanoahotels.com

LOCATION
Suva, Fiji

EMAIL
tanoaplaza@
connect.com.fj

PHONE/FAX
Ph (679) 331 2300
Fax (679) 330 1300

ADDRESS
Cnr Gordon & Malcolm Sts
GPO Box 112, Suva, Fiji

FACILITIES
Individually controlled air conditioned, IDD phone, satellite tv, tea/coffee facilities, and hairdryer, in room safes, writing desk and modem access, clock/radio, iron/ironing board.

CREDIT CARDS
All major cards accepted.

LOCATION
This nine-storey boutique style hotel is ideally located in the heart of Suva's business, finance and shopping areas, and is also conveniently located close to many leisure and sporting facilities in the capital.

ACCOMMODATION
48 Superior and 8 Deluxe Rooms and 4 Executive Suites provide excellent views of Suva Harbour and surrounding areas.

FEATURES
Purpose-built conference and function facilities together with an indoor and outdoor restaurant and bar. Pool, car parking, security and controlled access. In Room Dining, valet laundry service.

TROPIC TOWERS APARTMENTS

www.fijilive.com\towers

LOCATION
Suva Fiji

EMAIL
tropictowers@connect.com.fj

PHONE/FAX
Ph (679) 331 3855
Fax (679) 330 4169

ADDRESS
PO Box 1347
Suva Fiji

FACILITIES
Swimming pool,
air-conditioned rooms,
phones, satellite TV,
Internet facilities

CREDIT CARDS
Amex, Diners, MasterCard
& Visa

Situated 5 minutes walk to the city centre, the hotel has 47 spacious one- and two-bedroom apartments with private balconies.

All are self-contained with full cooking facilities, TV and video, radio, ISD phone and serviced daily. Also available car wash facility and laundry, babysitting service, coffee lounge, private bar, pool table, Internet access available, dial-a-meal service.

Rental cars can be booked at reception.

Self contained rooms from $F45 lodge rooms from $F30 – plus Government VAT Tax of 12.5%.

CAPRICORN APARTMENT HOTEL

www.capricornfiji.com

LOCATION
Suva Fiji

EMAIL
capricornsuva@
connect.com.fj

PHONE/FAX
Ph (679) 330 3732
Fax (679) 330 3069

ADDRESS
PO Box 1261
Suva Fiji

FACILITIES
Air conditioned, self-
contained, IDD phones, pool,
balconies, TV, central
location, conference facilities,
free in-house movies

CREDIT CARDS
All major cards accepted

34 self-contained apartments overlooking the private pool and landscaped gardens onto one of the finest views in Suva. All rooms are air conditioned, serviced daily, private balconies, ISD telephone, radio. 5 deluxe suites all 2 bedrooms and sitting room plus 4 – 1 bedroom and sitting room apartments with free in-house movies.

Situated in the heart of Suva at 7 Fort Street. Dial-A-Meal services delivered promptly. Continental breakfast available. Conference facilities available for up to 50 people, breakfast and bar facilities. Private parking and laundry services available.

See our website for rates and booking details: www.capricornfiji.com

SUVA MOTOR INN

www.hexagonfiji.com

LOCATION
Suva, Fiji

EMAIL
suvamotorinn
@connect.com.fj

PHONE/FAX
Ph (679) 331 3973
Fax: (679) 330 0381

ADDRESS
P.O. Box 2500, Government.
Buildings, Suva, Fiji

FACILITIES
Air-conditioned 2 bedroom
apartments or studio rooms,
swimming pool with slide.
Sky TV, Internet facilities,
tea/coffee-facilities, IDD
phones, restaurant and bar.

CREDIT CARDS
All major cards accepted.

FEATURES
45 modern two-bedroom and studio units set in a quiet peaceful, rainforest setting. Hydro-slide, swimming pool and cave spa. All rooms have Sky TV. Suitable for businesspersons, tourists or families. "Waterfall" Restaurant. Full bar facilities. Conference room. Evening Serenaders.

Very central location, within walking distance to city, Government Buildings, Central Business District and sports amenities, restaurants, night clubs and bars.

See website for rates and booking details. www.hexagonfiji.com.fj

SAVUSAVU VANUA LEVU

VANUA LEVU – The country's second largest island with 5556 square kilometres, is located north of Viti Levu. It was at one time the centre of the sandalwood trade, but now its primary economy is tourism and sugar, with copra a close second. Its primary port is Savusavu, but its principal urban centre is Labasa, which is also has a small port, and the island's principal airport. Comfortable visitor accommodation can be found in Labasa and Savusavu.

Savusavu is located 100 miles north-east of Suva, on Vanua Levu, the second largest island in the Fiji Group. Founded before the signing of the Deed of Cession, Savusavu township on the shores of a large picturesque, deepwater harbour was originally established as a centre for the sailing ships plying the coastline for cargoes of sandalwood and beche-de-mer, later it became the centre of the cotton boom. Today, Savusavu remains much as it did in its 'heyday', the hustle and bustle of progress appears to have passed it by. Savusavu's economy now relies on copra and the township serves an area that constitutes the major coconut producing area of Fiji. (Similar to the Coral Coast resort area on the main island of Fiji.) You may expect some rain between January and April but, even so, the sun is never far away.

Day temperatures range from 80 to 85, year around. The water is perfectly safe to drink, telephone communication is good world wide, there is a modern hospital and the roads are amongst the best in Fiji.

Savusavu Bay ranks amongst the world's finest natural harbours, and cruise ships visit regularly.

The Hibiscus Highway stretches 70 miles up the coast from Savusavu, offering some of the finest and most unspoiled scenery in the South Pacific, while the trans-insular road across to the main town of Labasa offers breathtaking views and indigenous rainforest. The atmosphere of the past lingers on everywhere, amongst a natural and friendly population.

Unusual attractions include the thermal springs at Nakama and the blowholes at Namale. Tours and scenic drives, bay cruises and fishing, reef-beach activities and local entertainment are all easily arranged. A tour of a working copra plantation is a unique experience.

Labasa pronounced, as Lambasa, is a busy Indian market town, which services Vanua Levu's major cane-growing area. Reminiscing about the Labasa Town, its beginning and development since 1922, brings fresh memories of those wonderful days and makes it possible to compare it with today.

Nasea Town was a village at the time, with earth road having deep side drains. During the spring tide you could fish in the middle of the commercial sites which were surrounded by cane, rice, coconut and cattle farms.

NAMALE RESORT & SPA

Namale
THE FIJI ISLANDS RESORT AND SPA

LOCATION
Vanua Levu, Savusavu, Fiji Islands

EMAIL
reservations@namaleresort.com

PHONE/FAX
Phone (679) 885 0435
Fax (679) 885 0400

ADDRESS
PO Box 244, Savusavu, Fiji Islands.

HOST
Mark Kitchen & Danielle Kenworthy

FACILITIES
Private individual luxury Bure (villa style) accommodation, all meals, all beverages including alcohol, round trip transfers to/from Savusavu airport, daily laundry service, Internet service

ATTRACTIONS
Freshwater swimming pools, snorkelling, hiking, water-skiing, tennis, horseback riding, volleyball, basketball, banana boat rides, croquet, badminton, kayaking, mountain bikes, visits to the village, tide pool exploration, coconut show, bowling, virtual golf, air hockey, 2 Jacuzzis, a putting green, scuba diving, sports fishing, Spa services.

Namale is extraordinary. This luxurious all-inclusive resort – with only Sixteen bures and Grand Villas sharing 325 acres of breathtaking paradise- provides an exquisite sanctuary of seclusion, romance and adventure. All have been lovingly built with the idea of bringing the outside in and maintaining the special Fijian Island style, while offering all modern amenities, modern bathrooms, beautiful sunset decks, lovely crisp white linens and flowing white curtains - with the end result of exotic hide-a-ways full of a special rustic charm. The two Deluxe Honeymoon Bures, and six Honeymoon Bures are each perched high on volcanic pinnacles. Six more Tropical Bures are set amongst lush tropical foliage that completes this picture of paradise. Each of the fourteen Bures has a spacious private deck with beautiful views of the rich blue ocean or the exotic rainforest gardens. And, for those looking for pure luxury with maximum privacy, we have two spacious beautifully designed and furnished Grand Villas that are positioned right at cliff's edge providing spectacular Koro Sea views and special additional luxury appointments.

The magnificent Main Bure – 60 feet high, is built in the traditional Fijian way and furnished with rich, big, overstuffed comfortable furniture and incredible attention to detail. This luxurious but unpretentious South Pacific Island style is continued throughout the resort. The mixture of rattan, voluptuous over-stuffed cushions, antiques, interesting objects'd art, with an overriding casualness has created a very welcoming and comfortable atmosphere.

JEAN-MICHEL COUSTEAU FIJI ISLANDS RESORT

www.fijiresort.com

LOCATION
Savusavu Bay Fiji
EMAIL
info@fijiresort.com
jmcfir@alphalink.com.au
WEBSITE
www.fijiresort.com
PHONE/FAX
US: (415) 788 5794
or (800) 246 3454
Australia: (613) 9815 0379
or 1300 306 171
ADDRESS
Private Mail Bag
Savusavu, Fiji
FACILITIES
Boutique, resident marine
biologist, day spa, private
island, tennis, 4 pools,
cultural host, business &
dive centre, Bula Club
for children

Winner of the 2004 Fiji Deluxe Accommo-dation award, this acclaimed luxury, lifestyle, eco sensitive resort boasts 25 elegant Fijian style bures-some have Jacuzzi, private pool and air conditioning. It is renowned for its surrounding multi-hued coral reefs, creative gourmet cuisine, cultural integrity, personalised service, nurturing and romantic ambience and its proximity to the interesting harbour town of Savusavu.

Dining is under the stars by lantern light, complimentary activities include yoga classes, guided snorkelling trips, kayaking, catamaran sailing, local village trips, rain-forest excursions and much more.

Guests of all ages experience the Fijian charm of yesteryear at this inclusive resort.

MOODY'S NAMENA

www.moodysnamenafiji.com

LOCATION
Namenalala Island
offshore Savusavu

EMAIL
moodysnamena@
connect.com.fj

PHONE/FAX
Ph (679) 881 3764
Fax (679) 881 2366

ADDRESS
Private Mailbag
Savusavu Fiji

FACILITIES
Tea/coffee-making, fans,
private picnics

100-acre private island, 6 enchanting hexagonal wood and bamboo bures perched on clifftops for panoramic views. King canopy bed, two ensuites (his/hers) each bure, coffee/tea facilities. Gourmet island cuisine. Superb snorkelling and scuba diving both offshore and on the Namena Barrier Reef.

Complimentary ocean kayaking, windsurfing, fishing (handline or trolling), trekking, birdwatching, canoes, beach volleyball, etc. Only extra is scuba diving.

FOR FURTHER INFORMATION
See our website for rates or email us direct.

KORO SUN RESORT & RAINFOREST SPA

www.korosunresort.com

LOCATION
Savusavu, Fiji Islands

EMAIL
res@korosunresort.com
info@korosunresort.com

PHONE/FAX
Ph (679) 885 0262
Fax (679) 885 0352

ADDRESS
Hibiscus Highway,
Private Mail Bag,
Savusavu, Fiji Islands

FACILITIES
18 bures/bungalows,
restaurant, bar, 9 hole golf
course, Rainforest Spa,
two swimming pools (one
with large water-slide),
dive shop, two tennis
courts, massage at
the Rainforest Spa.

ATTRACTIONS
Scuba diving, cultural
excursions, waterfall
adventure, deep
sea fishing, salt lake
kayak adventure.

CREDIT CARDS
JCB, MasterCard & Visa.

Koro Sun Resort & Rainforest Spa is Fiji's pre-miere adventure, dive, romance and rejuvenation resort. The 61-hectare property sits on a beauti-ful lagoon, with towering coconut palms encir-cled by a lush rainforest. The 18 private, fully air conditioned bures face an ocean panorama and views of the 9-hole golf course. Bures feature king-sized beds and natural palm wood and teak furnishings, romantic outdoor stone showers and your own private garden or screened in porch as well as a honeymoon bure. Walk on bridges over streams to your accommodation and enjoy the sweet scent of fresh ginger and fragipani flowers. Koro Sun's restaurant offers foods to please both adults and children, from island favorites, fresh fish, meats and vegetables to deserts while native drinks and cocktails are great for any time of the day. The menu choices change daily and your meal plan includes 3 meals per day with your choice off the menu. Children have their own menu so they can order your favorite foods.

MEALS & DRINKS

All meals are included in tariff.

GRAND EASTERN HOTEL

www.hexagonfiji.com

LOCATION
Labasa, Fiji

EMAIL
grest@connect.com.fj

PHONE/FAX
Ph (679) 881 1022
Fax (679) 881 4011

ADDRESS
P.O. Box 641, Labasa,
Fiji Islands.

FACILITIES
Air-conditioned rooms,
swimming pool, TV in all
rooms, tea/coffee-facilities, IDD
phones, restaurant and bar.

CREDIT CARDS
All major cards accepted.

FEATURES
Three accommodation wings with 24 units inclusive of four presidential suites. Our restaurant, the Colonial Arms, specialises in Vanua Levu seafood. We cater for businesspersons and corporate guests, tourists and families. We have meeting and conference facilities and you will find the Grand Eastern is the best place to stay whether for pleasure or business and for business functions. In the tradition of the grand hotels, the Grand Eastern Hotel caters for the traveller and businessperson alike. Providing an oasis of comfort and relaxation.
See website for rates and booking details.
www.hexagonfiji.com.fj

TAVEUNI

TAVEUNI – Known as the 'Garden Island' of Fiji, the country's third largest island boasts lush vegetation, spectacular waterfalls, miles of quiet sand beaches, and the country's national flower, the legendary Tagimoucia. Its primary economy is copra, but tourism also plays a dominant role with a major leisure development Soqulu, small eco-based projects around Taveuni and comfortable resort hotels. It is easily reached by air and sea from Viti Levu (mainland) and Vanua Levu.

The island of Taveuni is the third largest island in the Fiji archipelago. The International Date Line (180th Meridian) crosses the island within walking distance of the Garden Island Resort. However, for convenience sake, the date line has been moved so that all the Fiji Islands are under one time zone. The island is approximately 42 kilometres long and 15 kilometres wide. Taveuni's population of 12,000 (mostly native Fijians) resides in villages, the largest being the chiefly village of Somosomo.

In the high mountains of Taveuni there is a beautiful lake of considerable size, pouring through an outlet on the west, a stream which furnishes the township of Somosomo with a good supply of fresh water. A smaller outlet to the east discharges enough water to form a small cascade. A flowering plant called Tagimaucia is found only on the shores of this lake – any attempt to transplant it to lower altitudes has failed. The plant has bunches of flowers, red with a white centre, and is the most beautiful of all Fiji wild flowers.

A good motor road extends the full length of the lee or north-west coast from Vuna in the south to Wainibula in the north. There is an airstrip serviced by Air Fiji and Sunflower Airlines at Matei at the north of the island. Somosomo, on the west coast is a calling place for inter-island ships. There is a large hospital in the vicinity and several schools.

MARAVU PLANTATION RESORT

www.maravu.net

EMAIL
maravu@connect.com.fj

INTERNET
www.maravu.net

PHONE/FAX
Ph. (679) 888 0585 &
359 1819
Fax (679) 888 0600 &
359 1869

ADDRESS
PA Matei, Taveuni Island

FACILITIES
Spa, gym, beach,
swimming pool, horseback
riding, mountain bikes,
kayaks, snorkelling, deep
sea fishing, diving. Nearby
golf & tennis.

AMENITIES
Bar, lounge, library, laundry
service, air-condition,
ceiling fans, minibar, tea &
coffee making facilities,
CD-player, secluded
verandah.

ATTRACTIONS
Village- & eco-tours,
adventure treks via four
wheel drive, hiking tours
along the coast, jungle
trekking, islands &
snorkelling tours.

CREDIT CARDS
All major cards accepted

Maravu Plantation Beach Resort and Spa is a perfect Hideaway offering adventure and relaxation, culture and the unique experience to meet the people who have been here since ancient times. Maravu is tucked amongst 88 acres of coconut groves, lush tropical rainforest and a golden sandy beach. The setting of the Resort is spectacular and has only 20 elegant Bures (Villas) in a lush tropical garden to ensure space, freedom and privacy. They all are situated to face the tropical sunset, which you can enjoy from your large veranda. Maravu has Deluxe Bures and Honeymoon Bures with outdoor shower, sundeck and Jacuzzi as well as Planters Bure Duplex Units, all with high ceilings, hard wood and island décor. The top Bures are the Honeymoon Deluxe Suites and the Oceanview Spa Villas with a private yard containing an outdoor shower, a sundeck and a Plunge Spa Pool. All Bures except the Planters Bures are air-conditioned. Paradise is waiting to comfort you may it be finest dining with one of Fijiis best wine lists, world class diving in the Somosomo strait, spectacular waterfalls, or the famous volcano lake. Maravu's staff of over 50 will know you by name and guide you into any activities on the Resort like horseback riding, snorkelling or kayaking. This is a secluded tropical playground for you to relax at the white sand beach or around the pool, enjoy the hilltop sunset gardens, discover the underwater world snorkelling in crystal clear waters. Every week we invite for a Fijian Meke and Lovo feast where the speciality food is cooked in an underground oven. After the sunset, you may want to join in with the Maravu Band Boys, sitting around the kava bowl, sharing the ceremonial drink, made from pepper root and serenading beautiful Fijian melodies. Very attractive Packages are offered such as soft adventure, diving, honeymoon and wedding packages.

GET THE FIJI HOLIDAY FEELING, THE MOMENT YOU STEP ABOARD

With Air Pacific your holiday starts early. And with destinations all over the Pacific (Australia, New Zealand, Los Angeles, Japan, Hawaii, Vanuatu, Samoa, Tonga, Solomon Islands and Canada) you can enjoy the relaxed service, warmth and South Pacific tradition of caring we are famous for.

So step aboard Your Island In The Sky and get that Fiji holiday feeling!

AIR PACIFIC
FIJI'S INTERNATIONAL AIRLINE

SUSIE'S PLANTATION RESORT

www.susiesplantationresort.com

LOCATION
Taveuni, Fiji Islands

EMAIL
susies@connect.com.fj

PHONE/FAX
Ph (679) 888 0125
Fax (679) 888 0125
Australia:
Ph (612) 9281 5066
or toll free 1800 820 820
Fax (612) 9281 0660

ADDRESS
P.O. Box 69, Waiyevo,
Taveuni. Fiji Islands

FACILITIES
Pro Dive Taveuni dive
operation, licensed restaurant,
infinity pool, tours, Internet,
5-star bathrooms.

ATTRACTIONS
Unique deep water
frontage, scuba diving
specialists, marine park,
snorkelling, water sports,
Lava Tube & Rainforest
treks, whale watching, deep
sea fishing, horse riding.

CREDIT CARDS
All major cards accepted

ACCOMMODATION

Choose to stay in either our waterfront Traditional Fijian Bures or our multi capacity accommodations at the Divers Lodge, all have private balcony's and are individually landscaped, there is no escaping the natural beauty that abounds. From all accommodations magnificent red & gold sunsets over the Somosomo Strait can be viewed from your veranda hammock or at one of our many lookout points.

FEATURES

As one of the top 10 dive locations in the world this unbelievable Fijian paradise pertains to perfect unspoilt hard and soft corals, protected by the 1200m volcanic ridge that is the backdrop to Susies. Warm clear water welcomes all to embrace the brilliantly coloured tropical fish and shark dives are guaranteed, including hammers. The world class White Wall, Rainbow Reef, Orgasm Reef, The Stairway to Heaven & many more amazing sites are but minute's away waiting for you. Up to 10% discounts on all accommodation for Scuba Divers! Visit our live booking engine at www.prodive.com

QAMEA RESORT AND SPA FIJI

www.qamea.com

LOCATION
Taveuni Fiji

EMAIL
qamea@connect.com.fj

PHONE/FAX
Ph (679) 888 0220
Fax (679) 888 0092

ADDRESS
P.A. Matei Taveuni Fiji

FACILITIES
Airconditioning, fans,
mini-bar, tea/coffee-
making, pool, gym, spa,
restaurant, cocktail bar,
meet & greet
airport transfers

ATTRACTIONS
Private island, beachfront,
scuba diving, snorkelling,
great swimming at all
tides, watersports

CREDIT CARDS
All major cards accepted

ACCOMMODATION

Qamea is a breathtakingly beautiful island just three miles off Taveuni of dramatic mountains encased in tropical foliage, and totally unspoiled white sand beaches. A garden island in an azure sea, with spectacular soft coral gardens waiting just offshore. We are a luxurious and intimate resort with just 12 elegant air-conditioned oceanfront bures all discretely nestled among swaying palms and tropical greenery. Rates from US$590 double which includes all meals, and return transfers from Taveuni airport. The essence of luxury Fiji.

FEATURES

We are well known for some of the best cuisine in Fiji. The ambience of the resort makes it an ideal setting for honeymooners, divers and those that just want a private South Pacific getaway. No children under 13 years of age.

ACTIVITIES

Fiji's #1 rated snorkelling reef is just yards off our long white sand beach and our fully licensed scuba operation cater to all experience levels. Fully equipped gym, freshwater swimming pool, Guinot Institut.Paris Spa facilities, kayaks, sailing, windsurfing, village and waterfall tours, volleyball and more.

FOR MORE INFORMATION

See website for rates, specials and booking details.

QAMEA
FIJI

KADAVU

DIVING is first class on this island and all the resorts have dive operations. Trekking to some degree is also possible and overnight stays in villages can be negotiated through some of the resorts. Surfing, as mentioned in an earlier chapter, can also be quite good but rather inconsistent compared to Tavarua and Na Motu. Bird life is rich and no doubt you'll spot a Kadavu Parrot while you're on the island. You'll also be offered kava, which is exceptionally strong, on Kadavu. Finally, kayaking has become a big deal on Kadavu.

A kayaking holiday combines the best elements of Fiji – the natural beauty of the land and seascape plus the hospitality of the inhabitants. Though the scene is constantly changing, to the best of my knowledge kayaking trips are available in Taveuni, Vanua Levu, Kadavu and the Yasawa Group. For a first-person account of what it's like to go on a kayak trip check out Paddling Fiji's Kadavu Island.

Kayak Kadavu, not surprisingly, is based in Kadavu, Fiji's fourth largest island. Extremely remote, Kadavu is one of the least developed islands and has a spectacular array of bird life, including an indigenous parrot. Led by Michael and Melissa McCoy of Maui, Hawaii, they stress that the most important part of the experience is the cross-cultural dialogue with the Fijians. Travellers have the opportunity to visit villages, sip kava, watch a meke (traditional dance) and partake in a feast prepared in a lovo or underground oven. They tell me that they have a new route that starts at the top of Kadavu and follows the west shore. There are reportedly miles of perfect white sand beach, awesome calm waters, incredible seashell collecting and a couple of waterfalls. The kayak trip begins and ends at Dive Kadavu, a mid-range property located on a gorgeous beach. Guests may choose to cool their heels at the resort before or after the kayaking adventure.

WHERE TO STAY – Accommodation includes plantation-style hideaways, exclusive resorts, spacious traditional Fijian bures and dormitory share facilities. There are no restaurants at Vunisea, only a coffee shop at the airstrip which opens mornings only and there are two general stores selling canned goods.

There are no banks so change enough money before coming. Visitors normally book package holidays that include accommodation and meals.

NAGIGIA ISLAND RESORT

www.fijisurf.com

LOCATION
South-West Kadavu Island
by Cape Washington

EMAIL
sales@fijisurf.com

PHONE/FAX
Ph (679) 333 7774
Fax (679) 600 3052
Satellite Phone
(872) 762 941217

ADDRESS
PO Box 12, Vunisea,
Kadavu, Fiji

CONTACT
Taka Mashiko

FACILITIES
Private balcony, individual
bure, bure over the water,
fan cooled, wonderful views.

ATTRACTIONS
World class surfing, fishing
and diving, snorkelling,
broadband internet access,
windsurfing, licensed
restaurant and bar

CREDIT CARDS
MasterCard and Visa

Fly from Nadi or Suva daily to Vunisea Airport, Kadavu then enjoy a picturesque boat trip down the coast to Nagigia Island. Renowned for world-class surfing, fishing and scuba diving with several surfing breaks and uncrowded waves. Nagigia Island is the perfect getaway with beautiful scenery. Accommodation features bures right over the water. Some decks, you can jump into the water from. Weddings are a specialty. Other activities include: picnics on nearby white sandy beaches, snorkelling, kayak, paddleboard, hire surfboards, volleyball, table tennis, village tours, bush walks, island walks, reef walking, running tracks, cultural Fijian Meke, wake boarding, Nabukelevu mountain walk, video, DVD, playing cards, scrabble, drafts, chess, dominoes.

See our website www.fijisurf.com for full booking details and currect rates and specials.

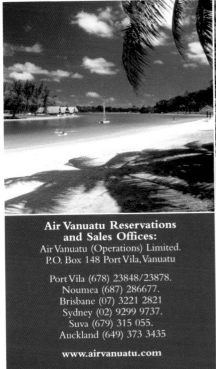

MAMANUCA

THE Mamanucas is a chain, or indeed chains, of islands west of Fiji's main island, Viti Levu. They provide white sand beaches, waving palms, blue waters and, at night, the cooling influences of the trade winds. Peace and tranquillity or, for the night owl, fun beckons on the Mamanucas.

The Mamanucas are volcanic outcrops pushed up from the ocean floor thousands of years ago. Some of them have a special significance in Fijian folklore; all of them have a special significance for the visitor.

From the air, the group is, in fact, two clusters of islands, known as Mamanuca-i-ra (or Leeward Mamanuca) and Mamanuca-i-cake (Windward Mamanuca). They are south of the long island chain known as the Yasawas and occupy the western margin of the lagoon between the Great Sea Reef and the Viti Levu coast.

The small northern or leeward islands are uninhabited; in the south, the windward islands have villages but most are used only for the cultivation of crops and the occasional fishing excursion.

Within the Mamanucas is the Malolo group, five kilometres inside the barrier reef and extending in a curve for about 120 kilometres. The biggest islands in this subgroup are Malolo, Malololailai (Little Malolo) and Qalito.

Malololailai is the hub for most of the traffic to and from the Mamanucas. It has a safe anchorage for vessels of varying sizes, shapes and styles. It boasts what can almost be described as a totally cosmopolitan community of Fijians, Indians, Europeans and other races and, importantly, it has an airstrip serviced daily from Nadi.

Fiji's Mamanucas are the epitome of the Pacific way of life. They are friendly and welcoming, their climate is warm and congenial. They represent history and tradition as well as the future with no fuss and no stress.

OUTER ISLANDS

THERE are hundreds more islands scattered around the main islands. Many of them are remote, making access difficult and often expensive. Rotuma is 600km north, and the Lau group stretches from north to south between the main islands and Tonga. Fiji's volcanic origins can be seen clearly in the shapes of the islands and their surrounding reefs. Boats are the local transport and villagers will often travel kilometres across open sea in very small boats.

LEVUKA: Historical walks, a colourful history and an interesting museum make Levuka a trip back in time. Located on Ovalau, it was established as a whaling settlement and soon became a centre for Pacific trading. It was also the capital of Fiji prior to Suva. The church, school, cottages, hotel and shop buildings hark back to the colonial past.

VATULELE: South of Viti Levu, the island is known for its rock paintings and the sacred red prawns that live in the tidal pools. The local women make traditional masi (tapa cloth).

DIVING: Ovalau has more than 50 mostly uncharted wrecks. There are superb soft corals and plentiful fishlife in all areas.

FISHING: Fishing is excellent, mostly hand-line or light tackle.

YACHTING: Cruising permits are required.

VILLAGE VISITS: These are generally arranged as part of an excursion. Devokula village on Ovalau Island is a traditional village providing day trips or overnight stays.

PICTURE: FIJI VISITORS BUREAU

WEDDINGS IN PARADISE

GETTING 'hitched' in Fiji has become quite a trend in this century, to the extent that many of the resorts and hotels are offering fabulous wedding and honeymoon packages to suit the bride & groom's needs.

Fiji Islands, the one truly relaxing tropical getaway, is a haven and a joyous destination for the 'about to be weds', newlyweds, romantic at heart, anniversaries, renewal of vows and re-kindling of longlost relationships. You can have your unique wedding, sensual honeymoon and re-kindling of lost love, just about anywhere in our peaceful, romantic, idyllic isles of Fiji. The options are endless, from underwater ceremonies to fun-filled relaxed island resort settings, love boats (cruises), secluded beaches, beautiful gardens, hilltops with the sun setting in the horizon, chapels, to the friendly welcome of the choirs. You'll capture the moments of a lifetime at the style/resort of your choice.

There are luxurious hideaways to affordable establishments, nightly entertainment, varied range of land and water-based activities, choice of elegant restaurants, sipping champagne and watching golden sunsets from your beachfront bures, clifftop decks set amidst cascading waterfalls in lush tropical surroundings, feel the waves lapping beneath your feet and much more.

Why wait, consider the peace and tranquillity of booking yourself a joyous celebration in the Fiji Isles.

ADVENTUROUS ECO-CULTURE

PICTURE: FIJI VISITORS BUREAU

THE Fiji Islands is one of the very few 'Edenic' places in the world today as it boasts miles and miles of extreme pristine beauty and is a nature lover's delight. It offers you the perfect escape to explore some of the best falls, tropical rainforests, as well as marvel at the exotic melting pot of customs of the Fijian, Indian, Chinese, Rotuman and other cultures that have made Fiji their home.

Fiji Islands is tailormade for relaxed adventure. You don't need to be a world-class athlete to participate in any adventure experiences that are available. You can experience the rush of jetboating, whitewater rafting or travelling at a more sedate pace on bamboo rafts (known locally as bilibili).

Basically, tourism in the Fiji Islands is divided into regions namely, the Nadi area, Coral Coast, Mamanucas, Sunshine Coast and Outer Islands. In all of these regions, you will never fall short of things to do and see. It awaits your discovery.

SMALL SHIPS, CHARTERS & CRUISES

THE joy of cruising the sparkling emerald and azure waters adjoining the Fiji Islands is not just the pleasure of experience untrammelled beauty, but also the realisation of childhood dreams of faraway places. Comprising over 300 islands, Fiji offers unsurpassed opportunities for exploration on both scheduled and 'make your own itinerary' charters. Experience world-renowned cruises to the magical Mamanucas, picture-perfect Yasawa Islands twice the setting for the movie 'The Blue Lagoon'.

See Blue Lagoon Cruises page 77.

SURFING, FISHING & DIVING

SURFING

BOARDS and accessories can be purchased or hired in one of a number of surf shops throughout Fiji. You should bring a hat, sunblock, rash vest, board shorts, booties and a small first aid kit. Treat cuts immediately as wounds left unattended will fester in this tropical climate. There are a number of good doctors and pharmacies in Fiji. Although the water does get fresh during the middle of the year (June/July/August) board shorts and rashy usually suffice. Springys are worn by some, as much for the fresh early morning surf as protection from the reef. If you have a helmet bring it.

FISHING

FISHING in Fiji is favoured all year round. There is simply great fishing for everyone! All methods of game fishing are available in Fiji – choice of group to instruct captain/crew. Overnight charter too is also available where the whole family can fish and catch a great amount of edible fish.

DIVING

FIJI offers some of the best scuba diving in the world. Labelled the Soft Coral Capital of the world by Jean-Michel Cousteau, it offers a comprehensive range of dive locations. Spectacular hard and soft corals, caves and grottos, an amazingly diverse marine life that includes large Pelagic species such as sharks and tuna, turtles and fish of all hues and sizes and internationally certified dive operations all ensure your dive experience will be a memorable one.

PICTURE: BLUE LAGOON CRUISES

PICTURE: FIJI VISITORS BUREAU

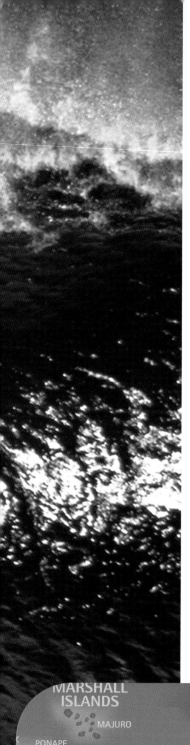

HAWAIIAN
ISLANDS

AS any fan of Magnum PI, Hawaii Five-O or even Baywatch Hawaii will know, the Hawaiian islands are rich in natural and spectacular beauty. Its many faces include the lush Na Pali Coast of Kaua'i; the fiery volcano of the Big Island; the historical charm of Lahaina, Maui; and the cosmopolitan atmosphere of Honolulu.

Hawaii's seven main islands – Oahu, Maui, Kauai, Molokai, Lanai, Niihau and Hawaii (together with the uninhabited Kahoolawe) – each offers a unique ambience and attraction for visitors. Author Mark Twain once pronounced Hawaii to be the loveliest fleet of islands that lies anchored in any ocean and not even the past 30 years of mass tourism have managed to change that.

Hawaii offers a natural sanctuary with everything from waterfalls to whales. There are accessible eco-adventures on land and sea. Since the first British frigates sailed into Hawaiian waters more than 200 years ago, visitors have been fascinated by Hawaii's unique environment: studying, drawing and being seduced by the natural riches native to her shores.

NATURE IN THE WILD

The young string of islands and atolls that make up Hawaii was developed in isolation, thousands of kilometres from the nearest landmass, through dramatic volcanic activity that continues to this day. The result is a unique masterpiece of natural diversity, where 21 of the world's 22 climatic zones are represented (everything from tropical rainforests to snow-capped summits), supporting an incredible 88 natural communities or eco-systems.

Hawaii Volcanoes National Park on the Big Island is an unforgettable showcase for Mauna Kea and Launa Loa, the two largest mountains on Earth (if measured from their ocean floor base, they rise 9144 metres). Then there is the still-active Mauna Loa volcano; the dormant, snow-capped Mauna Kea and its neighbour Kilauea, the world's most active volcano.

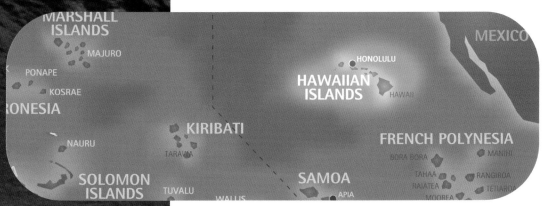

For more information on the Islands of Hawaii visit the website
www.pacifictravelfactfile.com

PICTURE: HAWAII...

PICTURE: JILL INNAMORATI-VARLEY

GEOGRAPHICAL LOCATION
Hawaii is located about 20¡ north of the equator in the Pacific Ocean. It is 4023 kilometres to the United States.

AIRLINES
International: Air New Zealand, Air Nauru, American, Continental, Hawaiian Air, Canadian Airlines, China Airlines, Japan Airlines, North West Orient, Korean Airlines, Qantas and a number of other international carriers all service the Hawaiian islands.
Domestic: Hawaiian Airlines, Aloha Airlines and smaller local airlines service the inter-island route.

ARRIVAL/DEPARTURE INFORMATION
Honolulu International Airport is the point of entry for all major international flights.
Visitors over 21 are permitted to bring in 1 litre of spirits or wine, 200 cigarettes or 50 cigars or 1.36kg of tobacco.
Conditions of entry are the same as those for the United States. Most visitors require a visa. However, Canadians need only proof of citizenship and citizens of Andorra, Argentina, Australia, Austria, Belgium, Brunei, Denmark, Finland, France, Germany, Iceland, Ireland, Italy, Japan, Liechtenstein, Luxembourg, Monaco, The Netherlands, New Zealand, Norway, Portugal, San Marino, Singapore, Slovenia, Spain, Sweden, Switzerland, the United Kingdom and Uruguay may stay up to 90 days without a visa.

Departure Tax: International Departure Tax from the Hawaiian Islands is US$38.50.

CURRENCY
The currency of Hawaii is the US dollar.

CLIMATE
The Trade Winds provide Hawaii with an ideal balmy climate, mild temperatures and moderate humidity. The temperature ranges from 18o to 30o Celsius.

ELECTRICITY
The electrical current is 120 volts, 60 cycles. Visitors are advised to purchase adaptors prior to arrival in Hawaii.

HANDICRAFTS
Many galleries and shops feature authentic Hawaiian arts and crafts.

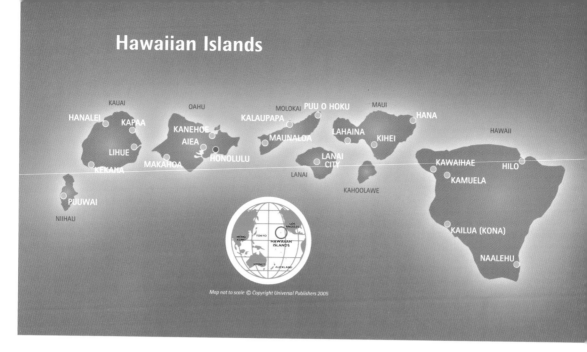

Hawaiian Islands

Map not to scale © Copyright Universal Publishers 2005

LANGUAGE

English is the official language. Hawaiian is the local language and, due to the large variety of tourists arriving from all over the world, many foreign languages are spoken at hotels and resorts.

POPULATION

Estimated population of the Hawaiian Islands is 1.5 million people and this is made up of Hawaiian, Japanese, Chinese, Filipino, Korean, Samoan and part-Hawaiian ethnic groups.

LOCAL CONSIDERATIONS

Medical services are readily available but expensive. Visitors should make sure they are well covered by sufficient medical insurance before leaving their home destination. Most hotels have resident doctors.

Dress is casual. Women in light, loose dresses, men in aloha shirts, shorts, sandals for day many religions and denominations are represented.

Tipping for good service is appropriate. It is customary to tip 15 per cent in a restaurant. Taxi drivers are usually tipped about 10 per cent of the fare. A four per cent State Tax is added to rooms, food, goods, etc. There is also a five per cent accommodation tax.

TELECOMMUNICATIONS

A network of underwater cable and satellite communication systems provide two-way voice, data, and television services to North America, Australia and Asia as well as other Pacific Basin areas. Telephone services throughout Hawaii are provided by a major company, GTE Hawaiian Telephone Co. Internet cafes are widely interspersed throughout the island.

TIME ZONE

Hawaiian time is 10 hours behind Greenwich Mean Time.

TRANSPORT

Taxis, car rental and regular bus services are widely available. For car rentals, drivers must be at least 21 years of age. Driving is on the right side of road. Pedestrians have right of way in almost all situations.

PICTURE: HAWAII VISITORS CONVENTION BUREAU

OAHU

WHERE ALOHA BEGINS

HOME of Honolulu, Waikiki and Pearl Harbor, Oahu is the most easily recognisable of the islands. Oahu is also the entrance to Hawaii with the Honolulu Internationl Airport. With a population of 875,000 people, it is the third largest of Hawaii's islands.

While Oahu was populated before 1000AD, it was added to the island kingdom in 1795 when King Kamehameha I fought the Oahu King's forces to surrender at the famous Battle of Nu'uanu Pali.

With its fine harbors, Oahu gradually became the state's political, economic, military, educational and cultural centre. Honolulu Harbor, discovered before 1800, became a key Pacific port for whale, sandalwood and fur traders. Pearl Harbor became famous when the United States set about establishing a key strategic presence in the Pacific Ocean.

By 1850, the Hawaiian Royal Court had moved permanently to Honolulu where it has remained the seat of government for the monarchy, republic, territory and state.

The city of Honolulu is a diverse and ongoing attraction with distinct and intriguing districts like the thriving downtown/Chinatown business district set alongside busy Honolulu Harbor. Chinatown has been a part of the city's history since the 1860s.

Hawaii's most visited attraction is the USS Arizona Memorial at Pearl Harbor, north-west of Honolulu, where 1.5 million visitors come each year to learn about the surprise Japanese attack on December 7, 1941 and to pay their respects to the 2335 dead US servicemen.

Oahu also boasts dozens of private or city-owned attractions that are simply pure fun vacation experiences. Luaus (Polynesian shows), dancing dolphins, sunset cruises, submarine rides, a world-class zoo and aquarium, garden tours and "ghost walks" all beguile visitors.

The island also boasts Byodo-in Temple which has beautiful Zen gardens and a three-ton brass bell. Visitors should not miss out on the US Army Museum of Hawaii, Waikiki Aquarium, Diamond Head Lookout and the Polynesian Cultural Centre.

KAUAI

PICTURE: HAWAII VISITORS CONVENTION BUREAU

BORN OF FIRE

NORTHERNMOST of the Hawaiian Islands and geographically the oldest, Kauai is the fourth largest of the islands. It was created by a massive volcano of which Mt Wai'ale'ale towers 1569 metres high at its eastern rim.

Kauai may well be the most recognisible of the islands as it has been the film location for more than 60 major movies and television films including South Pacific, Blue Hawaii and Jurassic Park.

The island has 145 kilometres of coastline and is remarkable for its spectacular and widely varied landscape, from desert-like Waimea Canyon – called The Grand Canyon of the Pacific – to the velvety-green Na Pali Coast, with cliffs rising to 810 metres.

Located just a 25-minute jet flight from Honolulu, Kauai is serviced by two inter-island air carriers with more than 45 regularly scheduled round-trip flights.

Captain James Cook's first Hawaiian landing was on Kauai, coming ashore at Waimea in 1778 – forever changing the status of this isolated group of islands. However, until 1810, Kauai remained an independent kingdom and only fell under the unified island rule of King Kamehameha after the death of King Kaumuali'i.

Kauai boasts a greater expanse of beach-per-coastline than any other island (with 43 white sand beaches). There are more hiking trails, it has Hawaii's largest coffee plantation and has the only navigable rivers in Hawaii.

Attractions are diverse and include Captain Cook's Landing, Waimea Bay, which remained for many years a favourite provisioning port with Pacific traders and whalers. Kalalau Lookout was once the home of peacocks preening their plumage in this tropical Eden and families cultivated terraces of taro – no one lives here now but it still provides one of the world's most beautiful views.

PICTURE: HAWAII VISITORS CONVENTION BUREAU

PICTURE: HAWAII VISITORS CONVENTION BUREAU

PICTURE: HAWAII VISITORS CONVENTION BUREAU

MAUI

UNIQUE SCENIC BEAUTY

MAUI is the second largest of the Hawaiian Islands. From Maui, the islands of Molokai, Lanai, Molokini and the uninhabited Kahoolawe can be reached by boat. They all group around Maui's southern and western shores, providing a unique scenic beauty.

Over 75 per cent of the island is wilderness. Sail to Lanai or Molokini for incomparable snorkelling and scuba diving, or go deepsea fishing for a real salty, satisfying seafaring challenge. Bike ride to Mt Haleakaka – an exhilarating downhill cruise from 3050 metres. Hike through lava deserts, tropical jungles, bamboo forests and towering mountain ranges. Maui is the whale-watching capital of Hawaii. Humpbacks congregate in the warm offshore waters annually from November through to April.

Famed as the magic isle, Maui's legends began many years ago when the world was young. The demigod Maui looked upon the people of his island and saw that the days were too short for them to finish their work and enjoy life because the sun flew so swiftly across the sky.

So Maui hid in the crater of the island's highest mountain and snared the fierce Sun god, making him promise to travel more slowly over Maui. To this day, the Sun keeps its word and even makes its mythical home in Mt Haleakala, the House of the Sun.

Island attractions include Baldwin House, a museum displaying an example of early island missionary homes, the Maui Zoological and Botanical Gardens, the Brig Carthaginian II Maritime Museum and the Humpback Whale National Maritime Sanctuary.

The art scene is world-renowned with scores of galleries, museum shops and a visual arts centre displaying contemporary, impressionist, abstract and traditional works – mostly inspired by the island.

"Maui Hands" shops allow local artisans to offer their amazing crafts notably in rare koa wood, hand-blown glass, and ceramics. For the shopping minded, some of the world's most famous fashion labels are represented.

DESTINATION RESORTS HAWAII

www.drhmaui.com

LOCATION
Wailea Resort, Maui

EMAIL
info@drhmaui.com

PHONE/FAX
Maui
Ph (808) 891 6249
Fax (808) 874 3554
Toll free U.S./Canada
1 (800) 367 5246

ADDRESS
3750 Wailea Alanui Dr.,
#B51 Wailea, Maui,
Hawaii 96753

FACILITIES
Pools, BBQ areas, air
conditioned, self-
contained, daily
housekeeping, free parking

ATTRACTIONS
Free night specials, golf &
tennis packages, beachfront,
golf course views, concierge
service, security

CREDIT CARDS
American Express, JCB,
MasterCard, Visa accepted

Destination Resorts Hawaii is the condominium rental and management company for six luxury condominium properties located in the exclusive Wailea and Makena golf and tennis resort communities on the south or "sun-coast" of Maui, Hawaii. The studio, one-, two-, three- and four-bedroom spacious condominiums in this portfolio of exclusive properties are distinguished by stylish decor, superlative appointments, fully equipped kitchens, air-conditioning, lush landscaping, and an amenities plan that includes daily housekeeping, concierge service and free long distance calls. Internet access is available in some units. Barbecues, swimming pools, a complete spectrum of activities, complimentary beach towels and preferential rates for tennis and golf round out the exceptional value you'll find at Destination Resorts' Wailea Ekolu Village, Wailea Grand Champions Villas, Wailea Ekahi Village, Wailea Elua Village, Polo Beach Club and Makena Surf. Choose from beachfront, ocean view or golf course condominium locations, and enjoy your private space and your "home away from home" vacation experience. Rates range from $175 plus tax to $1325 plus tax per night. Destination Resorts Hawaii offers car-condo packages and free night specials. For more information visit www.drhmaui.com or call (808) 891 6249.

PICTURE: HAWAII VISITORS CONVENTION BUREAU

PICTURES: HAWAII VISITORS CONVENTION BUREAU

HAWAII

ECOLOGICALLY DIVERSE

HAWAII, otherwise known as the Big Island, is the youngest and largest of the Hawaiian Islands and it continues to grow as long as lava spews from Mt Kilauea, the world's most active volcano.

The ancient Hawaiians arrived at Ka Lae, or South Point, and developed their civilisation for more than a thousand years before establishing contact with the western world. The island then became a busy seaport for traders and whalers from around the world. The Chinese were the first large group of immigrants to arrive, followed by waves of Japanese, Portuguese, Filipinos, Samoans, Okinawans, Koreans and Puerto Ricans – mainly lured there to work in the sugar fields.

Residents of the Big Island are very proud of their heritage and there is evidence of their ethnic pride everywhere – in the food, customs, architecture, language, arts and crafts and lifestyle.

Of all the islands, Hawaii's Big Island is the most ecologically diverse, with natural environments ranging from the desert plains of Ka'u and the rainforests above Hilo to snowcapped Mauna Kea. There are said to be 13 climatic regions on earth and the Big Island has all but two, the Arctic and the Saharan.

Hawaii Volcanoes National Park allows visitors to experience the sights of steaming calderas and lush jungle forests. Visitors will hear the legends of Madame Pele and walk through a lava tube. Self-guided trails take hikers through all terrains.

Tropical Hilo, the gateway to the Hawaii Volcanoes National Park area, is exceptionally lush with sweeping views from the sea to Mauna Kea. The district of Puna exports most of its exotic tropical flowers to all parts of the world. Tropical blossoms are everywhere and many gardens and nurseries are open to the public.

Hawaii's Big Island has nine natural spas to rejuvenate tired bodies and, for the more active, the island is Hawaii's golf capital with 18 golf courses.

WAIKIKI BEACHCOMBER HOTEL

LOCATION
Waikiki Honolulu, Hawaii

EMAIL
resv@waikikibeachcomber.com

PHONE/FAX
Ph (808) 922 4646
Fax (808) 923 4889
Toll Free Canada & USA
800 622 4646

ADDRESS
2300 Kalakaua Ave
Honolulu Hawaii 96815

FACILITIES
Pool, shops, boutiques, on-site laundry, private facilities

ATTRACTIONS
Central location, conference facilities, Don Ho Show & Magic of Polynesia offer nightly entertainment

CREDIT CARDS
All major credit cards accepted

ACCOMMODATION
500 rooms and suites with color TV and in-house movies, air conditioning, refrigerator, safe, direct-dial phones and ironing boards.

Large private balconies overlooking the ocean.

Non-smoking floors and handicap facilities available. Serviced daily.

Room rates from $245 to $980.

FACILITIES
Situated in heart of Waikiki, next door to International Market Place. Swimming pool, sundries shop, washer/dryer in building.

On-property parking, conference room seating 300, standing 400. Golf, tennis arranged.

Nightly entertainment (within the hotel) includes famous shows such as, Magic of Polynesia – Don Ho Show, Blue Hawaii (Elvis Presley impersonation).

3 times weekly there are hula dancing and ukelele lessons.

FOR FURTHER INFORMATION
See our website for full booking details and current rates.

ILIMA HOTEL

LOCATION
Waikiki, Hawaii

EMAIL
mail@ilima.com

PHONE/FAX
Ph (1808) 923 1877
(800) 801 9366
Fax (1808) 924 2617

ADDRESS
445 Nohonani St
Honolulu HI 96815

FACILITIES
Self-contained, cable TV, pool, laundry

CREDIT CARDS
All major credit cards accepted

99 spacious studios and suites, air conditioned, all with fully equipped kitchens and color cable TV with free HBO & Disney, radio, private lanais, coffee/tea maker, in-room safe, iron/board, hairdryer, daily maid service, pool, sauna, laundry facilities, fitness room and sundeck.

We have the largest rooms in Waikiki and are located 2 blocks from Waikiki Beach. Free high-speed Internet access and Cal King beds in all Deluxe Units.

Free parking, free local phone calls, voice mail and computer jacks.

Conference Center for up to 50 people, tour and travel desk. Rates from $US125 per night.

See our website for full booking details and current rates.

LANAI

PICTURE HAWAII VISITORS CONVENTION BUREAU

PICTURE HAWAII VISITORS CONVENTION BUREAU

SECLUDED ISLAND

LANAI, the sixth largest of the Hawaiian Islands, was once known as the Isle of Contentment. This, however, conflicts with the legend that says Lanai was once an evil place, overrun by demons. Once the evil spirits were driven out by Kaulula'au, an exiled son of a West Maui king, natives finally came to live on the island.

Lanai is 98 per cent privately owned by Castle & Cooke and they've developed the island as an exclusive resort destination. It is practically a private park with two very exclusive five-star resorts, each complete with its own classic championship golf course.

It is the smallest of the Hawaiian Islands that is open to visitors with daily flights in and out, and you can visit by boat or ferry from Maui, however, it is still very much a world apart.

Main attractions include the Luahiwa Petrographs. These inscriptions on 34 boulders on a steep slope overlooking the Palawai Basin are among the best preserved in all the islands. The petroglyphs are a mixture of ancient and historic styles.

On Lanai you can go horseback riding in the cool upcountry hills, across ranch lands where Hawaiian cowboys, paniolo, worked the herds and through eucalyptus forests where axis deer and wild turkey roam the trails.

PICTURE HAWAII VISITORS CONVENTION BUREAU

MOLOKAI

PICTURE: HAWAII VISITORS CONVENTION BUREAU

THE FRIENDLY ISLE

MOLOKAI is also known as "The Most Hawaiian Isle" a place where nature has carved rugged beauty and where residents and visitors enjoy a slow paced, truly Hawaiian pace. The ancients believed that this island possessed a spirituality unique in all the Hawaiian Islands and it remains that special place today.

Long ago, Molokai was known as the lonely isle because the power of its Kahuna priests was feared throughout the Hawaiian Islands. Warring island kings gave Molokai a wide berth and persecuted natives often fled here for refuge.

Growth and development on the island have been quite slow and there are no high-rises, no fast-food chains and just a single traffic light on the whole island.

The west-end of this long, narrow, mountainous island is dry with wide plains. The east end is a tropical rain forest, while the rough-hewn north shore features deep ravines in rich hues of green created by more than 6m of rainfall each year.

Prime attractions include the Molokai Ranch, 'Ili'ili'opae – a Hawaiian heiau that showcases traditional island culture; and Molokai's most famous site – Kalaupapa – a beautiful and secluded area that was once a leper colony administered by one of Hawaii's most venerated figures, Father Damien.

PICTURE: HAWAII VISITORS CONVENTION BUREAU

PICTURE: HAWAII VISITORS CONVENTION BUREAU

KIRIBATI

PICTURE: SOUTH PACIFIC TOURISM

KIRIBATI (pronounced Kiribas) is an independent Republic within the Commonwealth of Nations, located in the central Pacific Ocean, about 4,000 kilometres (about 2,500 mi) southwest of Hawaii. It is part of the division of the Pacific islands that is known as Micronesia. Kiribati consists of 33 coral islands divided among three island groups: the Gilbert Islands, the Phoenix Islands, and the Line Islands. All of the islands are atolls (ring-shaped islands with central lagoons) except for the island of Banaba in the Gilbert Islands. Of the 33 islands of Kiribati, 21 are inhabited. Most of the population is concentrated in the Gilbert Islands. Only one of the Phoenix Islands and three of the Line Islands are permanently inhabited. The capital of Kiribati is Tarawa, an atoll in the Gilbert Islands. Bairiki, an islet of Tarawa, serves as an administrative center.

Kiribati has a total land area of 811 square kilometres (313 square miles). The islands extend about 3,900 kilometres (about 2,400 miles) from east to west. From north to south they extend about 2,100 kilometres (about 1,300 miles), straddling the equator. Kiritimati (also called Christmas Island), one of the Line Islands, occupies 609 square kilometres (235 square miles) and has the largest land area of any atoll in the world. Kiribati's exclusive economic zone (area of the ocean in which it controls fishing and other rights) covers more than 3 million square kilometres (more than 1 million square miles).

Prior to 1994, the eastern and western islands groups were on either side of the International Dateline with a 23-hour time difference between them. President of Kiribati at that time decided to move the dateline for convenience which attributed a 2 hr difference between Islands in the Gilbert Islands Group and the (Line and Phoenix) Islands Group. This also marked Kiribati to become the first nation to see in the Third Millennium and Caroline was renamed Millennium Island to celebrate the occasion during the year 2000.

The majority of the atolls are barely more than six metres above sea level and surrounded by barrier reefs creating picturesque lagoons for fishing, snorkeling, scuba diving, swimming and other water sports. Professional scuba diving guide are available on both Christmas Island and Tarawa.

KIRIBATI
AT A GLANCE

KIRIBATI VISITORS BUREAU
PO box 487, Betio, Tarawa
Tel: (686) 26 003/26 004 Fax: (686) 26 193
Email: tourism@mict.gov.ki

PICTURE COURTESY OF SOUTH PACIFI

GEOGRAPHIC LOCATION
Kiribati is located in the Central Pacific between 173 and 177 East Longitude and 4 north and 3 South Latitude. From North to South, a distance of 800kilometres, and the distance east to west from Tarawa to Christmas Island is some 3,300 kilometres. They consist of 33 low-lying atolls of which 20 are inhabited.

AIRLINES
Scheduled airlines service Nadi, Fiji, Majuro in the Marshall Islands, Honolulu in Hawaii, Melbourne, Brisbane and Nauru. International airlines servicing Kiribati include Air Marshall Islands and Air Nauru. The domestic airline is Air Kiribati.

ARRIVAL/DEPARTURE INFORMATION
Tarawa and Christmas Island have international airports. Tarawa's airport is at Bonriki about 50 minutes from Betio.
There is a departure tax of A$20.00 for passengers aged two years. Airport taxes on the outer islands apply but are varied.
All visitors must be in possession of a valid passport and onward ticket and must have proof of sufficient funds to support themselves while staying in the country. A number of countries are exempt from holiday visas and citizens of Britain, New Zealand and Canada among others may enter without a visa for a maximum stay of 28 days.

CURRENCY
The unit of currency is the Australian dollar.

CLIMATE
Temperature varies between 25 and 33 degrees Celsius. The wet season extends from December to May. A gentle breeze from the easterly quarter is predominant.

ELECTRICITY
Power is supplied at 240 VAC, 50 hertz. Appliances with the standard Australian type three-pin plug will operate within South Tarawa.

HANDICRAFTS
Handicraft centres and shops located on South Tarawa and on Christmas Island provide a variety of local handicrafts for sale to visitors. Some of the handicrafts are shark tooth swords local fans, mats, trays and wooden spears.

LANGUAGE
The main language is I-Kiribati. On the capital Tarawa, English is widely understood but less so on the outer islands.

POPULATION
The 2000 census figures showed that the population of Kiribati was 84,494.

LOCAL CONSIDERATIONS
Normally very casual. The tropical climate and simple lifestyle of the islanders encourages cool, cotton, loosely fitting shirts and shorts for men. Women should not go out in shorts, short dresses especially on the outer islands. Bikinis and brief swimwear are also not acceptable.
Visitors are advised not to drink unboiled well water. Hepatitis is prevalent and it is wise to take precautions if staying for any length of time. The Tungaru Central Hospital at Nawerewere, on South Tarawa, provides medical services in an emergency. A pharmacy is located at the hospital but visitors are advised to bring their own prescribed medicines.

PICTURE COURTESY OF SOUTH PACIFIC TOURISM

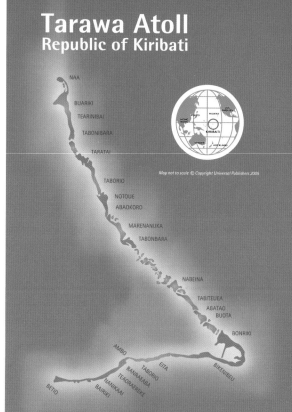

Tarawa Atoll
Republic of Kiribati

NAA
BUARIKI
TEARINIBAI
TABONIBARA
TARATAI
TABORIO
NOTOUE
ABAOKORO
MARENANUKA
TABONBARA
NABEINA
TABITEUEA
ABATAO
BUOTA
BONRIKI
AMBO
TABORIO
BIKENIBEU
BANRAEABA
EITA
TEAORAEREKE
NANIKAAI
BETIO
BAIRIKI

Map not to scale © Copyright Universal Publishers 2005

Tipping is not customary.

There are three types of water supplies - well water, desalinated water and rainwater tanks. Piped water supplies are chlorinated and it is advisable to boil all water before drinking.

TELECOMMUNICATIONS

Telecom Services Kiribati Limited (TSKL) provides facilities such as IDD, fax and telex. A limited number of islands have access to the public network. The rest of the islands are served by HF radio service.

TIME ZONE

Kiribati is 12 hours ahead of GMT that is, two hours ahead of Tokyo and 22 hours ahead of Honolulu, on the other side of the international dateline.

TRANSPORT

Overseas driving licences and international driving permits are recognised in Kiribati for a maximum period of two weeks after arrival.

Driving is on the left side of the road and the speed limit is 40 kilometres per hour in towns/villages but not exceeding 60 kilometres on the open highway.

A large fleet of privately owned buses operates an inexpensive mode of public transport.

Ships operate from Betio, Tarawa to all the outer islands transporting vehicles and passengers.

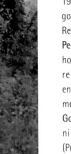

Flora and Fauna – The coconut palm is the most common form of vegetation. Other vegetation includes pandanus, pawpaw and breadfruit. Fisheries resources and rich of marine life can be found in profusion in all the islands, especially in the waters of Line and Phoenix island groups. Extensive populations of birdlife are found on Christmas Island and include shearwater, petrel, tropicbird, frigate birds, terns, noddys and the Christmas Island warbler, which is found only on Christmas Island.

A Brief History: Modern history of Kiribati begins with the arrival of Micronesians into the South Pacific, which took place between 200 and 500 AD. Tarawa was the scene of one of the fiercest engagements between the American and Japanese forces during the Second World War. Christmas Island was the base for early nuclear testing in the 1950's and is now a satellite tracking base as well as a thriving resort. Internal self-government was attained in two stages until it finally became a fully independent Republic on 12 July 1979.

People – The people of Kiribati live by values, which include the importance of family, hospitality, peace and tranquility and enjoy making time for conservation and time to relax. They are renowned traditional dancers and floorshows featuring such entertainment can be enjoyed during festive occasions at village Maneabas (traditional meeting house).

Government – Kiribati is a sovereign, democratic state and has a 42 member Maneaba ni Maungatabu (House of Parliament), elected every four years. The Beretitenti (President) is elected from among three or four candidates nominated by the Maneaba from its ranks. The Beretitenti chooses a twelve-member cabinet from the Maneaba. The country is a member of the commonwealth and adopts the Westminster model of government.

Economy – The country's economy is predominantly subsistence, with copra, seaweed and fisheries the main source of foreign exchange earnings. Revenue from the licensing of foreign vessels fishing in the Kiribati Exclusive Economic Zone (EEZ) contributes some $2-3 million per annum. Tourism plays a fairly modest role in the Gilbert Island group but in the Northern Line Islands especially Fanning Island and Christmas Island, tourism has a high priority. Revenue from tourism has been mainly generated from cruise tours in Fanning and Christmas Island. In 2003 Cruise tourism on Fanning Island contributed some AUD$1,041,145.00 from passenger head tax payments.

In addition, cruise tourism also generated extra income for the locals of Christmas Island & Fanning Island through sales of their handicrafts, local dancing performances and through local tour guiding.

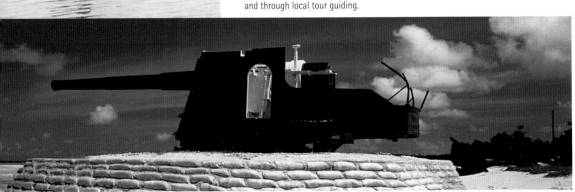

SCENIC ATTRACTIONS

Wildlife – Kiribati has wild life sanctuaries on Christmas Island and on most of the southern Line Islands. Extensive populations of birdlife are found on Christmas Island, and islands of the Line and Phoenix Group.

For full details or enquiries for visit purposes, please write direct to the Secretary, Ministry of Line and Phoenix Development, Christmas Island, Republic of Kiribati, the fax number (686) 81 278, Email: mlpg@tskl.net.ki or tourismxmas@tskl.net.ki

Cultural Center (Te Umanibong): A cultural centre at Bikenibeu, displays artifacts and other items of cultural and historic significance. Opening hours: 0800-1230, 1330-1615 from Mondays to Fridays only. For more details, please contact the Cultural Officer. Tel: (686) 28 283 Fax: (686) 28 334.

Historic Sites - Recent history is very apparent on some islands of Kiribati. The Islands' role in World War II is evident in the battle of Tarawa, during which thousands of American and Japanese lives were lost. Betio Islet where one of the bloodiest ever fought in World War II now left with memorable scars of war relics.

Abemama Island is an important historical site being the first island at which Captain Davis hoisted the Union Jack in 1892. It was also on this island that the famed Robert Louis Stevenson resided in 1889.

Butaritari Island, the greenest island, was famous for the traditional art of 'binekua', or the (calling of the whales to come ashore) by Kuma Villagers.

Handicrafts – Handicraft centres and shops located on South Tarawa and on Christmas Island provide a variety of local handicrafts for sale to visitors at these centres and shops:

Irekenrao Handicraft Shop, Bikenibeu
Atoll Handicraft Shop, Betio (near Kiribati Visitors Bureau Building)
Itoiningaina Handicraft Centre, Teaoraereke, Tel: (686) 21038

RAK Handicraft Centre, Tangitebu,
Tel: (686) 21132

AMAK Handicraft Centre,
Bikenibeu, Tel: (686) 28517

Kiribati Handicraft and Local Produce
Bairiki, Tel: (686) 22 193 or 22 195
Fax: (686)

Entertainment – We are renowned dancers and floorshows featuring such entertainment can be enjoyed during festive occasions or upon request, at a village Maneaba (meeting house) or at the hotels. Nightclubs have DJs and live bands playing a wide range of Local/Pacific Islands and English songs to keep guests and locals entertained. Recommended Nightclubs on South Tarawa for visitors are:

Royal Saloon - Nightclub & Bar. Opens Mon, Tues, Thurs from 5pm-10pm, Weds and Fri-Sat from 5pm-2am. Barbeque Nights on Wednesdays, Friday and Saturdays.

Emperor Saloon Nightclub. Opens Monday to Saturday from 6pm to 2am

Movie theaters are available on South Tarawa showing a wide range of international movies. You can also rent movies on DVDs, VCD and tapes at various video libraries on South Tarawa. On the outer islands movies are shown in the village maneabas' for the public.

TABUAERAN ISLAND & KIRITIMATI ISLAND

CHRISTMAS island (or Kiritimati Island) and Fanning Island (or Tabuaeran Island) both located in the Kiribati Line Islands Group have become very popular as new Cruise ship destinations for cruise passengers. Christmas Island receives surprise cruise tours from cruise ships on an irregular basis, and it is also very popular for diving and game fishing. Every year most American tourists come to Christmas Island to enjoy and experience the adventures in bonefish fishing and big trevally fishing. Fanning Island however is the very popular cruise destination with cruise visits provided by the Norwegian Cruise Line (NCL). NCL is currently operating a fixed cruise schedule with Fanning Island up until the year 2010. Every 10 to 11 days an NCL cruise vessel visits Fanning Island. On the island, passengers are welcomed with local dances, and participate in island tours, and activities such as sightseeing, fishing, snorkeling, and swimming in the clear blue lagoon. Cruise operators are advised that a Cruise Head Tax of $USD6.00 per passenger is charged, irrespective of whether their passengers land or not during their call.

For information on game fishing Christmas Island contact the Kiribati National Tourism Office.

Shipping Agencies of Kiribati (SAOK) proud agents of NCL and surprise cruises to Christmas Island and Fanning Island. Tel: (686) 26472, Fax: (686) 26430. Email: saok@tskl.net.ki

Sport and Recreation – Favourite swimming spots in Tarawa can found on both side of the Dai Nippon Causeway, the Ambo Lagoon area and off the small islets of North Tarawa. Your hotel will advise you on how to access local swimming spots. Facilities for the following holiday sports in Kiribati are available: basketball, soccer, volleyball, squash, tennis, canoe racing, jet skiing and other water sports.

Diving and Fishing Game – Game fishing, snorkeling and scuba diving plus scuba diving guide are available on both Christmas Island and Tarawa.

PRACTICAL INFORMATION

Local Transport – Large fleets of privately owned buses operate most efficient and inexpensive mode of public transport from the airport to the main centres on South Tarawa. Just flag one down anywhere on the main road and get off anywhere you wish. By the time you want to get off the bus just simply shout the word "I-kai" or "Taiaoka I-kai." If they sound their horn it means they are full. Do not worry another one will come along in a couple of minutes. Buses operate daily from Betio to Buota starting from 6.00am to 9.00-10.00pm.

Ships operate from Betio, Tarawa to all the outer islands transporting cargoes, vehicles as well as passengers. For more information on shipping services, please contact any of the following agencies.

KSSL – Kiribati Shipping Services Ltd.
PO Box 495 Betio, Tarawa, Republic of Kiribati.
Tel: (686) 26195 Fax: (686) 26204 Telex: (761) 77030, SCK
Email: kssl@tskl.net.ki

KIISS – Kiribati Inter Island Shipping Services
Tel/Fax: (686) 26 839

WKK Shipping
Betio, Tarawa, Republic of Kiribati
Tel: (686) 26 077

Inginimainiku Shipping Enterprises
Bikenibeu, Tarawa, Republic of Kiribati
Tel: (686) 28087 Fax: (686) 28539

Nikoraoi Shipping Betio
Tarawa, Republic of Kiribati.
Tel: (686) 26536 Fax: (686) 26367

The National Tourism Office may assist in obtaining schedules of other inter-island boats operating from outer islands to South Tarawa.

Motoring/Rental Cars – Persons hiring a rental car should be at least 17 years old. Small and medium size Toyota cars of Japanese made are available for rental hire. Make reservation at least 2 weeks in advance for your car through the Kiribati National Tourism Office.

Hire cars are available from:
Toyota Rent-a-Car, Bairiki, Tarawa
Tel: (686) 21090, Fax: (686) 21451

Otintaai Hotel Ltd, General Manager, Bikenibeu, Tarawa, Kiribati.
Tel: (686) 28 084, Fax: (686) 28 045 Email: otintaai@tskl.net.ki.

Kiribati National Tourism Office can arrange private rental cars upon request.

On Christmas Island – Pickup trucks with or without rear canopies are available for rent from the following companies which you may contact through the following:

Dojin, London, Tel: (686) 81346
Fax: (686) 81321 Email: dojin@tskl.net.ki

JMB Enterprises Ltd.
Main Camp Tel: (686) 81501 Fax: (686) 81501 Email: jmb@tskl.ent.ki
Dive & Sport Fishing Resort
Tel: (686) 81364, Fax: (686) 81246, Email: ote@tskl.net.ki

Water Supply – Three types of water supplies are available: Well water from fresh water lens, desalinated water and rainwater tanks. Piped water supplies are well chlorinated. However, it is advisable to boil all water before drinking or drink imported mineral water.

Laundry Service – Most hotels/motels provide laundry services.

ACCOMMODATION/RATES & TOUR OPERATORS

THERE are seven tourist hotels recommended by the National Tourism Office in Kiribati. Four are located on South Tarawa, one in Abaiang and two on Christmas Island. It is important to have a secure booking before arrival. Reservations can either be arranged through the Kiribati National Tourism Office or by contacting the hotels directly.

Rest Houses, Outer Islands: Numerous rest houses can be found on the majority of other islands. Although they may not be of international standard, they do present an interesting opportunity to experience life on the outer island without modern conveniences. The accommodation facilities are very basic and tariff is around $30.00 per night. If you wish to visit our outer islands, the Kiribati National Tourism Office may assist you in radioing ahead your arrival and reservation.

OTINTAAI HOTEL

GPO Box 270 Bikenibeu,
Tarawa Republic of Kiribati
Located on the edge of peaceful Tarawa Lagoon.
Phone: (68) 28 084 Fax: (686) 28 045
Email: otintaai@tskl.net.ki

The hotel consists of 40 air-conditioned rooms. All have coffee and tea making facilities. In addition there are excellent conference facilities available.

TARIFF

	East Wing	West Wing
Single room	$75.00/night	$80.00/night
Double room	$88.00/night	$90.00/night
Triple room	$95.00/night	$105.00/night
Extra person	$15.00/night	$15.00/night

+ 10 % Government Tax. Continental breakfast is inclusive of the room rates.

SPECIAL FEATURES

An excellent restaurant – Lounge bar caters for all international visitors. The hotel provides airport transfers and sightseeing tours are also available. Picnics, BBQ and traditional dances can be organized with prior arrangement.

CREDIT CARDS: Visa and MasterCard are accepted.

MARY'S MOTEL, RESTAURANT & BAR.

P.O Box 12, Bairiki Tarawa, Republic of Kiribati.
Tel: 9686) 21 362 Fax: (686) 21 164
Comfortable motel-style accommodation.
Tariff:

	Old Building	New Building
Single	$55.00/night	$77.00/night
Double	$66.00/night	$85.00/night

+ 10% Govt tax.

An excellent restaurant serving Japanese, Chinese and local dishes. The bar is an international meeting place for many visitors. New wing comprises 8 new rooms, all with air-conditioning, satellite TV, fridge, tea & coffee facilities, private showers, toilets, queen and single beds. Fishing trips, Jet Ski, and car rental are also available from Mary's on arrangement.

CAPTAIN COOK HOTEL

Main Camp, Kiritimati Island, Republic of Kiribati located within the Line Islands. Tel: (686) 81 230 Fax: (686) 81249 Email: cchxmas@tskl.net.ki or cchxmas@globalsatellite.us

The Captain Cook Hotel accommodations consists of 44 modern, simple, air-conditioned rooms, with 2 beds each and 10 attractive duplex bungalows, overlooking one of the most beautiful beaches on Kiritimati island. The room rates are AUD$90.oo per night, plus an extra AUD$23 per person per night for single supplement surcharge. Double occupancy is AUD$124 per night. The dining room serves excellent meals featuring Buffet styles, Lounge Bar, homemade bread carefully prepared seafood, also BBQ night, steak night, whole pig roasting and local dancing entertainment.

Daily meal cost: (in Australian Dollars): Continental Breakfast $5.00, Full Breakfast $9.50, Lunch $5to $20, Dinner $8 to $40, Night Luau entertainment $40.00/person

Fishing packages are also available through Frontiers, P.O Box 959 Wexford, P.A. 15090-0959, Toll-Free 800 245 1950 Tel: 724 935 1577 Fax: 724 935 5388 Email: info@frontierstrvl.com

MINI HOTEL KIRITIMATI ISLAND

London Village, Christmas Island
Republic of Kiribati, Central Pacific
Tel: (686) 81 371
Fax: (686) 81 336

Mini Hotel Kiritimati is located on Christmas Island, three and half hours flight time south of Honolulu, Hawaii. Meals are provided on a fixed menu featuring local, European and Oriental dishes. Vegetarian dishes are also served. There is also a bar with darts and a pool table. Accommodation is US$25 single and US$50 double. Meals are on a fixed cost of US$30 a day, which covers breakfast, lunch and dinner. For accommodation reservations only, please call or fax the numbers above. Bone-fishing (fly-fishing) packages are also available through PR Fly Fishing, Inc.

For this package contact: Tel: 001 804 823 1937 Fax: 001 804 823 1837 Email: msomers@prflyfishing.com Website: ww.prflyfishing.com

DIVE & SPORTSFISHING RESORT – CHRISTMAS ISLAND

Situated in London, Christmas Island. Is comprised of 6 rooms with 12 beds equipped with cooking facilities in case you want to cook your own meal. For reservations call Tel: (686) 81364, Fax: (686) 81246, Email: ote@tskl.net.ki

A package for 6 Nights is provided. Rates in (AUD$) include:

Single Occupancy $1,684.80, Double Occupancy $1,915.80, Single package for 4 $7,243.20, Double package for 4 $8,167.20

The package covers the following: Arrival assistance (Customs and Immigration), Airport Transfers, Accommodation for 6 nights, Three meals daily, Boat & Vehicle Hire, Tour Guiding, Local Dance and BBQ, Scuba/Snorkeling Diving Gear provided, Birdwatching, Surfing and windsurfing, Bonefishing/Trevally fishing.

MOLLY'S TOUR

Discover World War II – 'The Battle of Tarawa' and 'Kiribati Culture' through Molly's tour. P.O. Box 409, Betio, Tarawa, Kiribati, Central Pacific. Tel/Fax: (686) 26 409 Email: jaybe@tskl.net.ki

KIRIBATI HOLIDAYS

Discover the delights of Tarawa with Kiribati Holidays with their following organized tours: World War II tour, Cultural tour, North Tarawa Escape.

Other services available: Accommodation reservations, Flight confirmation/bookings, Car rental, Boat Hire and fishing trips, Group or private tours, Handicrafts and souvenirs.

Located near Hotel, Bikenibeu, P.O Box 212, Bikenibeu, Tarawa. Tel: (686) 28258 Fax: (686) 28989. Email: reservations@kiribatiholidays.com

TABON TE KEEKEE HOMESTAY

Situated just a short canoe journey away from bustling South Tarawa on the islet of Abatao, Tabon te Keekee Homestay is the way to experience traditional I-Kiribati family life.

Situated on the edge of the lagoon

3 traditional island guesthouses. Rates include: single $45, double $55 with breakfast/evening meal provided. Friendly atmosphere. Airport transfers available.

For more information/reservation contact Mr. Karea Baireti @ Kiribati Holidays Tel: (686) 28258, Fax: (686) 28989 Email: reservations@kiribatiholidays.com

LAGOON BREEZE LODGE

Located beside the lagoon in rustic and quiet surroundings. 8 double/twin ensuite rooms and 4 single ensuite rooms, including a self-contained chalet.

Comfortable rooms with fans and air-conditioning, fridge, table and chairs. A well-equipped kitchen/dining room with tea/coffee maker, gas cooker and microwave oven. Self-catering by guests or served meals.

Facilities include IDD telephone and fax, Internet, computer and laundry.

Services include: Free airport transport transfers, Arranging rental cars, Tour bookings, Kiribati Language lessons.

For more information and reservations contact Mr. Roniiti Teiwaki on Tel: (686) 28942, Fax: (686) 28941 or email: lagoonbreeze@tskl.net.ki or lagoonbreezelodge@yahoo.com

BUARIKI HIDEAWAY GUEST HOUSE

Naa Buariki is the last village of North Tarawa where you can find the perfect spot to experience the traditional life of an I-Kiribati. Lagoon and outer reef features the best diving and snorkeling spots on Tarawa with abundance of marine life.

The resort has 4 small double Guesthouses and one larger Guesthouse built over the lagoon all in traditional style. It also has a small restaurant and mini bar. Cooking is mostly in local and European style. Facilities available are BBQ house, shared kitchen, Office with telephone, Bathhouse with Shower).

Activities offered are: Snorkeling, Surfing, Sailing, Swimming, Fishing, Fun Water sports – jet ski, Exploring and village tours, Learning local skills, Scuba Diving can also be arranged.

Other Services: Boat transport to and from Buariki Hideaway Guest house is available on arrangement.

For more information/reservations contact: Mr. Mike Shrub, PO Box 8 Bairiki, Tarawa, Kiribati Phone Office: (686) 26250 e-mail: mike.kangare@tskl.net.ki or buariki@tskl.net.ki

For more information on Kiribati you can visit Mike Shrubs website: www.kiritours.com

SWEET COCONUT MOTEL

The motel is set right in the middle with direct access to both the lagoon and ocean shores. The main features of Sweet Coconut Motel are the coconut palms and the overlooking of the mighty South Pacific Ocean just a few from where you sleep. Sweet Coconut Motel also offers competitive rates covering full kitchen facilities, bathroom and singles, doubles or air-conditioned room services.

Rates plus Tax include: $25 per night (fan) single + breakfast provided, $35 per night (fan) double + breakfast provided, $45 per night air conditioned room, $850 per month for lodging.

Services like boat trips, transport, laundry and food can be arranged upon request for reasonable extra costs. The Sweet Coconut Village also incorporates a fitness studio holding private fitness classes right on the edge of the beautiful Tarawa Lagoon.

For bookings contact Mrs. Emily Karoua at Sweet Coconut Motel, P.O BOX 200 Bairiki, Tarawa, Republic of Kiribati. Tel: (686) 21487 / 22594 or call Emily on 28100 during working hrs.

BUOTA LODGE

Is situated in Buota on North Tarawa, where it is quiet and peaceful away from the bustling South Tarawa congestions. It is the perfect escape that couple would want to enjoy their honeymoon. Buota Lodge has a total of 3 self-contained rooms and rates are fixed with single and double occupancy of $50.00 per night.

For reservations please contact: Mrs. Aketa Scarlet Buota Lodge, Buota Tel: (686) 28906

TE MAEU LODGE

Is situated on the Oceanside of Eita on South Tarawa. The lodge features a total of 6 air-conditioned and non-air-conditioned rooms. Rates include: Single occupancy (air-condition) A$50.00, Double occupancy (air-condition) A$60.00 and fully furnished, Single & Double occupancy (non-air-condition) A$35.00

For reservations contact: Dr. Airam Metai. Tel: (686) 28501/28493 Fax: (686) 28501 Email: airam_metai@tskl.net.ki

RECREATION SITES

AMBO LAGOON CLUB

The Lagoon Club at Ambo is situated on a beautiful beach on South Tarawa, where swimming is possible at all times, except during the lowest tide. A traditional "Maneaba" provides shade, while drinks are available at the bar. What was once a formal colonial club with a golf course is now a tranquil, relaxed spot to rest your soul.

Bring some friends and your kids along and enjoy the recreational activities that are available: Swimming, Beach Volley Ball, Pool, Dart and playground (with slides, swings, climb-up-bars and a trampoline) for your Kids.

BIKETAWA PICNIC & CAMPING ISLET

Biketawa Islet situated in North Tarawa is a perfect place for picnics, camping, swimming and relaxing on its white sparkling sandy beach. Otintaai Hotel organizes day picnic trips to the islet every Saturday on the second week of the month with a fee of $10.00 adults and $7.50 for children under 8 years old, which covers your picnic package - Meal and return transport. Bar services are also available on every picnic trip so bring along some extra cash. For further information please contact Otintaai Hotel reservation desk @ Tel: (686) 28 084 ext 141.

Activities and Entertainment include: Camping & Fishing– bring your own camping and fishing gear, Canoeing, Village tour, Swimming and snorkeling, Wanderlust and sunlust, Beach volley ball.

CRUISE FANNING ISLAND WITH NORWEGIAN CRUISE LINE

Cruise with Norwegian Cruise Line and explore the untouched Paradise island of Fanning where the people are smiling, gentle, friendly and respectful of their beautiful culture.

Ashore at Fanning Island as an NCL guest you can choose to spend the day lounging in paradise, enjoying the Eden-like playground or exploring the fascinating unique culture.

The Local islanders offer tours of their homeland where you can visit the village's cluster of homes, the NCL Primary School, seaweed farms, and supply stores while learning about the island's history from the I-Kiribati perspective.

There is an open-air straw market that offers convenient souvenir shopping and a chance for you to interact with I-Kiribati people. You will also find a multitude of original gifts to take home including shell jewelry, ornaments, hand carved shark tooth knives, postcards, collectors' stamps, and dream catchers.

You can also enjoy a barbeque feast where local dance groups dressed in traditional grass skirts perform energetic and engaging shows, dipping back in time as they sing and perform the stories of their ancestral past.

For further exploration of the island, bicycles may be rented where you can discover the outer villages, meet inquisitive children, spot giant land crabs and breathe in the spectacular postcard perfect views of the island and sea.

Fanning island has one of the most pristine and perfect beaches in the world. Napali Beach on Fanning Island is NCL's private water sports beach located inside the lagoon. On Napali Beach, you can ride jet skis, sail hobby cats, rent paddle boats, try kayaking, or simply spend the afternoon floating in the shallow 87 F lagoon, while sipping on a rum cocktail and reflecting on this once-in-a-lifetime experience.

Scuba diving and Snorkeling trips along the outer reef gives a chance for the guests to explore and experience the rich underwater sea life, which includes colorful corals, giant parrotfish, butterfly fish, shy sea turtles, giant manta rays and reef sharks

For more Information & Reservations on cruise Fanning Island with NCL, visit Norwegian Cruise Line's website at www.ncl.com

If you need help either before you come or while in Kiribati please contact us at:

KIRIBATI NATIONAL TOURISM OFFICE

Ministry of Communication, Transport and Tourism Development, PO Box 487 Betio, Tarawa Tel: (686) 26003/26004, Fax: (686) 26193 Email: secretary@mict.gov.ki or sto@mict.gov.ki

Or if you want to contact our Christmas Island Branch their point of contact is: Tel: (686) 81091 or (686) 81198, Fax: (686) 81091 Email: tourismxmas@tskl.net.ki

KIRIBATI VISITOR'S BUREAU

Ministry of Communication, Transport & Tourism Development
PO Box 487, Betio, Tarawa.
Phone: (686) 26003/04 Fax: (686) 26193
Email: tourism@mict.gov.ki

LORD HOWE ISLAND

T AKEN in its entirety, Lord Howe Island has a most unique character. It is one of only four island groups in the world to be accorded World Heritage status for its "rare collection of plants, birds and marine life and exceptional natural beauty". Part of the Australian state of New South Wales, it lies 700 kilometres north-east of Sydney and 700 kilometres south-east of Brisbane. Lord Howe Island is 11 kilometres long and just less than 3 kilometres wide. Seven million years ago, a volcano erupted from the sea floor and pushed the island to the surface. With the ravages of marine erosion over time, Lord Howe emerged in its present shape, leaving a spectacular landscape of towering cliffs and mountains. The Admiralty Islets, Roach Island and Mutton Bird Island extend along the east coast.

An extensive coral reef shelters an expansive turquoise-shaded lagoon on the island's western side. Surrounding this landmass are marine parks protected by the Australian and New South Wales governments.

CALMING & PEACEFUL

AT the southern end of the island are the towering peaks of Mt Lidgbird (777 metres) and Mt Gower (875 metres). Much of the island is covered in forests, Banyan trees and Kentia palms. Discovered in 1788, it was not settled until the mid-1830s and today a large majority of the 390 permanent residents are descended from these original inhabitants. Visitor numbers are strictly enforced; with the extreme fragility of the eco-system, no more than 400 visitors are allowed at any one time.

With none of the distractions and hassles of big city life, Lord Howe Island really is an eco-friendly getaway that soothes the nerves and allows visitors to get back to nature. The sense of peace and serenity that engulfs visitors begins the moment they step from the aircraft. No traffic jams, no noise, no needless trappings of 21st century – Lord Howe Island is a step back to a quieter, more relaxing time.

LORD HOWE ISLAND
AT A GLANCE

LORD HOWE ISLAND
TOURISM ASSOCIATION
PO Box 141, Lord Howe Island
New South Wales, Australia 2898
Visitors Centre Toll Free 1800 240 937
Phone: (612) 6563 2114
Email: lhi.visitorcentre@bigpond.com
Website: www.lordhoweisland.info

GEOGRAPHIC LOCATION
Lord Howe Island is 550 kilometres east of Port Macquarie on the New South Wales (NSW) coast, and is part of the State of New South Wales.

AIRLINES
QantasLink has direct services from Sydney, Brisbane. Flying time under two hours. There are connecting services from Australian capital cities and most NSW and Queensland regional ports

ARRIVAL/DEPARTURE INFORMATION
There are no entry requirements, however a quarantine strategy has been developed to keep unwanted organisms off the island. You can do your part by not bringing plant material to the island, cleaning boots and shoes prior to arrival.

Quarantine – The unique flora and fauna of Lord Howe Island is protected by a recent quarantine strategy keep foreign organisms off the island. Do not take plant material to the island and clean boots and shoes before arriving at Lord Howe Island.

Departure tax is included in the airline ticket price.
There are no health regulations.

CURRENCY
The Australian dollar. The Commonwealth, Colonial State and Westpac have agencies. Credit cards are accepted widely but not everywhere. Cash or cheque-book as a back-ups are a good idea as there are no autotellers but some businesses have EFTPOS facilities.

CLIMATE
September to May is fine and warm to hot. The winter months of June to August can be cooler and sometimes windy. Daytime temperatures go up to about 27 degrees Celsius in summer, 16 degrees Celsius in winter.

ELECTRICITY
Same as the Australian mainland. 240V AC 50 cycles.

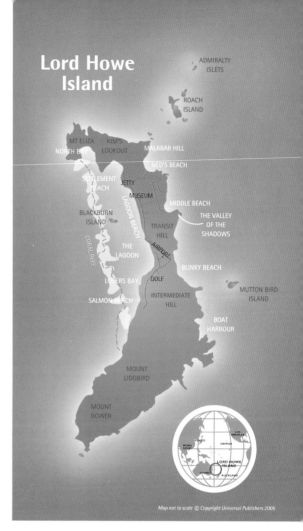

Map not to scale © Copyright Universal Publishers 2005

HANDICRAFTS/SHOPPING
A variety of stores carry clothing and souvenirs as well as groceries, fruit, vegetables, pharmaceutical lines, sandwiches and snacks. Prices may be slightly higher than on the mainland.

LANGUAGE
English.

POPULATION
There are 350 permanent residents, with a cap of 400 visitors per day.

LOCAL CONSIDERATIONS
Dress is casual, smart for evenings. Shoes for bush and reef walking. Sunblock and a shady hat, maybe a raincoat or windcheater.

There is a small hospital and dispensary situated on Lagoon Road. It is open 8am to 12.30pm Monday to Friday. The Doctor and nursing staff are on 24-hour call.

Religion - Anglican, Catholic and Seventh-day Adventist.

Tipping is not expected but is carried out at the discretion of visitors.

TELECOMMUNICATIONS
Beyond the reach of a mobile phone network, email and Internet facilities are available at the Visitor Centre 9am–4pm. Daily except Saturday.

TIME ZONE
Australian Eastern Summertime during daylight saving. Winter is 30 minutes ahead of Australian Eastern Standard Time.

TRANSPORT
There is no public transport and the accommodation properties meet flights and provide free transport for arriving and departing guests. There are bicycles and a limited number of cars for hire. A speed limit of 25 kilometres per hour is maintained. Bicycling is the most common form of transport.

FAR FROM THE CROWDS

JOURNEY THROUGH TIME

THE world is left behind at the departure gate. As the aircraft descends through the blue Pacific sky, passengers crane their necks to catch a glimpse of the dramatic scenery of Lord Howe Island.

The forest-swathed mountains at the southern end of the island provide the best way to orient visitors – Mt Gower at 875 metres above sea level is the highest point with nearby Mt Lidgbird at 777 metres. Lying 23 kilometres offshore is Balls Pyramid, a rocky outcrop some 548 metres in height.

The low-lying middle of the island shelters the small settlement while the north rambles gently upwards and culminates in the 208-metre Malabar Hill and Mt Eliza at 147 metres.

From the long stretch of Lagoon Beach, visitors can see exactly what the coral barrier protects, including a number of smaller beaches with such names as Lovers Bay, Salmon Beach and Old Settlement Beach.

MOUNTAINS AND VALLEYS

The Museum Complex & Visitor Centre. This superb new building opened in 2002, contains the Island's natural and human history. Coral Café for snacks. Open Sunday to Friday 9am to 4pm. Toll free call Australia 1800 240 937. Email: lhi.visitorcentre@bigpond.com

Visitors are never too far away from their accommodation, shops and restaurants. The compact nature of Lord Howe Island not only makes it easy to navigate but leisurely rambles and even a picnic atop some picturesque lookout are easily organised.

The people of Lord Howe are friendly, welcoming and eagerly supportive of the tourist trade. The island's beauty and its natural attractions are things of great pride and visitors come away with a picture of a well-preserved and actively nurtured paradise far from care but with all the facilities needed to make a holiday of a lifetime.

SOMETHING FOR EVERYBODY

A wide variety of activities, both passive and active, makes Lord Howe Island a great place to visit. Viewing the spectacular scenery from points throughout the island provides some stirring sights.

As there's only one road around the island, it's easy to navigate. For the truly adventurous, there's a guided climb to the top of Mt Gower. In essence, the southern part of the island with its sheer basalt cliffs tumbling down to the sea provides the most challenging of treks. At the northern end, there's plenty of beaches and secluded areas to explore.

Glass-bottom boat trips expose the truly remarkable wonders of the lagoon and the coastal extremities. The waters teem with more than 500 species of fish and serious sportsfishermen will be able to do battle with kingfish, yellowfin tuna and wahoo.

Diving, snorkelling, kayaking, surfing, swimming in the sheltered waters of the lagoon, or simply relaxing on the beach are all richly rewarding options. The 9-hole Lord Howe Golf Course provides some land-based activity although many visitors are content to meander the trails and get as far away from settlement as possible.

FLORA AND FAUNA

Ornithologists will be especially satisfied. In the cliff face below Malabar Hill, red-tailed tropic birds nest between September and May. Mt Eliza is the nesting place of sooty terns between August and March with activity so frantic that the summit is closed for the birds' protection. At Mt Gower, petrel and woodhens can be sighted in abundance. In all, there's some 32 species of birds to capture the imagination.

Another fascinating activity is feeding the fish at Ned's Beach on the north-eastern coast. An amazing variety of fish and marine life surge in close to shore for hand feeding.

Some 240 species of native plants are also found on Lord Howe Island, about 105 of which are endemic. These include the Kentia palm which is commercially grown and exported worldwide.

EARL'S ANCHORAGE

LOCATION
Lord Howe Island

EMAIL
Earlsanchorage@
bigpond.com

PHONE/FAX
Ph (612) 6563 2029
Fax (612) 6563 2030

ADDRESS
Earls Anchorage,
Anderson Rd. Lord Howe
Island, NSW 2898
PO Box 180 Lord Howe
Island, NSW 2898

FACILITIES
Self-contained, dining &
kitchen, bathroom &
laundry, living room, reverse
cycle air conditioning,
facilities for the disabled.

ATTRACTIONS
Snorkelling, scuba diving,
reef-walking, beachcombing,
hand feed fish, tennis, golf,
bowling, board & body
surfing, fine dining, nature
tours, canoeing & kayaking,
yachting, boating, walking,
cycling, bird watching, wind
and body surfing, climbing,
fishing, swimming

CREDIT CARDS
Bank/Master cards & Visa

This stunning new development, which opened in December 2004, boasts a tranquil, private and central location with convenient access to the main beaches on either side of the Island and close proximity to many scenic walks.

Earl's Anchorage is located in a cleared grassy field, like an oasis, surrounded by the famous Lord Howe Island Kentia palms, for increased privacy from neighbours and the road. Each self-contained bungalow named after a famous Australian yacht, have been purpose designed by Arcoessence Architects to take advantage of the sunny (northern) aspect.

Each generously sized bungalow is different, some more noticeably than others. Different roof shapes, window placement and proportions have been used to create interesting spaces. Every Living/Dining/ Kitchen has a northern aspect to maximise winter warmth, with direct access to a northern outside deck area. Each Living/Dining room has a unique ceiling shape from sweeping vaults to pitched, and we have carefully positioned each building to be separate and achieve a pleasant private outlook, while maintaining a connected 'village feel'

INCLUSIONS
All bungalows airconditioned, Daily housekeeping service, Beach towels & bath robes, Comprehensive mini bar, Fully equipped kitchens, Personal laundry facility, Dedicated phone line, Stereo CD player and Austar pay TV, Quality cotton linen and towels, Quality furnishings and appliances Airport transfers. We have a bungalow equipped with disabled facilities.

FOR FURTHER INFORMATION
See our website for full booking details and current rates.

PINETREES

www.pinetrees.com.au

LOCATION
Lord Howe Island

EMAIL
info@pinetrees.com.au

PHONE/FAX
Ph (612) 9262 6585
Fax (612) 9262 6638

ADDRESS
50 Clarence St Sydney
NSW 2000 Australia

FACILITIES
Tennis court, licensed
restaurant, bar, fridge,
tea/coffee making

CREDIT CARDS
All major cards accepted

Pinetrees is the ultimate full board holiday resort close to the lagoon, boatshed, surf beach and bowling club

ACCOMMODATION
Clean comfortable accommodation ranges from motel-style rooms with facilities to one bedroom suites and luxurious Garden Cottages.

FACILITIES
There is a restaurant, bar, boatshed, tennis court, bicycles and billiard room and snorkelling gear can be hired locally.

Pinetrees packs a picnic lunch or BBQ pack each day if you wish to go out to enjoy the island's many secluded beaches and picnic spots.

Pinetrees is centrally located on the Lagoon Beach and is close to all the island's attractions.

FOR FURTHER INFORMATION
See website for rates and booking details

WAIMARIE

www.lordhoweisland.info

LOCATION
Lord Howe Island

EMAIL
waimav@aol.com

PHONE/FAX
Ph (612) 6563 2057
Fax (612) 6563 2138

ADDRESS
PO Box 72
Lord Howe Island
NSW 2898

FACILITIES
BBQ, views, self contained,
beach towels, TV

For a quiet, relaxing holiday, Waimarie is set amid a lush sub-tropical garden with breathtaking view of mountains, lagoon and ocean.

An easy bicycle ride or walk to all Island attractions, Waimarie has two spacious one-bedroom self-contained fully equipped deluxe holiday apartments with television radio and laundry facilities.

Fresh rainwater.

Delightful BBQ area in garden setting, bicycles available, beach towels, TV, fans and hairdryers.

MARY CHALLIS COTTAGES

www.lordhoweisland.info

EMAIL
marychallis@
pacific.net.au

PHONE/FAX
Ph (612) 6563 2076
Fax (612) 6563 2159

ADDRESS
PO Box 69
Lord Howe Island
NSW 2898

FACILITIES
Self contained,
TV, radio, BBQ

Make the most of your holiday on Lord Howe by enjoying the hospitality at our cottages.

Right opposite Lagoon Beach – perfect for an early morning dip, and secluded in the palm forests.

Mary Challis has two one-bed self-contained cottages with covered decks, fully equipped kitchen, television, radio, library and BBQ.

Mary Challis is close to shops, beaches, Bowling Club and restaurants.

Seasonal rates available.

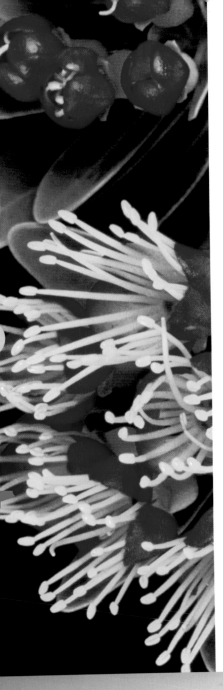

WORLD HERITAGE LISTED LORD HOWE

LORD Howe Island group and surrounding waters is one of a handful of places in the world to be awarded World Heritage Listing for its rare collection of plants, birds, marine life and exceptional beauty. This paradise, so accessible to Australians, is just 11kms long and barely 2kms wide. Most of the Island is covered in natural forests, with spectacular Banyan trees and Kentia palms. The marine park contains a spectacular range of habitats with acknowledged international significance, including the world's southern-most barrier coral reefs, associated lagoon system, sandy beaches and open ocean.

There is no pollution. No crowds. The walks are world-class, from level strolls, to the challenging climb to the peak of Mt. Gower.

Under the terms of the UNESCO Convention Concerning the Protection of the World Cultural and Natural Heritage (the World Heritage Convention) there has been established a World Heritage List of properties having outstanding universal value. These form part of the natural or cultural heritage of countries which are Party to the Convention.

In order to qualify for World Heritage listing for natural values, a property must meet one or more of the four natural criteria and fulfill the associated conditions of integrity. Lord Howe Island meets two of these criteria

1. The Lord Howe Group is an example of superlative natural phenomena.
2. Contains important and significant habitats for in-situ conservation of biological diversity.

The Lord Howe Island Group World Heritage Property which includes Ball's Pyramid and other Islands covers more than 145,000 hectares, the largest part of which comprises marine areas. A comprehensive plan of management has been prepared for the Island.

From the World Heritage perspective, the Lord Howe Island Group is considered to be an outstanding example of an island ecosystem developed from submarine volcanic activity, having a rare diversity of landscapes and biota. The high proportion of endemic species make the Group a superb example of independent evolutionary processes at work.

LORD HOWE

MARSHALL ISLANDS

WELCOME to Majuro Atoll, capital of the Marshall Islands. For our first time visitors, we say Iakwe. This is our native word of greeting and can mean either hello, goodbye, or love (literally, it is translated as 'you are a rainbow'). For those of you who have visited our attolls previously, we say bar iakwe or hello again.

The Republic of the Marshall Islands (RMI) is one of the most unique places in the world to visit, made up of 29 coral atolls and five single islands spread out over an exclusive economic zone of nearly 2,590,000 square kilometres (one of the largest in the Pacific). Located in the Central Pacific, in magnificent Micronesia, The Marshall Islands is a self-governing democracy in free association with the US. Independent since 1986 and a member of United Nations since 1991.

Majuro is home to some 50 per cent of the country's population. Indeed it is the country's most developed and urban atoll. Here you will find the major hotels and facilities. Here, there is an array of restaurants, bars and local craft shops. You will find the Alele Museum, which houses pictures and artefacts from the nation's past.

Nonetheless, even on Majuro, you can still get away from the crowds. Right across the lagoon from the main island are a series of smaller, mostly uninhabited islands that are perfect for a picnic, snorkelling or an overnight camping trip. You will be amazed at how pristine the marine life is along the lagoonal shores.

While you are here, we encourage you to take a little time to really see the Marshall Islands' other atolls, like Arno, Jaluit, Milli or Likiep, where small accommodation facilities are available. Here you can find Marshall Islanders living, for the most part, in the same form and fashion as they have for hundreds of years. While Western products and technology have slowly made their way into the outer atolls, the island culture and traditional lifestyle still prevail. Men still sail their traditional canoes while women continue to weave crafts from native materials.

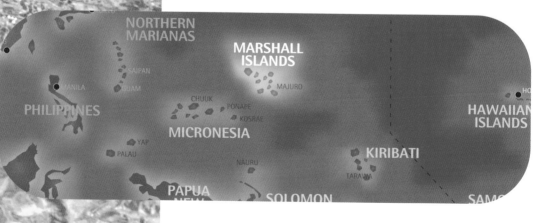

MARSHALL ISLANDS
AT A GLANCE

MARSHALL ISLANDS VISITORS AUTHORITY
PO Box 5, MH 96960
Republic of the Marshall Islands
Tel: (692) 625 6482   Fax: (692) 625 6771
Email: tourism@ntamar.com
Website: www.visitmarshallislands.com

GEOGRAPHIC LOCATION
The Marshall Islands is located about halfway between Honolulu and Australia and is accessible via Guam to the east and Honolulu to the northwest. Made up of 20 coral atolls and five single islands, it spreads out over an exclusive economic zone of nearly 2,590,000 square kilometres (one of the largest in the Pacific).

AIRLINES
While some of the most isolated islands in the world, they are easily reached via Guam or Honolulu on Continental Airlines and Aloha Airlines. The domestic carrier, Air Marshall Islands provides service from its hub on Majuro atoll to 24 outer atoll destinations.

ARRIVAL/DEPARTURE INFORMATION
Visa-free entry for all visitors staying less than 30 days. All visitors must have a valid passport and onward air or sea ticket.
Departure Tax: US$20 (out of Majuro - outer atolls have departure taxes ranging from US$2 to US$10).
Duty free allowance two litres of alcoholic beverages, 15 packets of cigarettes, 75 pieces of cigars, or 227 grams smoking tobacco.
Quarantine restrictions: Fruits, vegetables, plant products, birds, snails and other live animals or animal products.

CURRENCY
The local currency is the US dollar.

CLIMATE
Average temperature 27° Celsius, average rainfall 12-15 points per month.

ELECTRICITY
Voltage 110 volts.

HANDICRAFTS
Renowned for their originality and fine artistic quality, Majuro is the best place to shop for the hand-made, all natural and original Marshallese handicrafts. Busy Hands Club and Leipajid, all near the Assumption Church, Am Mon Keke (behind Payless) and the smaller stands at the airport offer 'Amimono' from all over the Marshall Islands.

LANGUAGE
Marshallese and English. Marshallese is described as belonging to the Austronesian language family, spreading from Madagascar and Easter Island.

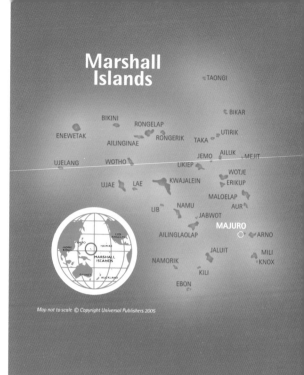

POPULATION
Approximately 60,000 with 25,000 in capital Majuro Atoll.

LOCAL CONSIDERATIONS
Dress is island style casual. Cool, loose fitting clothes accepted in most places. Sunscreen recommended, swimsuits, short shorts/skirts should not be worn in urban areas.
Majuro has one private medical clinic and one public hospital. Most outer islands have medical dispensaries.
Religion – Christian – Catholic, Protestant.
Tipping is optional.

TELECOMMUNICATIONS
Satellite, telex, telephone, cable, facsimile and electronic mail are available on Majuro. Communications with outer islands by radio. Jaluit Atoll and Bikini Atoll have satellite phone/fax systems available.

TIME ZONE
The Marshall Islands are 12 hours ahead of Greenwich Mean Time.

TRANSPORT
Taxis are a cheap way to travel Majuro, with prices ranging from US$0.50 to US$20.00 depending on distance. There are no current regulations for taxi prices on Majuro. In the island they use a ride-sharing taxi system which means you can hop on board the island-wide shuttle bus service, which departs every other hour from the RRE Hotel parking lot.

HISTORIC MARSHALLS

THE BEGINNINGS

THE Marshall Islands first emerged 70 million years ago when volcanic cores erupted at presently extinct hotspots south of the equator. Around 40 million years ago, while the Pacific plate continued to move in a northwesterly direction, the volcanoes began to subside. The islands were initially high, volcanic islands, but over the course of the ensuing 40 million years, they slowly sank back into the ocean from which they came, propelled by their own weight. Microscopic organisms called polyps, which thrive in warm waters with high salinity, salvaged the remaining rim of what was once a volcano to the extent that, with botanical seeds transported by birds and ocean currents, 3000 years ago small islets had taken form on the reefs, capable of sustaining life. These islets formed circular rings encircling sheltered lagoons, namely our beautiful atolls we today can share with visitors.

MARSHALLESE CULTURE

While dates and origins may still be arguable, the uniqueness of the culture, which evolved on these islands, is certain. Marshallese society was and for the most part, still is, stratified into three general classes. Iroij (chief), Alap (clan heads), and Rijerbal (workers). The Iroij have ultimate control of such things as land tenure, resource use and distribution and dispute settlement. The Alap's duties include maintenance of lands and supervision of daily activities. The Rijerbal are responsible for the daily work involved in subsistence, construction, agriculture, etc. In addition, land is divided into twelve categories, ranging from Imon bwij, land belonging to the whole lineage, to Kitdre, land given by a husband to his wife as a gift. Inheritance is matrilineal (passed through the mother).

THE PEOPLE

Marshall Islanders are known as one of the friendliest and most peaceful people on earth. Inherent to their culture are the important principles of caring for one another and kindness to others. These make the Marshall Islands one of the safest places to visit.

While local population is mostly indigenous, there are many mixed German, Japanese and American Marshallese.

UNIQUE CULTURAL SKILLS AND TECHNOLOGIES

Over the last 2000 or so years, Marshallese have developed, refined and perfected a number of unique skills and technologies, all of which illustrated their keen adaptation to the atoll and oceanic environment.

Fishing technologies, for instance, developed into one with very high specialisation. The wide range of fishing environments coupled with the great variation in fish species led to a diverse and highly specialised range of fishing techniques. Few other cultures in the world have developed as many fishing techniques and styles as the Marshallese.

Marshallese canoes, or wa, which range from small rowing canoes to massive high-speed voyaging canoes have amazed Westerners from Otto Von Kotzebuel, who visited the Marshalls in the early 1800s, to modern day world-class sailing enthusiasts. Marshallese canoes are recognised and revered throughout the Pacific for their advanced technical refinements, including the asymmetric hull, the lee platform and the pivoting midship mast.

HISTORY

Approximately 2000 years ago these islands were first discovered by skilled ocean voyagers who searched the horizons for new land. By the time the first European explorers arrived, in the mid-1500s, almost all 29 atolls were colonised, and the people here had developed their own unique language and culture.

A young nation politically, the Marshall Islands gained its independence in 1986, after a long history of colonisation by Germany, Japan and the United States.

The significant effects of this colonial history have contributed much to the shaping of the modern-day Marshall Islands. The Spanish were the first Europeans to sail into and explore the Pacific (with Magellan landing on Guam in 1521) and during that century at least eight Spanish ships sailed through the Marshall Islands. During these brief early visits, the Marshallese became some of the first Pacific Islanders to establish contact and initiate trade with Westerners.

WORLD WAR II

During World War II, the Marshall Islands served as the eastern defensive perimeter for the Japanese military forces in the Central Pacific. After taking control of the Marshalls from Germany in 1914, the Japanese steadily increased their military presence here and beginning in the late 1930s with the anticipation of war, they began to heavily fortify the atolls of Kwajalein, Wotje, Maloelap, Jaluit and later Mili and Enewetak. These heavy fortifications were intended to help launch air attacks on certain targets (such as Hawaii, Wake Island, Kiribati and Johnston atoll) and to serve as defence posts for Japan's more westerly strongholds.

The first attack on Japanese forces in the Marshalls by the US occurred in the early morning hours of February 1, 1942. The ensuing three years of fighting would prove to be some of the bloodiest in the whole of the Pacific. When the smoke cleared, what remained was an extravagant collection of war wrecks and relics unrivalled elsewhere in the Pacific.

SCUBA DIVING AND SNORKELLING

While almost a 2,590,000 square kilometres of ocean, over 800 reef systems and countless species of coral and marine life, the Marshall Islands are without question, a scuba diver's dream. The 100-plus foot visibility and year-round 27°C water temperature make diving here exceptionally pleasant.

One of the Marshall Island's key dive attractions is the abundance of WWII ship and plane wrecks. Atolls such as Bikini, Jaluit, Kwajalein, Mili and Wotje are home to dozens of famous wrecks that have just recently been explored by visiting divers.

With only three scuba diving operations based on Majuro and Bikini atolls, the vast majority of the country is just waiting to be discovered. If you're a diver who's looking to escape the crowds and to tread new waters, this is the place to be.

Indeed, there's nothing more memorable than discovering a new dive site, and naming it yourself. And nothing beats the thrill of finding a new wreck!

ENJOYING THE MARSHALL ISLANDS

SPORT FISHING

IF you're into sport fishing, look no farther. This is literally one of the 'fishiest' places you can visit. There's fly fishing on the reef flats for snapper, trevally or bonefish, and deep ocean trolling for the prized Pacific Blue Marlin. Whatever your interests, you'll find ample opportunity in these islands.

With such excellent fishing conditions, tournaments are a major activity in the Marshall Islands. Every September, Majuro Atoll hosts the most prestigious regional fishing tournament in Micronesia. Teams from all over the region join together for this tournament to compete and celebrate the sport of fishing.

MUCH TO SEE AND DO

You'll find a melting pot of international cuisine in the Marshall Islands. Whether it's Chinese, Korean, Vietnamese, Japanese, Indian, Western or local food, you can be assured that the selection of restaurants in Majuro atoll will be able to satisfy your palate.

Majuro also offers a variety of local bars and nightclubs all over the downtown area with karaoke, billiards and some with shuffleboard. You can put on your dancing shoes and stop by The Pub, Long Island Club, Island Disco, or Club Lanai, the places to go, every weekend.

Tour operators offer everything from dive charters, overnight camping trips, visits to a copra plantation where you can see copra made into coconut oil, soaps, baby oil and coconut fee. There are excursions to the atoll of Arno where you can tour the pearl farm, bike across jungles, ride the waves or just relax. Or, less than an hour by plane of six hours by boat are the picturesque islands of Mili Atoll. Pristine nature, WWII exploration tours, spectacular diving and your own bungalow.

Come see the Marshall Islands in
Beautiful Micronesia!!

"Pearl of the Pacific"

MARSHALL
ISLANDS

VISITORS AUTHORITY

Marshall Islands Visitors Authority

P.O. Box 5 Majuro, MH 96960

Tel: (692) 625-6482 Fax: (692) 625-6771

Email: tourism@ntamar.net

www.visitmarshallislands.com

www.magnificentmicronesia.com

NEW CALEDONIA

A TOUCH of France in the South Pacific sounds suspiciously like an advertising copywriter's dreamfest. But in the case of New Caledonia, it's pretty close to the truth. With the capital, Noumea, having such a vast range of French fine-dining restaurants, European-inspired duty-free shopping and an often overwhelming and leisurely joie de vivre, it's easy to see how the concept developed. Yet New Caledonia can be many things to many people and beyond the glossy resorts and charmingly Gallic influences, there's an authentic Pacific Island experience.

New Caledonia is located 1500 kilometres off the east coast of Australia and about 18,000 kilometres from France. This overseas territory of France comprises the Mainland, known as Le Grande Terre, the Isle of Pines (Ile des Pins) to the southeast, the Loyalty Islands (Mare, Lifou and Ouvea) to the east, the Belep archipelago to the northwest plus numerous smaller islands. Covering some 18,575 square kilometres, it consists of three provinces: North, South and Loyalty Islands.

SAILBOARDS & SAILFISH

The mountainous interior of Le Grande Terre rises to New Caledonia's highest peak, the 1639-metre Mt Panie. A coral barrier reef some 1600 kilometres long encloses the world's largest lagoon complex. A year-round sporting paradise, it hosts boating, sailing, swimming scuba diving, snorkelling and windsurfing, in fact, a list of activities that is almost endless.

Tourism plays a very important part in New Caledonia's economy after nickel production (the islands hold more than 20 per cent of the world's known nickel deposits). Tourism is largely concentrated around Noumea and the Isle of Pines, although there's much to explore north of the city and on the outlying islands.

Visitors will find a destination that differs remarkably from many others in the South Pacific – a strong indigenous culture flourishing alongside the vibrant French influences.

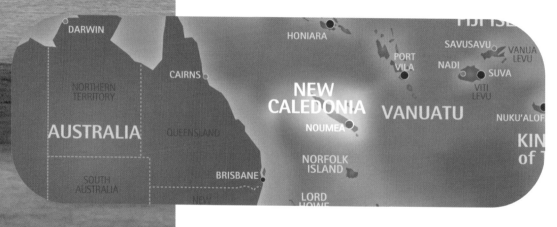

NEW CALEDONIA AT A GLANCE

NEW CALEDONIA TOURISM SOUTH
20 Rue Anatole France
Immeuble Noumea-Centre
Place des Cocotiers
BP 688-98845 Noumea Cedex,
New Caledonia
Tel: (687) 242 080 Fax: (687) 242 070
Email: info@nctps.com
Website: www.nctps.com
www.newcaledoniatourism-south.com

GEOGRAPHICAL LOCATION

Five hundred kilometers long, fifty kilometers wide, New Caledonia is the third largest island in the Pacific Region after Papua New Guinea and New Zealand. It is located in southern Melanesia, at a latitude of 19° - 23° south and at a longitude of 158° - 172° east.

AIRLINES

International: New Caledonia's national airline is Aircalin. Other airlines serving New Caledonia include Air France, Air New Zealand, Air Vanuatu and Qantas.
Domestic: Domestic flights are operated by Air Caledonie with regular services from Noumea to airfields on the island and the other smaller islands. La Tontouta (otherwise known as Tontouta International Airport), is 50 kilometres from Noumea.

ARRIVAL/DEPARTURE INFORMATION

A valid identity card is required for French citizens as is a return or onward ticket. If travelling on an EEC, New Zealand, Australian, Japanese or American passport, a visa is not needed for stays of up to three months.
Visitors may bring in 200 cigarettes or 50 cigars or 250 grams of tobacco, 1 litre of spirit and a reasonable quantity of perfumes for private use.

There are no health requirements. However, up-to-date vaccinations for diphtheria, tetanus and poliomyelitis are recommended.
There is no departure tax.

CURRENCY

As in French Polynesia, the local currency is the French Pacific Franc (CFP or XPF), it is divided into 1, 2, 5, 10, 20, 50 and 100 Franc coins and 500, 1000, 5000 and 10,000 Franc notes. All banks are French.

CLIMATE

New Caledonia enjoys a semi-tropical climate. The warm season extends from September to March with average temperatures of up to 27 degrees Celsius. The green season, from April to August, has average temperatures of around 20 to 23 degrees Celsius.

ELECTRICITY

The current is 220 volts 50 cycles.

HANDICRAFTS

Thursdays in the City markets and the Maison des Artisans are popular places to meet with local artisans and buy their wares. A wide range of French and European

goods including high fashion, leather goods, jewellery, perfume and china is available at duty-free prices. Known as the 'Paris of the Pacific'. There are about 40 duty-free shops, mainly in the centre of Noumea, offering reductions of up to 30 per cent on regular prices.

LANGUAGE
French is the official language but English is widely spoken. There are 30 different Melanesian dialects.

POPULATION
Around 220,000 inhabitants including Melanesian, European, Tahitian, Wallisian and Vietnamese. 204,863 (July 2001 est.) CIA.

LOCAL CONSIDERATIONS
Light, summer-style clothes are appropriate with casual but elegant dress for the evenings. In the cooler months, a sweater or light jacket is recommended.

Medical services consist of the central hospital in Noumea, the Centre Hospitalier Territorial (CHT), with regional hospitals in Koumac and Poindimie. There are also a number of private hospitals and clinics.

Religion - largely Roman Catholic, then Protestant although other religions such as Mormon, Baha'i, Muslim and Jewish are also represented.

There is no tipping.

TELECOMMUNICATIONS
The New Caledonian OPT (Office des Postes et Telecommunications) has branches all over the Territory, offering such services as telephone, fax and telex facilities.

TIME ZONE
New Caledonia is 11 hours ahead of Greenwich Mean Time (GMT).

TRANSPORT
An International Driving Permit is required to hire a car. Drivers must be aged 21 years or over. Cars drive on the right hand side of the road. High-speed inter-island ferry services operate from Noumea to the Isle of Pines and Loyalty Islands.

LA GRANDE TERRE measures some 400 kilometres long and 50 kilometres wide. Noumea, the charming and sprawling capital, occupies a spot at the south-western end of the island. Standing on the shoreline and watching sportspeople at play at Anse Vata and Pointe Magnin is to appreciate just how indulgent yet sophisticated paradise can be.

The markets held on the waterfront at the Baie de la Moselle bring in seafood and produce from throughout the islands. Other attractions include the Museum of Maritime History, the Neo-Caledonian Museum, which traces Kanak arts and traditions back thousands of years, and the Aquarium bring visitors face-to-face with the marine wonders of the lagoon and the sea beyond the reef.

One of New Caledonia's most impressive attractions is the Tjibaou Cultural Centre. Opened in 1997, it was designed by world-renowned, Italian-born architect Renzo Piano. Located on the Tina Peninsula, about 10 kilometres from Noumea, it covers eight hectares and celebrates Kanak culture. Its lofty, traditionally-inspired architecture encompasses permanent and temporary exhibitions, seminar rooms, a theatre for 400 people and a restaurant.

The southern end of La Grande Terre is lush and green while less frequent rainfall in the north gives it an altogether different appearance. Along the west coast there are numerous caves and rock formations formed by the constant pounding of the Pacific Ocean. White sand beaches backed by dense rainforest complete the picture.

Hienghene is considered one of the most beautiful spots on the island with an expansive lagoon surrounded by 120-metre-high cliffs. Melanesian villages, quaint churches and forests dot the coastline.

Although the northern region doesn't get as many visitors as Noumea, that's no reason to pass up one of New Caledonia's. There's much to explore and many rewarding experiences just waiting for visitors. The traditional lifestyle of the people provides an interesting contrast to Noumea's French-influenced appeal.

ABOVE &
BELOW
THE WAVES

A SYMPHONY IN CONTRASTS

TOURISTS dawdle along the promenade at Anse Vata beach, taking in the breathtaking ballet of windsurfers as they speed majestically across the lagoon. In the shade from the summer heat, groups of New Caledonians lend a European ambience as they play petanque. It's a stirring sight and one that visitors to New Caledonia will not soon forget.

In the best tropical traditions, it's the contrasts that mark the special nature of New Caledonia. The storefronts and street signage are in French, yet the ambience is very much marked by a leisurely and unhurried pace. The sun rises each day and sets with the certainty that the following day will be much the same – the lagoons will be crystal clear and sparsely populated by snorkellers and divers, the breeze will bring forth the sailboarders, the fishing boats will head out with anglers looking forward to their individual battles with the deep.

New Caledonia's lush interiors attract bushwalkers eager to rediscover nature. There are over 3000 indigenous species of vegetation, with about 70 per cent found nowhere else in the world. The Blue River Park, 60 kilometres south of Noumea, covers 9045 hectares and is a popular spot as are guided excursion to the forests around Mt Koghi.

Horseriding along the bush trails or by the seaside, golfing, bicycling – just about every activity under the sun is available in New Caledonia. In fact, there's so much to do that New Caledonia's reputation of being one of the most tranquil of holiday destinations could seem overpowered by the activity.

But that's not really possible. Not when there's a sunset to look forward to and another beautiful day in paradise just around the corner.

THE AZURE SEA

THE Isle of Pines was named by Captain James Cook in 1774 after its beautiful 60-metre-high Colmunar Pine trees. Long settled by the indigenous people of New Caledonia, in 1872 it became a prison for Communards – political prisoners sent from France after the Paris Commune uprising. The ruins of the jail can still be seen amid the dense vegetation that has reclaimed the site.

The extreme beauty of the island, with its expanses of white sand beaches, rainforest and turquoise lagoons, makes it renowned throughout the world. Areas of interest include Upi Bay and Saint-Joseph Beach (the perfect spot for excursions on traditional Melanesian outrigger canoes) and the 262-metres-high N'Ga Peak.

As compelling as its more obvious attractions are the many hidden delights of the Isle of Pines. These include the well-visited Grotte de la reine Hortense which is entered by way of the shady rainforest and the high-ceilinged cave houses – a tribute to the Virgin Mary.

NATURAL RAMBLES

Measuring 18 kilometres long and 14 kilometres wide, the Isle of Pines is a favourite spot for divers eager to get up-close-and-personal with turtles, crayfish and myriad tropical fish.

Around New Caledonia, there are numerous protected marine reserves with some spectacular dive sites including the Amedee Lighthouse Reserve (where divers can indulge in shark-feeding), La Dieppoise with the shipwreck of a Royal Navy vessel, the Hienghene Reef and Lifou Island. The outlying islands are well served for diving expeditions.

From July to September, humpback whales traverse the waters of New Caledonia. To witness these large mammals plough through the warm waters is to experience nature at its most compelling.

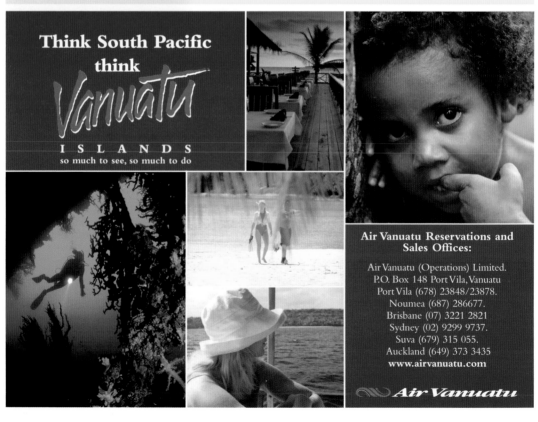

FAMOUS NEW CALEDONIA – TJIBAOU CULTURAL CENTRE

ngan jila ● centre culturel
Tjibaou

COMPLETED IN MAY 1998, **THE TJIBAOU CULTURAL CENTRE** IS A SPECTACULAR EDIFICE RISING ON THE TINA PENINSULA IN NOUMEA. IT IS NAMED IN RECOGNITION OF THE KANAK LEADER, JEAN–MARIE TJIBAOU, AND HIS CONTRIBUTION TO THE NATION'S CULTURAL DEVELOPMENT.

Expression of a nation's soul

The structure was designed by Renzo Piano, who was responsible for the Georges Pompidou Centre in Paris and Kansai International Airport in Japan.

A harmonious alliance of traditional Kanak and modern architecture. There are 10 pavilions connected along a spine evoking the central alley of a typical Kanak village.

The outdoor Custom Area has three traditional 'cases' or houses representing the three main regions of New Caledonia – the North, the South and the Loyalty Islands. Bwenaado 'case' houses an exhibition of artistic and historical items from the Kanak heritage and Jinu house illustrates the spirit of all the Pacific cultures with monumental sculptures.

A collection of contemporary Kanak and Pacific art is housed in the gallery space and the Mediatheque resource centre contains a wide range of documentary resources on Kanak and Pacific cultures.

In addition, there are three theatres for performances, the indoor seating

400 and two outdoor spaces holding 1000 and 4000.

The Tjibaou Cultural Centre is open from Tuesdays to Sundays, from 9.00am to 5.00pm (closed Mondays). The entry fee allows free access to the whole site including the exhibitions, the Kanak path, the tribal customs space and the media library.

In order to make the most of your visit, there are organised tours which depart 9.30am and 2.30pm Tuesdays to Sundays and last for approximately one hour.

The Tjibaou Cultural Centre can be reached by Blue Line Bus or by taxi, and visitors to New Caledonia should not hesitate to ask for information at their hotel's reception desk. Packages including a guided tour and return transport from hotels are sold by the following tour operators: Alpha International, South Pacific Tours, Arc en Ciel and Le Petit Train Touristique (The Little Train).

A range of quality arts, crafts and souvenirs specially selected for their originality is available at the shop.

TJIBAOU CULTURAL CENTRE
Rue des Accords de Matignon
BP 378-98845 Noumea Cedex
NEW CALEDONIA
Tel: +687 41 45 45
Fax: +687 41 45 56
Email: adck@adck.nc
Internet: www.adck.nc

RAMADA PLAZA NOUMEA

OPENING IN OCTOBER 2005

LOCATION
Ideally located on Anse Vata Bay, RAMADA PLAZA NOUMEA is close to downtown (10 minutes drive), to the domestic airport and to Tina Golf (15 minutes drive). Bus transfer drives you to Tontouta International Airport in 45 minutes

EMAIL
info@
ramadaplaza-noumea.nc

PHONE/FAX
Pre-opening office
Ph (687) 26.06.00
Fax (687) 26.17.20

ADDRESS
Pre-opening office
Rue Louis Blériot - Anse Vata Bay, BP 2557, 98846 NOUMEA - New Caledonia

RATES
See website for rates and booking details (April 2005)
www.ramadaplaza-noumea.nc

CREDIT CARDS
All major credit cards are accepted

ACCOMMODATION
188 spacious rooms including Junior Suites; Deluxe Suites, Executive Suites and Presidential Suites.

12 rooms for handicapped available.

All rooms equipped with air-conditioning, kitchen (except Superior Rooms), sprinkler, 220V electricity, direct telephone lines, flat screen TV with satellite channels, Internet connection, safety deposit box, mini-bar/refrigerator, hair dryer, ironing facilities, necessary Tea & Coffee making facility, kettle, microwave, coffee machine, toaster, blender mixer. Washing machine and dryer in all suites (except Junior).

FACILITIES & SERVICES
Room service, dry cleaning, laundry service, swimming pool with sandy beach, business centre, currency exchange, baby sitting, kids club, newspapers, activity desk, bus transfer to the airports, spa, fitness centre.

RESTAURANTS & LOUNGE
The Panoramic revolving restaurant is unique in New Caledonia. You'll enjoy a 360 degree view over Noumea while you savour a refined cuisine.

The Swimming Pool Snack, our relaxed poolside café, The bar is the convivial place to meet and also three private rooms available for your meetings and business lunches.

SPORTS & RECREATION
The activity desk will help you to organise your stay and propose many activities (water sports, car rental, excursions, scuba diving, horse riding...).

LE MERIDIEN NOUMEA

ADDRESS
Pointe Magnin, BP 1915
98846 Noumea Cedex
New Caledonia

PHONE/FAX
Ph (687) 26 5000
Fax (687) 26 5003

EMAIL
le.meridien@meridien.nc

**WORLDWIDE
RESERVATIONS**
Worldwide Central
Reservations
Australia (toll free)
1800 622 240,
New Zealand (toll free)
(0800) 454 040
Hong Kong (toll free)
(0800) 963 833
Tokyo (toll free)
(0120) 094 040,
USA/Canada (toll free)
(800) 543 4300
France (toll free)
(0800) 905 552

RATES
See website for rates and
booking details

CREDIT CARDS
All major credit cards
accepted

LOCATION

New Caledonia's premier deluxe hotel overlooks spectacular Anse Vata Cove in the heart of Noumea, 10 minutes from downtown shopping, 15 minutes from the 18-hole Tina golf course and steps from the Grand Casino de Noumea.

ACCOMMODATION

245 spacious rooms with private balcony including 15 suites, overlooking the ocean, gardens or pool.

FEATURES

Facilities
Air conditioning, beauty & massage centre, swimming pool, casino, duty-free shop, 24-hour room service, excursion services, business centre.

Restaurant and Bars
Four restaurants featuring French, Japanese and International Cuisine. Cocktails served in the Lobby Bar and light meals at the beachside Faré.

Function Rooms
An elegant ballroom offering natural daylight accommodates up to 400 guests and is divisible into two sections. There are two additional rooms with a capacity to accommodate up to 70 and 100 guests.

Sports and Leisure
Choose from tennis, table tennis, volleyball, petanque, golf, scuba diving (nearby), snorkelling, windsurfing, sailing, fishing, mountain bikes, canoeing.

NC NOUVATA PARK HOTEL

www.newcaledoniahotelsresorts.com

LOCATION
Anse Vata opposite the beach and close to the shops.

EMAIL
resa@nchotels.nc

PHONE/FAX
Ph: (687) 262 200
Fax: (687) 261 677
Reservations
(687) 260 512

ADDRESS
BP 137-98845
Noumea Cedex
New Caledonia

GENERAL MANAGER
Jean Francois Debon

FACILITIES
Tea & coffee-making mini-bars, TV, IDD telephone and dual port for internet connection, pool, gym.

CREDIT CARDS
AMEX, Visa, MasterCard, JCB, Jade.

310-room fully serviced four star property consisting of: NC Pacifique Tower: 120 rooms: 38 Standard Pool view rooms, 85 Standard Ocean view rooms.

Nouvata Superior Rooms: 74 comfortable superior rooms with balconies overlooking Anse Vata Beach.

Park Deluxe Rooms: 110 highly appointed deluxe rooms and six deluxe suites.

The hotel's rooms and suites are the largest in New Caledonia. All rooms have terraces and are air conditioned.

Three restaurants – Le Park, Le Lagon and Le Terrasse, a bar Le Recif and a banquet room, Venezia.

See our website for full booking details and current rates.

NOUVATA PARK HOTEL
NEW CALEDONIA

NC CORAL PALMS ISLAND RESORT

www.newcaledoniahotelsresorts.com

Coral Palms
ISLAND RESORT

LOCATION
Island Ilot Maitre|
15 minutes from Noumea

EMAIL
resa@nchotels.nc

PHONE/FAX
Ph (687) 285 320
Fax (687) 240 677
Reservations
(687) 260 512

ADDRESS
BP 4918 - 98847
Noumea Cedex
New Caledonia

GENERAL MANAGER
Philippe Bertho

FACILITIES
Overwater bungalows, TV, DVD, Jetskis, Boutique

CREDIT CARDS
AMEX, Visa, MasterCard, JCB, Jade.

Located on the island called "Ilot Maitre" is seven hectares in size and 15 minutes by water taxi from Noumea and surrounded by 200 hectares of Marine Reserve in which fishing is prohibited. Coral Palms Island Resort is a five-star property.

ACCOMMODATION
25 Overwater, 27 Ocean View and 17 Garden View Bungalows. All rooms offer IDD, air conditioned, mini bar, hairdryer, bathrobes, CD, TV stereo, Internet connection including individual phone numbers.

24-hour reception, boutique, library, conference facilities for up to 20 people Licensed restaurant and 2 bars, snorkelling, jetski, Hobiecat, sailing, canoes, pedal boats.

NC CASA DEL SOLE

www.newcaledoniahotelsresorts.com

Casa Del Sole
NEW CALEDONIA

LOCATION
A few minutes to the waterfront at "Anse Vata Baie"

EMAIL
valerie.defossez@nchotels.nc

PHONE/FAX
Ph (687) 258 700
Fax (687) 258 711
Reservations
resa.casa@nchotels.nc

ADDRESS
Baie des Citrons, BP 3340
98846 Noumea-Cedex
New Caledonia

GENERAL MANAGER
Valerie Defossez

FACILITIES
Beachfront – close to all waterfront activities, TV, self contained, laundry and balconies.

CREDIT CARDS
AMEX, Visa, MasterCard, JCB, Jade.

ACCOMMODATION
128 fully furnished one-bedroom or two-bedroom apartments with panoramic views over "Baie des Citrons" or "Anse Vata Baie".. These luxury serviced apartments are ideal for extended stays with weekly and monthly rates. Each apartment includes an open-plan dining and living room, television. The kitchen contains a dishwasher, microwave, cooktop with oven, fridge, washer/dryer, ironing board and iron, & fully stocked with china, glassware, cutlery and linen. Air conditioned bedrooms have a queen-sized bed and twin beds in the second bedroom of the larger apartments. The lounge room also has a foldaway sofa bed. The main bedroom has an interconnecting bathroom. All have private balconies.

BEST WESTERN LE PARIS

LOCATION
City - 10 minutes away from the beaches

EMAIL
leparis@canl.nc

PHONE/FAX
Ph (687) 28 17 00
Fax (687) 28 09 60

ADDRESS
B.P. 2226 - 98846
Noumea Cedex - New Caledonia

FACILITIES
Entirely renovated in 2002. Air conditioned, TV (satellite), IDD phones, tea/coffee making. Best Cafe Restaurant

ATTRACTIONS
Between tourist area and business district. Ideal location for shopping or professional and business meetings

ACCOMMODATION
48 comfortable and soundproofed rooms recently renovated with individual air conditioning. Each room has luxuriously appointed bathroom with bath or shower. All the rooms are fully equipped with : desk (data port), telephone, colour television (+satellite), radio, in-room safe, refrigerator, coffee and tea facilities, ironing facilities... According to your needs, cribs and additional beds will be placed at your disposal.

HOTEL FACILITIES & SERVICES
24 hour reception, International reservations of Best Western hotels, meeting room (8 persons), lounge (20 persons), luggage room, room-service for breakfast till 9.30 am, laundry and dry cleaning service, Fax and Email service, General information service: excursions, car rentals, airport transfers.

RESTAURANT & BAR
Restaurant "The Best Cafe" open from 6.30 am till 9.30 pm featuring French cuisine from light meals to excellent dining.

CREDIT CARDS
All major credit cards accepted.

RATES
See website for rates and booking details. Special rates (long stay, groups or business) on request.

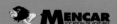
NOVOTEL SURF NOUMEA

NOVOTEL
Accor hotels

LOCATION
Anse Vata Beach Noumea

EMAIL
novotelnc.resa@offratel.nc

PHONE/FAX
Ph (687) 28 6688
Fax (687) 28 5223

ADDRESS
Rocher à la Voile
BP 4230-98847
Noumea Cedex
New Caledonia

FACILITIES
3 restaurants, bar, pool, conference and reception rooms, Internet, fitness centre, boutique, hairdresser, and beauty centre

ATTRACTIONS
Located between Noumea's two finest beaches, offering a great choice of water sports. Casino. City centre 10 minutes by car.

CREDIT CARDS
All major credit cards are accepted

Amid the coconut palms and araucaria pines of the Rocher à la Voile promontory, between Noumea's two finest beaches, the Novotel Surf offers 238 rooms and suites with a view onto one of the most beautiful lagoons in the world.

For your holidays or business trip, the Novotel Surf complex is a great place to stay in Noumea and offers you wide choice of facilities and activities: water sports, 3 restaurants, bar, boutique, conference and reception rooms, fitness center, casino, etc.

LE MERIDIEN ILE DES PINS

www.iledespins.lemeridien.com

Le MERIDIEN
ILE DES PINS

ADDRESS
Baie d'Oro, BP 175
98832 Vao, Ile des Pins
New Caledonia

PHONE/FAX
Ph (687) 46 1515
Fax (687) 46 1516

EMAIL
meridien.idp@meridien.nc

WORLDWIDE RESERVATIONS
World Wide Central Reservations

Australia (toll free)
1800 622 240

New Zealand (toll free)
(0800) 454 040

Hong Kong
(0800) 963 833

Tokyo (toll free)
(0120) 094 040

USA/Canada (toll free)
(800) 543 4300

France (toll free)
(0800) 905 552

RATES
See website for rates and booking details

CREDIT CARDS
All major credit cards accepted

LOCATION
Situated at spectacular Oro Bay with its natural turquoise lagoon, white sand beach and surrounded by majestic Norfolk pines, Le Meridien Ile des Pins is the island's only luxury resort.

ACCESS
A 20 minute flight with domestic carrier AIR CALEDONIE from Noumea's Magenta airport.

ACCOMMODATION
Total 39 rooms and bungalow suites including: 25 bungalow suites, 4 Premium bungalow, 10 deluxe guest rooms. Each bungalow suite consists of an outdoor terrace, living area, master bedroom, spacious bathroom and a dressing area. Premium bungalow suites are located on a clifftop offering a panoramic view on the Oro bay. Each deluxe guest room includes a private outdoor loggia, spacious bedroom and bathroom.

FEATURES
Facilities
Air conditioning, ceiling fans, TV, video players, safe, CD player, personal bar, IDD telephone, coffee & tea-making facilities, hairdryers, laundry.

Restaurants and Bars
La Pirogue Restaurant & Terrace, La Boussole Bar & Terrace.

Sport and Leisure
Swimming pool, table tennis, billiards, snorkelling, petanque, volley ball, canoe/kayaks, pedal boats, bicycles, games room and library.

Services
Room service, airport shuttle, resort boutique, excursion desk, massage and beauty treatments.

WELCOME TO THE NORTHERN PROVINCE

AUTHENTIC and endearing, the Province of a hundred faces harbours treasures of many types just waiting to be discovered. Beyond the magical landscapes you will meet men and women who form a harmonious mosaic. The North is the land of the smile and of sharing, of new atmospheres where nature is intact and fiercely preserved.

HOW TO GET THERE

Three alternatives for getting to the Northern Province from Noumea: by car (saloon or four-wheel drive, depending on your chosen route): contact rental companies; by bus: contact the bus station (Tel. 24 90 26) for routes and timetables; by air: departing from Noumea Magenta airport, going to Koné, Koumac, Touho and Belep. Contact Air Calédonie or your travel agency.

PRACTICAL INFORMATION

State of the roads: all roads in the Northern Province are suitable for most vehicles. Certain sections remain unsealed. Drive carefully.

Petrol stations: fuel can be found in all villages, but certain are at quite a distance from each other. Pay attention to opening and closing times: stations tend to open early in the morning, but also close quite early. Be prepared.

ACCOMMODATION

The Northern Province offers a large range of accommodation for tailor-made holidays. The choice goes from *** hotels with bungalows and activities, to traditional gîtes, authentic and of good quality. These are relatively inexpensive but don't forget to book ahead: the tradition in Caledonia is to prepare meals for those who have ordered, but booking is not automatic.

RESPECT

Custom: When near a tribe it is advisable to enquire before visiting a site: it could be sacred or taboo. In the same way, when visiting a tribe take a small gift (piece of cloth, tobacco, money) to give to those who receive you.

Dress: Out of respect and decency, one does not go topless on the beach and avoid walking around in a swimsuit away from the beach.

YOUR STAY STARTS AT THE VILLAGE

You'll find a warm welcome when you call at our office at the Village. We will help you with your accommodation and your itinerary according to your budget and your wishes. Already, you can begin to discover the North: its hospitality, its natural beauty, its gentle way of life.

THE WEST COAST

By taking the road North, nowhere else is there such a richness of landscape and men. By just following the RT1 from Poya, one penetrates a world where tribes and villages follow each other on. Along the West coast, the long plains slide between the lagoon and the mountain chain, showing savannah where the niaouli is king. Magnificent bays, edged by coconut groves, stretch along the shore. It is the place for first meetings with the Broussards (Bushies) and first exchanges in the tribes.

THE FAR NORTH

At the extreme North the atmosphere is quite different. The whole world seems to belong to you when viewing the two coastlines from the top of a pass, looking out over the mountain chain and the lagoon.

THE EAST COAST

A very different spectacle attends the visitor on the East Coast. Steep massives side by side with entrancing and majestic tropical vegetation, tribes here invite you to discover a different world of custom and legends. And then there is the amazing light, long bays edged with coconut groves and rivers.

STAYING IN A TRIBE

Staying in a tribe is being immersed for a time in the Melanesian world. It is the most authentic way to meet Kanak people, sleeping in a case (thatched hut) after tasting bougna around the fire and listening to stories and legends. The inhabitants of the tribes also suggest guided hikes or horse rides along the most enchanting pathways. The women will show you how to weave or do basketwork and one can also go fishing.

ONE SIDE TO THE OTHER WITH KONE-TIWAKA

The cross-country Koné-Tiwaka road shows its assets to advantage with four rest areas and picnic places installed by the Northern Province with the help of neighbouring tribes. They offer resting spots for walkers and serve as a point of departure for activities such as hikes or horse rides.

CAMPING: STAYS AT SMART PRICES

If you like sleeping in a tent the campsites of the North have plenty of surprises for you.

There are many camping sites in the Northern Province: you will be spoilt for choice. Located in superb spots, by the edge of the sea or at the foot of a waterfall, the majority have toilet and shower blocks and some have shelters and electricity.

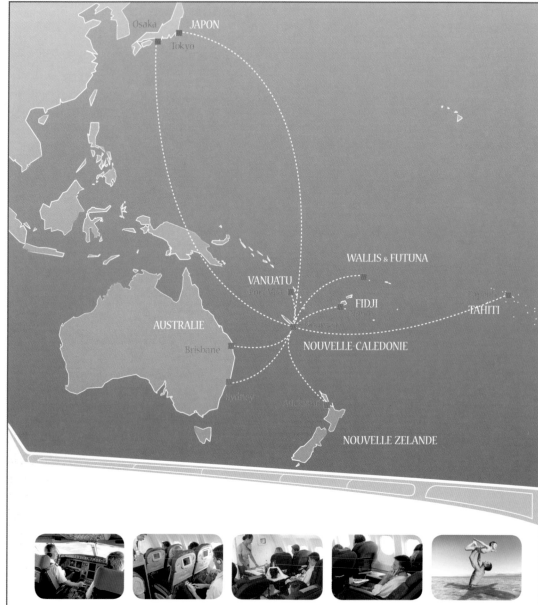

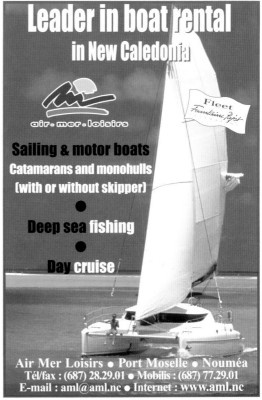

NIUE
UNDISCOVERED

O K, two's company, three's a crowd! If you subscribe to this thought, then you might want to tie your knot away well from the mad world. Then just think of Niue – this tropical island is but a stone's throw away, yet it's a world apart. It's politically stable and famous as being of one of the world's safest destinations. It hasn't been ruined by commercialism, but you'll never lack for the creature comforts you'll need and expect.

Best of all, it's an eco-tourist's paradise.

Originally settled by migrating Tongans, Samoans and Cook Islanders, Niue evolved a unique culture and language, similar to, but quite separate from its neighbours. That makes more sense when you realise that the land itself is totally unlike that of its neighbours.

The name 'Niue' translates as 'Behold! The coconut!', a reference to the fact that this rocky island could sustain the coconut palm, thereby making it a land worth inhabiting. Polynesians benefit immensely from this plant and have ingeniously evolved innumerable uses of it.

Unlike its neighbours it avoided adapting the traditional Polynesian power hierarchy of priests and chiefs, and instead, relied on family or clan based units united under a 'democratically' elected monarch. This made Niueans very independent, both of each other and from their neighbours, and they remain so today.

CLOSE TO HOME, YET A WORLD APART.
Just three hours northeast of New Zealand and you're a whole world away. Inside and out, up, down and under, nothing on our planet Earth comes close to Niue.

NO CROWDS – EVER!
There are less than 90 hotel rooms in Niue, so sometimes the number of visiting whales out-number the visiting humans. Seriously. All in a country four and half times the size of Rarotonga. A quarter of Niue is virgin rainforest, and guided walks will help you explore this safely!

You'll have all the space and time you need to do your own thing, but whatever you choose to do, you won't have to queue to do it.

PICTURE CHARLES COOPER, COURTESY NIUE TOURISM

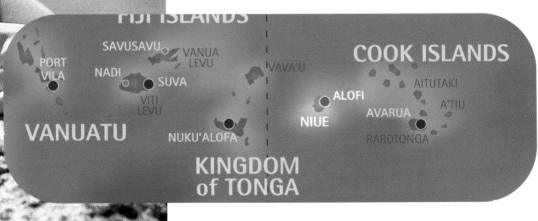

FIJI ISLANDS

SAVUSAVU
VANUA LEVU
PORT VILA
NADI
SUVA
VITI LEVU
VANUATU
NUKU'ALOFA

VAVA'U

COOK ISLANDS
AITUTAKI
ALOFI
A'TIU
AVARUA
NIUE
RAROTONGA

KINGDOM
of TONGA

NIUE TOURISM OFFICE
PO Box 42, Alofi, Niue Island
Tel: (683) 4224/4394 Fax: (683) 4225
Email: niuetourism@mail.gov.nu
Website: www.niueisland.com

PICTURE: COURTESY NIUE T

PICTURE: COURTESY NIUE TOURISM

GEOGRAPHIC LOCATION
The tropical island of Niue is situated 19°south of the Equator. It's 2200 kilometres northeast of New Zealand, 386 km's east of Tonga and 900 kilometres west of Rarotonga in the Cook Islands.

AIRLINES
Only Polynesian Airlines fly to Niue and there are only two flights per week. One direct flight leaving Auckland, New Zealand at 0150 hrs NZ time every Saturday, arriving in Niue at 0500 hrs Friday morning (Niue is over the international dateline, so, -23 hours behind NZ time). Another flight arrives in Niue at Monday 0210 hours, ex departs Apia 0100, Samoa leaves 0300 hours and onwards to Auckland NZ arrives 0630 hours Tuesday.

ARRIVAL/DEPARTURE INFORMATION
Passports are essential, and genuine tourists are given a free 30-day tourist visa upon arrival provided you have an onward ticket. Extensions are available upon application to the Immigration Office before arrival. Contact PO Box 67 Alofi, tel. (683 4349 fax 4336.
A universal NZ$25 departure fee is payable at the airport, but children under 12 are exempt.
The following duty free items can be imported into Niue by persons 18years and older without incurring duty: 200 cigarettes or 227grams of tobacco or 50 cigars, three bottles of spirits not exceeding three litres. Duty free beer bottles from Apia, Samoa are not allowed. Restricted prohibited imports prohibited are firearms and ammunition.
Taxes - Niue has no sales or accommodation taxes, no GST and no VAT.

CURRENCY
Niue uses the New Zealand dollar ($NZ).

CLIMATE
At 19° south of the equator, tropical Niue is never cold and has only two seasons– wet, from December to March, and dry, from April to November. It has an average annual temperature of 25° Celsius and a medium humidity that peaks at 88 per cent. Average rainfall is 218 cm's per annum, and it rains about 170 days per year.

ELECTRICITY
240 volts, 10amp, three pin plug, same as New Zealand.

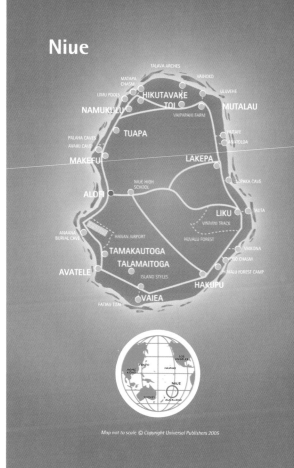

Niue

TALAVA ARCHES
VAIHOKO
MATAPA CHASM
LIMU POOLS
HIKUTAVAKE
ULUVEHE
NAMUKULU
TOI
MUTALAU
VAIPAPAHI FARM
PALAHA CAVES
TUAPA
MATAFE
AVAIKI CAVE
ANATOLOA
MAKEFU
LAKEPA
NIUE HIGH SCHOOL
PAKA CAVE
ALOFI
LIKU
TAUTA
VINIVINI TRACK
ANAANA BURIAL CAVE
HUVALU FOREST
HANAN AIRPORT
VAIKONA
TAMAKAUTOGA
TO CHASM
TALAMAITOGA
VALU FOREST CAMP
AVATELE
ISLAND STYLES
HAKUPU
VAIEA
FATIAU TUAI

TOKYO
LOS ANGELES
HONG KONG
HAWAII
NIUE
SYDNEY
AUCKLAND

Map not to scale © Copyright Universal Publishers 2005

POPULATION

The entire population of about 1500 people live in only 14 widely dispersed villages. The rest of the island comprises virgin rainforest and farmland.

LANGUAGE

Niueans are multi-lingual, fluent in both Niuean and English, so it's unlikely a visitor would find anyone who doesn't speak English.

LOCAL CONSIDERATIONS

There are 90 hotel rooms in Niue, so sometimes the number of visiting whales out-numbers the visiting humans. Medical & Dental Centre - Tel: (683) 4100, Fax: (683) 4265. On call emergency service available for emergency cases only. Monday - Friday 9:00am - 4:00pm. Closed for lunch 12:00 - 1:00, 7:00pm - 9:00pm. Weekends 9:00am - 11:00am.

A quarter of Niue is virgin rainforest, and guided walks will help you explore this safely.

Niue is a place where crime is almost unheard of, where anyone can feel totally safe walking around after dark, where personal belongings are respected.

There is nothing carnivorous or poisonous or even large enough to harm you.

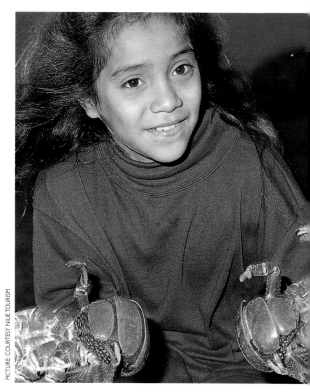

PICTURE: COURTESY NIUE TOURISM

NIUE
UNSPOILED

ONE OF THE WORLD'S SAFEST DESTINATIONS

NIUE is a place where crime is almost unheard of, where anyone can feel totally safe walking around after dark, where personal belongings are respected. Our politically stable tight-knit community affords protection to everyone.

MORE THAN YOU CAN IMAGINE.
MUCH MORE THAN YOU'D EVER EXPECT.

You'll have everything you need to be more than comfortable, but you'll rediscover what's been lost in this modern world. We're proud that our home is one of the safest countries on Earth. Crime, graffiti, drugs and pollution are almost heard of. We don't need traffic lights so we don't have any.

We also don't have anything on Niue that's carniverous or poisonous or even large enough to harm you, so you can amble anywhere, anytime, in safety. But be careful - it's an addictive feeling!

UNSPOILED POLYNESIA

We can't change what's been done elsewhere, but we'll prevent it ever happening here. Niue's a place where Nature hasn't been broken. Where it's normal for strangers to wave at each other, all the time. Where the sweet sound of laughter mixes with the drumming ocean waves. Where everything stops at 4 PM and no-one understands the meaning of the words 'hurry' and 'rush', so it pays not to use them!

UNREAL EXPERIENCES

Swim with whales and dolphins. Walk through flocks of butterflies in virgin rainforest. Dive within spectacular underwater cathedrals. Drift beneath avenues of perfumed frangipani. Discover tiny swimming coves teeming with coloured fish. Explore the most breathtaking caves in the South Pacific with ease. Gaze upon breaching whales 80 metres from your breakfast table. Snorkel over bright corals in warm tropical water acclaimed as being amongst the clearest in the world.

Niue will reveal to you so many things previously trapped in your imagination. Liberate them and discover them in Niue.

NIUE
UNBELIEVABLE

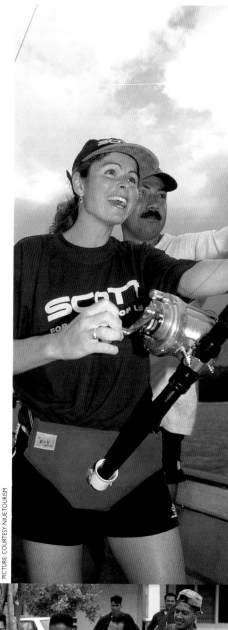

PICTURE: COURTESY NIUE TOURISM

LEGENDARY FISHING

NIUE is a raised atoll, not a sandy one, so very deep water is just a stone's throw from land. Game fishing is plentiful, and all manner of big ones await the anglers keen and strong enough to tempt them to strike. We take it all for granted, but some folks come here just to fish.

THE BLUEST OF WATER

Niues' water's are so clear they're rated as amongst the very best visibility in the world - frequently in excess of 50, and even up to 70 metres.

It is because Niue is made of porous limestone that it has no lakes or streams, so all rainwater filters quickly through this rock into the sea & in doing so has carved out an exquisite & unique environment to explore   - caverns, caves and cathedrals!

Snorkelling and diving is a spectacular encounter with a mind-boggling array of marine life, including turtles, dolphins, whales in season, hard corals and all manner of fish.

Niue seems to burst out of the deep Pacific Ocean and the island's shelf sharply drops off within a hundred metres from dry land in places, so you don't have to travel far to be in very, very deep water.

Additionally there are several stunning in-shore swimming areas like Matapa Chasm & Limu that offer a gentle   introduction to the marine world beyond the outer reef.

Some were formerly reserved exclusively for Niuean Kings, so you'll be keeping good company in these waters.

PICTURE COURTESY NIUE TOURISM

NIUE
UNFORGETTABLE

WHALE ENCOUNTERS

ELSEWHERE in the world, you can spend hours chasing them around the open ocean. But here on Niue, the whales practically come to you.

Many Humpback whales, both pods and individuals, shelter in the bays around Avatele and Tamakautoga.

These are very deep waters, and so whales can often be seen, between June to October, for hours on end, a mere 50 metres! (150 feet!) from the waters edge.

We don't know of any other place in the world where humans can get this close to whales without leaving land.

You can stay dry and watch them from anywhere along our southwest coast, or the comfort of the Cliffhanger Bar at the Matavai Resort.

Because of the very low levels of people visiting Niue, it's even possible to go swimming, snorkeling or diving with the whales.

If you're brave, Niue Dive can get you out nearer to them. Naturally, getting this close carries risks that you must accept responsibility for, but to many people it's the best thing they've ever done.

DOLPHIN ENCOUNTERS

Dolphins are permanent residents, and much safer to swim with – when they are there! Niue Dive can also take you out to see them, but this is not a retail experience – 'dolphins on demand' is something that only happens in zoos. Ours are free to roam & have habits that make finding them reasonably easy.

Above or below the water, not a thing on this Earth comes close to...

UNFORGETTABLE

NIUE

www.niueisland.com

undiscovered unspoiled unbelievable®

NORFOLK ISLAND

HOME of the iconic Norfolk Pine, Norfolk Island is a gently-paced drop in the Pacific Ocean with a relaxing atmosphere and remarkable history entirely its own. Norfolk Island is an external territory of Australia with its own legislative assembly and even its own unique language ñ a mix of Tahitian and old English. This is spoken alongside English by most of the islandís population, many of whom are descendants of the HMS Bounty mutineers and their Tahitian wives.

For such a charming place, Norfolk Islandís history is a brutal one. After accommodating two penal settlements between 1788 and 1856, Norfolk became home to the Bounty descendents who immigrated here from Pitcairn Island on June 8, 1856.

This date continues to be the most significant on Norfolk Island's annual calendar of events. It marks the public holiday of Bounty Day, or Anniversary Day, when Norfolk Islanders commemorate the arrival of their forebears. The celebrations havenít changed over the generations and the food, friendship and clothing styles all reflect 19th century traditions. Impressive features on the day include the re-enactment of the Pitcairn peopleís landing and the procession march that follows.

Norfolk's first settlement heritage is beautifully preserved in and around the island's historic capital of Kingston. Situated at the southernmost end of Norfolk, the Kingston Precinct is where the first convict settlement began, and today it remains mostly as a 19th century village, with many of its buildings containing excellent museums. Elegantly refurbished buildings line Quality Row, which leads to a fascinating cemetery at the eastern end. The walls of the infamous pentagonal prison, hospital and Crankmill still stand, and beneath the Crankmillís floor are rumoured to be hundreds of undiscovered artefacts.

Norfolk Island's history comes alive with countless stories of mythological proportions. Like the gruesome tale about Bloody Bridge, the old rough-stone bridge near the Kingston cemetery. Legend has it that convict labourers murdered their overseer and bricked his blood-soaked body into the bridge as they built it. Unfortunately for them the blood oozed through the still-damp mortar and their heinous crime was discovered.

This amazing story is simply one of the captivating tales that will hold you spellbound on Norfolk Island.

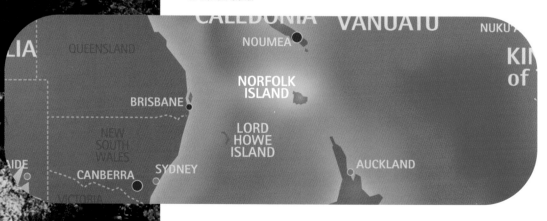

NORFOLK ISLAND
AT A GLANCE

NORFOLK ISLAND TOURISM
PO Box 211
Norfolk Island 2899
Tel: 6723 22147
Fax: 6723 23109
Email: info@norfolkisland.com.nf
Website: www.norfolkisland.com.nf

PICTURE NORFOLK ISLAND TOURISM

PICTURE NORFOLK ISLAND TOURISM

GEOGRAPHIC LOCATION

This small 3855 hectare island is under the authority of the Commonwealth of Australia. It is 1610 kilometres ENE of Sydney and 1456 kilometres ESE of Brisbane.

AIRLINES

International: Norfolk Jet flies from Australia ex Sydney & Brisbane. Norfolk Jet flying out of Melbourne January 2004. Air New Zealand flies from Auckland. Charters are available from Noumea.

ARRIVAL/DEPARTURE INFORMATION

The international airport is 1.5 kilometres from the Burnt Pine Shopping Centre.

Visitors may bring in: 1 litre of alcohol and 200 cigarettes. However, on the island, spirits tend to be 20-50 per cent cheaper than on the mainland. A special concession for visitors entitles airline ticket holders to a once-only 30 per cent discount off marked prices for a maximum of three litres of spirits.

Australian and New Zealand passport holders have access to Norfolk Island.

Visitors who are not Australian or New Zealand citizens will be required to obtain an Australian visa or an Electronic Travel Authority (ETA) that is valid for 30 days longer than the period of intended stay in Norfolk Island. If visiting Australia enroute to Norfolk Island, travellers will need to hold a multiple entry visa.Australian citizens can opt to use a Certificate of Identification obtainable through the Australian Post Office.

Departure Tax - there is an AUD$30 per adult over the age of 16 years Norfolk Island Government Departure Fee. This fee cannot be paid prior to arrival on the island but can be paid at the NI Visitors Information Centre prior to departure day on the island.

The importation of fresh fruit, vegetables, flowers and plants or seeds are strictly prohibited. The importation of pork and poultry products from New Zealand is also prohibited.

CURRENCY

The currency is the Australian dollar. Most major credit/bank cards are accepted on the island.

CLIMATE

Subtropical. Average rainfall 1328mm per year. Summer days from 24 degrees but not exceeding 28.4 degrees, nights 19-21 degrees. Idyllic days mid-winter, with temperatures ranging from 12 at night to 19-21 degrees during the day.

PICTURE: NORFOLK ISLAND TOURISM

ELECTRICITY

240 volts AC, 50 cycles, three-pin plug. As electricity is made locally by diesel generators, a power-surge protection device is advised for electronic equipment, particularly computers.

POPULATION

Around 1800. Two-thirds of the residents are directly descended from the original Pitcairners (from HMS Bounty).

LANGUAGE

English is the main language. There is a native language called Norfolk, which is derived from the speech of the HMS Bounty mutineers and their Tahitian wives and companions who settled Pitcairn Island in 1790.

LOCAL CONSIDERATIONS

Comfortable and casual day and night. It's wise to pack a sweater and light nylon jacket, strong shoes for walking and a torch for night outings. Remember a hat and sunscreen.

Religion – Church of England, Catholic Church, Unity Church and Seventh-day Adventist are all present on the island.

There is a 21-bed public hospital with excellent facilities and ambulance service. Medical insurance is recommended.

Tipping is not customary on Norfolk Island. The island residents are friendly, helpful and obliging.

TELECOMMUNICATIONS

International IDD telephones, telegrams and fax services are available. Public IDD coin-operated booths are available. Local calls are free. Only Norfolk Island phone cards are accepted. Mobile telephones are not operable on Norfolk Island.

TIME ZONE

Norfolk island is 1.5 hours ahead of Australian Eastern Standard Time. In summer, there is a 30-minute difference ahead of Sydney and 1.5 hours difference behind New Zealand. There is no daylight savings on the island.

TRANSPORT

There is no public transport system. Taxis are available. Hire cars are inexpensive. A current driver's licence is required.

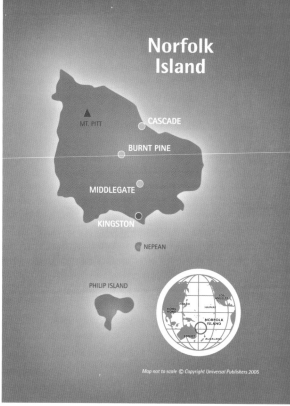

Norfolk Island

MT. PITT
CASCADE
BURNT PINE
MIDDLEGATE
KINGSTON
NEPEAN
PHILIP ISLAND

Map not to scale © Copyright Universal Publishers 2005

PICTURE: NORFOLK ISLAND TOURISM

SIMPLY BEAUTIFUL NORFOLK

HISTORY ABOUNDS

NORFOLK Island, still simply beautiful with pristine landscapes enhanced by a blanket of Norfolk Pines that have seen many centuries of life on this distinctly different holiday destination.

Under the authority of the Commonwealth of Australia, but with its own Legislative Assembly, Norfolk Island has a total land area of 35 square kilometres and lies 1140 kilometres east of Brisbane, 1120 kilometres northwest of Auckland and 800 kilometres south of Noumea.

What really will surprise you is its people, the Norfolk Islanders, descended from the Bounty mutineers and their Tahitian wives with a unique dialect derived from the old English and Tahitian languages. Discovered by Captain Cook on his South Pacific travels, the island was first settled as a penal colony in 1788.

Abandoned in 1814 it was again home to the unredeemed from 1824 to 1856. This second settlement provided the ultimate punishment for the most recalcitrant convicts.

Even today it requires little imagination to picture the horrors inflicted on these poor souls. When down town in Kingston, visitors can walk freely through the convict settlement buildings and cemetery or take a 'walk & talk' tour with the museum curator. View the Crankmill, the remains of the prison. Government House, Quality Row Georgian cottages and a host of other interesting historic sites.

Following the vacation of the penal settlement in 1856 the people of Pitcairn Island were transported on the Morayshire to Norfolk Island and it is these descendants of the Bounty mutineers who make up the majority of the population today. Familiar names from history such as Adams, Christian, McCoy, Quintal and Young are among the famous of these and with so many shared surnames nicknames are listed in the phonebook to help with identification. On Bounty Day, June 8th, the Norfolk Islanders commemorate their heritage, bringing it back to life in vivid style.

NATURAL ATTRACTIONS

The island is largely devoted to national parks and reserves that offer wonderful structured walking trails highlighting spectacular views. One of the most popular walks takes you to Captain Cook's Monument, following the cliff top where you will enjoy splendid views of Cathedral Rock, Bird Rock, Moo-oo Stone and Green Pool Stone. At the trail's end, 100 metres above the ocean, a lovely tree-shaded area provides picnic tables and barbecues. Another walk leads you to the summit of Mt. Pitt, the highest point on the island, where breathtaking panoramas give the true perspective of this island paradise.

From the summit of Mt. Pitt can be seen the larger of the outer lying islands, Nepean and Philip. Soft adventure trekking tours to Philip Island serve to dramatically illustrate the devastation man can inflict on nature while demonstrating the power of good management practices to restore the equilibrium within the environment.

Like any subtropical island the beaches are another lure. Almost every day from mid September through May offers pleasant beach weather, with December to April the very best months. From Emily Bay into Slaughter Bay the lagoon is sheltered behind a coral reef. A great spot for swimming, snorkelling, or just simply lazing about under the many pines on the grassed foreshores. The marine life on the reef is abundant with colourful tropical fish, striking coral varieties and a multitude of other life forms.

The natural topography of Norfolk forms a network of valleys and ridges with more than 130 kilometres of road leading you through a maze of rural and bush-clad scenes to end on secluded beaches, stony coastlines or amazing cliff tops reserves.

Picnic and barbecue areas are located all around the island to enhance your experience of the Norfolk way of life.

ACTIVITIES GALORE NORFOLK

LET NORFOLK SURPRISE YOU

GET into the action on Norfolk through audience participation and dress up as a convict for the night or become a part of the Murder Mystery dinner party, wander amongst two centuries of gravestones by starlight or experience the thrill while airborne on a scenic flight over the island. Get head down and observe myriad marine life under Slaughter Bay through a glass-bottomed boat or take on the big fellas out on a blue-water fishing charter. Enjoy the local poet's stories told under the stars in the creatively lit bush setting of wonderland by night. Take a stroll with the museum's curator around Kingston's penal settlement to admire and learn about the cruelty dished out to those incarcerated there in the 19th century, or sing for your supper on a Sunday during the Chapel visit. Attend a sampling of the locally manufactured liqueurs ... and so the list of action-packed activities goes on – call at the visitors information centre for more details.

For those who are sporting minded, Norfolk offers a range of international venues. The Point Hunter golf course with resident professional creates an experience in itself by its very location amongst the Georgian buildings of the Kingston valley. Picturesque views across Anson Bay are afforded the shooter on the Clay Target range, while all-weather courts at the Cheryl Tennis Club enhances one's game plan. There is a host of friendly fellow bowlers at the lawn bowls club and two squash courts await your pleasure at the Leagues Club. An abundance of other sports is catered for – enquiries are welcome at the visitor's information centre for details.

For the more adventurous, try the wonderful array of dive sites dotted around the small rocks and islets off Norfolk's coastline, where many subterranean caves and colourful coral display abound. Philip Island trekking presents a dramatic picture of how devastating man's folly can be while demonstrating to all the power of cohesive environmental management to restore the natural beauty of the island. Off-road 4Wdriving tours get up close and intimate with the uncharted tracks of the island while bushwalking takes the quieter approach on structured trails through the peaceful flora and fauna of our national parks with spectacular views of the outer rock bird sanctuaries on the eastern coastline. Experience memory lane unfolding while riding in a carriage drawn by two magnificent draft horses or explore the options of other horse riding activities that are graded to accommodate all levels of competency.

Touring opportunities will unashamedly pamper you while familiarising your senses with the beauty of Norfolk Island. A variety of 12-day tours giving general or special interest opportunities to mix and mingle with the people is available from a number of operators. You will come to recognise many of the characters portrayed in the different settings and get to be acquainted with the colourful personalities behind them. There are many smaller tours going behind the hedges, visiting farms and industry, or playing tag-a-long through the penal settlement. You can soak up the pure fresh air on a breakfast walk or relax over a glass or wine at the sunset fishfry.

The people of Norfolk have a rich cultural heritage of which they are proud and there are multitudes of occasions when you can become part of their way of life.

A group of Norfolk Islanders has collectively developed progressive dinners where you enter their homes to encounter this firsthand. Certain restaurants feature traditional island style cuisine while the Mutiny on the Bounty Show mimics the events leading up to their becoming a separate community on Pitcairn Island. The very essence of their being is depicted at Cyclorama and the exploits of years past can be viewed on film evenings. A locally written and produced play set in the old penal colony court house tells an amusing story in the trial of fifteen and the various museums harbour collections of artefacts from the early settlement eras. Special occasions celebrate Bounty Day, A&H Show Day, Foundation Day and Thanksgiving Day, the dates for which can be accessed through www.norfolkisland.nf

Let Norfolk keep surprising you with the unhurried pleasure of a remedial massage, a soak in the hot pool or a full facial before the shear enjoyment of eating out at one of the numerous sidewalk or al fresco cafés that nestle into the environment around the island. Indulge in classic dining at one of the dozen or more restaurants offering excellent food and wine over a variety of styles and tastes. Eateries to take out cater to those requiring pizza, fish & chips, Chinese, Thai, etc.

Stroll through Burnt Pine and go broke saving money on tax-free shopping. A plethora of globally sourced goods is offered in more than 50 stores, from footwear to hats, teapots to cameras, art to souvenirs and perfume to fishing tackle. Special discounts apply to visitors on liquor and tobacco products at specific outlets.

Join us for some memorable events throughout the year. Bounty Day on June 8th celebrates the arrival of the Pitcairn Islanders to Norfolk Island with parade and community picnic. A musical feast commences in May with the Country Music festival followed by ballroom dancing, line dancing and later Rhythm on the Rock in December during jazz week. For the studious there's a Writer's & Readers Festival in July. A variety of sporting carnival, dot the calendar and theatre week provides some special interest in September.

Rest & relaxation ... read a book, lie on the beach, study the stars or wake to a special silence filled only with the singing or birds. Watch the sun set over a glass of fine wine, stroll through the Botanic Gardens, play bridge, chess or scrabble ... whatever your aspiration or vision Norfolk has the environment to meet it. Norfolk Island will surprise you ... we invite you to experience it, fulfill the desire to have a real stress free holiday and capture memories that will live with you forever.

FISHING AT NORFOLK

YOU have probably heard a lot of stories about the fishing at Norfolk Island. Well, they're all true! Fishing is a paradise for the keen fisherman as well as the novice. Norfolk has no harbour so boats have to be raised and lowered by crane into the water. The boats vary in size from 5 to 8 metres and take up to 5 fishermen.

The main fish is the 'Trumpeter', a reef fish that lives in among the coral. Also caught are rock cod, snapper, kingfish. trevalli and grouper. All gear is supplied, but if you wish you are welcome to bring your favourite rig.

Trolling: Trolling is done for surface fish such as kingfish and yellowfin tuna. All gear is supplied and some good catches have been taken with plenty of excitement.

Fishing: The reason for Norfolk's abundant fish stocks are the ocean currents swinging from the equator and across from Australia bringing a rich array of baitfish which is followed by tuna, kingfish, mahi mahi, wahoo, bonito and marlin.

There are four commercial fishing tour operators on the island and they provide regular tours to the rock shelf surrounding Norfolk Island to give visitors the opportunity to experience deepsea fishing. Species caught on these expeditions include trumpeter, rock cod, snapper, grouper and trevally.

Our friendly fishing tour operators supply all the bait and tackle you need, and their vast knowledge of the local waters and best fishing spots assures you of a good feed of local fish upon your return.

Rock fishing is a very popular pastime on the island. Many of the best rock fishing spots can only be reached in good weather and at low tide. Given the dangers associated with rock fishing around Norfolk Island, it is advisable to seek the guidance of an experienced local fisherman.

Fishing with Ian

Ian and Joan Kenny are famous for their fishing trips, island cruises, private charters and their special island-style fish fry!

Mystic II is equipped with the following: CB radio, mobile phone (Norfolk only), life vests, GPS, colour sounder, EPIRB and flares. Length: 7.3 metres. (23 feet) Deep Vee
Engine: 165 Hp Merc Stern Drive. Big Game Fishing: 5 Rods All Penn Equipment, 3.24kg Rods and 2.37kg Rods, 1 Game Chair

Phone/Fax: (6723) 22 386
Email: kenny@norfolk.net.nf

Come and Enjoy!

SHOPPING AT NORFOLK

TAX-FREE SHOPPING

Norfolk Island has become one of the leading tax-free shopping destinations for Australians and New Zealanders. In fact, some visitors come to Norfolk just to shop!

You will be amazed at the shopping bargains! Income, company, GST or sales tax is not applicable and the local shop proprietors ensure that the shoppers are the big winners by passing on the savings.

You don't have to travel the world to buy something special, our shopkeepers have done it for you and it is available at tax-free, GST-free prices – at better than normal duty free.

We have all that you find in a duty free shop plus many extras i.e. shoes, clothes, knitwear, figurines, dinnerware, giftware, collectables, sporting goods, toys, electrical goods, crystal, silverware, cosmetic and perfumes.

Just about everything you could ever want to buy is on Norfolk Island.

There are more than 70 tax-free shops in Burnt Pine at the heart of the island, many of them specialising in a diverse range of quality merchandise which is not readily available in Australia or New Zealand.

The shopping precinct is centrally located, so that you can stroll from one shop to another at your leisure.

Designer labels are commonplace in these shops as you will find on a short stroll along the main street.

GOVERNOR'S LODGE RESORT

www.governorslodge.nlk.nf

LOCATION
Queen Elizabeth Avenue, Norfolk Island

EMAIL
res@governorslodge.nf

PHONE/FAX
Ph (6723) 24 400
Fax (6723) 24 300
Freecall 1800 181 608

ADDRESS
PO Box 898 Norfolk Island
2899 South Pacific

FACILITIES
Tennis courts next door, swimming pool (heated in winter), heated spa (all year round), Signature restaurant (Soon to reopen) featuring local prime beef, fresh fish and produce. Dave Bailey's Café for light meals, coffee, casual dining, post masters & al fresco dining.

The Governor's Lodge Resort is the newest and most luxurious resort on Norfolk Island with a 4.5-Star rating. It covers four hectares with beautifully landscaped gardens and majestic Norfolk Pines.

50 Executive one-bedroom cottages, separate dining/ lounge areas in a stand-alone cottage with verandah, 4 deluxe one-bedroom cottages, separate dining/lounge areas in stand-alone cottage with spa and verandahs with rural views and 1 special needs one-bedroom cottage executive style, makes up our accommodation complex. Our comfortable bed sizes are king, queen and king singles, with sofa beds available for a third person sharing. All bedrooms and lounges have ceiling fans and for winter, gas heaters. All cottages have Sky Television for sports, news and movies. ISD telephones, radios, hairdryers, kitchenette with fridge, microwave, kettle and toaster. The tennis courts next door are available to our Guests.

This exclusive resort has an inviting swimming pool, heated in winter, with a separate all year heated spa. Swim, relax in the sun around the pool.

Our superior Restaurant features a range of local product for fine à la carte dining, with a comfortable and relaxed bar to enjoy pre-dinner drinks or your coffee and liqueurs.

For further details please call toll free 1800 181 608.

THE COLONIAL OF NORFOLK ISLAND

www.colonial.nf

LOCATION
Queen Elizabeth Avenue Norfolk Island, ten minutes from town

EMAIL
reservations@colonial.nf

PHONE/FAX
Ph (6723) 22 177
Fax (6723) 22 831

ADDRESS
PO Box 70 Norfolk Island
2899 South Pacific

FACILITIES
TV and radios, fridges, coffee & tea, making facilities, IDD direct-dial phones, ceiling fans, hairdryers, irons & boards, guest laundry

Accommodation at The Colonial is available in a range of rooms, including the Executive Poolside Rooms.

Beautifully landscaped grounds and delightful décor complement the colonial architecture.

Only minutes from the town shopping centre, the hotel has a secluded charm and character. It is home to one of the Island's finest dining establishments – Annabelles Restaurant – set in the lush richness of the gardens, it offers superb à la carte dining, popular theme nights and live entertainment most evenings.

The Colonial also offers Norfolk Island's largest dedicated convention complex. Ideal for small meetings, conferences and large functions, the modern convention rooms cater for up to 150 guests.

Cocktail bar, swimming pool, guest barbecue facilities, tour information, coffee lounge, lobby shop, postal service, theme nights, complimentary coach service, tennis, lawn bowling, gymnasium, golf (one round), manager's "Monday Sunset" cocktail party, "Islanders" arrival drink, courtesy coach to the shopping centre.

See our website for full booking details and reservations www.colonial.nf

Norfolk Pines Group

Norfolk Island's widest variety and highest quality range of accommodation.
For all information and bookings please contact:
NORFOLK PINES GROUP
PO BOX 169 NORFOLK ISLAND, SOUTH PACIFIC 2899
PHONE: (6723) 22 114 FAX: (6723) 23 014
EMAIL: borrys@norfolk.nf INTERNET: www.norfolk-pines-group.nf

The Natural Choice in Accommodation and Rental Cars

BLIGH COURT HOLIDAY COTTAGES

In Grassy Road – at the base of Mt. Pitt. Close to shops, restaurants and the National Park. Bligh Court cottages is a popular smaller property suited for families and small groups. The newest cottage has been built for the disabled with all fittings. Beautiful gardens create a relaxed home-away-from-home feeling. Appointments include full kitchen, queen size beds and TV. All cottages come with a bonus rental car included in the accommodation package.

DAYDREAMER HOLIDAY APARTMENTS

In Grassy Road. One and two bedroom fully self-contained apartments offer well equipped ground level "walk-in" suites set in spacious grounds some with tranquil, idyllic valley views. An excellent covered guest BBQ and entertaining area, where the proprietors also hang bunches of bananas for all guests use, is set in the beautifully maintained gardens. All apartments come with a bonus rental car included in the accommodation package.

ISLANDER LODGE HOLIDAY APARTMENTS

Five fully self-contained and well equipped one-bedroom apartments on a hillside overlooking the Kingston historical area. They command magnificent panoramic views of the convict settlement ruins and the foreshores of Emily and Slaughter Bays with volcanic Philip and Nepean Islands in the background. You also have a grandstand view of the golf course and Cemetery Bay. All apartments come with a bonus rental car included in the accommodation package.

WHISPERING PINES LUXURY COTTAGES

Nestling in the foothills of Mt Pitt and the National Park are 7 two-bedroom hexagonal private cottages with contemporary interiors clad in Norfolk pine. Each offers stunning views, tranquillity and complete privacy. They are self-contained with fully equipped kitchen, lounge, dining area, ensuite bathrooms, radio, TV, laundry and outdoor barbecue entertaining area. All cottages come with a bonus rental car included in the accommodation package.

OCEAN BREEZE HOLIDAY COTTAGES

Ideally located high in the centre of the Island, our self-contained one bedroom cottages have broad panoramic ocean views to the south and extensive views of Mt Pitt to the north. All cottages are tastefully furnished including king size beds, modern full kitchens, en-suite bathrooms, in-house laundry, TV and video. Our guests can enjoy picturesque barbecues in our outdoor entertaining area with tennis court and swimming pool. All cottages come with a bonus rental car included in the accommodation package.

The Natural Choice in Accommodation and Rental Cars

CUMBERLAND HOLIDAY APARTMENTS

LOCATION
Taylors Road
Norfolk Island
South Pacific

EMAIL
bookings@
cumberlandclose.com

PHONE/FAX
Ph (6723) 22 721
Fax (6723) 23 264

ADDRESS
PO Box 46 Norfolk Island
2899 South Pacific

HOSTS
Rael & Angela Donde

FACILITIES
BBQ area, laundry, transit
lounge, free rental car,
movies, free tennis,
tropical gardens

ATTRACTIONS
golf, tennis, squash,
beaches, fishing,
kayaking, biking, 4WD
tours, musuems, clifftop
BBQ, forest walks, mini-
golf, glass-bottom boat,
diving, snorkeling

CREDIT CARDS
Visa, MasterCard,
Bankcard, JCB, Amex

Complimentary car (excluding insurance), transfer, continental BreakfastPack, chocolates, bottle of wine, and tennis.

Location: set in tranquil, tropical gardens, the property is centrally situated, an easy 3-minute stroll to tax-free shops, cafes & restaurants, yet only a 5-minute drive to the white-sand beaches, golf, forest-walks & historical-area.

Facilities: Exclusive resort of 3$^1/_2$ & 4-star self-contained, luxury, quality appointed, guest houses, each with its own private, sunny veranda overlooking fruit and palm trees. Enjoy lingering breakfasts. Retire to fluffy heavenly beds. Wake to steamy showers and Egyptian cotton towels. Fully-equipped kitchens, DVD&CD players, in-house movies, massage, internet, recreation & BBQ areas, laundry, transit lounge and Italian restaurant. Choices range from the economical studio to 1-&-2 bedroom units, to Cumberland-House, a modern, spacious 4-bedroom home. Also, the private EastWing, with 3 connected ground floor units sleeping up to 8-persons with 4 bedrooms, 3 bathrooms & 3 living rooms, private courtyard.

POINCIANA COTTAGES

LOCATION
Norfolk Island

EMAIL
poinciana@ni.net.nf

PHONE/FAX
Ph (6723) 22 547
Fax (6723) 22 911

ADDRESS
PO Box 460
Norfolk Island 2899

FACILITIES
Self-contained, central
location, cable TV/video
phones, email facilities

HOSTS
Peter & Jackie Pye

Locally-owned, small property with fully self-contained spacious one-bedroom cottages for up to three persons. Centrally located (5 min. walk to airport / 10 min. to CBD) with valley and mountain views. BBQ facilities. Separate bathroom and laundry. Full cooking facilities including convection microwave, dishwasher, crockery, cutlery etc. Serviced weekly, full linen provided. Children welcome - cots available. We recommend Aloha Rent-a-car for competitive prices and friendly service. Medium-sized automatic vehicles included in tariff - insurances are $10.00/day. Vehicles must be confirmed at a time of reservation and drivers must hold a current driver's licence.

FANTASY ISLAND RESORT

LOCATION
Norfolk Island

EMAIL
info@fantasynorfolk.com

PHONE/FAX
Ph (6723) 23 778
Fax (6723) 23 779

ADDRESS
PO Box 441
Norfolk Island 2899 So.
Pacific via Australia

ATTRACTIONS
Norfolk's newest 4-star
rated luxury resort in the
centre of town. 10 modern
units opposite Post Office
and Visitor's Bureau

Situated in the heart of the tax-free shopping centre, choose from studios, 1- and 2-bedroom units, each with private balcony and magnificent ocean views. Set in 4$^1/_2$-acres of landscaped grounds with tropical fruit trees and shrubs. A poolside BBQ / entertaining area. Tour operator on site. Guest laundry with washer, dryer and tub. Covered carports adjacent to each unit. Resident owner/manager. Smoking or non-smoking rooms have king or twin beds with IDD phones, cable TV, kitchens (kitchenettes in studios) and spacious lounge/dining area in 1- and 2-bedroom units with modern tropical decor. Late model auto rental cars included, and transit lounge for late departures. Studios start at $140, up to $280 for a 2-bedroom unit for 4 (incl car).

CASTAWAY HOTEL & APARTMENTS

Castaways is one of the larger properties on the Island, but still boutique by comparison to other destinations.

Castaways has location, right in the main township yet down a quiet driveway and spread amongst mature, glorious sub-tropical gardens.

The choice is yours as to what type of accommodation. There are Garden hotel rooms, Superior hotel rooms and one- and two-bedroom Apartments. Some of the Apartments have been designed specifically for the physically handicapped.

The Hotel's "Christian's Restaurant" has some great theme dinner nights. There is a log fire lounge. A car is included in the soft months.

HIGHLANDS LODGE & COTTAGES

Highlands is an up-market property located in the middle of the Island adjacent to the National Park.

The property consists of some 50 acres, some beautiful bush, and the balance rolling grasslands and manicured gardens. In the main B&B Lodge each room has its own en-suite bathroom and a dedicated separate lounge.

There is exquisite cuisine from the licensed restaurant.

The one- and two-bedroom cottages are all individuals, handcrafted in rich timber.

Have a hit of tennis or swim in the pool or just relax and rest on your king size bed. A car is included all year around.

PANORAMA GARDEN APARTMENTS

Panorama Garden Apartments is located in the historical penal settlement area of Kingston.

The property has stunning views over the rural rolling hills, over the lagoon, past the reef and out to Philip Island.

You have a choice of Kingston view apartments (direct sea views) or valley view apartments (sea views from your balcony). There are one- and two-bedroom apartments. Apartments have all the holiday necessities including full kitchens, heaters, fans, IDD phones, microwaves, hair dryers, electric blankets and king size or queen size beds.

A car is included all year around.

HAYDANBLAIR HOUSE

Haydanblair House is a substantial executive-style home suitable for several couples or a large family get together or for somebody wanting large amounts of space.

It is set on five acres of rolling grass lawns, bush and plantations.

There is a fully equipped kitchen, 25-foot-high ceilings in the sunken lounge, separate dining room, a TV room, mezzanine music area and extensive verandahs.

A car is provided all year around

Haydanblair House is situated 2kms from the shopping centre, 500 metres from the National Park and 4kms from the beach.

H. Martin Estates has almost all accommodation styles covered on Norfolk Island, including hotel, lodge, apartment, cottage and executive home varieties. Our family looks forward to your inquiry at our central booking reception desk.

H. Martin Estates

PO Box 15, Norfolk Island, South Pacific, 2899
Tel: (6723) 22625   Fax: (6723) 22785   Email: hmartinres@ni.net.nf
Website: www.h.martin-estates.nf

NORFOLK HOLIDAY APARTMENTS

LOCATION
Taylors Road Norfolk Island

EMAIL
norfolkholidayapartments
@norfolk.nf

PHONE/FAX
Ph (6723) 22 009
Fax (6723) 23 804

ADDRESS
Taylors Road, Norfolk Island

FACILITIES
King size beds,Full kitchens,
microwave, hairdryers, picnic
baskets, beach towels, TV, DVD

ATTRACTIONS
2 min drive to the beach and
5 min walk to the shops,
cafes and tour companies

CREDIT CARDS
Mastercard,Visa, BankCard

This property will impress, rated 4 star and positioned in a central location. These apartments are in a tranquil setting overlooking quiet valley views and the sunset. Exceptional quality, all apartments are spacious, and furnished with modern decore. All bedrooms have ensuite bathrooms. We have a covered guest BBQ area suitable for large groups or small individual dining. A transit lounge for your comfort if an early checkout is required. You will appreciate everything you see here.

HOSTS

Proprietors, Ray and Sue Sills

SHIRALEE

website: www.shiralee.nf
email: bookings@shiralee.nf

Four star Executive Cottages

Luxurious, Private, Spacious and Fully Equipped Individual Self-Contained 1 & 2 Bedroom Cottages with IDD phones, TV & Videos, BBQ, hairdryer, laundry, transit lounge. Serviced Daily

Centrally located 2 minutes walk to shops, club and restaurants

**Reservations contact your Travel Agent
or Mike & Barbara Hehir**
Taylors Road PO Box 448 • Norfolk Island 2899
Telephone: int + 6723 22118 • Facsimile: int+ 6723 23318

FLIGHTS FROM BRISBANE AND SYDNEY
BUSINESS AND ECONOMY CLASS SEATING

HEAD OFFICE ~ NORFOLK ISLAND

Taylors Road PO Box 270 Norfolk Island 2899
Ph: Int + (6723) 24313 Fax: (6723) 24314
Email: sales@norfolkjet.nf

BRISBANE OFFICE

4/97 Creek Street Brisbane QLD 4001
Ph: (61) 7 3221 6677 Fax: (61) 7 3211 9823
Email: sales@norfolkjet.com.au

www.norfolkjet.com.au

NORFOLK ISLAND
YOUR ISLAND HOME

Only a short flight away, Norfolk Island is ideal for stretching all your senses, with it's friendly locals, rich history, adventure activities and tax free shopping. Enjoy the island's unspoilt beauty, comfortable accommodation and stylish eateries. All you have to do is relax, settle in and appreciate it.

Norfolk Island Tourism   www.norfolkisland.nf
Phone (int) 6723 22147   Email info@norfolkisland.nf

NORFOLK
ISLAND

PAPUA NEW GUINEA

To many, Papua New Guinea remains the world's last frontier. It is a land of the last living ancient civilisation. It is also a diverse mix of old and new, with Port Moresby a thriving business harbour and air hub and areas where the majority of the population lives, undeveloped terrain that is difficult to access. There are more than 5 million people living on Papua New Guinea's 600 islands. Originally inhabited by Asian settlers more than 50,000 years ago, the first European contact was by the Portuguese explorer Jorge de Meneses in 1526, who named the island Ilhas dos Papuas (Island of the Fuzzy Hairs). The Spanish renamed it New Guinea after its inhabitants' supposed similarity to those of Guinea in Africa.

Following various explorers such as de Bougainville and Cook, New Guinea was left alone for several centuries. In 1824, the Dutch added the island to their East Indies empire. Germany took possession of the northern part of the island in the 1880s and Britain soon followed declaring a protectorate over the southern region.

COLONIAL HISTORY

In 1906, British New Guinea became Papua, and administration of the region was taken over by newly independent Australia. With the outbreak of WWI, Australian troops promptly secured the German headquarters at Rabaul, subsequently taking control of German New Guinea.

Post-war, the eastern half of New Guinea reverted to Australia and became the Territory of Papua & New Guinea. Indonesia took control of Dutch New Guinea in 1963 (incorporating it into the Indonesian state as Irian Jaya). PNG was granted self-government in 1973, and full independence was achieved in 1975.

Today, a modern economy exists within Papua New Guinea with the rich natural resources of the region including gold, copper, oil, coffee, tea, copra and palm oil. Co-existing with this economy is a traditional non-monetary barter economy that existed long before Europeans arrived on the Papuan shores.

Papua New Guinea

Lorengau
Manus Is.
Kabuti M'bunai
Manus

Wutung
Musu Vanimo
Osima Leitre
Imbrinis Sissano
Bewani Aitape
Kilifas Paup Suain
Imonda Yakamul
Amanab Lumi Dreikikir Dagua
Kamberatoro Yankok Nuku Maprik Wewak
Green River Abrau Yilui Bainyik Passam Kaup Darapap
Ama Burui Korogo Angoram Marienberg Watam
May River Ambudti Pagwi Timbunke Kanduanam Awar
Yapsiei Yesimbit Yamen Yip Bogia
Amboin Yaminbot Ninas Tung Hatzfeldthafen
Avieme Annanberg Ulingan
Tabubil Telefomin Oksapmin Atome Sumasuru Josephstaal Sarang Wadau
Oslobip Lake Porgera Simbai Magila Matukar
Kopiago Laiagam Wabag Kompiam Madang
Koroba Tari Kandep Tagan Baiyer River Tabibuga Ato
Ningerum Honinabi Margarima Tambul Wapenamanda Walium Bibi
Kiunga Nipa Mt Hagen Kerawagi Kundiawa Dumpu
Lake Poroma Minj Chuave Gumine Goroka Gusap
Lake Kutubu Talibu Benabena Kaiapit
Murray Simo Kagua Pangia Gumine Lufa Henganofi Kainantu
Keketa Karimui Okapa Aiyura Kanbaire
Kasua Komaio Erave Lake Gurimatu Obura Yanuf Erap
Kaviananga Nanase Tebera Wabo Wonenara Nadzab Bukaua
Pikiwa Waira Kikori Marawaka Tsile Lae Busama
Emeti Kalam Baimuru Iori Menyamya Mumeng Salamaua
Suki Bebisa Misiki Akoma Iriu Kaintiba Asekr Bulolo Kui
Goe Balimo Kenewa Wau Morobe Doha
Serki Wasua Kerema Malalaua Garaina Aro Manau
Weam Iamara Buk Kukipi Girabi Guari
Morehead Sewerimabu Miaru Maipa Ioma Oure
Gubam Malam Iokea Beipa Tapini Garara
Wando Tonda Sibidiri Orioma Bereina Woitape Popondetta
Bula Boze Daru Kainuku Bakoiudu Kokoda Sangara Inonda
Mari Tais Togo Poukama Kabuna Sigule Eroro Waiwa
Hisiu Loloua Ilimo Afore
Lea Lea Iawop Awoma
Boera Dorobisoro Safi

PORT
MORESBY
National Capital
Sogeri Gaire Bulidobu Aimare
Kwikila Potuna Amau
Hula Kupiano Tutubu Abau

Bamaga Australia

Sepik
Highlands
Madang
Morobe
Gulf
Manus

Air Niugini Country

Nobody knows Papua New Guinea like Air Niugini

Alotau (675) 641 1100	**Lihir** (675) 986 4008	**Rabaul** (675) 982 9033
Boroko (675) 325 9084 / 3541	**Madang** (675) 852 2699	**Tabubil** (675) 548 3325
Goroka (675) 732 1444	**Manus** (675) 470 9092	**Vanimo** (675) 857 1014
Hoskins (675) 9893 5077	**Mt Hagen** (675)542 1444	**Waigani** (675) 325 1055
Kavieng (675) 984 2135	**Porgera** (675) 547 9500	**Wewak** (675) 856 2233
Lae (675) 472 1892	**Port Moresby** (675) 321 2888	

Celebrating **30** *years of service to Papua New Guinea*

Air Niugini

PAPUA NEW GUINEA TOURISM PROMOTION AUTHORITY
Level 5, Pacific MMI Building,
Champion Parade, PORT MORESBY,
Papua New Guinea
Tel: (675) 320 0211
Fax: (675) 320 0223
Email: info@pngtourism.org.pg
Website: www.pngtourism.org.pg

GEOGRAPHICAL LOCATION

Papua New Guinea lies within the tropics south of the Equator and 160 kilometres north of Australia. With a landmass of 473,189 square kilometres, the country includes the eastern part of New Guinea Island, the second largest island in the world, plus some 600 outer islands, atolls and coral reefs.

AIRLINES

International: Air Niugini and Qantas
Domestic: Air Niugini, Airlink, Airlines of PNG, Islands Nationair, Trans Niugini Airways, MAF, Regional Air.

ARRIVAL/DEPARTURE

Jacksons International Airport is the gateway to Papua New Guinea, eight kilometres from the centre of Port Moresby. Mt Hagen Provincial Airport has been declared the international port of entry because of the mining activities in the Highlands provinces.

A 60-day tourist visa can be obtained from Papua New Guinea Diplomatic Missions or Australian Missions at a cost equivalent to K75.00. Visas can also be obtained on arrival for a fee of K75.00 and can be extended for a further 30 days for a fee of K200.00. Business entry visas are valid for 12 months from the date of issue.

Certification of vaccination against yellow fever or cholera is required for travellers over one year of age coming from infected areas. Malaria is a serious health risk and so anti-malarial precautions are strongly recommended. HIV/AIDS is a growing global epidemic and travellers are advised to take extra care.

CURRENCY

Currency is the Kina which is divided into 100 toea. There are K50, K20, K10, K5 and K2 notes and a K1 coin.
Travellers cheques and international credit cards are accepted at major hotels and restaurants.

CLIMATE

Warm to hot and humid throughout the year. There is a rainy season, which varies from province to province, however, in general, the dry months are from May to November. The weather patterns vary greatly because of mountain and valley configurations, which influence the prevailing airstreams. Temperatures on the coast vary between 25 and 30 Celsius all year round, and in the Highlands the temperature can reach 20 Celsius, but can be very cold at night.

ELECTRICITY

The current on the national grid is 240 volts AC. Some hotels have 110volt outlets in guestrooms.

HANDICRAFTS

A wide range of traditional crafts are made in many different local styles. Masks, wooden bowls, string bags, baskets, drums, story and spirit boards can be found. Heritage items made before 1960 are restricted and must be inspected by National Museum staff before an export permit can be issued. Export of Bird of Paradise plumes, stone artefacts ? except stone axes ? is prohibited.

LANGUAGE

Over 800 different languages are spoken. Melanesian Pidgin and Hiri Motu are the two most widely used, but English is the official language in education, businesses and government circles.

POPULATION

5.5 million people.

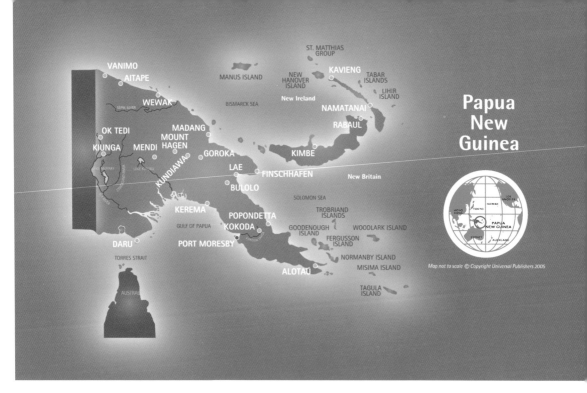

LOCAL CONSIDERATIONS

Dress code is informal and casual with shorts and open-neck shirts worn throughout the year. In the Highlands sturdy walking shoes are recommended and a sweater or jacket for cool evenings. Female dress should always be modest.

Dental, medical and hospital services are available in major centres. Medical clinics and posts are run by church and government bodies in remote areas.

Religion - Christianity is dominant although local traditional beliefs and ceremonies are maintained in more remote areas.

Tipping is neither expected nor encouraged in this Melanesian culture.

TELECOMMUNICATIONS

Modern satellite communications with ISD and STD dialling is available in most parts of the country. Telex and facsimile services are also available except in very remote areas where high frequency radio is in use.

TIME ZONE

PNG is 10 hours ahead of Greenwich Mean Time (GMT).

TRANSPORTATION

Mostly by air across PNG but a good road network links the Northern zone and the Highlands region. Because of rugged country between the Northern zone and Port Moresby there is no road link.

In Port Moresby and major towns rental cars, local boats and ferries, taxis and local buses are all readily available.

EXPERIENCE PAPUA NEW GUINEA

THERE are four main regions of the island of Papua New Guinea: Southern, Momase, Highlands and the New Guinea Islands.

SOUTHERN REGION

THE Southern region is made up of six provinces: Central and National Capital District, Western, Gulf, Milne Bay and Oro, home of the infamous Kokoda Trail. The country's capital city, Port Moresby, is situated on the magnificent Fairfax Harbour. It is home to the National Parliament, National Museum, Botanical Gardens and the Catholic Cathedral – built in the Haus Tambaran (traditional house of the spirits) style. Other attractions of the region include the sites of fighting between the Japanese and Allied troops of World War II in Milne Bay and the Oro provinces. The famous Kokoda Trail is one not to be missed. You can choose to start trekking either from the Central or the Oro side of the trek. The world's largest butterfly 'the Queen Alexandra Bird Wing' is found in the Oro province.

MOMASE REGION

THE Momase region includes Morobe, Madang, East Sepik and Sandaun provinces. Lae in Morobe province is the country's second largest city and gateway to the Highlands provinces as well as Madang province. Madang is one of the prettiest towns in the Pacific.

HIGHLANDS REGION

THE remote Highlands region is home to the greatest proportion of the population. There are many tribes and 60 discovered language groups. Both Asaro mudmen and the Huli Wigmen come from this part of the country.

ISLANDS REGION

THE New Guinea Islands provinces include East and West New Britain, New Ireland, North Solomons and Manus. Rabaul in East New Britain is known for the locals dressed in traditional ornaments dancing over blazing flames called the Baining Fire Dancers. Dancers perform over flames after nightfall in a ritual show of thanksgiving to the gods and release of spirits in the night.

Papua New Guinea

Ambua Lodge

Malolo Plantation Lodge

Karawari Lodge

Sepik Spirit

The Surprising Paradise

To capture the essence of Papua New Guinea is to fully experience the rich natural and cultural diversity that has created this surprising paradise. From the jungle highlands to the teeming coral reefs, Trans Niugini Tours welcomes you to four unique destinations from which you can explore this incredible country.

Set amongst exotic birds, exquisite flora and the exhilarating mountains of the highlands, Ambua Lodge offers a breathtaking location surrounded by rich tradition and culture.

Perched high on a mountain ridge, Karawari Lodge overlooks pristine tropical rainforests and the Karawari River, a slender link to the outside world.

For a dramatic contrast, cruise on the *Sepik Spirit*, a floating lodge that takes

small select groups of travellers to the mysterious middle reaches of the Sepik River allowing them to experience an unforgettable adventure including traditional village life and culture.

The picturesque seaside setting of Malolo Plantation Lodge offers snorkelling and sea kayaking among the colourful coral reefs and marine life as well as informative cultural experiences.

Each Trans Niugini Tours destination offers friendly professional service to make your Papua New Guinea experience even more memorable.

The New Ambua Lodge Airport is now open for commercial traffic and is connected to **Ambua Lodge** by a new nature trail. Visitors are now able to travel directly from

Karawari Lodge or Mt Hagen by charter aircraft to **Ambua Lodge Airstrip**. All inclusive retail tariff.

Bensbach Wildlife Lodge – located on the river westwards in South West Papua New Guinea, the lodge has eight twin bedded rooms with comfortable accommodation for 16 guests. Activities include birdwatching, Barramundi fishing, wildlife tours to see herds of deer and wallabies.

MV Sepik Spirit – operates schedule three-night cruises along the Sepik River and its tributaries.

Malolo Plantation Lodge – located on the north coast offers snorkelling, nature tours and village visits.

For more detailed information, brochures and tariffs contact Trans Niugini Tours.

trans niugini tours.

PO Box 371, Mt. Hagen
Ph: +675 542 1438 Fax: +675 542 2470
E-Mail: service@pngtours.com Web Site: http://www.pngtours.com
Australia Toll Free: 1 800 634 773

ECHO F031

TREEHOUSE VILLAGE DIVING & RESORT
www.treehouse.com.pg

LAE INTERNATIONAL HOTEL
www.laehotel.com.pg

LOCATION
Kavieng, New Ireland,
EMAIL
info@treehouse.com.pg
PHONE/FAX
Ph (675) 984 2666
Fax (675) 984 2693
ADDRESS
PO Box 506, Kavieng, NIP,
Papua New Guinea
HOST
Capt. Alun Beck & friendly Staff
FACILITIES
7 x Beach Front Bungalows,
TreeHouse Suite and Loft,
TreeHouse Restaurant & Bar
ATTRACTIONS
Diving & U/W Expeditions, one
day Highway Tour, snorkelling,
cycling, culture, fishing,
surfing, Rain-Forest walks.
CREDIT CARDS
Amex, MasterCard, Visa.

The TreeHouse provides a unique friendly Melanesian experience in harmony with the environment. Staying at the Treehouse provides the simple comforts, but the real South Pacific. Our activities feature a range of world class diving from corals to palegics, a range of rainforest walks, coastal tours, Malagan culture, fishing, cycling, snorkelling and more. The TreeHouse has international phone connections and we can book hire cars, travel and other activities. For the ultimate dive experience... our 6 day U/W Dive Expeditions depart regularly through out the year. We are 2 degrees from the equator with an 'Endless Summer'.

LOCATION
Lae, Papua New Guinea
EMAIL
laeinter@global.net.pg
PHONE/FAX
Ph (675) 472 2000
Fax (675) 472 2534
ADDRESS
4th Street Lae
Papua New Guinea
FACILITIES
Coffee/tea-making,
iron/board, satellite TV, air
conditioning, licensed
restaurants, pool, BBQ.
ATTRACTIONS
Gym, business centre,
Internet access, conference
facilities, tennis.

ACCOMMODATION
18 brand new 2 bedroom apartment in addition to the hotel rooms. All fully self contained hotel rooms have coffee/tea-making facilities, iron/board, satellite TV, air conditioning and telephone. 24-hour room service available.
FEATURES
Combining the luxury of resort-style accommodation with the needs of today's corporate traveller. Laundry and dry cleaning available.
ACTIVITIES
Tennis court, swimming pool, BBQ area, child-care facilities, gym, Internet/email access, secretarial services, 3 conference rooms, car rental service, airport transfers, 24-hour security.
FOR FURTHER INFORMATION
See our website for full booking details and rates.

Airlines PNG

Come fly our way with Airlines PNG
Together an adventure,
Explore the spirit of this land
With our friendly service
And welcome smile
Sit back and relax
As we travel each mile.
We're reaching out to far and near.
Come fly with the best,
Airlines PNG Come Fly Our Way.

Airlines PNG OFFICES

Operations:
Charters/Medivacs
Tel/Fax: (675) 325 9330
Email: ops@apng.com

Reservations/Sales:
Tel: (675) 321 3400 or 325 2011
Fax: (675) 321 4191
Email: pomtravel@apng.com

Administration:
Tel: (675) 325 2011
Fax: (675) 325 2219
Email: apng@apng.com

Cargo:
Tel: (675) 325 2011 ext 180/181
Fax: (675) 325 2219
Email: cargo@apng.com

www.apng.com

Paradise Adventure Tours

On the trail of the astonishing birds of paradise.

Visit Papua New Guinea in 2005 with Paradise Adventure Tours. The Only Ultimate Adventure Holiday Destination On The Planet With Untouched & Unspoiled Environment!

PAPUA NEW GUINEA WILD AND STILL BEAUTIFUL

PO Box 1356, Mt Hagen, Western Highlands Province. Papua New Guinea Tel; (675) 542 1696 Fax; (675) 542 1660 Mobile; (675) 685 1719 Email: travel@paradisetours.com.pg Website: www.paradisetours.com.pg

GRANVILLE MOTEL
BOROKO

LOCATION
Boroko, Papua New Guinea

EMAIL
granvill@online.net.pg

PHONE/FAX
Ph (675) 325 7155
Fax (675) 325 7672

ADDRESS
PO Box 1246, Boroko, N.C.D. Papua New Guinea

FACILITIES
Air conditioned, self-contained, cable TV, licensed restaurant.

CREDIT CARDS
All major cards accepted.

Half a kilometre from the airport, and fifteen minutes to Port Moresby, or Boroko or Waigani.

128 air-conditioned rooms and self-contained units with cable TV, refrigerator, tea/coffee making, ISD telephone and daily maid service.

Our licensed restaurant is open 7 days, offering local and European dishes. Relax at the bar or air-conditioned pokies room. Hire cars and chauffeur-driven limousine available. Conference Centre with 6 rooms – one of which can cater for up to 250 people. An 18-hole golf course is nearby. Half and full day tours or dive trips can be arranged. We have 24-hour office and security.

Nobody knows PNG like we do...

DIVE...TREK...EXPLORE...RELAX

Call us anytime for the most exciting holiday packages on this planet

Papua New Guinea offers an abundance of amazing holiday options, so when you want to arrange the perfect getaway, talk to the experts.
www.nghhols.com
Fax +612 9267 6118

Sydney   +612 9290 2055
Brisbane   +617 3221 5777
Cairns   +617 4039 2251
Australia   1300 850020
Email info@ngholidays.com

NIUGINI HOLIDAYS

BIRD OF PARADISE HOTEL - GOROKA

www.coralseahotels.com.pg

LOCATION
Overlooking the town centre, adjacent to the GPO

EMAIL
thebird
@coralseahotels.com.pg

PHONE/FAX
Ph (675) 731 3100
Fax (675) 732 1007

ADDRESS
PO Box 12 Goroka

Qantas Frequent Flyers get a special rate and earn points with every kina spent.

Qantas Frequent Flyer program

52 modern rooms with shower/bath, 10-channel satellite cable TV including CNN and AXN, fridge, IDD phone, tea and coffee-making facilities and room service. Conference facilities cater for up to 100.

Amenities include à la carte Lahani Restaurant, Deck Bistro, bar and Enzo's Pizzas. Heated swimming pool also has soda bar and children's play area. Rent-A-Car, TNT Cargo are on the premises. Business centre located off reception and there is free email access for all guests between hours of 5-10pm daily. Also a fitness centre and squash centre. Free airport transfers.

Car (Hertz) and accommodation package available which is excellent value.

ELA BEACH HOTEL - PORT MORESBY

www.coralseahotels.com.pg

LOCATION
Ela Beach Road, Port Moresby CBD

E-MAIL
elabeach
@coralseahotels.com.pg

PHONE/FAX
Ph (675) 321 2100
Fax (675) 321 2434

ADDRESS
P.O. Box 813, Port Moresby NCD

Overlooking picturesque Ela Beach yet within walking distance from downtown Port Moresby. Completely renovated, this classic hotel now offers Premier rooms and 1 & 2-bedroom serviced apartments. Popular with the corporate traveller who wants more than just another hotel room. Each room and apartment has modern individual split-system air-conditioning, cable TV, fridge, IDD phone with easy plug-in for Internet access, tea and coffee making facilities and room service.

Beachside Brasserie is the most popular place in town for either a business meal or to relax at a weekend brunch. The hotel offers 24-hour reception, free car parking, guest laundry, pool with an adjoining sauna, spa, massage and hairdressing salon, free airport transfers on request. Free e-mail access for all houseguests between 5-10pm each day. Two conference rooms cater for up to 150 comfortably plus a stylish Board Room.

COASTWATCHERS HOTEL - MADANG

www.coralseahotels.com.pg

LOCATION
Coastwatchers Avenue, Madang

EMAIL
coastwatchers
@coralseahotels.com.pg

PHONE/FAX
Ph (675) 852 2684
Fax (675) 852 2716

ADDRESS
PO Box 324
Beautiful Madang

Qantas Frequent Flyers get a special rate and earn points with every kina spent.

Qantas Frequent Flyer program

Surrounded by Madang Golf Club, Pacific Ocean and town centre, our Motel-style property has 32 rooms with individual a/c, ceiling fans, shower, cable TV, fridge, IDD phone, tea and coffee-making facilities and room service.

Verandah-style Coasties Restaurant and Bar has ocean views and Enzo's Pizzas. There is 24-hour reception, free car parking, guest laundry service, pool, free airport transfers. Rent-A-Car is on the premises.

There is free email access for all guests between 5-10pm. Conference facilities cater for up to 150.

Car (Hertz) and accommodation package available which is excellent value.

GATEWAY HOTEL - PORT MORESBY

www.coralseahotels.com.pg

LOCATION
Adjacent to Port Moresby Airport and a ten-minute drive to the city centre

EMAIL
gateway
@coralseahotels.com.pg

PHONE/FAX
Ph (675) 327 8100
Fax (675) 325 4585

ADDRESS
PO Box 1215, Boroko NCD, Port Moresby

Qantas Frequent Flyers get special rate and earn points for every kina spent.

Qantas Frequent Flyer program

Fine dining Ani Ani Restaurant plus Rattle'n'Hum Pizzeria and bar, plus Enzo's Pizzas.

Reception has 24-hour foreign exchange desk. There is free car parking and a laundry and dry cleaning service. Swimming pool.

Rent-A-Car, Trans Niugini Tours and a beauty salon located on the premises.

Business Centre has Internet with free email for guests between 5-10pm daily. Free airport transfers. Conference facilities cater for up to 250.

Car (Hertz) and accommodation package available which is excellent value.

HIGHLANDER HOTEL - MOUNT HAGEN

www.coralseahotels.com.pg

LOCATION
Wahgi Parade, Town Centre

EMAIL
highlander
@coralseahotels.com.pg

PHONE/FAX
Ph (675) 542 1355
Fax (675) 542 1216

ADDRESS
PO Box 34, Mt Hagen

Qantas Frequent Flyers get special rate and earn points with every kina spent.

Qantas Frequent Flyer program

Rooms have 10-channel satellite cable TV including CNN and HBO, fridge, IDD phone, tea and coffee-making facilities and room service. Conference facilities accommodate 150.

Amenities include sub-tropical flower gardens, Palmuri Restaurant and Enzo's Pizzas, Poolside and several bars. Reception has 24-hour foreign exchange desk.

Free car parking; laundry service; heated swimming pool, tennis courts; Rent-A-Car on the premises. Business Centre offers Internet access and guests have free email access between 5-10pm. Free airport transfers.

Car (Hertz) and accommodation package available which is excellent value.

HUON GULF MOTEL - LAE

www.coralseahotels.com.pg

LOCATION
Milfordhaven Road, next to Lae Botanic Gardens

EMAIL
huongulf
@coralseahotels.com.pg

PHONE/FAX
Ph (675) 472 4844
Fax (675) 472 5023

ADDRESS
PO Box 612, Lae

Single-storey motel-style property has 40 rooms with individual air conditioning, ceiling fans, shower, cable TV, fridge, IDD phone, tea and coffee making facilities and room service.

Conference facilities cater for 75.

There is a restaurant plus bars, 24-hour reception, free car parking, laundry and dry-cleaning.

Swimming pool is located in a friendly Melanesian setting.

Car (Hertz) and accommodation package available which is excellent value.

Conference room for up to 24 at a u-shaped table, or 40 theatre style.

MELANESIAN HOTEL - LAE

www.coralseahotels.com.pg

LOCATION
Second Street, across the street from Lae GPO and the city's business centre

EMAIL
melanesian
@coralseahotels.com.pg

PHONE/FAX
Ph (675) 472 3744
Fax (675) 472 3706

ADDRESS
PO Box 756 Lae

Qantas Frequent Flyers receive special rates and earn points with every kina spent.

Qantas Frequent Flyer program

65 rooms with air conditioning, shower/bath, satellite cable TV, IDD phone, tea and coffee-making facilities and room service. Conference facilities cater for up to 250.

Hotel has Salamaua's à la carte restaurant and Coffee Shop plus bar and Enzo's Pizzas. Reception has 24-hour foreign exchange desk.

Free car parking; laundry and dry cleaning service. Swimming pool in a lush tropical setting. Beautician & hairdresser on the premises.

Business centre offers free email for guests between 5pm and 10pm daily.

Car (Hertz) and accommodation package available which is excellent value.

LAMINGTON HOTEL - POPONDETTA

www.coralseahotels.com.pg

LOCATION
Popondetta Town Centre

EMAIL
lamington
@coralseahotels.com.pg

PHONE/FAX
Ph (675) 329 7222
Fax (675) 329 7065

ADDRESS
PO Box 27, Popondetta

16 rooms with individual air conditioning, ceiling fans, shower, cable TV, fridge, IDD phone, tea and coffee-making facilities and room service in a single-storey motel-style property.

Paia's Restaurant and bar on the premises.

24-hour reception, free car parking, guest laundry service, Rent-A-Car on the premises.

Airport transfers available on request.

Car (Hertz) and accommodation package available which is excellent value.

Conference room for up to 24 at a u-shaped table, or 40 theatre style.

NICHE ADVENTURES

VISITING Papua New Guinea is like paying a visit to paradise. The rugged terrain and spectacular scenery provide a backdrop for unlimited adventures and experiences, including cultural heritage, bird watching, canoeing, fishing trips and diving.

Canoeing: Travelling by motorised dugout canoe up the Sepik River is a great experience and the best way to appreciate the scenery of the river system and the culture of the people. There are guesthouses all along the Sepik River to stay in and meet the local people and admire their carvings and story boards.

Cycling: Introduced by Australia's Melbourne Grammar School, Cycling the Buluminski Highway in New Ireland Province is an annual event. Cycling on the highways is an option all year.

Kayaking: Recently introduced as a water sport in Papua New Guinea, kayaking is available in several regions including Lorengau in Manus province and from resort bases in Madang, Port Moresby and Kavieng.

Bird watching: Of the 43 species of birds of paradise, 38 are found in Papua New Guinea. The vast areas of tropical rainforest provide perfect habitats for a wide variety of bird life. Some of the favourite places are Ambua Lodge, Tari, Kiunga and the Moitaka and Baiyer River sanctuaries.

Worldwide Contacts

Let Air Niugini show you the world...

International Offices

Australia Wide
Local call: 1300 361 380

Sydney
Somare House
100 Clarence Street
PO Box 5293
Sydney NSW 2001
Australia
Tel: (61 2) 9290 1544
Fax: (61 2) 9290 2026
Email:
sales.sydney@airniugini.com.pg

Brisbane
Level 4
99 Creek Street
GPO Box 2216
Brisbane QLD 4001
Tel: (61 7) 3221 1544
Fax: (61 7) 3220 0040
Email: sales.brisbane@airniugini.com.pg

Cairns
Shop 2 Tropical Arcade
4-6 Shields Street
Cairns QLD 4870
Australia
Tel: (61 7) 4031 1611
Fax: (61 7) 4031 3402
Email: sales.cairns@airniugini.com.pg

Manila
3rd Floor
Fortune Office Building
160 Legaspi Street
Legaspi Village
Makati City
Philippines
Tel: (63 2) 891 3339 /40 /41
Fax: (63 2) 891 3393

Tokyo
6th Floor Chiyoda Kaikan
1-6-17 Kudan Minami
Chiyoda-Ku
Tokyo. 102-0074 Japan
Tel: (81 3) 5216 3555
Fax: (81 3) 5216 3556
Email:info@air-niugini.co.jp
Website:www.air-niugini.co.jp

Port Vila
Vanuatu Travel Services Ltd
Tel: (678) 22836
Fax: (678) 233583

Kuala Lumpur
Abadi Aviation Services
Tel: (60 3) 242 4311
Fax: (60 3) 241 2322

Honiara
Guadalcanal Travel Service
Tel: (677) 20336
Fax: (677) 23887
Email: kevin@gts.com.sb

Auckland/Fiji/Cook Islands
Walshes World (NZ) Ltd
Tel: (64 9) 379 3708
Fax: (64 9) 302 2420

Jakarta
P.T. Ayuberga
Tel: (62 21) 8356 214-217
Fax: (62 21) 835 3937

Hong Kong
Niugini Travel Service
Tel: (852) 2524 2151
Fax: (852) 2526 7291

Taipei
Cha May Travel Service
Taipei, Taiwan
Tel: (886 2) 500 7811
Fax: (886 2) 500 7970

Singapore
101 Thomson Road
#11-03 United Square
Singapore. 307591
Tel: (65) 62504868
Fax:(65) 62533425
Email: airng.sg@pacific.net.sg

Air Niugini

Stockholm
Discovery Leisure Group AB (DLG)
Kungsholms Krykoplan 6
S112 24 Stockholm
Sweden
Tel: (46) 8 6517410
Fax: (46) 8 6538030
Email: sales.stockholm@airniugini.com.pg

Frankfurt
Mr Rudiger Knospe
Tel: (49) 69 634095
Fax: (49) 69 6313332
Email: sales.frankfurt@airniugini.com.pg

Los Angeles
Mr Kerry Byrd
Tel: (1 949) 752 5440
Fax: (1 949) 4716 3741
Email: sales.usa@airniugini.com.pg

Seoul
Sharp Inc
Tel: (82 2) 734 7100
Fax: (82 2) 734 7108

United Kingdom
Flight Directors
Flighthouse
Fernhill Road, Horley, Surrey
RH6 9SY, UK
Tel: (44) 0870 24 00 767
Fax: (44) 0870 24 02 208
Email: airniugini@flightdirectors.com

UNIQUE CULTURE

PAPUA New Guinea is extremely rich in local culture throughout the regions. The Highlands is the most densely populated area in the country with more than 60 separate languages and peoples, including the colourful Huli wigmen and Asaro mudmen who can be seen in costume in cultural shows. Local singsings are exhibitions of dances accompanied by the beat of 'kundu' drums.

Singsings are common all over the country the Goroka and Mount Hagen cultural shows are so popular that bookings to see them need to be made a year in advance. Port Moresby is the gateway to all experiences in Papua New Guinea and is known for the exciting Hiri Moale festival depicting the epic voyages undertaken by the Motuans of the Central Province who traded clay pots for sago in the early trade days.

This unique barter system ensured the survival of the Motuans and, in return, provided the Gulf people with quality clay pots for domestic use as clay quality was poor in the Gulf. The show is a diverse representation of groups with around 500 entertainers as well as contemporary performers, music, dance and theatre.

The National Mask Festival is held in July in Rabaul each year. Another fascinating cultural event is the Yam festival in the Trobriand Islands of the Milne Bay province. The festival highlights the workmanship of the Trobriand Islanders who use traditional methods of planting and harvesting yams.

You can visit the Trobriand Islands aboard the MV Melanesian Discoverer, a tourist vessel operated from Madang by the Melanesian Tourist Service. Cruising aboard this comfortable and spacious vessel, passengers are able to make dinghy trips out to local villages on the coast. Here you meet friendly locals and the Trobriand's craftsmen will tempt you with some of Papua New Guinea's finely carved storyboards and souvenirs.

One can also cruise the Sepik River on the Melanesian Discoverer. The Sepik is one of Papua New Guinea's natural treasures in terms of art and craftsmanship. Like the Trobriands, the Sepiks convert imaginative pictures and dreams into reality through carving and other crafts. Samples of Sepik art and culture are often exhibited overseas. An option for exploring the evergreen flood plains of the mighty Sepik in comfort and style is aboard the MV Sepik Spirit which explores the extensive river networks along the Sepik, Blackwater and Karawari rivers. Guests can travel by dinghy through small river canals to walk into local villages to experience the lifestyles of the local Sepik communities.

Local customs of Papua New Guinea are Melanesian-based but each region is distinctly different. The Malagan carvers of New Ireland, for example, have a complicated process of initiations and rituals while if your idea of adventure is witnessing locals dressed in traditional ornaments dancing over blazing flames, then Rabaul in the East New Britain Province is the place to be. The Baining Fire dancers perform over flames after nightfall in a ritual show of thanksgiving to the gods and a release of spirits into the night.

The local villages along the Buluminski Highway in New Ireland province hold the secret to calling white sharks to the surface and this breathtaking experience is offered to visitors and tourists who wish to stay in local guesthouses. The island provinces, the first places in Papua New Guinea to interact with early missionaries and traders, are also famous for their church choirs. Apart from all the customs and traditions of this untouched paradise, the remains of two world wars and Papua New Guinea's many volcanic vents offer extra dimensions of interest.

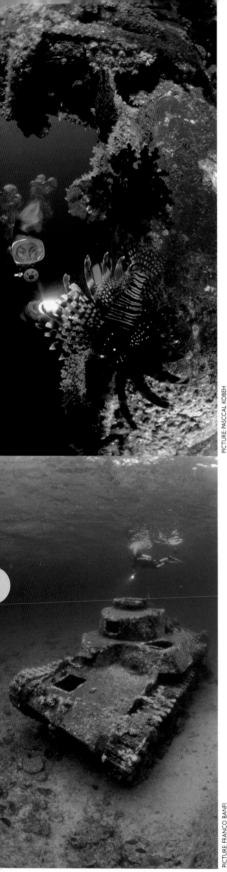

PICTURE PASCAL KOBEH

PICTURE FRANCO BANFI

DIVING

PAPUA New Guinea is home to some of the world's most spectacular diving – as many as the Carribbean. Located in the centre of the Asia-Pacific region, it is said to have twice as many marine species as the waters of the Red Sea and up to 10 times as many as the Carribbean. Significantly PNG is located in the 'bulls-eye' of marine diversity with the highest diversity of tropical fish and coral in the world.

PNG has become known as the 'underwater photographers' paradise' with many international award-winning photos being taken in PNG waters. PNG is surrounded by the Bismarck, Coral and Solomon Seas, whose constant movements feed and enrich the marine environment. From tiny colourful nudibranchs to the magnificent whale shark – divers encounter a stunning array of species.

The immense diversity of dive sites includes barrier reefs, coral walls (drop-offs), fringing reefs, sea grass beds and coral atolls. Wreck dive sites provide a collection of ships and aircraft from WWII. The water temperature varies from 26°C along the edge of the Coral Sea, to 30°C in the Bismarck Sea.

One can dive in Papua New Guinea all year round. Diving is offered by resort dive centres and live-aboard dive boats. Land-based operations offer resort courses and have fully-equipped dive shops with gear for hire. The majority operate on small to medium sized properties with an emphasis on personal attention in a relaxing environment. While live-aboard dive boats range in size between 45' and 120' with differing levels of amenities, the excellent quality of diving service is synonymous with each operation. Several operators offer nitrox and rebreathers and most boats have facilities for cameras and E6 processing.

PNG has its own hyperbaric recompression facility located in Port Moresby which is supported by all members of the PNG Divers Association (PNGDA). The chamber is situated in a private hospital and is maintained by Hyperbaric Health Australia.

In recognition of the importance of preserving the marine eco-system, members of the PNGDA actively promote the use of moorings on regularly-dived sites. The need to practice sensible diving and respect the underwater environment is emphasized, with a clear message: look but don't touch.

So come and Experience Papua New Guinea!

Papua New Guinea Divers Association Inc. (PNGDA)

P.O. Box 1646 Port Moresby NCD Papua New Guinea.

Tel: +675 321 3913 Fax: +675 321 5650

Email: pngdive@online.net.pg Web: www.pngdive.com

FISHING

PAPUA New Guinea's fishing grounds are unique for their natural and pristine state. There are many areas which have been fished by sports and game fishing anglers and those which are fished are under no pressure from fishing enthusiasts. The best lure is often not knowing what might bite in the spot where you are fishing.

In dense jungle rivers and estuaries, the mighty Papuan Black Bass will challenge any angler intruding into his domain. This monster is found no where else in the world and, as those lucky few who have a big one will tell you, is just about the toughest fish in any river, anywhere! They love crunching lures, so leave anything less than XOS behind.

Barramundi and Jacks abound in many rivers and are also keen lure takers. In the rivers and creeks you may have the opportunity to meet the locals and swap a few stories. If you are lucky you might see a traditional village or even a singsing.

For those who prefer the blue water, the underwater predators of Papua New Guinea's Bismarck, Coral and Archipelago Seas offer all of the known tropical species in abundance. We have Blue, Black and Striped Marlin, Sailfish, Yellowfin Tuna, Wahoo, Mahi mahi, Mackerels, Sharks and the biggest and meanest GT's and Doggies you have ever seen.

The beautiful, warm blue waters offer everything from exciting reef fishing to magnificent days chasing birds, bait and tidelines at sea. Evenings can be spent anchored at remote coral quays and beaches under tropical sunsets, or in the many fishing clubhouses throughout Papua New Guinea telling tall tales with other anglers.

Get serious and start planning your fishing venture into some of Papua New Guinea's unknown ground for that big bite.

So for your next fishing experience, come visit our way www.pngtourism.org.pg

SURFING

AS a surf destination, Papua New Guinea is relatively new to surf enthusiasts.

Pioneers have found one thing is certain – that is the breaks here are just as challenging as any others they face elsewhere.

Papua New Guinea has unlimited surfing potential year round. On the southern side, ten minutes out of Port Moresby, is Sero Surf Club (Taurama Point) where the main barrier reef stretches along the southern seaboard all the way to the Milne Bay Province.

From June to September during the south-east season the waves range from 3 to 6 feet, with the best waves in the early morning. 100km to the east of Port Moresby is Hula Beach. Other surfing spots are being explored around the Milne Bay Province area. Bougainville Island and the Gazelle Peninsula in the East New Britain Province have quality waves ranging from 3 to 6 feet along the coral atolls, including point and beach breaks.

The northern side of Papua New Guinea has premier surfing locations with waves on the mainland and offshore islands generated by the monsoon swells from mid October through to late April. Consistent quality waves ranging from 3 to 8 feet, and occasionally to 6 feet waves can be found at Madang and Wewak. The most consistent waves are in Vanimo, which vary from beach breaks to point and island reef breaks. Accommodation and transport is readily available from Vanimo Beach Hotel, Sandaun Motel and Vanimo Club located on the doorstep to Vanimo's premier surf location.

Around Kavieng in New Ireland Province are numerous reef setups which provide good and varying surf breaks. Just off Kavieng town is Nusa Island Retreat, an environmentally low-impact facility that provides accommodation, meals and boat transport to the surrounding islands and their breaks.

The waves in this region and around Nusa Island Retreat are well established and known in international surfing circles – Nusa Island Retreat limits the number of surfers staying at any one time and is often fully booked during the surf season.

Surfing Association of Papua New Guinea Inc.
P.O. Box 240 University, National Capital District Papua New Guinea.
Tel: +675 326 0884 Fax: +675 326 1648
Email: abelcorp@online.net.pg Web: www.surfingpapuanew.org.pg

TREKKING

PAPUA New Guinea has long been a popular destination for trekking, mountain climbing and bushwalking. With largely unspoilt mountains, rivers and forests, cultural interests and remnants of World War 2 including the infamous Kokoda Track, Papua New Guinea is ideal for both experienced trekking and weekend bushwalking.

The Highlands region is famous for its tall mountains with scores of readily accessible peaks. Mt Wilhelm, at 4509 metres, is the most popular target for mountain climbers with good road access to Kegsugl village from Kundiawa and National Parks huts for climbers to stay in. Recently a focus of PNG Tourism Promotion Authority sponsored guide training activities, the Mt. Wilhelm region is becoming the focus for individual and guided trekkers. While it is accessible, Mt Wilhelm is not easy and guides are necessary to assist climbers.

The islands have good potential for long distance coastal treks, with villages providing the ideal campsites. The interior of the islands and coastal regions offer largely undisturbed rainforests and cross-island treks are possible with small towns as the starting and finishing points.

The Old Bulldog Trek and the famous Camel Rally follow the mountain roads, while Kokoda is the starting point for the world-famous Kokoda Track trek. In World War 11 the Kokoda Track was the scene of bitter fighting and the track is now a national park. The record for completing the track is less than 24 hours, however the usual trek time is about 10 days with Kokoda being the usual start point. Many trekkers carry their own packs, however carriers/guides can be hired in villages along the route. There are a number of points along the track where light aircraft airstrips and regular or chartered flights are available so trekking the Kokoda Track can be undertaken in sections. Several tour companies offer organised tours along the track and for safety reasons this is advisable.

ECO TOURISM

A GREAT percentage of Papua New Guinea's land mass is covered with a dense blanket of rainforest including an exotic tangle of vines, creepers, flowers, plants and trees. Wild orchids blaze against a verdant green background of rainforest canopy and Papua New Guinea has a greater number of orchid species than any other country in the world. The National Capital Botanical Gardens in Port Moresby is well-known for its extensive collection of Papua New Guinean orchid species and large hybrid orchid houses.

The bird life is prolific and most famous bird is the Bird of Paradise. These brilliantly-coloured birds perform fantastic ritualistic and mating dances and, of the 43 known species in the world, 38 are found in Papua New Guinea.

Most animals here are marsupials and relatives of those found in Australia. Although not indigenous to PNG, pigs are a valuable resource and important status symbol among the tribes of the Highlands. Rusa deer are a more recent arrival, first brought into Irian Jaya by Dutch colonists.

There are about 200 species of reptile including 13 different turtles and 100 different types of snake. Papua New Guinea also has a multitude of insects. In 1978, the Insect Farming and Trading Agency at Bulolo in Morobe Province was established by the PNG Division of Wildlife to initiate and control the local insect farming industry and further market it overseas. It ensures strict controls of quality and accompanying scientific data. It is the only organisation permitted by the Papua New Guinean Government to farm and trade insects and research workers at the IFTA have discovered many new species. Special areas of research have included detailed studies of all native birdwing butterflies and a study of the conservation strategies needed to save Queen Alexandra's birdwing, orthinoptera alexandrae, the largest known butterfly in the world which is found only in Papua New Guinea's Oro Province.

THERE IS SOMETHING NEW AND EXCITING FOR EVERY VISITOR TO PAPUA NEW GUINEA

PAPUA NEW GUINEA TOURISM PROMOTION AUTHORITY

The Papua New Guinea Tourism Promotion Authority invites all enquiries as we welcome you to the most beautiful and culturally diverse destination in the entire Pacific Region.

- Take a cruise on the luxurious Sepik Spirit along the mighty Sepik River.
- Voyage on the Melanesian Discoverer to some of PNG's most fascinating destinations.
- Stay at Karawari Lodge by the Sepik and go hunting for artifacts.
- Fish for giant Barramundi in remote Bensbach National Park. Hunt wild deer with or without your camera in Western Province.
- Visit the National Museum and Art Gallery, Port Moresby.
- Experience the unique culture of the Trobriand Islanders – Milne Bay Province.
- The diving has never been better, nor the surroundings more tranquil, than at Walindi Resort, Kimbe, West New Britain Province.
- Reel in a monster, gamefishing from Ajim Island Resort, West New Britain Province.
- Marvel at the Asaro Mudmen near Goroka in the Eastern Highlands.
- Look out for a whole new world from Lakwanda Lodge in the Tari Basin, Southern Highlands.
- See the famous Huli Wigmen and magnificent orchids while you stay in cosy Ambua Lodge, Southern Highlands Province.

- For your next fishing adventures visit Lindenhafen and Baia Fishing establishments in West New Britain.
- Be astounded by smoked, mummified bodies perched on cliff burial ledges. Enjoy considerably more comfort at nearby Pine Lodge, Bulolo, Morobe Province.
- Escape the real world on Mansava guest-house off Kavieng. If you love diving you may wish never to leave.
- Let the magnificent Coastwatchers Memorial Lighthouse welcome you to beautiful Madang, full of history and a hive of resorts and activities for the visitor.

For more information on these destinations and many more, contact your travel agent

PAPUA NEW GUINEA
E X P E R I E N C E

PAPUA NEW GUINEA TOURISM
PROMOTION AUTHORITY
Level 5, Pacific MMI Building,
Champion Parade, PORT MORESBY,
Papua New Guinea
Tel: (675) 320 0211 Fax: (675) 320 0223
Email: info@pngtourism.org.pg
Web: www.pngtourism.org.pg

SAMOA

THE 'Treasured Islands' of Samoa are the crowning jewels of the South Pacific. Samoa as a tourist destination is now known as 'The Treasured Islands of the South Pacific'. Surrounded by the warm crystal-clear blue waters of the Pacific Ocean, here travellers will find islands blessed with natural beauty, a tropical paradise where the environment is pristine, the people friendly and hospitable and a living culture treasured by all.

Discover what the great writers of the 18th Century, including Rupert Brooke and Robert Louis Stevenson found during their visits to Samoa. Brooke described Samoans as "The loveliest people in the world, moving and dancing like gods and goddesses, very quietly and mysteriously, and utterly content" and also described Samoa as "sheer beauty, so pure that it is difficult to breath it in". Robert Louis Stevenson, on the other hand, found a home in the idyllic islands of Samoa, after searching the world for paradise. Samoa's natural wonders of waterfalls, rainforest, mountains, extinct volcanoes, lava fields and miles of white sand beaches beckon the adventurer seeking peace and quiet away from the hustle and bustle of modern society.

The Samoan people are eager to play hosts to visitors from afar and share their hospitality. Their living culture, the Fa'a Samoa (the Samoan way), virtually unchanged for more than 3000 years is centred around the extended family unit full of love and respect for all.

Experience a holiday destination like no other, uniquely tropical, exciting and distinctively Samoan.

Explore our website www.visitsamoa.ws and discover all the elements you need for putting your holiday together and come and visit Samoa, The Treasured Islands of the South Pacific.

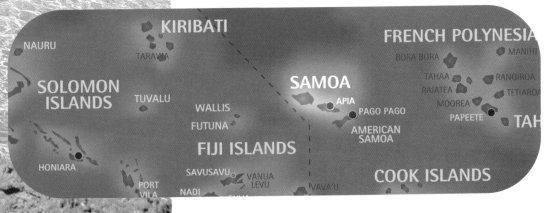

SAMOA
AT A GLANCE

SAMOA TOURISM AUTHORITY
PO Box 2272, Apia, Samoa
Tel: (685) 63 500/63 540
Fax: (685) 20 886
Email: info@visitsamoa.ws
Website: www.visitsamoa.ws

GEOGRAPHICAL LOCATION

Samoa is located east of the International Dateline between longitudes 171o and 172o west and latitudes 13o and 14o south of the Equator.

AIRLINES

International: Samoa's national airline, Polynesian Airlines, operates services to Samoa from New Zealand, Australia, Hawaii, Fiji, Tonga and American Samoa. Other international airlines flying to Samoa include Air New Zealand, Air Pacific and Samoa Air. Polynesian Airlines operates regular domestic services from Fagalii Airport near Apia, to Maota and Asau on the island of Savai'i.
Faleolo International Airport is located 35 kilometres west of Apia, the capital of Samoa.

ARRIVAL/DEPARTURE INFORMATION

A written declaration is required for every visitor entering Samoa.
Firearms, ammunition, explosives, drugs and indecent publications of any kind are prohibited.
Visitors do not require an entry visa for stays up to 30 days although an onward or return ticket and valid passport (six months or more) are required. An entry visa is only required for visits longer than 30 days. To apply, contact the nearest Samoa High Commission or Embassy. One litre of spirits and 200 cigarettes per person may be brought in duty free
Samoa is free of all tropical diseases. A vaccination for yellow fever is required if arriving within six days of

leaving or transiting infected areas.
Departure Tax is S$40. Children under 12 years of age, free.

CURRENCY

The Samoa decimal. A number of hotels, restaurants, tour operators and general merchants have EFTPOS (Electronic Funds Transfer Point Of Sale) terminals for easy payment. These terminals accept all major credit cards.

CLIMATE

Samoa's climate is pleasantly warm with an average maximum temperature of 29 degrees Celsius. From May until November, hot conditions are tempered by south-east trade winds. The rainy season extends from November to March.

ELECTRICITY

240 volts / AC 50 cycles but can be converted to 110 volts in most hotels.

HANDICRAFTS

Handicrafts such as kava bowls, floor mats, tapa cloth, and necklaces are an important part of Samoan culture and make wonderful souvenirs. In Apia, handicrafts can be found in the markets and at a number of stores around town. Major hotels also have souvenir shops.

LANGUAGE

Samoan is the national language, but English is the official language of business.

POPULATION

The population of Samoa is approximately 164,000. Samoa has the largest proportion of full-blooded Polynesian people in the world.

LOCAL CONSIDERATIONS

Light summer clothing is appropriate all year round, with a light sweater for the cooler evenings. Smart casual eveningwear is appropriate for hotels and restaurants. Visitors should not wear bathing suits in Apia or in the villages. No nude or topless (for women) swimming or sunbathing. Women are recommended to wear a lavalava (sarong) or dress, rather than shorts or trousers, if they attend church.
Medical Services – Tupua Tamasese Meaole Hospital,

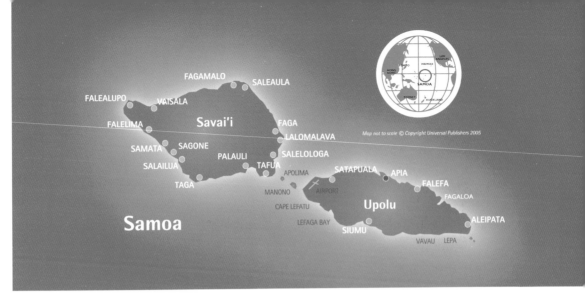

Samoa's main hospital, is located in Apia. Another new hospital is the privately owned Medcen hospital located near the Robert Louis Stevenson Museum at Vailima.

The main religious denominations in Samoa are Congregational, Anglican, Catholic, Methodist, Seventh-day Adventist, Baha'i, Latter Day Saints and Jehovah Witness. Sunday in Samoa is dedicated to God, with families usually attending church in the mornings followed by a family to'onai (lunch) and resting for the remainder of the day. Visitors are welcome to attend religious services and enjoy the choir singing and sermons.

There is a 12.5 per cent tax on accommodation, food and drinks.

Tipping is not mandatory but a gift for excellent service would be well appreciated

TELECOMMUNICATIONS

Samoa has an up-to-date telecommunications system. Telephone, telex and fax facilities can be accessed at Samoa Communications on Beach Road, Apia. Cybercafes can be found throughout the main tourist areas.

TIME ZONE

Samoa's time zone is three hours behind U.S. Pacific Time and 12 hours behind Greenwich Mean Time.

TRANSPORT

Visitors require their driver's licence to be validated for use in Samoa. This can be obtained at the Traffic Section of the Police Department on Ifiifi Street, Apia, near the Harbour. The cost is S$10. Drive on the right-hand side of the road. Speed limits are 25 miles per hour in town and 35 miles per hour between villages. There is an extensive bus service on both Upolu and Savaii, providing inexpensive transportation for local people and an experience to remember for visitors. A passenger and vehicle ferry service operates between Upolu and Savai'i.

SAMOA

THE basis of Samoan life is aiga, the family, which covers a broad range of extended family in the Polynesian style. There are more than 362 villages in Samoa and 18,000 matais, the male or female elected or inherited heads of the families. The village council is made up of matais headed by a high chief and each village has a ceremonial orator chief, tulafale.

The island culture, known as Fa'a Samoa, is steeped in traditions and protocols which vary from village to village. Visitors are not expected to know these intricacies but it is appreciated when attempts are made to try to understand. Sa (curfew evening prayers) takes place between 6pm and 7pm for 10 – 20 minutes, often marked by a bell or the blowing of a conch shell and visitors should avoid walking or driving through villages during Sa. Sunday is a special day of rest and prayer and some beaches and scenic spots are closed.

If you are invited into a Samoan house (fale), you should leave your shoes outside and sit cross-legged on the floor tucking your legs under yourself or covering them with a mat so as not to point your feet at others. Never stand inside a fale when elders are seated.

Wear bathing suits for swimming and sunbathing but cover up in the streets of Apia and the villages. Skimpy clothing isn't recommended in Samoa and for church a light-coloured dress or lavalava is appropriate.

Independent Samoa's population of about 175,000 lives principally on the island of Upolu, with 35,000 residing in Apia. Savai'i, the largest of all the Samoan islands, is home to 45,000 people. The other inhabited islands are Manono and Apolima, which lie in the 18km strait between the two bigger islands.

Samoa was the first Pacific Island nation to gain independence in 1962. The Head of State, currently His Highness Malietoa Tanumafili II, holds office for life and is chosen from one of the four Samoan royal families.

Samoa lies near the equator so has a pleasantly tropical climate with a year round average temperature of 29°C.

The warmest months are December to April, the southeast trades making May to November cooler and drier.

Samoa is a country of natural, unspoiled beauty with so much to offer its visitors.

You can 'do your own thing' or there are several tour companies who will help you experience Samoan customs and show you the sights. Picture postcard, white sandy beaches, rugged mountains, virgin rainforest and plantations, sparkling waterfall, lava fields and blowholes; there's something for everyone and a wide range of activities to enjoy.

Bustling with beaches
Wild with waterfalls

Just add mountains, rainforests, caves, blowholes, lava fields, cascading rivers and the most welcoming and friendly people in Polynesia and you have the secret recipe for a most exciting and adventurous South Pacific vacation. "See you in Samoa!"

Samoa
The Treasured Islands of the South Pacific

SAMOA TOURISM AUTHORITY
Head Office
P.O. Box 2272, Apia, SAMOA
Phone: (685) 63500/63540
Facsimile: (685) 20886
Email: info@visitsamoa.ws
Website: www.visitsamoa.ws

NEW ZEALAND
Samoa Tourism Authority
Level 1, Samoa House, 283 Karangahape Road
P.O. Box 68423, Newton, Auckland
Tel: (09) 379 6138,
Fax: (09) 379 8154
Email: samoa@samoa.co.nz

AUSTRALIA
Samoa Tourism Authority
Level 9, 99 York Street, Sydney
NSW Australia 2000
Tel: (02) 9279 4808, Fax (02) 92991119
Mob: 0411753544
Email: samoa@ozemail.com.au

UPOLU ISLAND

THE main island in the Samoa Group is Upolu, home to the nation's capital of Apia, which is the hub for all activities from dining out, bars and clubs to movie theatres and natural wonders galore. Apia is a hive of activity during the day with the markets and locals going about their daily business to the night where Beach Road comes alive to the aromas wafting through the air and the sounds of local music from the bars and clubs.

APIA

The Samoa Tourism Authority has information about historic monuments, which are scattered around in Apia, such as the Robert Louis Stevenson Museum, the 1962 Independence Memorial, the German, British and American Memorials, and the tombs of several influential Samoan figures.

THINGS TO DO AROUND UPOLU

For the more adventurous there is a huge range of activities to do on Upolu, from taking a work-out at the local gym to playing a round of golf, diving the blue Pacific Ocean, surfing the huge reef breaks or fishing in the luxury of a game fishing boat where you are guaranteed to catch a fish or two.

For nature lovers, there are numerous walks and tracks to choose from in the national parks located on the island. Take a local guide and venture into the village plantations and visit some stunning and dramatic waterfalls.

There is a number of adventure and guided tour operators located in Apia that offer a range of activities to suit your fitness level.

Or you may simply want to lie on a beach and enjoy the peace and quiet. The sand is pure white and the ocean temperature a warm 29° Celsius.

GETTING AROUND UPOLU

Nothing beats the freedom of exploring Upolu at your own pace and there is a huge range of rental car companies to choose from in finding the right vehicle for your needs. One important rule to remember when driving around Samoa is that we drive on the right-side of the road.

For inexpensive transport catch a local bus. Nothing can compare to this experience with the music playing and locals singing along during the journey. It's a great way to meet people and make new friends.

SAVAI'I ISLAND

Savai'i is the largest island in the Samoa Group and of total contrast to the main island of Upolu. Here life moves at a slower pace and the dramatic landscapes from vast lava fields to lush rainforest offer visitors a tranquil setting from the fast pace of Apia.

The main town on Savai'i is Salelologa, not as big as Apia, but still the commercial hub for the island with its post office, banks, shops and market place. It is here at the wharf where travellers catch the inter-island ferry between the two main islands.

THINGS TO DO ON SAVAI'I

Just like Upolu, Savai'i offers all the natural wonders, from dramatic volcanic peaks and waterfalls to forest canopy walkways and breathtaking sunsets. For the adventurous who enjoy the water there is diving in some spectacular spots and surfing at some isolated and huge reef breaks. Savai'i is also home to the largest stone pyramid in Polynesia and awe inspiring blow holes. The beaches on Sava'i are just as beautiful as those on Upolu.

There are a number of adventure and tour operators based on Savai'i who offer a wide range of guided tours around the big island.

GETTING AROUND SAVAI'I

A lot of visitors to Savaii find the biggest island of the Samoa group, unspoilt and beautiful. For a good sightseeing tour of the island, it is advisable to take a rental car tour of Savaii, and visitors will get to see many attractions of the island at their own pace. Some hotels on Savaii and tour operators also conduct organised tours around the island, visiting the lava field at Saleaula village, turtle farm at Satoalepai, canopy walkway at Falealupo, Taga Blow Holes and many other attractions Savaii has to offer. There are also local buses that go to most villages on the island, which is even more fun to travel on. It is a great way to meet people and make new friends.

AGGIE GREY'S HOTEL & BUNGALOWS

www.aggiegreys.com

LOCATION
Apia, Samoa

EMAIL
aggiegreys@
aggiegreys.ws

PHONE/FAX
Ph (685) 22 880
Fax (685) 23 626

ADDRESS
PO Box 67
Apia, Samoa

FACILITIES
Air conditioned, private balcony, tea/coffee facilities, IDD phones, TV, laundry, restaurants, bar, pool, coffee shop, laundry service, business centre, hair salon

ATTRACTIONS
Waterfront location, Island floor show, gym & health club, diving courses, Palolo deep marine reserve

CREDIT CARDS
All major cards

ACCOMMODATION
156 rooms, 2 suites and 26 island style bungalows (Fales). All rooms are air conditioned with private balcony or patio. Tea and coffee-making facilities. Direct dial telephones, television, complimentary in-house movies, mini-bar, 24-hour room service, 24-hour concierge, valet and cable TV.

FEATURES
Beach Road overlooking Apia Harbour. 10 minutes from town and 35 kms from the International Airport. Fine Dining restaurant, Island restaurant, Marlon Brando coffee lounge, 3 cocktail bars, child minding/baby sitting service, same-day laundry and dry cleaning, full tour desk and inbound service, outdoor pool, business centre, conference facilities. The 'boardroom' can accommodate 70.

ACTIVITIES
Gym and health club, diving courses on request, kids playground and club, complimentary off site golf for hotel guests, hair salon, hotel gift shop, Palolo Deep Marine Reserve (5 minutes walk). Mountain Bikes for hire. Set in lush tropical gardens, Island floor show and Island feast, traditional Samoan barbecue night. Seafood extravaganza night. 300 staff with true Samoan friendliness and warmth. Truly the legend of the south seas. Extravagant Wedding packages available, Eco-Tour packages available. The hotel that became a legend in the South Pacific offers you the unique chance to be part of the legend of the South Seas.

FOR FURTHER INFORMATION
See our website for full booking details and current rates.

AGGIE GREY'S LAGOON BEACH RESORT & SPA

www.aggiegreys.com

LOCATION
Faleolo, on the stunning north/west coast of Upolu - on the edge of a white sand beach and blue lagoon.

EMAIL
resort@
aggiegreysresort.com

PHONE/FAX
Ph (685) 45 611
Fax (685) 45 626

ADDRESS
PO Box 67, Apia, Samoa

FACILITIES
Air-conditioned, private balcony/patio, IDD phones, colour TV with free in house movies, laundry, restaurants, bars, freshwater pool, café, conference centre, historic wedding chapel, water activities centre, daily maid service, 18 hole championship golf course and country club.

ATTRACTIONS
Pearly white sand beach, stunning lagoon with easy access to nearby islands of Savaii, Apolima and Manono. Spread over 224 acres of lush tropical gardens and an 18 hole championship golf course. Marine activities are plentiful and local tours available from the resort.

CREDIT CARDS
All major cards

ACCOMMODATION
140 deluxe ocean view rooms and suites all with stunning beach and lagoon views. Each deluxe room features central air conditioning, 3 IDD telephones, Internet and modem access as well as iron/ironing board, hairdryers, in room safes, satellite television with 8 complimentary in house movie channels playing 24 hours 7 days a week, plus 24-hour valet and room service. There are 4 family rooms and 4 rooms adapted for physically disabled guests.

FEATURES
Stunning location overlooking pearly white sands and a sparkling blue lagoon, also bordered by an 18 hole championship golf course. Signature 'South Pacific' Restaurant with fine dining and spectacular theme nights including Fia Fia buffet and dance show. Poolside al fresco café, Bloody Mary's Bar and Solent Poolside Bar. Horizon pool, activities hut, Manaia Polynesian Spa, Dolphins Kids Club - open daily available for children 3-16yrs, babysitting services, historic wedding chapel, tour desk, car hire, conference facilities.

ACTIVITIES
18 hole championship golf course, Penina Country Club, freshwater infinity swimming pool (lagoonside), 2 x floodlit tennis courts, Fautasi Water Sports Centre, snorkelling, catamaran sailing, paddleboats, windsurfing, water skiing, jet ski hire, PADI Dive courses, daily Activities Programme; and daily excursion tours to the other side of Upolu Island and into the Apia township. A great range of romantic wedding packages are also available.

FOR FURTHER INFORMATION
Please visit our website for full resort information, booking details and current rates.

INSEL FEHMARN
HOTEL APIA, SAMOA

www.inselfehmarn.ws

LOCATION
Apia Samoa

EMAIL
insel@samoa.ws

PHONE/FAX
Ph (685) 23 301
Fax (685) 22 204

ADDRESS
PO Box 3272
Apia Samoa

FACILITIES
Rooms: Garden,
Superior,
Executive & Suite.
Kitchenettes,
tea amenities,
IDD phones. Restaurant
and bar, poolside bar &
lounge, business centre,
conference rooms,
convenience store,
laundrette,
swimming pool,
floodlit tennis courts.

OTHER SERVICE
Shuttle service to town

CREDIT CARDS
Amex, Diners, Master
Card & Visa

ACCOMMODATION & FEATURES

In a tradition of excellence, this well maintained Property in Samoa, offers 54 spacious air-con rooms, complemented with international hotel amenities. All rooms contain kitchenettes, a convenience to travellers. For the pampered, the 'Admiral Suite' is perfectly inviting and comfortable.

Rates from USD$85 per night

Business centre, conference facilities, catering, room service, laundry/dry clean services, complimentary downtown shuttle, airport transfers and rental cars, provide a comprehensive package for business and holiday travellers. For family - a home away from home.

Other hotel facilities include the Peleiupu restaurant and bar offering international cuisine and a delightful 'Island BBQ' featuring local seafood and steaks. Guest can enjoy meals in an air-con room or relax on the terrace overlooking the swimming pool and beautiful Samoan sunsets. Forgetting your toothpaste is not a problem as the hotelís convenience shop provides various sundries from personal care to eggs and butter. The guest launderette offers do it yourself laundry. The hotel field, swimming pool, and floodlit tennis courts provide other activities for guest relaxation. While swimming, enjoy our poolside lounge and bar.

What is in a name you might ask? The proprietor and builder, Fritz J. Kruse II, built the hotel on a piece real estate left by his German grandfather, F. J. Kruse I. Check out this family's fantastic story at out website.

SINALEI REEF RESORT

www.sinalei.com

LOCATION
Siumu, South Coast
Samoa

EMAIL
sinalei@lesamoa.net

PHONE/FAX
Ph (685) 64300 or 25191
Fax (685) 20 285

ADDRESS
PO Box 1510
Apia Samoa

FACILITIES
Air conditioned, direct-
dial phone, ensuite
bathrooms, refrigerator,
private patio,
shuttle bus to Apia,
9 hole golf course

ATTRACTIONS
Natural rock swimming
pool with cascading
water, beachfront
location and 33 acres
landscaped gardens

CREDIT CARDS
Amex, MasterCard
& Visa

ACCOMMODATION
27 individual fales with 6 varying categories;

Garden view fale, Ocean view fale, Ocean view fale suite, beach side fale, Honeymoon Pool Villa and Presidential Suite.

ACTIVITIES
Tennis, diving, fishing, glass bottom cruises, snorkelling, kayaking and golf.

FEATURES
Laumosooi Fale Restaurant - Tropical Dining for buffet breakfast, lunch and dinner serving International as well as local cuisine. Ava I Toga Pier Side Bar and Restaurant - features fresh local seafood and wood fire oven baked pizzas...then end the day with a dip in the fresh spring pool at the end of the jetty. Enjoy a tropical cocktail at Uncle Harry's Pool side Bar while relaxing in the natural rock pool.

Enjoy the Wednesday night Fiafia entertainment featuring the Sinalei Staff and the spectacular fire knife performance by the youth of the local district. BBQ Island Night at Ava I Toga every Saturday night and be serenaded by Sinalei's String Band.

FOR FURTHER INFORMATION
See our website for current rates and booking details, or email us direct.

HOTEL KITANO TUSITALA

www.kitano.ws

LOCATION
Apia Samoa

EMAIL
kitano@kitano.ws

PHONE/FAX
Ph (685) 21 122
Fax (685) 23 652

ADDRESS
PO Box 101
Apia Samoa

FACILITIES
Air conditioned,
2 swimming pools,
tennis courts,
safety deposit boxes,
cable TV,
in-house entertainment

CREDIT CARDS
Amex, Diners,
MasterCard, Visa

ACCOMMODATION
Fully air-conditioned & internationalized guests room has shower & bathtub, TV, fridge, teakettle, telephone, radio, alarm clock, optical fiber line, all with veranda faced tropical garden. Also available 1 suit, 2 family rooms and 8 kitchenette for long stay.

FEATURES
Even 5 M walk to center of Apia, still hotel is in calm, surrounded by tropical garden in 14 acres premises, that luxury space offer the relaxation of Samoa with full food service as room service, 3 restaurants & 1 bar with light up pool & garden. Especially FiaFia Dinner Show, every Thursday is most memorable attraction in Samoa

ADDITIONAL SERVICE
Travel agent & rent car, business center, gift shop, massage clinic, coin laundry, tennis court, mini golf, Tree House News Paper, mineral water, rubber slipper.

CONFERENCE FACILITY
Only capable hotel to have conference in Samoa with 5 compounded by 350 capacity main hall, 1 dining hall plus 3 small meeting rooms.

SA'MOANA RESORT

www.samoanaresort.com

LOCATION
Salamumu Beach Samoa
EMAIL
info@worldsurfaris.com
PHONE/FAX
Ph (617) 5444 4011
Fax (617) 5444 4911
ADDRESS
PO Box 180 Mooloolaba
Qld 4557 Australia
FACILITIES
Private facilities, restaurant bar, TV & video/dvd lounge, pool & ping pong table, swimming pool, golf practice nets, kids playground.
ATTRACTIONS
Surfing, gourmet cuisine, beachfront location, snorkelling, game fishing etc
PACKAGES
All inclusive Surf packages, All inclusive Game Fishing packages, General Tourist package

ACCOMMODATION
Caters for up to 24 guests in high quality fales with private facilities. Singles, couples, groups and families are all catered for.

FEATURES
Sa'Moana Resort is fast gaining reputation as having the best food in Samoa. Highly acclaimed Australian chefs have introduced a very innovative menu that is receiving rave reviews.

Choice of bed & breakfast or full board packages available. One night per week is the traditional Fia Fia Feast.

ACTIVITIES
Surfing: full time Australian surf-guides to take surfers to some of the world's best reef-breaks by fast boat. Samoa offers uncrowded perfect waves and Sa'Moana Resort's surfing expertise.

Game Fishing:
Expert Game Fishing tours available.
Hire Cars can be arranged on request.

JT'S TRAVELLERS INN
www.samoa-jtstravelinn.com

LOCATION
Apia, Samoa

EMAIL
jtscomplex@samoa.ws

PHONE/FAX
Ph (685) 22 221
Fax (685) 29 193

ADDRESS
PO Box 6572, Apia, Samoa

HOST
Hennie Tonu'u

FACILITIES
Air conditioned rooms
available, Restaurant & Bar
onsite

ATTRACTIONS
Centrally located

CREDIT CARDS
MasterCard, Visa

JT's Travellers Inn is Apia's newest bed and breakfast accommodation facility located in Fugalei just two minutes from Apia's main shopping centre and markets.

Family owned and managed by Hennie Tonu'u, JT's Travellers Inn is an offshoot of the successful JT's Sportsbar and Cafe which is one of Apia's popular bars, frequented regularly by locals, ex-pats and tourists alike.

Both the Travellers' Inn and Sportsbar & Cafe are conveniently situated together onsite. The Sportsbar & Cafe contains a fully licensed bar and restaurant.

APIA CENTRAL HOTEL
www.samoahotels.ws/ahkams.htm

LOCATION
Apia, Samoa

EMAIL
ahkams@lesamoa.net

PHONE/FAX
Ph (685) 20 782
Fax (685) 20 782

ADDRESS
PO Box1299
Apia Samoa

ACCOMMODATION
Apia's best kept secret! Private, comfortable and filled with Samoan hospitality. Apia Central Hotel's 22 self-contained air-conditioned units are conveniently located in the heart of Apia, providing easy access to amenities for all your holiday and business needs. Rental cars, tours and airport transfers can be arranged upon request.

Mini fridge, television, telephone, hot water, tea and coffee making facilities, conference room, bar and restaurant, entertainment courtyard, laundromat.

HOTEL MILLENIA SAMOA
www.hotelmilleniasamoa.com

LOCATION
Apia, Samoa

EMAIL
info@hotelmilleniasamoa.com

PHONE/FAX
Ph (685) 28284/28286
Fax (685) 28285

ADDRESS
PO Box 214
Apia, Samoa

FACILITIES
Air-conditioned, local &
cable TV, refrigerator,
phone, licensed bar,
restaurant. Internet access.
24-hour reception. car
rental and taxi service
available.

CREDIT CARDS
Amex, MasterCard & Visa

ACCOMMODATION
A range of accommodation is offered from standard to twin deluxe.

ATTRACTIONS
Located at Sogi Point the hotel has views that catch the sunrise over famous Apia Bay.

FEATURES
Licensed restaurant with extensive menu. Sip a chilled cocktail in the Tiafau Cocktail Bar. Five minutes walk to the town centre.

TATIANA MOTEL
Your home in Paradise

ACCOMMODATION
26 self-contained air-conditioned rooms double or queen beds, en suite bathrooms, fridge, kitchenette, telephone, wardrobe, TV (incl. cable TV), Radio/alarm clock and hot water. 14 backpacker rooms twin bed (to single beds) ceiling fans, common room, communal kitchen and rest rooms. Maximum of two people per unit. 3 open bungalows (fales). Single mattress with protective nettings and shared facilities

FEATURES
You have a choice of the two best locations in the heart of Apia. One site is two minute walk to the central market and main town center and the other near the Robert Louis Stevenson home and now museum (five minutes ride to Apia). Enclosed in a lush garden surrounding each site. Tatiana Motels the most competitive prices for self-contained rooms, and top quality backpacker rooms. A wide variety of rooms are available depending on your budget and preference. Complimentary tropical breakfast and 12.5% tax is inclusive in rates quoted. Honesty and sincerity is our policy.

* Internet Access is available to all guests

ATTRACTION
Spacious with beautiful garden surroundings. Tatiana Motel offers a natural cool atmosphere to kick back and relax. Centrally located to plan and explore the hidden treasures of Samoa. We will help you. Just ask. Also, Free Complimentary tickets to the popular RSA Night Club where you can boogie to the sounds of the 2 famous Tatiana Band and the RSA Band LIVE. Learn and experience the true beauty of the Samoa Living Culture called "Fa'asamoa" with real Samoans at Tatiana.

See you at TATIANA MOTEL

FOR FURTHER INFORMATION:
visit our website
www.tatiana-motel.com
for current rate and special offers or email
tatiana.motel@lesamoa.net
or Ph: (685) 26829
Fax: (685) 30699
Located in Apia, Samoa

APIA
RENTALS

LEADING THE WAY IN SAMOA

For professional service, attention to detail and outright value for money.

We have a price that will suit your budget. Be it daily or weekly rates, you'll find your dollar buys more miles with us.

Our attentive staff will happily assist in providing the right vehicle at the right time.

If you are visiting our islands, we can offer competent advice about interesting places to see and visit.

ADDRESS	PHONE/FAX	EMAIL	HOURS	CREDIT CARDS
Vaea St., Saleufi PO Box 347, Apia, Samoa	Ph: (685) 24 244 Fax: (685) 26 193	apiarentals @ipasifika.net	Monday to Friday 7.30am – 4.30pm Saturday 8am – 12pm	Amex, MasterCard & Visa

SOLOMON ISLANDS
DISCOVER SOMEWHERE COMPLETELY DIFFERENT

TWENTY-FIVE million years ago, volcanic activity raised the first of what is now the Solomon Islands above the waves. And throughout its history, volcanoes – and other unceasingly violent conditions far below the Earth's surface – have continued to play an important part.

A double chain of islands, with a landmass of approximately 27,540 square kilometres and covering about 1.35 million square kilometres of ocean, the Solomon Islands comprises 922 individual islands of which some 350 are inhabited. The landscape for the most part is mountainous and draped with almost impenetrable rainforest that covers almost 80 per cent of the islands. Located along what is known as the Pacific Ring of Fire, there are several active volcanoes as well as numerous uplifted atolls, islands of coral which have been lifted above sea level by the numerous earthquakes that continue to impact on the region.

WILD AND UNTAMED

It's a strangely beautiful environment, wild and untamed yet holding many surprises that are unique to the area. In this nation largely untouched by modern development and tourism, continue traditions that have changes little in hundreads of years, visitors will find a landscape molded by the uncompromising hands of nature.

Located 1450 kilometres south-south-east of New Guinea and approximately 1860 kilometres north of Australia, the Solomon Islands comprises nine provinces – Guadalcanal, Malaita, Choiseul, Isabel, Western, Central, Rennell and Bellona, Makira and Temotu. The six main islands are Malaita, Guadalcanal, Santa Isabel, New Georgia, Makira and Choiseul.

There's a wide variety of cultures present in the Solomons with over 80 distinct cultural and ethnic groups, scattered over the 990 individual islands comprising the Solomon Islands. The Solomon Islands is also the only country in the Pacific region to have three different racial groups present, which are the predominant Melanesian race, Polynesians and Micronesians. Most of the population lives in small villages, following a traditional lifestyle that keeps the 21st century at bay. Hunting, fishing and subsistence farming are the main activities but visitors will find the Solomon Islanders to be warm and generous hosts, friendly and at ease.

SOLOMON ISLANDS
AT A GLANCE

SOLOMON ISLANDS VISITORS BUREAU
PO Box 321
Mendana Avenue, Honiara
Solomon Islands
Tel: (677) 22 442
Fax: (677) 23 986
Email: info@sivb.com.sb
Website: www.visitsolomons.com.sb

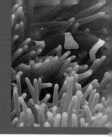

GEOGRAPHICAL LOCATION

The country is located between 5º – 12º south latitude and 150º – 170º east longitude.

AIRLINES

There are five international flights per week. Two services from Brisbane on Tuesdays and Thursday mornings by Solomon Airlines, one service from Nadi on Thursday nights by Solomon Airlines, two services from Port Moresby on Mondays and Fridays by Air Niugini. Domestic flights to provinces such as Malaita, Western and Ysabel on a daily basis and one or two flights per week to provinces such as Renbel, Choisuel, Makira and Temotu. Solomon Airlines provides regular services to about 27 airstrips in nine provinces. Henderson Airport is 13 kilometres from Honiara.

ARRIVAL/DEPARTURE INFORMATION

American, British, Commonwealth and EEC visitors may obtain a visitor's permit on arrival for a period of 30 days (extensions may be issued). No fees apply. All visitors must have current return or onward tickets and should be in possession of adequate funds in support of their stay. Enquiries at the Division of Immigration at PO Box G26, Honiara, Solomon Islands. Fax: 677 22 964 or the nearest consulate.

Visitors require immunisation if originating or having passed through disease-infected or epidemic countries. Malaria medication is recommended.

Duty free limits are 200 cigarettes or 250 grams of tobacco, two litres of spirits or equivalent, also other dutiable goods that do not exceed SI$400.00

Departure tax - SI$40.00.

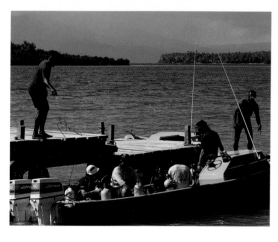

CURRENCY

The Solomon Island Dollar. Denominations are in $50, $20, $10, $5 and $2 notes, and $1, 50, 20, 10, 5, 2 and 1 cent coins.

CLIMATE

Hot and humid year-round with the green season occurring December to March.
The average temperature is 29 degrees Celsius

ELECTRICITY

The Solomon Islands Electricity Authority operates a continuous 240/415 volts hertz electrical supply in Honiara and other major provincial centres.

HANDICRAFTS

Local artifacts can be bought direct from local artisans throughout the islands as well as from numerous souvenir outlets. Local handicrafts of note include Kerosenewood carvings, shell jewellery, basket, bags, hats and mats woven from pandanus or coconut palm leaves. One of the most dramatic of Solomons handicraft is the Nguzunguzu carving, which once adorned the bows of war canoes.

LANGUAGE

Predominantly English-speaking although locals speak Melanesian pidgin. There are 90 vernacular languages nation-wide.

POPULATION

The total population of the Solomon Islands is 409,042 (1999 census). The population is made up of Polynesians,

Micronesians, Europeans, Asians and Melanesians, who make up about 90-95 per cent of the population.

LOCAL CONSIDERATIONS

Dress - take light and airy clothing. A sweater for the rare cool evening. Female dress should be modest in public. Bikinis and other beach or swim wear are most appropriate for the pool, sea or beachfront. However, because of the strong cultural sensitivity of the local people, it is considered offensive to walk around town with such clothing.

There is a 10 per cent tax on accommodation and restaurant bills.

The Central Hospital in Honiara is the major medical facility in the Solomon Islands. The nine provinces are served by mini hospitals and village clinics. Munda in the Western Province has a hospital run by the United Church of Solomon Islands and the Seventh-day Adventist church also runs a hospital in the Malaita Province.

There is a wide range of religions including the Church of Melanesia (Anglican), Catholic, Seventh-day Adventist, Baha'i, Baptist and Jehovah Witness.

Tipping is not at all encouraged in any tourist facilities. Your courtesy, a spoken word of expressing appreciation with the service received and a display of respect are well received.

TELECOMMUNICATIONS

The Solomon Telekom offers a wide range or telecommunication facilities. There are a number of Internet café's in Honiara and at Gizo in the Western Province. Phone cards are available from the Solomon Telekom Head office as well as selected outlets in town, which can be used at the numerous public phones around town and the provinces.

TIME ZONE

11hours ahead of Greenwich Mean Time.

TRANSPORT

In Honiara and bigger provincial centres like Auki (Malaita) and Gizo (Western) public buses and taxi services are readily available for use. There are a number of radio-controlled taxi services some of which operates on a 24-hour basis. In all provinces, outboard motor canoes are the most common form of transport.

HISTORIC SOLOMON ISLANDS

SHAPED BY NATURE

WHILE volcanoes and earthquakes shaped the Solomon Islands over thousands of years, the most cataclysmic events of recent times were man-made. World War II came to the Solomons with a vengeance and much of the destruction centred on Guadalcanal. At 5302 square kilometres, Guadalcanal is the largest of the Solomon's numerous islands. From August 1942 until February 1943, the Battle for Guadalcanal pitched the Allies against the Japanese and extracted heavy losses on both sides; the Japanese alone lost 24,000 men.

Today, reminders of the heavy fighting are everywhere to be seen. Just off the coast of Honiara, the Solomon's capital and the largest town on Guadalcanal, lies Iron Bottom Sound. It's so named because literally hundreds of ships and aircraft litter the ocean floor, providing divers with a wide range of wrecks to explore. Organized tours are available for visitors to see the World War II battlesites, monuments or memorial sites, and relics, which are scattered throughout the islands and particularly around the capital Honiara and the nearby island group of Florida.

Strewn across the island (as on many of the Solomon's islands) are further reminders of the war together with monuments to many of the individual battles. Most of the war sites are accessible on day trips from Honiara.

QUIET PURSUITS

From the 410-metre-high Mt Austin, the expansive view over Honiara gives little of Guadalcanal's history away. Inside town, visits to the Solomon Islands National Museum and the National Art Gallery give a splendid overview. China Town, the Honiara Main Markets and Watapamu Village within the Botanic Gardens are also highly recommended.

The coastal plain to the east of Honiara is one of the very few in the Solomons. Continue east, beyond Aola, which was the original capital of the island, and visitors will arrive at the spectacular Marau Sound. Diving and snorkelling are probably the best ways to appreciate this coral wonderland populated with countless thousands of brightly coloured fish, rays and sharks.

LOCAL CULTURE

Solomon Islands is known for its forms of traditional bamboo music as well as wooden drum beating, which are unique only to the Melanesian group in the Solomons. Black magic and traditional practices that have been practices for thousands of years are still happening today under Christian radar in many parts of the country. There are man-made islands still visible and inhabited today in various parts of the country, which were built without any engineering formulas but still withstand the very few strong hurricanes that hit the country in history.

THE ISLANDS OF SOLOMON

FARAWAY AND REMOTE

FOR the adventurous, there are some remarkable things to see and do in the Solomon Islands. Malaita Island, for example, is the second largest island in the Solomons and the focal point of Malaita Province. Within Langa Langa Lagoon on the east side of the island, and the 36-kilometre-long Lau Lagoon on the west, can be found numerous artificial islands created from coral and dirt. Providing a unique location for some of the island's traditional inhabitants, they also house some of the region's last shark-callers. Believing their ancestors have a spiritual affinity with sharks, practitioners beat stones underwater to bring sharks into shore for ritual feeding.

South of Guadalcanal is the Rennell and Bellona Province. The islands of the same name are coral atolls lifted permanently above the waves by volcanic activity. Encompassing some 690 square metres, East Rennell is the largest raised atoll in the world and has been listed as a World heritage site.

At the northern end of Iron Bottom Sound is Savo, part of the Central Province. Towering some 485 metres above the waves is an active volcano which last erupted in 1840. Among some of the other volcanoes worth visiting is Santa Cruz, part of the Temotu Province, the easternmost of the Solomons. Just north of Santa Cruz is the 800-metre-high Tinakula Island, considered to be the Solomon's most active volcano.

LAY BACK UNDER A WIDE BLUE SKY

For the less adventurous nature-lovers, there's Marovo Lagoon. Measuring 35 kilometres across and up to 50 kilometres wide, it is the largest lagoon in the world. It's also the most beautiful, an opinion canvassed by author James A. Michener. It can be found in the New Georgia group, at the core of the Western Province.

The town of Gizo is the administrative centre of the province and nearby is Kennedy Island (often referred to as Plum Pudding Island) where John F. Kennedy and the crew of PT 103 swam to safety after a Japanese attack.

HONIARA HOTEL

LOCATION
Honiara, Solomon Islands

EMAIL
honhotel
@welkam.solomon.com.sb

PHONE/FAX
Ph (677) 21 737/21 738
Direct Ph (677) 23 412
Fax (677) 20 376

ADDRESS
PO Box 4, Honiara,
Solomon Islands

FACILITIES
Swimming Pool, Dive
Shop, Gift Shop, Licensed
Restaurant & Bar, Live
Local Entertainment.

ATTRACTIONS
Some of the best diving in
the world can be found
off the beaches around
Honiara and nearby
islands in the historic Iron
Bottom Sound.

CREDIT CARDS
Amex, MasterCard & Visa.

Smiling faces and warm island hospitality are a distinctive trait of the Honiara Hotel, which is located in tropical surroundings only a few minutes from the city centre.

Perched on a hilltop with breathtaking ocean views and modern facilities are the hotel's new 'Paradise Wing' rooms, increasing the hotel's guest accommodation and setting an even higher standard with their large balconies overlooking Honiara and the historic Iron Bottom Sound.

New too is the hotel's Flamingo Lounge and Night Club and two restaurants – Club Havanah serving Pacific, Italian and French cuisine and the Boucanier Restaurant with its a la carte international menu.

Our accommodation features air-conditioning, satellite TV, in-house video, radio, IDD telephones, private bathroom, fridge and tea and coffee making facilities.

Other hotel facilities include a poolside terrace, bar and souvenir shop while the experienced staff at the Coast Watchers Dive shop provides quality dive and snorkeling services. The Honiara's friendly receptionists can also help with enquiries about other activities including local tours, including the famous 'WWII Guadalcanal Battlefields tours and boat rides offshore to war wrecks, rich coral reefs, stunning walls of colour and dramatic caverns. They also specialise in conferences, banquets, cocktail parties and wedding receptions.

TAWAIHI ISLAND RETREAT

www.tawaihiislandretreat.com

LOCATION
Tawaihi Island
Katou-Marau Sound
East Guadalcanal, 9°
South Latitude, 160° East
Longitude

EMAIL
tawaihi@hotmail.com
tawaihi@tawaihi.com
guardtrav@solomon.com.sb

PHONE/FAX
Ph (677) 30 584,
(677) 22 586
Fax (677) 26 184

ADDRESS
PO Box 1945
Honiara, Solomon Islands

ATTRACTIONS
Diving, fishing, yacht safe
touring, snorkelling, bush
and village walks, island
visits, birds, bats,
butterflies, paddling,
cultural performances.

ACCOMMODATION
Spacious waterfront leaf roof bungalows, queen
and single beds, dressing and bathrooms, verandah, tasteful wall decorations, power electric and
water, all with spectacular island views. Eight
minutes boat ride from Marau airfield. As a jet
setter you can be assured of the ultimate of exotic yet rustic resorts with your hosts Peter and Dee
Prichard.

FEATURES
International and Oceania cuisine. Choice of beverages, emphasis on seafood caught fresh.
Acclaimed most beautiful soft adventure eco
tourism location in Solomon Islands. Guadalcanal
Island in a world you never knew still existed.
Warm, clear tropical waters, marine life, flora and
fauna in abundance. Shy but friendly villagers
steeped in culture. In what world could you ever
better us? Tawaihi Island Retreat.

Guadalcanal Province Highlights
- Experience the fabulous retreat at Tawaihi and
the beautiful Tavanipupu Island resort to the east
of Honiara in Marau Sound – the gems of the
Solomon Islands.

- Ideal resting place Marau Sound for visiting
yachts and boats – located 9° south latitude and
160° east Longitude.

UEPI ISLAND RESORT

www.uepi.com & www.kayaksolomons.com

copyright: Peter Lange. www.fotofish.at

LOCATION
Marovo Lagoon
Solomon Islands

EMAIL
info@uepi.com

PHONE/FAX
Ph (613) 9787 7904
Fax (613) 9787 5904

ADDRESS
PO Box 149 Mt Eliza
Victoria 3930 Australia

FACILITIES
Diving, beachfront,
snorkelling, fishing,
sea kayaking.

Uepi Island has the unique combination of
sandy beach on one side of the island, and
fringing reef merging into magnificent
2000m drop-offs on the other.
Accommodation is in 6 bungalows, 2 units
and 2 guestrooms, all with either absolute
beachfront or with spectacular water views.
The snorkelling is truly remarkable with
access immediately from the resort.
Activities include jungle walks, cultural trips,
lagoon, open-ocean and river fishing. Paddleboards, windsurfers and inflatable kayak are
available FOC.
Sea kayaking trips now available for 1/2 day
to 10-day fully guided expeditions of the
Marovo Lagoon.
World-class scuba diving on walls, drop-offs,
WWII wrecks and reefs – complete facility
with resident Dive Instructors.

SOLOMON ISLAND HIGHLIGHTS

WESTERN PROVINCE HIGHLIGHTS.

- Magnificent aerial views of verdant islands and the proposed world heritage site of Marovo Lagoon.
- World class diving and snorkelling at a variety of sites including coral reefs, deep sea and WWII wrecks.
- Driving and excursion centres in main tourist spots at Gizo, Munda, Uepi Island Resort and the Shortland Islands.
- Kolobamgara Island, an archetypal conical volcano with a crater rim, 1770m high.
- Megapod birds and skull shrines on many small lagoon islands.
- Numerous eco-lodges and eco-tourism villages with a culture and nature based activities unique to each area.
- Meeting local artisans at work on their high quality and traditionally oriented artefacts and handicrafts.
- Fishing at some of Solomons best fishing grounds with local experts.

GUADALCANAL PROVINCE HIGHLIGHTS.

- Exploring Guadalcanal WWII battle sites and memorials on organised tours or individual.
- Visiting the bustling Honiara CBD with various shops, handicrafts shops, hotels and restaurants.
- Diving and snorkelling on coastal areas of the Honiara outskirts.
- Experience the retreats offered by Tavanipupu Resort on the East of Honiara.

MALAITA PROVINCE HIGHLIGHTS.

- Auki, relaxing provincial centre with numerous shops, the Malaita Centre Culture and History, restaurants and a number of budget accommodations.
- Day excursions to the artificial Islands of the Langalanga Lagoon or a trip to explore the attractions of Lau and Are Are Lagoons.
- Stronghold of ancient tradition, including dolphins and shark calling.
- Langalanga Lagoon, the main centre for manufacturing of shell money and boat building.
- The isolated and untouched nature and people of the Kwaio language group, some of whom are still hunters and collectors.
- The isolated Polynesian atolls of Sikaiana and Ontong Java.

CENTRAL ISLANDS PROVINCE HIGHLIGHTS.
- Strolling around the historical town of Tulagi, which serves as Solomon Colonial Capital.
- Exploring the numerous caves on the Ngella Islands, which are believed to be storing buried treasures.
- Megapod birds and thermal spring on Savo Island.
- Diving and snorkelling in the Florida and Russell Islands group.
- Visiting the RIPEL Coconut oil processing mill and staying at the Yandina Plantation Resort.

YSABEL PROVINCE HIGHLIGHTS.
- Explore Buala, the relaxed provincial capital surrounded by forest and coconut plantations.
- Stay at ecotourist villages near Buala where you'll see traditional dances, go on guided bush walks and learn pidgin.
- Visit Kia, the northern village guarding three inlets, where houses are built on stilts.
- Take a turtle-monitoring trip in the Arnavon Islands, one of the largest nesting grounds for the endangered hawksbill turtle.

MAKIRA/ULAWA PROVINCE HIGHLIGHTS.
- Carved housetops and inlaid bowls.
- Tour the copra mill near Kirakira the province's capital.
- Black sand beaches on Makira.
- Turtle nesting beach on Santa Ana Island.
- Custom houses at the traditional village of Natagera, Santa Ana.

Rennell & Bellona Province Highlights.
- Visit Lake Te Nggano on Rennell, which is the largest lake in the South Pacific and haven for bird life and proposed site for World Heritage site.
- See the soaring cliffs of Rennell and Bellona, which are, raised coral atolls.
- Experience the unique culture including Polynesians traditions.
- Visit ancient burial places, caves and temples of the legendary Hiti people.
- Explore caves on the Bellona, the scene of many fables.

CHOISUEL PROVINCE HIGHLIGHTS.
- Explore off the beaten track, free from tourist development.
- Abundant deserted sandy beaches where turtles swim and breed.
- Traditional crafts, including pottery and bukaware weaving.
- Ndolos, the carved stone burial chambers of Choisuel Island.
- Home of Kesa, an unusual currency.

TEMOTU PROVINCE HIGHLIGHTS
- Travelling by boat – the only way to get around the isolated province.
- Visiting distant Tikopia and Anuta, both virtually unaffected by modern life.
- Red feather money, one of the world's unique currencies.
- Tinakula, the most active volcano in the Solomons.
- Snorkelling in Santa Cruz's 'West Passage'.
- Tapa cloth which is made locally from tree bark.
- Mendana rooster hunting.
- Banana fibre basket weaving.

A WORLD YOU NEVER KNEW STILL EXISTED.

The Solomon Islands

– discover somewhere completely different –

Unspoiled... untouched... undeveloped

A little known natural South Pacific Paradise three hours from Brisbane. But it's not for everyone. It's for the new breed of of eco tourist. Thoughtful travellers worldly enough to expect the unexpected ...and find joy in simple natural realities

The Solomons are ready and waiting for you

Solomon Island Visitors Bureau
Mendana Avenue PO Box 321
Honiara Solomon Islands
Phone (677) 22 442
Fax (677) 23 986
Email info@sivb.com.sb

TAHITI & HER ISLANDS

HIGH islands, and low islands, Tahiti and Her Islands display all the forms created by bountiful nature. Lush green high islands with their peaks in the clouds surrounded by barrier reefs or no reef and with beaches of black basalt sand or white coral sand. Mountains, with all the colours of Gauguin, are blue, violet or brown depending on the angles of the light as they range majestically over this tranquil ocean of a faraway blue. The sky also plays its part, with sunrises and sunsets at times taking on fabulous colours ranging from pale yellow to scarlet red in short but intense moments that the traveller may burn into his holiday memory banks. The mountainsides flow with impetuous waterfalls and there are numerous exuberant valleys just asking to be hiked. And there are mountains sculpted out over centuries of erosion offering unique panoramic views to be contemplated ad infinitum, such as in Cook's Bay in Moorea or the Bay of Virgins in the Marquesas.

Low islands, atolls ringed around with internal lagoons of fairytale colours ranging from oh-so-light jade green and show such a luminous turquoise offering of authentic postcard colours. Multitudes of little islands inhabited by birds, countless beaches one after another. Coconut trees, shells, plentiful fish, sun and an intense feeling of happiness...

All these islands, 118 in all, are different from each other. Each has its special charms. Moorea is not Bora Bora and Bora Bora is not Manihi, but all these islands are gently rocked by the trade winds, these sweet and gentle winds that make the coconut palms rustle. And, depending on the season, they will be cooled by the 'maraamu', the south wind that blows in the southern winter.

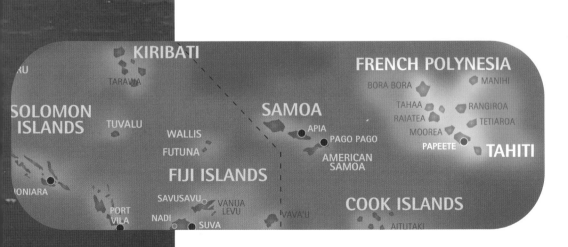

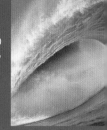

TAHITI & HER ISLANDS
AT A GLANCE

TAHITI TOURISME, POMARE BOULEVARD
Paofai Bldg, entry D, PO Box 65 Papeete,
Tahiti, French Polynesia
Tel. (689) 50 57 00
Fax. (689) 43 66 19
Email: tahiti-tourisme@mail.pf
Websites: www.tahiti-tourisme.com
www.tahiti-tourisme.pf

GEOGRAPHIC LOCATION

The island of Tahiti in the Society Islands group is located at 17o 32' S. and 149o 34' W., halfway between California (6200 kilometres) and Australia (5700 kilometres). Tahiti is 8800 kilometres from Tokyo and 7500 kilometres from Santiago de Chile.

AIRLINES

International: Air Tahiti Nui, Air France, Air New Zealand, Qantas Airways, Air Calin, Hawaiian Airlines and LanChile provide international services to Tahiti.
Domestic: Air Tahiti flies from Tahiti to 38 islands on a very regular basis. Flights on request are possible with Wan Air. Air Moorea shuttles between the islands of Tahiti and Moorea in less than seven minutes. There are also charter flights with Air Archipels.

ARRIVAL/DEPARTURE INFORMATION

Faa'a Airport is about five kilometres from Papeete.
200 cigarettes or 50 cigars, two litres of spirits or two litres of wine are duty-free.
French nationals require only a National Identity Card for a stay in French Polynesia. However, it is essential to hold a valid passport in case of transit via the USA. Travellers are seriously advised to be in possession of a passport valid for six months longer than their return date. They need a return airline ticket to their resident country or to at least two more continuing destinations.
and sufficient funds to cover their planned stay.
No vaccinations required unless travelling from yellow fever, plague or cholera areas.
A Tourist Development Tax applies on hotels, cruises and any other establishments of equal characteristics.
Value Added Tax: 10 per cent on tourist services and six per cent on hotels.

CURRENCY

The French Pacific Franc (CFP) is on parity with the French Franc (about 100 CFP's for every US dollar).

CLIMATE

Tahiti and her Islands enjoy a tropical climate; the maximum number of hours of sunshine is close to 3000 per year in the Tuamotu. The temperature, which is always pleasant, is cooled by the trade winds of the Pacific that

Tahiti
and Her Islands

blow throughout the year. The average ambient temperature is 27° Celsius. Austral and Gambier, farther away from the equator in the archipelagos down south, enjoy cooler temperatures.

ELECTRICITY
110 or 220 volts (60Hz), depending on the island and type of accommodation.

HANDICRAFTS
A wide variety of flowers, food, pareos, hats, mother of pearl, art objects and souvenirs is available at craft and souvenir shops. Tapa cloth (made from breadfruit, banyan or paper mulberry trees) is mainly used for ceremonial occasions these days and makes a colourful souvenir. Black pearls from the Tuamotus are highly prized.

LANGUAGE
French and Tahitian are the two official languages. English is also widely spoken particularly in tourist areas.

POPULATION
There are 220,000 inhabitants, 75 per cent Polynesian, 15 per cent European and 10 per cent Chinese.

LOCAL CONSIDERATIONS
Bring summer clothes, beachwear, sports wear and boat wear, all preferably in cotton. Have something warm available for the cooler evenings and sandals, sneakers and/or boat shoes for the feet. Essentials are swimming costumes, sunglasses, hat, sunblock cream and a powerful anti-mosquito lotion.
Medical services: There is a public hospital, as well as some private medical centres in Papeete while the main tourist islands also have at least one medical centre.
Religion is largely Protestant and Catholic.
Tipping is not expected.

TELECOMMUNICATIONS
Papeete Central Post Office, located near the Yacht Wharf and Bougainville Park, is open weekdays from 7am to 3pm and on Saturdays from 8am to 11am.There are numerous card-operated call boxes located throughout most of the islands. Cybercafes can be found in Papeete and Bora Bora.

TIME ZONE
Tahiti and her islands are 10 hours behind Greenwich Mean Time (GMT). This is 12 hours in summertime or 11 hours wintertime difference from Paris and two hours behind the United States Pacific Coast.

TRANSPORT
Taxis and buses are a popular form of transport on the main island of Tahiti. On the outer islands car and scooter rentals are available and 'Le Truck" open-air buses are an inexpensive means of getting around.

Visit Air Tahiti website at www.airtahiti.aero

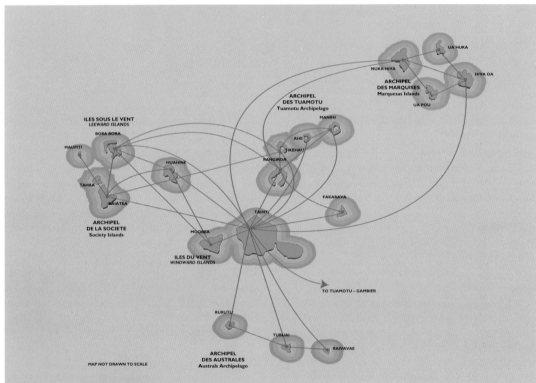

And contact us for more information
and your comments to:
Reservation@airtahiti.pf
Fax: (689) 86 40 99
PO Box: 314 – 98713 Papeete
TAHITI – French Polynesia

АС AIR TAHITI

ECO-TOURISM

A WALK ON THE GREEN SIDE

WHENEVER one hears the name "Tahiti and Her Islands" one invariably associates it with images of coconut palms and lagoons. Tahiti and her high island groups of the Marquesas, the Austral and the Society Islands offer keen visitors far more attractions than just beaches and warm water. High above, much higher above, at times accessible easily only by 4-wheel-drive vehicles, and sometimes viewable with even greater effort after a long mountain hike, stands the mountain peak often wreathed in cloud and always magnificently awaiting those who allow themselves the time to explore her. The spectacle of secret valleys with their cool waters, their stones, and their abundant flora as well as their canyons, their peaks and ridges show quite another face of Polynesian beauty.

The animal life and the flora are unique to this part of the world and there are many endemic species. On the highest peaks, the plant life that only grows at over 2000 metres in altitude is totally original.

We invite you to join us in tracking down these special wild plants, in the secret hope that at some point in your stay we could see you hiking on a mountain adventure.

Whether high or low, the bounteous nature of Tahiti and Her Islands certainly produces all varieties of islands. From the green cloud-covered peaks of the high islands either with or without a barrier reef to the black basalt sand or white coral sand. The mountainsides are running with rushing waterfalls and many rewarding valleys highly conducive to hiking.

A PORTRAIT: TAHITI & HER ISLANDS

118 ISLANDS, 5 ISLAND GROUPS

TAHITI'S 118 fabulous islands are scattered across five far-flung archipelagoes, each with their own particular character and whose inhabitants have adapted the 21st century to the ancient rhythms of the ocean and the sun.

The Society Islands (made up of the Leeward Islands and the Windward Islands) is a group of high tropical islands, the main one of which is Tahiti, the largest of the Polynesian islands, with Papeete as its administrative capital. This group also includes the famous islands of Moorea, Huahine, Raiatea, Tahaa, Bora Bora and Maupiti.

The Tuamotu group is a collection of low islands or atolls. Here is a very special world, situated between sky and sea.

Each island is encircled on its lagoon by a ring of coral. It is an environment favorable to pearl farming.

Rangiroa, Tikehau, Manihi, Fakarava are the ones most frequently visited.

The Marquesas is a group of high islands near the equator whose steep mountains are inhabited by horses, goats and pigs. The most well-known are Nuku Hiva, Hiva Oa, Ua Pou and Ua Huka which offer the tourist among many numerous points of interest, a magnificent arboretum.

The Austral archipelago, situated far to the south, includes high islands with nature in the wild.

There is a variety of tropical plants and plants from temperate regions also. This environment is favourable to market gardening.

A special attraction on the Austral Islands occurs every year from June to October when the whales meet in the warm, shallow waters.

The Gambier archipelago, consisting of the high island of Mangareva and its fringe of islands, which are the eroded remains of its former gigantic crater, is situated in the far eastern corner of French Polynesia. Rarely visited, it is a good place to grow pearls and is endowed with many large pearl farms.

TAHITI

TAHITI is a mountainous island dominated by the peak of Mount Orohena (2,241m) and standing alongside the other famous silhouettes of Aorai (2,066m), Diadem (1,321m), a name given by Dumont d 'Urville, and Mount Marau (1,493m).

The capital city, Papeete, is situated on the northwest coast with a harbour sheltered by reefs. The city of Papeete, which is the political and economic heart of the country, stretches around a narrow coastal strip and up the mountainside in the north and in the west of the island that is now being covered by luxury residences.

In the form of a huge circle, the big island Tahiti Nui is criss-crossed by deep, beautiful valleys and is connected to the equally mountainous little Tahiti Iti by the narrow Taravao isthmus. The mountains of Tahiti offer curious visitors charming walks in natural valleys of light and shade in the cathedral of fern trees. You will see impressive waterfalls and discover mysterious grottoes and archaeological sites steeped in legends. The high valley of the Papenoo River, which leads to the Maroto pass and to the Vahiria crater lake (whose eels have ears!), together with the nature reserve of the Feuna ai'here and its coastal cliffs at Pari on the peninsula, will awaken a sense of marvel in hikers and those who love wild and unadulterated nature. The rocky coastline on the west side of Tahiti has spectacular views and long black sand beaches of basaltic origin swept by ideal surfing waves. The road twists and winds its way past splendid gardens with their hibiscus hedges, with au ti (cordylines), with bougainvillea or birds of paradise, sometimes under the shade of majestic breadfruit trees whose fruits were at the heart of the story of the "Mutiny on the Bounty".

RESTAURANTS

Papeete is renowned for its fabulous restaurants with such a variety of foods to cater for every taste and budget from 'Les Roulottes', mobile diners which set up shop each afternoon along the boat dock and serve hot meals until the wee hours of the morning. These colourful food-wagons provide good, fast food at reasonable prices, as well as a bar stool to sit and watch the waterfront scene of Papeete-by-night to the beautiful upmarket restaurants in some hotels.

SIGHTSEEING

Visit the various and spectacular mountains and waterfalls, take one of the tours around the island and through the city, go fishing, trekking inland, horseback riding. Tahiti is abundant with picturesque parks and gardens. Talented local artists display their crafts in art galleries or visit the history of Tahiti and her islands at the museum.

RADISSON PLAZA RESORT TAHITI

www.radisson.com/aruefrp

LOCATION
Lafayette Beach

EMAIL
sales-tahiti
@radisson.com

PHONE/FAX
Ph (689) 488 888
Fax (689) 488 889

ADDRESS
BP: 14 170 - 98701 Arue,
Tahiti

FACILITIES
Restaurant, pool bar, cocktail
bar, room service, beach, pool
(800m²), Jacuzzi, fitness
centre, hair and beauty salon,
day spa, sauna, laundry service,
business centre, boutiques, air
conditioning, safety box, tea
& coffee facilities.

ACTIVITIES
Yoga, Aquagym, fitness
classes, Polynesian dance,
snorkelling and kayak and a
large choice of water
activities and land activities.

CREDIT CARDS
AMEX, JCB, Visa,
MasterCard, Diners.

Experience the true meaning of paradise in Tahiti's newest 5 star Resort. The Radisson Plaza Resort Tahiti is the ideal place to explore the unique culture and spectacular natural wonders of French Polynesia. Set amidst a tropical garden landscape on the exotic black sands of Lafayette Beach, the resort features a range of deluxe accommodation, including 86 ocean view rooms, 52 suites and 27 duplex suites, all feature a Lanai, a large covered balcony creating an external living room environment and stunning panoramic views over beautiful Matavai Bay.

An ideal base for island or diving day cruises, the resort features unique excursions and packages featuring the exotic east coast of Tahiti. Soak up the warmth of the Tahitian sun, laze around the lagoon pool and Jacuzzi and after your swim, relax at the pool bar for a cold refreshment, or choose from the tantalising array of contemporary cuisine infused with French Polynesian fare. Revitalise and rejuvenate the mind, body and soul at Tahiti's first purpose built day spa and health club. Offering traditional treatments using natural local products, Le Spa is a place of harmony. Radisson Plaza Resort Tahiti offers the perfect destination to enrich your mind, body and soul.

HOTEL LE MANDARIN

LOCATION
Papeete, Tahiti
French Polynesia

EMAIL
chris.beaumont@mail.pf

PHONE/FAX
Ph (689) 503 350
Fax (689) 421 632

ADDRESS
PO Box 302
Papeete, Tahiti
French Polynesia

FACILITIES
Bar, restaurant, room
service, laundry, ice
machine, tour desk, car
hire, phone,
menu bar, fridge, TV,
tea/coffee facilities

ATTRACTIONS
Central location, videos,
suitable for business
people, air-conditioned

CREDIT CARDS
Amex, Diners, JCB,
MasterCard & Visa

ACCOMMODATION
The hotel consists of 37 beautifully decorated rooms all equipped with air conditioning, colour TV including linkage to numerous international channels and video, mini-bar, refrigerator, direct-dial telephones and private bathroom. Tea/coffee facilities, hairdryer.

FEATURES
24-hour reception, private meeting rooms suitable for small conventions: equipment at your disposal – fax, photocopying, bilingual secretarial services. Car rental – excursion desk.

Hotel 'Le Mandarin' is situated in the heart of Papeete business – shopping centre, opposite the Town Hall within walking distance from all conveniences. Ideally suited for the business person.

SPECIAL FEATURES
Two air-conditioned restaurants serving European and French cuisine and specialising in Chinese including authentic Cantonese-style cooking, with live music each Fri/Sat nights. Every Sunday Chinese buffet – brunch. Honeymoon packages available.

FOR FURTHER INFORMATION
See our website for current rates, booking details and cancellation policy.

HOTEL KONTIKI PACIFIC

www.tahiti-tourisme.pf

LOCATION
Waterfront
Papeete Tahiti

EMAIL
kontiki@mail.pf

PHONE/FAX
Ph (689) 541 616
Fax (689) 421 166

ADDRESS
BP 111 Papeete Tahiti
French Polynesia

FACILITIES
Air conditioned, phone,
fridge, TV, private
bathroom

ATTRACTIONS
Central Papeete, night
club and discos,
gambling club

CREDIT CARD
All major cards accepted

ACCOMMODATION
The Kontiki Pacific is a modern hotel in the heart of downtown Papeete. The hotel has 44 rooms, of which 20 are waterfront. All have private balconies with views of the ocean and Moorea or the mountains.

FEATURES
2 bars, nightclub, laundry, ice machine, hotel tour desk to help booking rental car hire and sightseeing tours. Rates from CFP11,000.

ACTIVITIES
It is just few blocks from the shopping and business centre, airlines, travel agents and marketplace. Across the street is the Moorea boat terminal and 10 minutes from the airport. Our Royal Flush gambling club opens daily for guests and visitors. Honeymoon packages are available.

FOR FURTHER INFORMATION
Phone, fax or see our website for current rates, booking details or cancellation policy.

HOTEL TIARE TAHITI

www.hoteltiaretahiti.com

LOCATION
Papeete, Tahiti

EMAIL
hotltiaretahiti@mail.pf

PHONE/FAX
Ph (689) 500 100
Fax (689) 436 847

ADDRESS
BP 2359-98713 Papeete
Tahiti, French Polynesia

FACILITIES
Air conditioned, IDD
phones, cable TV, private
bathroom

ATTRACTIONS
Downtown, central
locations, friendly staff

CREDIT CARDS
All major credit cards
accepted

ACCOMMODATION
The Hotel Tiare is a hotel with 38 deluxe rooms consisting of 3 panoramic, 17 oceanview and 18 standard rooms. Most rooms have private balconies with magnificent views over Papeete Harbour and Moorea with wonderful sunsets.

Rates:	Standard	CFP13,500.
	Seaview	CFP15,000.

FEATURES
The hotel Tiare Tahiti is an ideal place for either holiday or business. Opened in 1997 with a touch of Polynesian elegance and in the most perfect location. The staff will await you with a warm welcome and the service is excellent.

Right on the seafront in the centre of Papeete's business and restaurant area. Restaurant, laundry, ice machine, tour desk able to organise rental cars and all sporting tours and excursions to the outer islands, diving, fishing, helicopter tours.

FOR FURTHER INFORMATION
Phone, fax or see the website for current rates, booking details or cancellation policy.

MOOREA

TRADITION has it that Moorea was the dorsal fin of the great fish of Tahiti. History tells that the god Hiro, desirous of Rotui, the most beautiful mountain of the island and the place where spirits of the dead pause before their descent of the underworld, wished to make off with her one night to his home in Raiatea. But the warrior Pai put him to flight, throwing his spear which passed through the other famous mountain known from that day as Moua Puta (Pierced Mountain). The sculptured beauty of Cook's Bay ranged with chiselled mountain peaks, including the very lovely Rotui, is paralleled by its twin bay of Opunohu whose dark waters reflect the steep mountainsides. Formerly known as Aimeho, a high priest gave her the name of Moorea after having had a bad dream of a giant and a very beautiful yellow lizard. An important Domain of the royal Pomare family, Moorea was the birthplace of the Protestant Church with the printing in the nineteenth century of the first Bible in the Tahitian language. The scenic beauty and its history are not the only attractions of this island also known for its gentle, easy life style and its high quality of pineapples. Its many white sand beaches, the wide variety of its coral sea bed and the richness of its underwater life make Moorea a very special destination.

FOOD & RESTAURANTS
A broad and interesting variety of foods including French, Chinese and delicious local styles is available in a number of restaurants.

SIGHTSEEING & TOURS
A circle island tour takes about 4 to 8 hours, with visits to small villages and stops to photograph the spectacular view of Moorea's mountains, valleys, lagoons and bays. the Moorea highlights tour passes through Opunohu valley, with stops at the stone 'marae' temples and archery platforms, used by Polynesian royalty in pre-Christian days.

TRANSPORTATION
Le Truck transports passengers between the ferry dock in Vaiare and their hotels for a nominal fee. Taxi service is available at Moorea airport. From Tahiti, Moorea is serviced several times a day by ferries and fast catamarans and by Air Moorea in less than 10 minutes from Tahiti's airport.

HOTEL LES TIPANIERS

www.lestipaniers.com

LOCATION
Moorea French Polynesia

EMAIL
tipaniersresa@mail.pf

WEBSITE
www.lestipaniers.com

PHONE/FAX
Ph (689) 561 267
Fax (689) 562 925

ADDRESS
BP 1002
Moorea French Polynesia

FACILITIES
Ceiling fans, IDD phones, safety box, hot & cold water, games room, laundry

ATTRACTIONS
Beachfront, swimming, diving, Tahitian dances, famous beach restaurant serving French, Italian & Tahitian specialties.

CREDIT CARDS
Amex, Diners, JCB, MasterCard & Visa

ACCOMMODATION
The resort comprises 22 beachfront and garden bungalows. 13 bungalows have kitchens. Maximum person per bungalow is 6 for vanilla bungalow.

Also available is "Tipaniers Iti", situated 5kms from the main hotel and has 5 bungalows with full kitchens. Special rates for long stays.

FEATURES
One of the best restaurants on the island with magnificent views, white sandy beach, tropical gardens. Two cocktail bars.

ACTIVITIES
Boat pier, water skiing, snorkelling excursions, snorkel and scuba diving, deepsea fishing, island tour, motorboat shuttle service to Motu, horseback riding, hiking, rent a car (island touring), canoes, bicycles, volleyball, ping pong.

For a relaxed barefoot kind of holiday in Moorea.

FOR FURTHER INFORMATION
Phone, fax or see website for current rates, booking details and cancellation conditions.

CRUISING

ANOTHER LOOK

FLOATING hotels, ranging from the superbly comfortable to the highly luxurious, constantly ply the waters of French Polynesia. Passengers can rest assured that they will be pampered as they cruise around these golden islands, discovering their diversity from their best side - the ocean.

Great luxury liners offer 10-day or week-long cruises to the Leeward Islands out of Papeete while, based in Raiatea, smaller vessels, still with modern comfort, propose delightful intimate cruises on a 4-5 day plan. There are also discovery cruises available to the Leeward Islands, as well as dive cruises , eco-tourism cruises, and surfing cruises organised in the Tuamotu Islands, so you can savor the delights of these fabulous islands onboard well appointed catamarans.

For those who wish to venture farther to the enchanting Marquesas Islands, a mixed cargo vessel, will admirably fulfill your desire to discover the six main islands and their fantastic scenery.

SCUBA DIVING

RICHES FROM THE OCEAN DEPTHS

THE first glimpse of Tahiti and Her Islands gained by the travelling diver, when arriving by plane, reveals the riotous jade and turquoise tones of lagoons and the tumultuous tangle of reefs, with their passages and rocky outcrops plumbing the great blue depths of the ocean. It is an exhilarating sight, though immediately tinged with the frustration that this visit will be all too short. While still aloft, you drink in the incredible beauty of Polynesia's living contours laid out across the surface of the ocean. Here are riches only rivaled by the great bio-diversity of the islands. And there are 118 of them in total! Each one of these oases of life emerges out of the blue desert of the ocean, each with its own many-faceted features, its own underwater intensity and its own special powers.

How long need one wander through this aquatic paradise in order to experience all the possibilities of this rich underwater world? Undoubtedly, for much longer than a single visit would permit. For many years now, with their great passion for this realm, Polynesian men and women have frequented these treasures, have studied them intently, filmed them and now offer to share their secrets with as many others as possible, whilst still mindful of the urgent need to protect them. These are the folk you will meet in their local dive clubs. They will be your highly skilled guides on your next underwater adventure.

Welcome to the magic of our lagoons.

CHARTER BOATS

ADVENTURE IS AT HAND

THIS vacation formula is becoming very popular in Tahiti and Her Islands, both within the lagoons and between the groups of such diversely different islands.

It is based upon motor boats, some specialising in deepsea game fishing and others on private luxury cruises from the larger Society Islands. They offer fishing trips, day trips that include picnics, half-day and sunset-watching trips. Longer cruises can be made on request.

Single-hull and catamaran sailboat companies, based in Tahiti, Moorea and principally in the Leeward Islands, offer the choice of chartering with or without a skipper or hostess for a weekend or a few days, but more typically on a weekly basis.

Dive cruises, laze-about cruises, discovery or honeymoon cruises - there really is a very wide range of options for you to choose as you cruise in comfort past white, pink and purple sand beaches that fringe the unreal colours of the lagoons of the fabulous Leeward Islands or the sparkling atolls of the Tuamotu.

Having your own private yacht is a great alternative. It's like taking your hotel along with you!

BORA BORA

A VOLCANO on one of the most beautiful lagoons in the world, Bora Bora, "the Pearl of Polynesia", remains that place of your dreams. The proud silhouette of its mountainous heart is made up of three peaks, the highest of which, "Otemanu" at 727 metres figures in the legend of Pahia. The island still takes pride in its warrior expeditions, their invasions by stealthy paddling of days of old, and its former control of Raiatea, its age old rival. Bountiful nature has graced this island with a lagoon of translucent waters and immeasurable beauty, ringed by a rosary of heavenly islets. One of these motu is the site of the airport, while others have luxury hotels on them. One exception is the Toopua motu with a hill more than 100 metres high where there are echoing rocks called "Hiro's bells". The charm of Bora Bora goes way back in history and artists, painters, writers, philosophers and pleasure seekers follow in their footsteps of Alain Gerbault, Herman Melville and Paul Emile Victor.

SIGHTSEEING & TOURS

The island has a multitude of activities and views available. See the underwater splendours of the lagoon from a glass-bottom boat, or hire scuba or snorkelling gear. Sports fishing offshore Bora Bora yields record catches of marlin, yellowfin tuna, sailfish, waho and mahi mahi, and many boats are available to hire, as well as waterskiing and sailing. There are also helicopter tours and mountain sightseeing tours.

TRANSPORT

Le Truck, taxi services and taxi boats on Bora Bora. Also cars, scooters, bicycles and boats are available for hire. Bora Bora is serviced by two ferries and by Air Tahiti (several flights daily).

BORA BORA LAGOON RESORT & SPA

www.boraboralagoon.com

LOCATION
Bora Bora French Polynesia

EMAIL
info@bblr.pf

PHONE/FAX
Ph (689) 604 000
Fax (689) 604 003

ADDRESS
Motu Toopua
Bora Bora, French Polynesia

FACILITIES
Two restaurants, two bars, beaches, infinity pool, Maru spa, fitness centre, games room, tennis courts, boutique, meeting room, internet access, lush tropical gardens

ATTRACTIONS
Beachfront location, safe swimming, scuba diving, snorkelling, shark feeding and other watersports, jeep tours, panoramic views, hiking

CREDIT CARDS
Amex, Diners, MasterCard & Visa

ACCOMMODATION
This award-winning Orient Express Hotel consists of 77 luxurious bungalows in Overwater, Beach and Garden locations. All bungalows feature air conditioning, minibars, tea and coffee facilities, safes, IDD telephone, TV with DVD player, separate bath and shower and private terraces. Overwater bungalows feature glass topped coffee tables and private access to the lagoon. New to the resort are three 1-bedroom suites and a two-bedroom presidential villa, all with their own private swimming pools. Daily laundry service, dry cleaning, and twice-daily maid service.

FEATURES
Fabulous location with best views of Mt. Otemanu. Located 15 minutes by boat from the Bora Bora Airport on its own private island. Complimentary 3 minute shuttle boat ride to the main village of Vaitape. Otemanu Restaurant features fine dining overlooking the lagoon; Café Fare offers lighter fare for lunch and is located near the pool. Hiro lounge provides entertainment nightly. Traditional Tahitian Feast presented each week.

ACTIVITIES
Enjoy one of the largest swimming pools in Bora Bora, the air conditioned fitness center or the unique tree-house style Maru Spa, located in its own tropical oasis along the edge of the lagoon. Along with the resort's array of complimentary activities, guests can partake in a wide variety of optional activities such as private motu picnics, sunset cruises, jet ski tours, scuba, shark feeding and much, much more.

HONEYMOONS

LOVE AND ROMANCE

WHAT could be a more exciting and romantic destination than this island, Garden of Eden, lying at the end of the world between the infinite horizon of the deep blue sky and the warm crystal-clear waters of the tropical ocean – this island so far from the hectic pace of smoggy cities, caressed by the trade winds that rustle the palm trees and rocked by the incessant rhythm of the waves? This is the island of love, the Garden of Delights tasted by the first couple on earth. Wouldn't this be the ideal place to let your love grow?

Couples can experience an enchanting, authentic setting where even breakfast is served from a canoe right at the balcony of your bungalow, built out over the jade and turquoise waters of the lagoon.

Or, to celebrate your years of happiness together, why not relive your wedding in romantic style? Embraced by island song and dance and enveloped in flowers of a thousand perfumes, right in the heart of a Tahitian village.

Every detail contributes to make these moments unforgettable and will etch images of great happiness in your memory forever.

RANGIROA & MANIHI

RA'IROA

RA'IROA gets its name 'huge sky' from its great length. It is the largest atoll here and one of the four largest in the world, with more than 240 motu separated by more than 100 hoa, small channels that make up its ring of coral and, in the centre of the inside lagoon, is the Paio motu. The incomparable brilliance and colours of the lagoon, from jade-green to violet completely overwhelm the visitor who discovers this long ribbon of islets way out in the middle of the Pacific Ocean.

On the northwest side of the atoll is Avatoru, the main village opposite the Fara motu whose lagoon is said, according to the legend, to have been breached by the two twins "Moana-tea" ("Peaceful Ocean") and "Moana-uri: (Wild Ocean"). The main Government buildings are to be found here, including the Mayor's Office, the Post Office, the Pearl Industry Research Centre and two churches. The other village is Tiputa, situated at the eastern end of the motu, near the second main reef entry point, has houses ringed with bleached coral and fenced with flowering hedges. A road surfaced with crushed coral or tar seals links the two villages and their neighbourhoods.

MANIHI

Manihi is an atoll in the Tuamotu Archipelago, 520km (322 miles) northeast of Tahiti. Its clear lagoon, which is 3.5 miles wide by 19 miles long, has a deep navigable pass through the reef and shelters several black pearl farms. Most of the 769 population live in Turipaoa village beside the pass. Activities are naturally centred around the lagoon and, no matter where you stay, your hosts will arrange boat trips to show you around the lagoon, visiting the fish parks and pearl farms, with picnics on a 'motu' and line or spear fishing.

RAIATEA & TAHAA

ACCORDING to Polynesian tradition, Raiatea, formerly known as Hava'i, "the sacred island" was the first inhabited island and Hiro a descendant of the creator god Taaroa and Oro was its first king. The many legends that arise from mythology lend a mysterious and magic atmosphere to the various places of interest. Mt Temehani at 772 metres, a sort of Polynesian Olympus and "fragrant paradise", where the strange and unique "Tiare apetahi" plant is found, watches over this island that is still untouched by the turbulence of modern life. Its mountain range divides the island from north to south. Its many waterfalls, the deep and narrow Faaroa Bay and its fertile valleys are equally attractive as its charming lagoons with its many islets.

In the northern part of the same lagoon, the island of Tahaa, according to legend, was detached from Raiatea by a sacred eel possessed by the spirit of a princess. This island of soft mountain shapes and filigree coastline has been nicknamed "the vanilla island" because of its many vanilla plantations.

The market at Uturoa, the commercial centre and port of call for cruise liners, is loaded with produce of the land and sea, especially on Wednesday and Fridays, the market days. Nature smiles on these two islands whose high quality vanilla and copra is well-known. The main companies for both charter and pleasure vessels have set up office here to ensure you of some magical boat trips.

FOOD & RESTAURANTS
Local cuisine as well as French, Chinese and Italian food are offered by a number of local restaurants and snack bars. Small hotels have restaurants on the premises.

SIGHTSEEING
Small hotels offer a variety of sightseeing tours as well as lagoon excursions or horseback riding.

TRANSPORTATION
Raiatea is serviced by Air Tahiti (several daily flights), two ferries and a fast catamaran. A taxi stand is located near the market in the centre of Uturoa. Rental cars are available through local operators. Bikes are available through some hotels. Lagoon transfers are available between Raiatea and Tahaa.

HUAHINE

THE secret island or rebel island, there is no shortage of adjectives to indicate the wild but attractive nature of this island known for its fierce warriors and its resistance to change. Consisting of two islands, Huahine Nui in the north and Huahine Iti in the South, it is separated by a hollow channel said to be the god Hiro's canoe. This mountainous island, but with soft shapes, has magnificent indented bays and some lovely white sand beaches. The islands dotted around the lagoons are given over to growing melons and there is a varied and abundant supply of fruit and vegetables from these fertile soils. Huahine is also the proud owner of one of the largest and best archaeological preserved sites: the Maeva marae, which is a group of a number of large marae at the foot of Mount Mouatapu and on the shores of lake Fauna Nui. Legends also abound in this island desired by Hiro and now adopted by artists in search of their roots.

In the boutiques in the hotels and in some of the shops on the island, original creations can also be found, paintings on silk, scarves, cushions and pareus. Varied local handicrafts, including pottery, dishes, lamps, vases, handpainted clothing and pareus, and jewellery from mother-of-pearl and seashells. Roti Tarona Artisan Center sells 'tifaifai' quilts and wall hangings, woven hats, sculpted bowls, handpainted clothes, 'monoi' oil and sea shells.

Maeva village Archaeological sites: This old fishing village, built beside Lake Fauna Nui, is an open-air museum, with its stone 'marae', fish weirs and sacred Matairea Hill.

Circle Island Tour: Mini-bus tours around Huahine-Nui, Huahine-Iti or both islands can be arranged through your hotel or pension.

Car, bicycle and boat rentals available. The hotels and pensions provide mini buses at a charge from the airport and return. Le Truck services operate between the centre of Fare and each village, co-ordinating their runs with the ferry schedules and school hours.

Huahine is serviced by two ferries and a rapid catamaran and by Air Tahiti (several daily flights).

OTHER HIDDEN PARADISES

NUKU HIVA, MARQUESAS ARCHIPELAGO

NORTHERN group of Marquesas, 330 square km, population: 2375. The biggest of the Marquesan islands, the "roof beam" of the "Great House" has a mountain range dominated by Mt Tekao (1224 metres) that runs the length of the desert lands in the west where the airport has been built. The centre consists of the Toovii plateau (800 metres) which extends out as a large agricultural region in pasture, fields and forests. The highly indented coastline features bays, capes, rocky points and cliffs with villages at the heads of the bays. Taiohae, under the imposing shadow of Mt Muake (864 metres), the administrative capital and seat of the archbishopric, is in a sheltered harbour location guarded by two rocky islets, the "Sentries" of the East and the West.

HIVA OA, MARQUESAS ARCHIPELAGO

Southern Marquesan group, 320 square km, population: 1837. The largest of the southern islands, Hiva Oa, the master pillar or finial post of the "Great House" has always been the rival of Nuku Hiva.

The island is shaped like a seahorse and has a mountain range running southwest to northeast whose main peaks, Mt Temetiu and Mt Feani form a real wall around Atuona. Atuona, a peaceful little port at the head of Taaoa Bay, also known as Traitors Bay, has emerged from obscurity due to having had the privilege of being the last resting place of Paul Gauguin and of the singer Jacques Brel. The tombs of these famous personalities are on the side of the Calvary cemetery looking out across the bay and are places of great pilgrimage.

FAKARAVA, TUAMOTU ISLANDS

Rectangular-shaped Fakarava is the second largest atoll in the Tuamotu, 60km (37 miles) long by 25km (15 miles) wide. Rotoava village, located near Ngarue pass (one kilometre wide), is home to most of the atoll's 467 population, with only a small settlement in Tetamanu village.

TIKEHAU, TUAMOTU ISLANDS

Tikehau is an almost circular atoll, with an interior lagoon 26km (16 miles) across and a pass for small boats through the coral reef. When Jacques-Yves Cousteau's research group made a study of the Polynesian atolls in 1987, they declared the lagoon of Tikehau to contain the most fish. Fish parks earn an income for many of the atoll's 400 inhabitants.

TONGA

THERE are many reasons to visit Tonga. Long expanses of golden beaches, crystal-clear water, dramatic coastal scenery and volcanic peaks, a languid lifestyle that makes other Pacific islands look hectic in comparison, the warm and welcoming nature of the Tongan people, and myriad idyllic backdrops in which to snorkel, yacht, fish and simply laze away another perfect Pacific day.

The Kingdom of Tonga comprises 170 islands (only 37 of which are inhabited) stretching 425 kilometres across the South Pacific. Tonga lies about 775 kilometres south-east of Fiji and 3220 kilometres north-east of Sydney. Located just to the west of the International Date Line, Tonga is the first Pacific nation to greet the new day.

Think of Tonga as being divided into four main regions. In the south is the Tongatapu island group, where the capital, Nuku'alofa, can be found. One hundred kilometres north is the Ha'apai group followed, another 100 kilometres on, by the Vava'u group. At the extreme northern end of Tonga, 300 kilometres from Vava'u, is the remote Niuas group.

Tonga is notable for being the only Pacific nation never to have been subjugated by foreign powers as well as being the last remaining Polynesian monarchy. The population is immensely proud of their Royal family, especially King Taufa'ahau Tupou IV. The King's birthday is celebrated during the first week of July with the Heilala Festival, one of the biggest celebrations on Tonga's calendar.

It is believed the Polynesians arrived in Tonga more than 3000 years ago and the first of the hereditary rulers, known as the Tu'i Tonga, governed from around 960AD. Dutch travellers entered the area in the early 1600s although it was renowned explorer Abel Tasman who became the first European to set foot on Tongatapu and Ha'apai in 1643. Captain James Cook visited in 1773, 1774 and 1777; although he blissfully misunderstood the wildly rapturous reception he received, he nonetheless bestowed on Tonga the label of The Friendly Islands.

In 1875, Tonga was united to a central monarchy under King George Tupou I. The current king is the first monarch's grandson.

TONGA
AT A GLANCE

TONGA VISITORS BUREAU
PO Box 37, Nuku'alofa
Kingdom of Tonga
Tel: (676) 25 334
Fax: (676) 23 507
Email: info@tvb.gov.to
Website: http://www.tongaholiday.com

GEOGRAPHICAL LOCATION
The Kingdom of Tonga is located on the eastern edge of the Indo-Australian Plate, between latitudes 15.5o South and 23.5o South and longitudes 173o West and 177o West. It is comprised of 176 coral and volcanic islands, thirty-six of which are inhabited

AIRLINES
International: Royal Tongan Airlines, Air New Zealand, Polynesian Airlines, Air Pacific provides services from Sydney, Auckland, Fiji, Samoa, Los Angeles and Hawaii. Domestic: Royal Tongan Airlines has many daily flights linking Vava'u, Ha'apai, 'Eua and the two Niuas. Tonga's second domestic air carrier, flyNiU Airlines operates to Vava'u and Ha'apai. There are two major international airports, Fua'amotu International Airport on Tongatapu and Lupepau'u International Airport on Vava'u.

ARRIVAL/DEPARTURE INFORMATION
Two litres of liquor and two cartons of cigarettes may be imported duty free. No restrictions of other travel items, as Tonga is a duty-free port.
Bona-fide tourists and business persons may enter Tonga for a period not exceeding 30 days providing immigration authorities are satisfied that the visitor holds a valid passport, an onward air or sea ticket, proof of adequate funds and relevant health certificates. If visitors wish to extend their stay, permission must be requested from the Principal Immigration Officer.
A valid yellow fever certificate and a valid cholera certificate are required by all travellers over one year old who have been in an infected area prior to arrival in Tonga.
Any food, seeds, flowers, or goods made from animal or plant parts must be declared on arrival. For details of prohibited items contact your airline or TVB office.
Departure tax of T$25.00 is payable at the airport.

CURRENCY
Tonga's currency is the pa'anga, and its economy is a feudal system.

CLIMATE
From December to April, the weather is hot and humid, with considerable rainfall. The cool dry season, with average temperatures of up to 22 degrees Celsius, runs from May to November. Tradewinds blowing during this season makes for pleasant days and cool nights.

ELECTRICITY
The electricity is 240 volts. Visitors should be warned to change the voltage of their electrical appliances, as the voltage here is higher.

HANDICRAFTS
One place where the cultural experience can be seen at its very best is at the Tongan National Cultural Centre. You can visit a museum, purchase handicraft, take part in a kava ceremony, see some of the best dancers in the land and taste a genuine Tongan feast. The adjacent gallery offers contemporary art and genuine cultural handicrafts. See tapa and canoe making; woodcarving; basket weaving and mat making.

LANGUAGE
Most Tongans understand and speak some English so few problems should be experienced.

LOCAL CONSIDERATIONS
Bathing suits and bikinis are fine for the beach and poolside but are frowned upon if worn in public. Tonga law prohibits any person from appearing in a public place without a shirt.

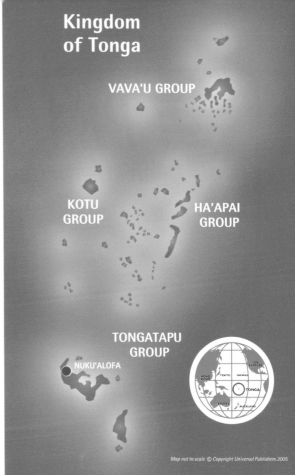

Kingdom of Tonga

VAVA'U GROUP

KOTU GROUP

HA'APAI GROUP

TONGATAPU GROUP

NUKU'ALOFA

Map not to scale © Copyright Universal Publishers 2005

For police, fire brigade and hospital services, ring 911.
The Government provides comprehensive medical and dental facilities to residents and visitors. Modern hospitals can be found in Nuku'alofa, Ha'apai and Vava'u. There are also dispensaries, chemists and pharmacies available. Religion – Christian, although virtually every denomination is represented in Tonga.

Tongans do not expect tips, though no offence will be caused if special service is rewarded in this way.

POPULATION
(1996 Census): Tongatapu - 66,577; Vava'u - 15,779; Ha'apai - 8,148; 'Eua - 4,924; Niuatoputapu - 1,283; Niuafo'ou - 735. In total, Tonga has a population of some 97,446 people.

TELECOMMUNICATIONS
There are two telecommunications company, the Tonga Telecommunications Commission and the Tonfon Co. Ltd. They link Tonatapu to the world with the latest satellite system, email, fax, and telephone (ISD), mobile phones and cable services. There are a few Internet cafes and Business Centres in town.

TIME ZONE
Tonga is 13 hours ahead of Greenwich Mean Time and 18 hours ahead of New York.

TRANSPORT
A temporary Tongan driving licence may be obtained from the Central Police Station providing you have a current driving licence. Cost is T$10.00. A current passport is required. The main forms of transport on land are buses, vans and taxis. There are regular ferry services to the outer islands.

ABODE OF LOVE: TONGATAPU

ON perfect blue-sky Sundays, Tonga goes to church. The day is dedicated to worship; churches as grand as St Mary's Cathedral and the Basilica of St Anthony of Padua, in the capital city of Nuku'alofa, as well as each and every outlying place of worship, attract royalty and commoners alike. The massed voices of the Tongan people, renowned for their singing skills as much as their enthusiasm, reverberate through the streets. The Tongan people take the time to celebrate the bounty that life in this beautiful corner of the Pacific brings forth in all its glory.

The pace of life, graceful and unhurried at the best of times, slows even further. Visitors find many of the attractions and restaurants closed for the day and fall back on Tonga's natural diversions – on sailing the wide blue ocean, hiking through rainforest or isolated ancient reminders of the islands' past, watching whales gambol in the warm waters or scores of bright tropical fish spearing haphazardly through the coral formations, or simply just finding that perfect untouched beach and working on a deeper tan.

There's plenty more of the same thing to look forward to and tomorrow, as someone once said a long way away, is another day.

A majority of Tonga's population lives on Tongatapu. It is where the capital, Nuku'alofa, can be found, as well as the home of the King of Tonga, the seat of government and the commercial and public heart of the country. Meaning 'Abode of Love', Nuku'alofa has some pretty reminders of the colonial past.

CAPITAL ATTRACTIONS
The Royal Palace is a charming Victorian-era residence which was prefabricated in New Zealand and erected in 1867, with a second-storey addition dating from 1882. Surrounded by an impressive barrier of Norfolk pines, the Royal Palace is now simply a figurehead with the King and Queen now installed at Fua'amotu Palace near the airport. Parliament, which meets from May to October, occupies another building prefabricated in New Zealand; it opened in1894 and is still in use.

One of the more important stops in the city is the Tonga National Center. Showcasing Tongan culture in all its diversity, it comprises a collection of Polynesian-inspired buildings where visitors can watch demonstrations of canoe making, woodcarving and basket-weaving, amongst many other activities. Guided tours are held throughout the week, along with barbecue lunches, dinners and fashion shows.

Of particular interest is the manufacture of the ta'ovala, the distinctive Tongan traditional dress. Made from finely woven pandanus-leaf, it is worn by both men (who secure it with a coconut-fibre cord) and women (distinguished with a kiekie waistband). The valas is the skirt also favoured by both men and women, which is worn under the ta'ovalas.

ROYAL CAPITAL

ANCIENT REMINDERS

NEAR the city are the Royal Tombs, where Tongan royalty has been buried since 1893. Farther east of the city is an ancient reminder of Tonga's earliest rulers.

The mysterious Ha'amonga 'a Maui is a stone archway weighing some 12 tons and measures 5 metres high by 6 metres wide. Although numerous theories abound, nobody really knows its original purpose. Scholars and historian feel a little certain about the nearby 2.7-metre-high slab called the 'Esi Makafaakinanga, which many seem to agree was a meeting place for royalty. A long-standing tradition is the sacred status accorded the flying foxes which nest at Kovavai in western Tongatapu. Thousands hang from casuarina trees during the day and fly out over the island at night searching for food.

Nature lovers should also check out the Tongan Wildlife Centre near Keleti in the south, and the Toloa Rainforest Reserve in the east.

FAR-FLUNG OPTIONS

Spreading north of the Tongatapu group is the Ha'apai islands, followed farther north by the Vava'u group. At the northern extremity of Tonga is the Niuas group. Access is easy with daily flights via Royal Tongan Airlines.

Ha'apai and Vava'u in particular are well suited for tourism and have much to offer both the first-time and experienced visitors. The Niuas group offers something completely different – a wild and volcanic vision that takes visitors back thousands of years to the region's geological birth.

Experienced dive masters throughout Tonga know the best places to explore the underwater wonders. From reefs spilling over with colourful and exotic marine life to hidden treasures of every imaginable dimension, even the most travelled of divers will come away from something new and wonderful. Sailing provides the means by which an exploration of the farthest flung reaches of the Kingdom can be traversed. From June until November, it's possible to observe the mating rituals of humpback as well as new-born calves warily taking their first new voyages in the warm waters.

Fully grown, the humpback weigh about 40 tonnes and to watch a pod of whales ply the waters is an experience like no other. Curious about the world they inhabit, whales will not shy away from sailing ships. Rather, they will present an up-close view that will travel in the memory forever.

And at the end of the sailing day, when the gentle Tradewind caresses the sails and the setting sun casts a golden-hued light, settle back with a locally made Royal beer or the juice of the immature coconut and reflect on how good life can be. There's few better places on Earth than the Kingdom of Tonga, whether its; spent in the worldly comforts of a resort, on a deserted stretch of white sand beach or far from the hustle and bustle on board a stately sailing ship.

THE EDGE OF THE WORLD

In the extreme north of Tonga lies the Niuas. The volcanic islands of Niuatoputapu, Tafahi, and Niuafo'ou (Tonga's northern-most island) are located midway between Vava'u and Samoa.

As difficult as it is to get to, it also ranks as one of the most exciting experiences of a lifetime. Niuafo'ou is a collapsed volcanic cone with the centre of the island dominated by Vali Lahi, a lake measuring some five kilometres across and up to 84 metres deep.

At this most isolated of locations, against the dramatic reminders of Earth's most basic primordial violence, visitors feel like they're on the edge of the world. Civilisation becomes an abstract concept, something left far behind. There's only nature – the wind and the unpredictable sea – to rely upon.

Of course, if your sense of adventure is fulfilled by the Discovery Channel, then Tonga still has a lot to offer. Aside from the conventional water sports, surfing is very popular. In May to September, the southern swells are renowned, while northern swells crank up in December to February. One of the most renowned beaches for surfing is Ha'atafu Beach on Tongatapu.

Although the Tonga Golf Club at Tongatapu has the Kingdom's only golf course, there's more than enough sporting possibilities to keep visitors more than occupied. Once the novelty of whale watching, mountain climbing, hiking, snorkelling, scuba diving, swimming and yachting fades, there's Tonga's rich and vibrant culture to explore.

After that, visitors will need another holiday to just get over it all.

INTERNATIONAL DATELINE HOTEL

www.datelinehotel.com

LOCATION
Waterfront
Nuku'alofa

EMAIL
idh@kalianet.to

PHONE/FAX
Ph (676) 23 411
Fax (676) 23 410

ADDRESS
PO Box 39 Nuku'alofa
Kingdom of Tonga

CONTACT
Ms. Lucy Niu

FACILITIES
Air conditioning, private bath, coffee/tea making facilities, Internet facility, IDD phones, fridge/minibar, satellite TV, licensed restaurant, cafe and bar, laundry, duty free shop, conference facilities, pool.

ATTRACTIONS
Waterfront residential, location, cultural performances, sightseeings, day cruising & fishing, friendly & efficient service

CREDIT CARDS
All major cards accepted

International Dateline Hotel is the best Hotel in Tonga, located in Nuku'alofa, Tongatapu, the capital of Tonga Island Group in South Pacific, within a few minutes walking distance from the central business district and has an ocean outlook to the North with the accommodation rooms overlooking the sea, sunrise and islands dotting the horizon.

ACCOMMODATION
After upgrading to and expansion of the International Dateline Hotel and re-commissioned by July 2003, total 126 guest rooms comprising the old 76 rooms and suites, new expanded 50 Suites composed 1 Royal Suite, 6 Executive Suites and 43 deluxe Superior rooms, plus a new conference hall, meeting rooms, two restaurants, business centre, duty-free shop and other commercial outlets are available. All rooms are air conditioned with refrigerator, coffee and tea-making facilities, mini-bar, ISD phone, colour TV, in house movies, international/domestic channels.

ROOM RACK RATE
Effective: 01st April 2005 - 31st March 2006

	Standard	Superior	Suite
Single	90	120	190
Twin, Double	105	140	190
Triple	120	150	-
Family	180 interconnecting rooms		

	Deluxe Superior	Executive Suite	Royal Suite
Single	190	400	2,600 (USD)
Twin, Double	220	450	2,600 (USD)

Note:
a) The room rate is quoted in Tongan Paanga except the Royal Suite is quoted in USD.
b) The room rate subject to 17.5% local taxes

International Dateline Hotel reserves the right to the Rate and Conditions.

FRIENDLY ISLANDER HOTEL

www.papiloa.com

LOCATION
Nuka'alofa, Tonga

EMAIL
papiloa@kalianet.com.to

PHONE/FAX
Ph (676) 23 810
Fax (676) 24 199

ADDRESS
Vuna Avenue, PO Box 142,
Nuku'alofa, Tonga

HOST
Mrs Papiloa Foliaki

FACILITIES
Lounge bar, restaurant,
squash courts, fresh-
water swimming pool,
conference and
meeting rooms.

Thinking about a vacation, why not come over to "Papiloa's Place" situated in the most beautiful and safest places in the world in Tonga. Appreciate and Experience Nature in it's natural form. The only remaining Polynesian Kingdom, and the only country in the Pacific never colonised.

ACCOMMODATION

Bungalows/Fales and Hotel Units. All accommodations are situated amongst the tropical gardens within the Friendly Islander property. Our Bungalows/FALES with Air-conditioning, private shower, fridge, tea/coffee making facilities and telephone or, our HOTEL UNITS containing basic kitchen facilities, private shower and toilet, table fans and telephone.

Both types have either one or two bedrooms and sleep between two to five persons.

BACKPACKER ACCOMMODATION

Yes, backpackers are welcome at the Friendly Islander too ... in a shared room with kitchen and bath facilities.

FAFA ISLAND RESORT

www.fafa.to

LOCATION
Nuku'alofa, Tonga

EMAIL
fafa@kalianet.to

PHONE/FAX
Ph (676) 22 800
Fax (676) 23 592

ADDRESS
PO Box 1444
Nuku'alofa, Tonga

FACILITIES
Licensed restaurant &
bar, boutique, library,
boat transfers, tour desk

ATTRACTIONS
Whitesand island
location, snorkelling,
diving, surf skiing, fishing

CREDIT CARDS
Amex, Diners,
MasterCard & Visa

ACCOMMODATION

13 beautifully appointed fales (bungalows) right on the beach, built in traditional Tongan style. The 8 superior fales and 5 new deluxe fales (incl. 2 specially designed and secluded honeymoon fales) have a spacious main room with a king size bed or twin beds and an extra room with single or bunk bed. The verandah is a few steps away from the sea. The bathroom is semi open with a private garden.

FEATURES

Situated 3.5 miles north of Nuku'alofa, (30 minutes sailing in Resort's own motor sailing boat) on a 7ha palm-covered island which is protected by a coral reef. A restaurant, open air cocktail bar, expansive verandah, boutique and library. A Robinson Crusoe hideaway where the only things warmer than the sun are the smiles.

ACTIVITIES

Nature walk, snorkelling, surf skiing, sailing, fishing, excursions to deserted island, scuba diving. Weekly Polynesian floorshow. Full Free Use of twice daily operating motor sailer (transfers only to be paid once), use of snorkelling gear, surfskis, volleyball, French boule, library and tour desk service.

FOR FURTHER INFORMATION

See our website for current rates, cancellation policy and booking details.

HEILALA HOLIDAY LODGE

www.heilala-holiday-lodge.com

LOCATION
Tofoa/Nuku'alofa
Kingdom of Tonga

EMAIL
quick@kalianet.to

PHONE/FAX
Ph (676) 29 910
Mob (676) 15 416
Fax (676) 29 410

ADDRESS
PO Box 1698, Nuku'alofa
Kingdom of Tonga

FACILITIES
Restaurant, coffee garden,
swimming pool, tv/game
room, conference room

CREDIT CARDS
Visa & MasterCard

Situated in exotic surroundings only 3kms south of Nuku'alofa city, with good bus and taxi services available. We provide you clean and cozy lodging with a friendly and personal service.
We offer a total of 10 units, ranging from Standard rooms to Tongan and Superior fales (bungalows). A complimentary breakfast is also served at our restaurant each morning and make sure (when you book in advance) to request for your complimentary International airport pick and and town (info) Tour. Some other services we provide are airport transfers, island tours, advice and arrangement for activities, luggage storage, and seasonal tropical fruits from our garden.
Rates range from US$20 to US$60 per night.

WATERFRONT LODGE

Waterfront Lodge

LOCATION
Nuku'alofa, Tonga
EMAIL
waterfro@kalianet.to
PHONE/FAX
Ph (676) 24 692, (676) 25 260
Fax (676) 28 059
ADDRESS
PO Box 211, Nuku'alofa, Tonga
HOST
Daniela and Paki Orbassano
FACILITIES
Air conditioning, king-size
bed, private verandah with
outdoor table and deck
chairs, IDD phone, Internet
access, satellite TV, mini-
fridge, tea and coffee
facilities, continental
breakfast included.
ATTRACTIONS
IDD prepayed phone card,
safety deposit box, foreign
exchange, car rental, airport
return transfer, tours and
island activities.
CREDIT CARDS
Amex, MasterCard & Visa.

The Waterfront Lodge offers the best private accommodation in the capital. The Lodge boasts a beautiful seaview, excellent services and luxury accommodation.
This charming property of eight large rooms is under Italian management and believes in paying special attention to each and every guest.
The atmosphere is intimate and home-like and the staff warm and friendly.
The guestrooms are inviting and luxurious, well appointed with Italian facilities and paintings by Gauguin, Hopper etc.
The Restaurant, arguably the most popular in the capital, features a large selection of seafood, homemade pasta and delicious desserts.

HOTEL NUKU'ALOFA

www.matangitonga.to

LOCATION
Nuku'alofa Tonga

EMAIL
sanft@kalianet.to
hotelnuk@kalianet.to

PHONE/FAX
Ph (676) 24 244
Fax (676) 23 154
Fax (676) 26 833

ADDRESS
PO Box 32
Nuku'alofa Tonga

FACILITIES
Air conditioned, fridge,
tea/coffee-making,
internet access

CREDIT CARDS
Amex, Diners,
MasterCard & Visa

Right in the heart of Nuku'alofa, this centrally located hotel has 24-hour reception, 10 large air-conditioned rooms which have refrigerators, tea/coffee-making facilities and are serviced daily.

All rooms have direct-dial international telephone. There is access to full secretarial services, including arrangements to make appointments.

Licensed restaurant serving the finest in international and local cuisine.

Prices: $94-$112. All rates are subject to government tax.

VAVA'U

NATURE'S PARADISE

A NATURE lover's paradise, the Vava'u group comprises some 34 islands, 21 of which are inhabited. It is widely regarded as Tonga's most scenic region. With an area of 115 square kilometres, the main island, also called Vava'u, is home to Tonga's second largest port, Neiafu. The entry is one of the most dramatic in the South Pacific.

Ships approach Neiafu by the 11-kilometre-long Ava Pulepulekai Channel to the landlocked Port of Refuge Harbour. Tonga's second largest town, Neiafu supports a large itinerant 'yachtie' population. When cruise ships come to port, the entire town is awash with the colour and excitement of a market-town ambience.

For those visitors fascinated by water sports, Vava'u is the place to stay. There's extensive charter boat operations and, from July to October, it's the place to watch humpback whales mate and calve. The sight of these enormous creatures of the deep at play is something visitors will remember forever. Snorkelling, scuba diving, sports fishing, and sea kayaking are all favoured pastimes.

GOING SWIMMINGLY

Under the waves, the extreme visibility – down some 30 metres through the clear, clean waters – makes journeys out to remote underwater caves and mysterious shipwrecks a delight.

The Vava'u Festival is held in the first week of May and has all manner of events ranging from the sporting to the cultural. Organised around the birthday of Crown Prince Tupouto'a (on 4 May), it includes a game fishing tournament and yacht race.

The search for high-quality and handsomely-made handicrafts becomes a special treat on Vava'u. Some of the islands in the groups have been settled for more than 2000 years and handicrafts have become something of a tradition. Shopping opportunities abound and it's possible to meet with the artists, weavers and artisans and purchase something unique. Like the rest of Tonga, Vava'u is a duty-free port with duty-free shopping at its most varied in Neiafu.

THE TONGAN BEACH RESORT

www.thetongan.com

LOCATION
Vava'u, Tonga

EMAIL
holidays@thetongan.com

PHONE/FAX
(676) 70 380

ADDRESS
PO Box 104 Neiafu,
Vava'u, Tonga

FACILITIES
Private facilities of hot
and cold showers,
electric ceiling fans,
fridges, tea/coffee
making, library, beach
towels & laundry service.

ATTRACTIONS
Beachfront location,
snorkelling, scuba diving,
sport fishing, swimming
with whales, sailing,
mountain biking,
deserted island
excursions and romantic
tree house.

CREDIT CARDS
Visa & MasterCard

ACCOMMODATION
12 recently refreshingly refurbished sun-dappled
rooms (twin, double or triple and including two
interconnecting rooms).

FEATURES
Situated a 15-minute boat ride (or 10km by road)
away from the township of Neiafu, The Tongan is
in the enviable position of having a beachfront
location on the island of 'Utungake with safe
swimming and snorkelling at all tides.

ACTIVITIES
"Where you can do it all ... or nothing at all" – we
can organise your outings for you and you will be
collected from our wharf as the local operators
pass by the resort to take you the short boat trip
for snorkelling and deserted island excursions,
scuba diving, sport fishing or swimming with
whales.

FINANCE
See our website for current rates, forms of payment and reservation details.

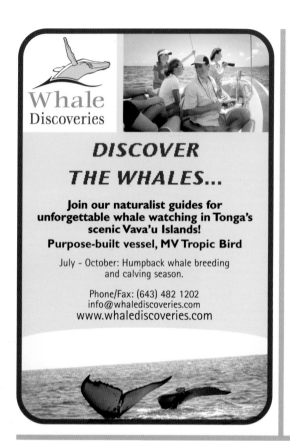

'EUA

UNSPOILT & AGELESS

'EUA lies 40 kilometres off the coast of Nuku'alofa. A ten-minute flight from Tongatapu brings visitors to the island; the ferry trip takes about two hours. Covering about 90 square kilometres, it is Tonga's third largest island.

The village of 'Ohonua, where the ferry from Nuku'alofa docks, is the centre of activities.

Hilly and thickly forested, it represents an age-old view of Tonga, offset with high cliffs at the northern end of the island. Anokula in northern 'Eua has a spectacular view above cliffs that drop away 120 metres. A little farther north is the Kahana Spring where the water is the clearest and purest in the kingdom.

Matalanga 'a Maui is great pit hidden in a plantation in the middle of island towards the southern end. There's a legend associated with it, of course, and it revolves around the god Maui. Climbing down into the pit, with its towering forest walls, is a special experience.

The birdlife around the Hafu Pool delights ornithologists. Amongst the many attractions is Tufavai Beach, considered to be the best place to laze away a few hours in the sunshine.

HA'APAI

STARTLING BEAUTY

THE Ha'apai islands group lies at Tonga's geographical centre. In the main, the 51 islands are low-lying coral atolls. The islands of Lifuka and Foa are joined by a causeway; at Pangia, on Lifuka Island, can be found the administrative centre of the region.

Other islands worthy of attention include Luahoko and Nomuka, which have some startlingly beautiful coral outcrops up to 45 metres high. Hunga Tonga and Hunga Ha'apai are volcanic islands which have remained peaceful for hundreds of years.

It was on Lifuka that Captain James Cook landed and his subsequent interaction with the locals led him to describe the surroundings as the Friendly Islands. At nearby Tofua, Fletcher Christian and the Bounty mutineers cast Captain William Bligh adrift on a journey that would extend some 6500 kilometres.

With an area of 110 square kilometres, there's enough long white beaches and beautiful areas for everybody to explore.

GRACEFUL ATTENTIONS

The friendliness of the people is legendary and this carries through to the present day with visitors enjoying a warm, generous welcome that continues throughout their stay. Independent travellers really consider the Ha'apai group to be a best-kept-secret and one that they hope will never be 'discovered' by mass tourism.

With its abundant wildlife and pristine natural beauty, Ha'apai is rapidly acquiring a reputation as an eco-tourism destination. Certainly, the staggering variety of marine – said to encompass some 1600 species of tropical fish alone – marks it as one of life's most impressive experiences.

Deepsea fishing for such prized catches as marlin, spearfish and tuna, brings in sportspeople from around the world.The dramatic nature of the region is marked by the volcanic peaks of Tofua and Kao to the west.

SANDY BEACH RESORT

LOCATION
Ha'apai, Kingdom of Tonga

EMAIL
sandybch@kalianet.to

PHONE/FAX
Ph (676) 60 600
Fax (676) 60 600

ADDRESS
PO Box 61, Pangai
Ha'apai, Kingdom of Tonga

CONTACT
Sigrid & Jurgen Stavenow

FACILITIES
Fridge, coffee/tea making, radio, fans, balconies, beach towels, rattan furniture, hot & cold water, shower, restaurant, bar, library

ATTRACTIONS
Beachfront location, fantastic swimming at all tides, whale watching tours
from August-November, Diving

CREDIT CARDS
Amex, MasterCard & Visa.

ACCOMMODATION
This first class resort comprises 12 bungalows situated in natural surrounding with balconies directly on the beach. Large luxury tiled room for 2 people with built-in wardrobes. The resort is not designed for children.

FEATURES
Located at FOA island in the unspoiled heart of Tonga, 10km north of Lifuka island Airport with access by car. Daily air service (except Sunday) from/to Nuku'alofa and several flights from/to Vava'u by Royal Tongan Airline.

On the most beautiful beach in Tonga, which allows swimming and other watersport activities at all tides. There are large numbers of beautiful reefs all within swimming distance, providing an abundance of colourful marine life

The fully licensed restaurant serves first class cuisine specialising in fresh fish and lobster.

Main building with bar, terrace (watching the sunsets with classical music).

No public bar, TV, discotheque/nightclub, traffic-noise etc! A dive base operates from the resort.

COURTESY ACTIVITIES
Return airport transfer by car. Snorkel/masks, bicycles, kayaks, canoes, guided kayak tours and bush and reef walks, shuttle to Pangai, Tongan Cultural Show.

EXTRA-FEE
Horseback riding, daytrips by boat to outer Islands. Scuba Diving Base: 'Happy Ha'apai Divers' at the resort.

FOR FURTHER INFORMATION
Phone, fax or see our website for rates, booking details and cancellation policy.

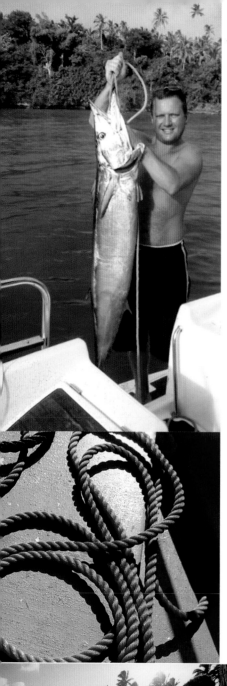

FISHING

TONGA is widely regarded as a 'fisherman's Kingdom' and it has the largest game fishing fleet in the South Pacific. With seven operators and nine boats - all between 25 and 35ft and all in survey - your chances of catching the mighty Blue Marlin in Tongan waters are better here than almost anywhere else in the world.

Game or sports fishing is easy and you have the luxury of day trips, as the fishing grounds are so close to the main settlements. The average charter is for 10 hours, the boats take four anglers, the tackle is first class and ranges from 12lb to 130lb and about 85 percent of catches are tag and release. Salt-water fly-fishing has tremendous potential while other species you are likely to catch are Marlin: On average reports are two to three Billfish shots a day per boat, Saltfish: Lots of Sails and they are both in offshore and inshore waters. Big Mahimahi: 15kg - 20kg has been consistent, especially Bulls. Wahoo: Plentiful in open water but go to the drop off areas at 40m-80m. Yellow Fin: Some good caught out wider, with fish up to 20kg being caught in the in-shore waters. Big Eye Tuna: Catching these fish by standard trolling methods is not that common. Dog Tooth Tuna: Good fishing fish around 15kg-25kg are being caught, particular at Fatamunga Island (South Bank).

Tonga consists of a string of islands stretching almost 425 kms and that means going from shallow to deep water (the Tongan trench, at 10 miles deep is the second deepest trench in the world) and you are never far from drop offs.

Sea Mounts - Nuku'alofa and Ha'apai) - there are three sea mounts close to the fishing grounds and a large reef system close to land. In Ha'apai you get the added attraction of Tofu and Kao volcanoes which dominate the horizon.

Drops offs - Vertical walls run 8kms to 11kms long and 700 metres deep. Distances between the 150 metre and 1000 metre drop off is at 50 metres. Expansive coral banks, 30 metres to 100 metres deep covers about 10 sq kms.

SAILING

THE waters around the Tonga group of islands of Vava'u are widely regarded as some of the best sailing waters in the world. Deep water, fine breezes, great anchorages, interesting restaurants miles from anywhere and space. Space to enjoy your sailing holiday, especially knowing that you will not have to be fighting for a spot at some tightly packed marina late in the afternoon.

The yachties are a special part of life in the 'capital' of Vav'u, Neiafu, and every Friday night they are out on the Port of Refuge Harbour pitting their racing sailing skills against the locals before dining at the waterfront restaurants of Ana's and the Mermaid.

A well-marked channel leads you away from Neiafu Harbour into the group of islands with more than 40 safe anchorages at your disposal. About a 20 minute sail will take you by the Tongan Beach Resort on your portside.

Down the track about four miles and Swallow's Cave comes into view on the western end of Kapa Island. Off to the west of Kapa is Tu'ungasika, a distinct pillar like island with awesome dive sites. From this point you have a choice of travelling south to Hunga Island on the west side or the east side. From the west you will pass an entrance 100 ft wide and 10ft deep into a calm sheltered lagoon. And not far away is Foiata Island. Going the other direction will lead you down a channel that has the legendary Mariner's Cave on the port side. The channel will take you into whale watching territory for humpbacks between July to the end of November - and often well into December.

'Euakafa is a larger uninhabited island with beautiful white sandy beaches and great snorkelling. South of here you can venture to some of the more remote smaller islands to find rare bird life in action. The tiny islands are only day anchorages.

Leave a chance for a last stop at Port Maurelle, the most popular place to anchor because of its central location and gorgeous sunsets.

MARINE & DIVING

IF it happens on the water, in the water or near the water...then Tonga is one destination that covers all marine activities. Ocean kayaking, whale watching, swimming with the whales, fishing, sailing, surfing, diving and snorkelling are offered by visitors by a band of truly professional operators.

Tonga is one of the few places in the world where you can swim with the mighty humpback whale and for many people it is a highly emotional experience. Tough young men have been known to weep after swimming with these amazing mammals.

The whale season extends from July to November and often in to December while other marine activities go on all year.

The diving industry is growing year after year as the word reaches out of the tremendous choice of dives. Many of the dives can be performed by all divers; a few of the dives need divers with a whole lot of experience. Each island has its special dive sites and they vary from the caves of 'Eua in the south to the wonderful coral gardens of Vava'u.

The magnificent clarity of the waters, the sprinkling of so many islands that means always somewhere sheltered to dive, the great sites and friendly people....the pretty soft corals, the lovely crinoids, the many underwater caves, the walls, overhangs, gorgonian fans and diverse fish life, the pretty coral shoulder areas and the unbelievably blue waters...all add up to a diving destination that is second to none.

The 'Green Wall' of Ha'ano Island has a long drop that plunges towards the great depths of the Tongan Trench, covered with a type of algae known as 'sea grapes', as well as soft corals: red, yellow, purple and white in colour. It's a fast flowing drift dive where you come to meet grey reef sharks and schools of tuna.

Tonga is definitely one of the world's best dive spots. It has drop-offs, sea mountains, caves . . . in fact, it has so many dive sites that it fulfils every wish a diver can have.

TREKKING

THE best trekking in Tonga can be found in 'Eua where you can walk through pristine forests in the 'Eua National Park, explore the rugged southern coastline, see panoramic views of the cliffs and beaches, descend through the rainforest to the sea or perch on the cliffs as seabirds fly past.

There are caves and chasms and waterfalls with pools to cool you off. 'Eua is the place in Tonga for feeling the sense of discover, remoteness and adventure.

'EUA NATIONAL PARK: LOOKOUT TRACK HIKE

This is an easy three-hour return walk from the forest nursery up to the Lokupo and Lauua Lookouts for spectacular views of the coat, cliffs and circling seabirds.

'EUA NATIONAL PARK: LOKUPO FOREST & COASTAL TREK

One of the best full day treks in the Pacific. A guide is essential as the trail descends steeply through tropical forest to Lokupo Beach then follows old lava flows and volcanic boulders to join the Veifefe Track. Great for fit people who are keen on nature and a bit of adventure it takes about seven hours and is not suitable for children under 12 years.

LAKUFA-ANGA: SOUTHERN LEGENDS HIKE

This hike takes you through fertile 'gardens' brimming with crops - taro, squash and cassava, through a small patch of forest and out onto the grasslands of the southern tip to the island. A place of legends and your guide will recount the stories as you walk. The trip takes about three hours.

FANGATAVE CAVES & BEACH TREK

A trek for the more adventurous as it involves scaling down (and later back up) some rock ledges. No technical climbing is involved and the scrambling up and down the ledges is fun and undertaken safely with guides. Hidden at the base of the cliffs is a spectacular sea cave system with fluted columns, stalactites and stalagmites. It takes about five and a half hours and is quickly becoming the most popular day trip on 'Eua.

ToursHideaway can arrange tours and treks. Phone: (00676) 50254 or 50255 Fax: (00676) 50128. Email: hideaway@kalianet.to

Tonga Visitors Bureau
and Representative Offices

Head Office – Tonga

Tonga Visitors Bureau
PO Box 37
Nuku'alofa, Kingdom of Tonga
Te: (676) 25 334
Fax: (676) 23 507
Email: info@tvb.gov.to
Website: www.tongaholiday.com

United States of America

Tonga Consulate
Suite 604, 360 Post Street
San Fransisco, Ca 94108
Tel: 781 0365
Fax: 781 3964

United Kingdom

Tonga High Commission
36 Moylneux Street
London WIH 6AB
Tel: 724 5828
Fax: 723 9074

VANUATU

RECALLING BALI HAI

VANUATU and its volcanic island of Ambae was immortalised by writer James Michener during World War II when, from his post on Espiritu Santo, he watched the island mysteriously disappear into the morning mist – it was the beginning of Bali Hai in his imagination and South Pacific to the world. For more than two generations Bali Hai has conjured visions of mystique and a magical, primitive Paradise.

Ambae is an exceptionally beautiful island and its legendary disappearing act is quite true. When seen from the east coast of Santo, the island is a clear blue pyramid rising from the ocean in the early morning light. But as the sun climbs higher, except for rare clear days, the island quickly disappears behind a glare of sea haze.

The country of Vanuatu is a Y-shaped archipelago of volcanic islands and submarine volcanoes in the South Pacific Ocean. There are more than 80 islands making up the archipelago, although many are no more than small islets or rocky outcrops. Of these, there are 13 major islands and nine have active volcanoes.

SWAYING PALMS

The largest islands, Espiritu Santo and Malekula, are on the western side of the archipelago's Y-shape. Ambae lies between the outstretched arms of the "Y" and the islands of Efate, Tanna, Erromango and Aneityum are located to the south.

Vanuatu is rich in underwater and underground caves formed by volcanic activity and the erosion of limestone and ash. Some caves, such as those at Siviri on Efate Island, stretch inland for miles. In recent years, a series of underground fresh water caves have been discovered in Espiritu Santo which are becoming increasingly popular with divers.

An unusual feature of the local geology is the formation of beach rock. In places like Santo, this beach rock has welded not only sand, but the remains of WWII machinery dumped at places like Million Dollar Point into one long beach of naturally cemented war refuse. Also on show is rock embedded with tens of thousands of Coca-Cola and 7 Up bottles.

Tanna is the country's most famous kava-producing region and home of the John Frum cargo cult. It also has Mount Yasur volcano which is considered one of the world's most accessible volcanoes, providing easy access to the crater for visitors. Erromango is best known for its giant kauri trees and sandalwood.

VANUATU
AT A GLANCE

VANUATU TOURISM OFFICE
PO Box 209, Pilioko House
Lini Highway, Port Vila , Vanuatu
Tel (678) 22 515/685/813
Fax (678) 23 889
Email: tourism@vanuatu.com.vu
Website: www.vanuatutourism.com

spirits or 1.5 litres wine, plus 100 cigarettes or 250 grams of tobacco or 50 cigars.

All food, fruits, animal products and plants must be declared upon entry into Vanuatu. Many such items are allowed though; some require a valid quarantine certificate from the country of origin.

It is wise to confirm flights 72 hours prior to departure. Your hotel reservation desk can assist or call the relevant local airline office direct.

For stays not exceeding 30 days, bona fide visitors who are nationals of Commonwealth countries, EU countries, Fiji, Japan, Norway, Philippines, South Korea, Switzerland and the United States. Visas are only obtainable from the Immigration Department, PMB 092, Port Vila, Vanuatu. Tel: (678) 22 354. Fax: (678) 25 492.
Email: vanuatuimmigration@vanuatu.com.vu
Website: www.vanuatutourism.com
Passenger Service Charge (departure tax) is VUV 2800 per person over the age of 12 years for international and VUV 400 for domestic for Port Vila, Espiritu Santo and Tanna. VUV 250 on the outer islands.

GEOGRAPHIC LOCATION

Previously known as the New Hebrides, Vanuatu forms an incomplete double chain of islands stretching from the north to the southeast, some 900 kilometres north of Sydney in Australia and 800 kilometres west of Fiji. The capital, Port Vila, is located 17 degrees 44 minutes South latitude, 168 degrees 19 minutes East longitude.

AIRLINES

International: Air Vanuatu has regular services from Auckland, Brisbane, Sydney, Noumea and Nadi. Other airlines operating to Vanuatu include Air Caledonie, Solomon Airlines and Air Pacific. Domestic: Vanair services all major islands in the country.
Bauerfield Airport is 10 minutes from the capital of Port Vila. Two other airports soon to receive international flights are Pekoa in Luganville on Espiritu Santo and White Grass Airport on Tanna.

ARRIVAL/DEPARTURE INFORMATION

Passengers over 15 years of age: 200 cigarettes or 250g of tobacco or 50g cigars or 100 cigarettes, 1.5 litres alcohol and two litres wine, 25cl litre eau de toilette and 10 centilitres perfume
A total of 50,000 vatu (approx $A600) in unused goods
Visitor personal effects are entered duty free One litre of

CURRENCY

The local currency is the Vatu. Although Australian dollars are accepted by many shops, restaurants and hotels in Vila and a few in Luganville (Santo), they are not readily accepted outside of town or throughout the islands.

CLIMATE

The dry season is May to October with an average temperature of 23 Celsius. The green season is from November to April with an average temperature of 28 Celsius.

ELECTRICITY

220-280 volts 50Hz AC.

HANDICRAFTS

There are some fine examples of traditional and contemporary crafts available including baskets and mats, carvings, shell and bead necklaces, head-dresses, ankle rattles, carved bowls, masks and tree fern figures. Traditional handcrafts sold to visitors are usually small copies of those created for traditional ceremonies such as gade-taking.

LANGUAGE

Bislama, French and English. 115 'Mother tongues' are in common use.

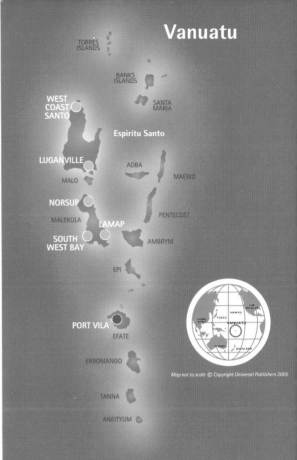

Vanuatu

POPULATION
Melanesian people born in Vanuatu are known as Ni-Van-uatu. The total population is around 190,000 (186,678 in the 2000 census). Many other nationalities also live here.

LOCAL CONSIDERATIONS
Light and casual but not too brief in public places. Tropical clothes for evening wear - no ties.

No vaccinations are required but anti-malarial precautions are recommended for visits to the outer islands.

Hospital facilities exist in Port Villa and Luganville, Espiritu Santo.

Neither tipping nor bargaining is considered as civilised behaviour. If you wish to express gratitude, send a T-shirt from your own country or a post card.

TELECOMMUNICATIONS
Worldwide satellite communications, 24-hour telephone, fax, email and Internet services are widely available. Internet cafes operate in Port Vila and Luganville.

TIME ZONE
11 hours ahead of Greenwich Mean Time.

TRANSPORT
Driving is on the right and cars and vans are available for hire. Taxis are plentiful and metered. Mini buses offer a frequent but not timetabled service - just flag one down and say where you want to go. The fare is VT100 a trip within Port Vila town limits and VT 200 to villages or areas out of town. Most inter-island travel is by air. Cruise ships call regularly.

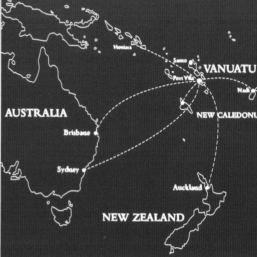

HUB OF ISLANDS MUCH TO DO

VANUATU is one of the widest spread of the Pacific Isles. Prior to independence from the United Kingdom and France in 1980, it was known as the New Hebrides. It was named after the Scottish islands by Captain James Cook in 1774.

A long history of inter-island and inter-village trading has given Ni-Vanuatu (the people of Vanuatu) several languages. However, more than 113 distinct languages and many more dialects are found throughout the group.

When Europeans arrived a lingua franca evolved. Its name, Bislama derived from the Bech-der-mer (sea cucumber) traders who developed a form of Melanesian Pidgin throughout the Pacific.

Main islands in the group are Espiritu Santo, Efate, Tanna, Erromango Pentecost, Ambrym, Ambae, Epi and Malekula. Each has its own attractions.

EFATE

EFATE – CENTRE OF THE ACTION

EFATE is home to the capital, Port Vila. Port Vila is the international gateway for Vanuatu and Efate is thus the more developed of the islands. There is a wide range of accommodation, great restaurants, nightlife, shopping and activities.

Port Vila is said to be the most beautiful capital in the Pacific. It lies on a horseshoe-shaped bay on the south-west coast of the island of Efate (pronounced "ef-art-ay"). Free of skyscraper office blocks, the sleepy capital is set within a magnificent natural harbour. Port Vila is a charming potpourri of cultures, blending elements of Melanesian, English, French and Chinese tastes.

Along the main street there are duty-free shops, restaurants and handicraft galleries. Port Vila Market comes alive every day, except Sunday when the stall holders return to spend a day with their families. Wander through rows of tropical fruits, vegetables, flowers, shells, artifacts and souvenir stalls. Savor the aroma of brewed coffee and freshly baked pastries tinged with the scent of blooming frangipani.

Within walking distance of the centre of town, a range of resorts offers a dozen different ways to cool off. Swim, snorkel or scuba dive. Try sailing, windsurfing, kayaking, fishing or even view the colorful coral in the harbor from a mini semi-submarine. Day and evening Cruises, exciting Jet boat adventures and Fishing charters all operate from the harbor's sea wall.

The harbour is so clean that the annual Vanuatu Ocean Swim is held here, swimming a 3.5km course around an offshore island.

There are many unusual things to do close to town such as the easy climb to view and swim in the Cascades waterfall along with a broad range of half and full day tours which explore Port Vila and Efate.

UNEQUALLED BEAUTY

Havannah Harbor on the northwest side of the island was the original European settlement but malaria and drought brought the early settlers 31 kilometers away to Port Vila. Moso Island forms the outer edge of Havannah Harbor, the largest natural harbour on the island of Efate. The harbour itself is undeveloped and strikingly beautiful with deep, clear waters.

All around Efate there are things to do or see. Driving around the island, visitors pass lonely coastlines, small villages, war relics, coconut palms and herds of grazing Charolais cattle. There are beach and island resorts within an hour's drive – bathe in a hot mineral spring or shower beneath a cascading waterfall, paddle or fish in a large freshwater lake, play a few rounds of golf or go horseback riding along a deserted beach. There are daily bus tours of the island and scenic plane flights or you can charter a sailboat and see it at your own pace from the water.

Vanuatu's Premier Tour Operator

Destination Pacific Islands
Ph: +678 22595 Fax: +678 22587
Email: destinationpacis@vanuatu.com.vu
www.destinationpacific.vu

Make a date with lady luck at the Palms Casino

Blackjack, Roulette, Baccarat, Slots, Link Jackpots.
Fun, friendly, fully air conditioned and licensed.

OPEN 11.30 am till late.
Located at Le Méridien Resort

PALMS CASINO B.P. 1111 - Port Vila, Vanuatu - Tel : (678) 24 310
Fax : (678) 22 394 - Email : casmanager@vanuatu.com.vu

Vanuatu AdVentures in Paradise

Tours and Travel · Inbound or Outbound · Shore Excursion Agents

Largest Professional Inbound Tour Operator in Vanuatu
Quality Transport and Service

- Airport Transfers by air-conditioned buses or limousine
- FIT Travel
- Groups

- Incentive & Conference
- Cruise Ship Excursions
- Full range of all-day and half-day tours

Phone: (678) 25 200 Fax: (678) 23 135
Email: paradise@vanuatu.com.vu
PO Box 1383, Port Vila, Vanuatu
Website: www.adventuresinparadise.vu

LE LAGON RESORT VANUATU

LOCATION
Port Vila, Vanuatu

EMAIL
res@lelagonvanuatu.com.vu

PHONE/FAX
Ph (678) 22 313
Fax (678) 23 817

ADDRESS
PO Box 86
Port Vila, Vanuatu

FACILITIES
Air conditioned, safes, room service, colour TV, tea & coffee-making, ironing board, IDD telephones, mini-bar, conference, seat up to 220 people, 24-hour reception desk, kids club free for 3 to 12-year-olds.

ATTRACTIONS
Scuba diving, croquet, white sandy beach, a wide range of free non-motorised watersports.

CREDIT CARDS
Amex, MasterCard & Visa

ACCOMMODATION
140 fully air conditioned and serviced rooms including bungalows and idyllic overwater island suites. Enjoy garden or tranquil lagoon views from your balcony or patio. Amenities include hairdryers, free in-house movies, iron and ironing boards, mini-bar, IDD telephones, colour TV, tea/coffee-making facilities, fridge and ceiling fans. In-room safes in all the rooms.

FEATURES
Vanuatu's leading resort for families and couples. Situated on 30.4 hectares of tropical gardens alongside the turquoise waters of Lagoon, with views to the magnificent Pacific Ocean. A true Melanesian cultural experience with its stunning location, cultural evenings and activities, along with traditional villages nearby.

ACTIVITIES
Free activities including tennis, scuba diving lessons in the pool and volleyball. Swim at the private white sandy beach, pool or outdoor spa.

There is a wide range of non-motorised watersports including catamaran sailing, windsurfing, outrigger canoes, kayaks, surf skis and snorkelling at no charge.

RATES
See our Website at www.lelagonvanuatu.vu for full booking details and our current rates.

SUNSET BUNGALOWS

www.sunset-bungalows.com

LOCATION
Port Vila, Vanuatu

EMAIL
sunsetbungalows
@vanuatu.com.vu

PHONE/FAX
Ph (678) 29 968, 29 969
Fax (678) 29 970

ADDRESS
Po Box 145,
Port Vila, Vanuatu

FACILITIES
Fully air-conditioned,
room service, laundry
service, restaurant, beach
barbecue.

ATTRACTIONS
Free water sports
activities, 10 minutes from
the airport, three minutes
from the city, shopping
close by, horse riding.

CREDIT CARDS
MasterCard & Visa

FEATURES

Traditional in design and tasteful in layout, Sunset Bungalows are set on the peaceful expanse of a tropical lagoon. In the surrounds of lush vegetation is a haven of absolute relaxation and one best suited to adults over 18 years of age.

The resort's spacious terraced bungalows offer outstanding views and private lagoon access and include air conditioning, mosquito nets, TV with three English-speaking channels, direct dial international telephone and Internet access, in room safes, mini bar and tea and coffee making facilities.

There are 10 over water, 46 square metre bungalows, four with shower or angle bath (specify when booking), four with cooking facilities and two suites with angle bath. In addition the resort has a 15 metre swimming pool with its own waterfall, an over water restaurant specialising in seafood, bilingual trained staff, the free use of water sports activities including canoes and pedal boats and access to public transport, massage and beauty services.

LE MERIDIEN PORT VILA

www.lemeridien.com

LOCATION
Port Vila Vanuatu

EMAIL
reservations@meridien.com.vu

PHONE/FAX
Ph (678) 22 040
Fax (678) 23 340

TOLL FREE
Australia 1800 622 240
New Zealand 0800 454 040
USA/Canada 1800 543 4300
France 0800 402 215
UK 0800 0282 840

ADDRESS
PO Box 215
Tassiriki Park
Port Vila Vanuatu

FACILITIES
Casino, safety deposit boxes,
tour desk, kids club,
babysitting services, business
centre, drug store, car rental,
24-hour room service

CREDIT CARDS
Amex, JCB,
MasterCard & Visa

ACCOMMODATION

Most of the 155 guest rooms over look lush tropical gardens or Erakor Lagoon. Our 10 exclusive Lagoon Bungalows are built in charming Melanesian style on a private island with spa bath, spacious living area and private sundeck with direct access to Erakor Lagoon.

FEATURES

Private white sand beach and conveniently located 5 minutes from Port Vila town and 15 minutes from Airport. La Verandah offers both international à la carte and buffet dining. Live music each evening in the Lobby Bar.

Vanuatu's largest pool has a swim-up bar and the Poolside Grill. Romantic tropical weddings to suit. Two spacious function rooms for up to 250 people theatre-style or 320 for cocktails.

ACTIVITIES

Kids club, Penguin Club, is open daily and is free for kids from 3-12 years. The Resort offers free non-motorised watersports including catamarans, sailing, kayaking, surf skis, canoeing and introductory scuba dive lessons in the pool. Two tennis courts, night tennis (new floodlights), and a 9-hole golf course and Vanuatu's only international Casino.

BLUEWATER ISLAND RESORT

www.bluewaterisland.com

LOCATION
Bluewater Island, 20kms from Port Vila

EMAIL
info@bluewaterisland.com

PHONE/FAX
Ph (678) 27 588
Fax (678) 27 604

HOST
Richard Kontos

FACILITIES
Transfers available, supermarket, licensed restaurant, in-house movies, watersports/recreation.

ATTRACTIONS
Cultural Events, Aquariums.

CREDIT CARDS
Bankcard, MasterCard, Visa, American Express

Located approximately 20 kms from Port Vila, at the mouth of the Rentapao River, Bluewater Island Resort extends over 40 hectares of tropical gardens. Dotted with dwarf coconut palms and multicoloured bougainvillea, this delightful haven exudes peace and tranquillity. With its own private island on the edge of the lagoon, one might be tempted to stay forever.

The Resort includes an ocean front restaurant, specialising in the freshest of seafood. Local delicacies such as the coconut crab, lobster, prawns are regularly available as well as an extensive menu of international cuisine.

Bluewater Island Resort offers a wide range of facilities for the active leisure seeker from tennis to windsurfing to game fishing (on request).

With traditional kava Nakamals built of local materials, a vast conference/ballroom on the resort, cultural activities and festivities are plentiful.

Bluewater Island Resort also boasts its very own Bluewater Aquariums. It is by far one of the last places on earth where you will hand feed sharks without having to get into the water. An experience not to be missed!

HIDEAWAY ISLAND RESORT & MARINE SANCTUARY

www.hideaway.com.vu

LOCATION
Port Vila, Vanuatu

EMAIL
info@hideaway.com.vu

PHONE/FAX
Ph (678) 22 963
Fax (678) 23 867

ADDRESS
PO Box 1110
Port Vila, Vanuatu

FACILITIES
Sand & coral beach, restaurant, bar, dive shop, sailboat

ATTRACTIONS
SCUBA diving, snorkeling, swimming, Underwater Post Office

CREDIT CARDS
MasterCard, VISA, Amex

ACCOMMODATION
Large Studio & One bedroom low-bank waterfront bungalows with fridge, tea/coffee making facilities. Twin share rooms & quad share dorms, ideal for the budget conscious. Only 15 minutes from town. Dive, wedding & group packages available. Beach restaurant & bar. Gift shop.

ACTIVITIES
PADI dive shop with full service rental & instruction. Beach volleyball, snorkeling, kayaks & sailboat. The world's only Underwater Post Office.

MARINE SANCTUARY
Snorkel right from the beach and handfeed thousands of tropical fish, or even mail a waterproof Underwater Postcard!

FOR FURTHER INFORMATION
www.hideaway.com.vu

IRIRIKI ISLAND RESORT

www.iririki.com

LOCATION
Port Vila Bay, Vanuatu
EMAIL
reservations@iririki.com
PHONE/FAX
Ph (678) 23 388
Fax (678) 23 880
ADDRESS
PO Box 230
Port Vila, Vanuatu
Sales Office Australia
Iririki Island Resort
PO Box 607 S
South Melbourne 3205
FACILITIES
Air conditioned, direct-dial phone, tea & coffee-making, in-house video. Room service & mini bars, hairdryers, pool, Internet access in all rooms
ATTRACTIONS
Private island, theme nights, own reef, snorkelling, sandy beach
CREDIT CARDS
American Express, MasterCard & Visa

ACCOMMODATION & AMENITIES
70 individual Island Bungalows, elevated above the ground to capture stunning tropical/water views. Harbour View Bungalows enjoy bay views from the gently sloping hillside location. Garden view are surrounded by tropical gardens. All bungalows are air conditioned. Waterfront bungalow enjoy uninterrupted water views.

FEATURES
The premier Resort in Vanuatu, located on a private Island and 3 minutes by free Resort Ferry to the Port Vila Waterfront. The feature of the Resort is Micheners Restaurant. A la Carte dining is offered nightly and the views across the harbour are stunning. The Resort caters for couples, singles and children over 12 years of age.
Iririki has a true Melanesian feel and the relaxing feel of the Lobby and Bali Hai bar that leads you out to the pool deck will have you immediately relaxed feeling like you have been on holidays for weeks.

SPORTS & LEISURE
Our Complimentary Watersports activities: Catamarans, Swimming, Kayaking, Sailboards, Canoes. Snorkelling equipment is also available free to guests for exploring 'Snorkeller's Cove' on Iririki Island. Para Sailing, Deep Sea & Reef Fishing can be arranged at the tour desk. Nautilus Dive offers Free Introductory Dive lessons.

MELANESIAN PORT VILA

www.melanesianportvila.com

LOCATION
Port Vila Vanuatu
EMAIL
melanesian@vanuatu.com.vu
PHONE/FAX
Ph (678) 22 150
Fax (678) 22 678
ADDRESS
PO Box 810
Port Vila Vanuatu
FACILITIES
24-hour reception, 24-hour room service, in-room safes, TV, in-house movies, IDD phones, tour desk, lobby shop, laundry, fridge with mini bar, bureau de change, conference rooms, 2 restaurants, 3 bars, coffee & tea-making, swimming pool & kids pool, 2 tennis courts with night lights, Club 21 Gaming Lounge
CREDIT CARDS
Amex, JCB, MasterCard & Visa

ACCOMMODATION
Choose from 52 air-conditioned rooms – 16 fan-cooled rooms with kitchenettes or 12 fully self-contained 1 and 2 bedroom apartments. There is also a presidential suite available. All accommodations have private balconies overlooking pool and gardens. All rooms are equipped with cable TV, complimentary in-house movies, IDD telephone, refrigerator, mini bar, tea/coffee making, iron & ironing board, hairdryer and ensuite bathrooms.

FEATURES
Situated only just minutes walking distance to the town centre, shopping, business, restaurant and beaches, making it the ideal place for either short or longer stays. Famous Italian/Mediterranean restaurants 'Gino's' is open 24 hours daily. Poolside Bar and Grill open daily for light meals. An ideal hotel location for either the business or a family holiday.
Two tennis courts and the famous Club 21 gaming lounge are all situated on the premises.
A free continental breakfast is provided for all guests.

ACTIVITIES
In addition to our tennis courts and pool our tour desk is able to provide excellent guided tours and activity programmes to suit anyone.

FOR FURTHER INFORMATION
Visit our website.

BENJOR BEACH CLUB

www.benjor.vu

LOCATION
Port Vila, Vanuatu

EMAIL
benjoraustralia
@ozemail.com.au

PHONE/FAX
Ph/Fax (678) 26 078

ADDRESS
Port Vila, Vanuatu

ATTRACTIONS
fabulous snorkelling, wedding chapel, tennis court, BBQ facilities, giant checker board, petanque court, volley ball, glass bottom kayaks, 200 metre golf driving range, phone/Internet on request, babysitting, ceiling fans, tea/coffee, DVD, laundry service, restaurant & bar

CREDIT CARDS
Amex, MasterCard, Visa

Located on 23 acres, with 600 metres of oceanfront, Benjor Beach Club is a fabulous boutique Resort which can cater for both romantic getaways and family fun. We are only 10 mins from town and only 5 mins from Hideaway Island, Botanical Gardens, Seahorse Riding Ranch, Port Vila Golf Course and the fabulous Cascades Waterfalls. Choose from 1 Bedroom, Studio (with kitchenette and spa bath), or 4/5 bedroom Luxury Villas. Let us organise your wedding, honeymoon or simply a relaxing stay in one of the world's true paradises!

PARADISE COVE RESORT

www.paradisecoveresort.net

LOCATION
Port Vila, Vanuatu

EMAIL
paradisecove@
vanuatu.com.vu

PHONE/FAX
Ph (678) 22 701
Fax (678) 22 693

ADDRESS
Box 389 Port Vila Vanuatu

AMENITIES
Tea and coffee, ceiling fan, cooking facilities, breakfast included, airport transfer, town transfer, public phone, laundry, baby sitting, massages, swimming pool

CREDIT CARDS
MasterCard, Visa, Anz access.

ACCOMMODATION
Situated on its own private beach with wonderful snorkelling, Paradise Cove Resort offers ten spacious bungalows in a tropical garden for a relaxing holiday in a peaceful and quiet atmosphere. Each bungalow features one or two bedrooms, living room, bathroom and a shaded verandah with deck chairs and hammock. A few steps from the beach there is a bar and restaurant serving local food and international menu.
The resort has its own private bus running day and night transfers.

ACTIVITIES
Snorkelling, diving, glass-bottom kayaks, bush walking, beach volley, mountain bike rentals, all tours and excursions.

ERAKOR ISLAND RESORT

www.erakor.vu

LOCATION
Port Vila

EMAIL
resort@erakor.vu

PHONE/FAX
Ph (678) 26 983
Fax (678) 22 983

ADDRESS
PO Box 24, Port Vila, Vanuatu

FACILITIES
Tropical walking tracks, free watersports for inhouse guests, secluded beaches, open air chapel, romantic dining, regular entertainment, scuba diving, snorkelling excursions, tour desk

CREDIT CARDS
Amex, MasterCard & Visa

Erakor Island Resort is a beautiful unspoiled Island paradise, situated on its own private 16 acres surrounded by white sandy beaches and crystal clear water. Having just completed major refurbishments, Erakor consists of 21 superb absolute waterfront bungalows, a new overwater restaurant/cocktail bar, new watersports centre and a new dive lodge. The Resort has a 24-hour complimentary ferry from Port Vila, which is only a 5-minute bus ride away. Enjoy the beauty of staying on a quiet tropical island with easy access to everything off the island, Erakor offers all the facilities of a major resort, but in a relaxed and secluded atmosphere of its own ... pure seclusion without isolation! Sole island hire is available for groups.

BUYING REAL ESTATE IN VANUATU

THERE are no restrictions on foreigners buying property. You do not need a Vanuatu Investment Promotion Authority (VIPA) Investor's Certificate or a business licence. If a purchase requires a business licence then you would need a VIPA approval and a business licence in your name, or in a local company's name. Property is registered as a leasehold title. The Minister of Lands is the Lessor in the urban areas, and in many rural leases where the customary ownership is not yet established. There is no requirement for property owners or holders of Vanuatu residency permits to reside in Vanuatu.

The maximum term of a lease is 75 years. Many leases are 50 years from their creation or from Independence on 30 July 1980. In 2003 Parliament passed a law enabling any urban lessee to surrender their existing lease title, and either extend a lease that is currently less than 75 years up to 75 years or, where a lease is already for a period of 75 years, to renew the lease for a full period of 75 years from the date of renewal for a payment of fees. The Vanuatu Strata Title Act means it is now possible to strata title existing buildings and to create strata titles for new apartment and commercial buildings.

Commercial banks accept leasehold titles as security for loans. Mortgages and 'Cautions' are registered on the leasehold titles, as they would be on freehold and leasehold titles in other countries. Banks typically require 20 per cent for residential loans and up to 50 per cent for commercial loans from the borrower. Ten per cent is the standard contract deposit when a sale agreement is exchanged between a buyer and seller. Deposits are held in trust, till settlement. The law does not oblige purchasers to use a solicitor but it is wise to seek legal advice and representation, especially if you are entering the Vanuatu market for the first time.

VAT (currently 12.5 per cent) is not payable by the purchaser on residential property. VAT is payable by a builder if they sell a house they have built or if a property developer creates a land subdivision for sale. As a rule VAT is payable by the purchaser on the sale of commercial property and can be claimed back if it is a registered VAT entity. A 'one – off' sale of a commercial property where the seller is not registered for VAT and has not claimed back VAT for expenses on the property may not be subject to VAT. Specific enquires should be made to the VAT Office, or to a solicitor or a professional dealing with VAT issues.

The usual outgoings on property in Vanuatu are: -
1.   Municipal Property Tax (in the Urban Zones) paid every six months.
2.   Annual Lease ('ground') rent
3.   Insurance
4.   Rent Tax on residential property (or VAT on commercial) is 12.5 per cent of gross income.

Private parties can agree to a sale in any currency. There are no restrictions in sending foreign currency into or out of Vanuatu.

There are no restrictions on a foreigner selling property in Vanuatu. If a vendor is up to date with their outgoings and lease rent they will be able to obtain the Lessor's Consent to transfer the title. Encumbrances such as mortgages are discharged at settlement.

The vendor has no costs in a sale transaction except agents commission and legal fees. There are no fees or taxes on the sale, unless VAT is applicable.

NB: Laws, Government regulations and fees may be subject to change from time to time so it is advisable to seek advice as to the current situation.

TANNA

UNSPOILT BY TIME

ACCORDING to archeologists, people moving southward through central Vanuatu first occupied Tanna in about 400BC. Captain James Cook was the first European to come to Tanna in August 1774, after seeing the glowing light of the island's volcano in the sky.

Today, the approximately 20,000 inhabitants have retained much of their original custom and culture with the exception of one group – the John Frum cargo cult. The cult is thought to be the response to the sudden and mysterious appearance in their midst of foreigners, principally Americans, during World War II. Its belief system is that there are gods responsible for such magical goods as jeeps, the refrigerator and Coca-Cola.

However, the typical islanders recognise the importance of their old customs and many have turned their back on modern ways preferring the traditional way of life. The Nekowiar or Toka ceremony is generally the largest and most impressive. The festival is held every three to four years and goes on for three days and nights.

INSIDE THE EARTH

The village hosting the ceremony tries to better the previous one in the quantity of food and gifts (pigs, mats, etc.) offered to the guest villages. A beauty contest takes place where women and men elaborately paint their faces. Other ceremonies include the annual yam festival, circumcision rituals and marriages. Such ceremonies feature the unique Tannese face painting that is seen frequently in photos and posters on Vanuatu.

The Mount Yasur volcano is the island's most famous site and is considered to be the safest and most easily accessed volcano in the world. Four-wheel-drive transport takes visitors to within 150 metres of the crater rim with a 10-minute walk to the brink of the broiling maelstrom below. It is a live volcano and a tour at night when the fiery display of erupting lava is the most spectacular.

Tanna also has a coffee plantation which produces one of the country's best known exports – Tanna Coffee.

VANUATU

FRIENDLY BUNGALOWS TANNA

www.friendly-bungalows-tanna-vanuatu.com

WHITE GRASS OCEAN RESORT

www.whitegrassvanuatu.com.vu

LOCATION
South East Tanna

EMAIL
friendlybungalows
@vanuatu.com.vu

PHONE/FAX
Ph (678) 26 856
Fax (678) 26 856

ADDRESS
PO Box 601
Port Vila Vanuatu

FACILITIES
Tours and transfers by 4WD
arranged. Most currencies,
credit cards and travellers
cheques accepted

Tanna's most unique resort, situated in a small corner of paradise and surrounded by custom villages. Our individually designed and decorated bungalows are built beside the ocean, in a true Melanesian style. Each has its own bathroom with shower and WC. They are comfortably furnished, with terraces and hammocks.
The resort is only 6km from the magnificent Yasur volcano, 4km from the hot springs of Sulphur Bay and the John Frum village. Our beach and reef offer excellent swimming and snorkelling, in crystal clear waters. The restaurant serves a variety of French, English and Island-style meals with a wide choice of drinks.

LOCATION
Tanna Island, Vanuatu

EMAIL
whitegrasstanna@vanuatu.
com.vu

PHONE/FAX
Ph (678) 68 688
Fax (678) 68 677

ADDRESS
PO Box 5
Lenakel
Tanna Island, Vanuatu

FACILITIES
Restaurant, bar, tennis,
badminton, volley ball, 3-
hole pitch n putt golf, gift
shop, laundry, tour desk,
4WD safari tours.

ACCOMMODATION
An ideal starting point from which to explore this extraordinary island, White Grass Ocean Resort is situated only minutes from the airport, with 12 Melanesian style bures overlooking the Pacific Ocean. Set amongst 6 acres of beautifully landscaped gardens, the resort has many activities on site and offers Virgin Reef snorkelling, sea kayak safaris, mountain bikes and many 4WD safari tours including Mt Yasur Volcano, custom villages and underwater caves. The restaurant serves the freshest lobster and seafood and is designed to take full advantage of the amazing ocean views and sunsets.

"If paradise exists, then this must be the front door."

VILLAGE ACCOMMODATION and SAFARIS

Your Vanuatu Inbound operator for all your soft adventure needs

Discover the islands of fire and magic

ISLAND SAFARIS of *Vanuatu*

For all your travel needs throughout the islands:

Cultural, nature and adventure tours
Domestic air reservations & ticketing
Hotels in Vila and all islands, airport transfers
The widest choice of tours to the outer islands
Quick and efficient, reliable information and booking service

PO Box 133, PORT VILA, Vanuatu
Tel: (678) 23288 Tel/Fax: (678) 26779
email: islands@vanuatu.com.vu
For further information consult our website: www.islandsvanuatu.com

PACIFIC TRAVEL FACT FILE 30TH EDITION 313

ESPIRITU SANTO ISLAND

ACTIVITY MECCA

AN hour's flight north from Port Vila is the largest island in the Vanuatu group. In the 17th century, the Espiritu Santo islands were the first of the Vanuatu group be discovered by Europeans. Visually stunning, the jewel-like islands have powdery-white sand beach fringed with coconut palms.

During World War II, the writer James A Michener was stationed on Santo and such was its effect that he was inspired to write the legendary 'Tales of the South Pacific' – the source for the musical South Pacific.

During the course of the war, more than 100,000 troops and support staff were stationed on Espiritu Santo and the liner-turned-troopship SS President Coolidge and the destroyer USS Tucker sank in Santo Harbour. These ship wrecks and the surplus military equipment the US Army dumped at Million Dollar Point make the region a mecca for scuba divers in the South Pacific. Exploring Fresh-water caves is also becoming popular with the recent discovery of connecting sinkholes and caverns.

The surrounding isles and coast line offer exceptional coral gardens, contributing to the numerous sand beaches which range in color through powdery white, gold, orange and to black on the nearby isles of volcanic rock.

The jungle reveals expeditions through caves and ravines where trekking and floating along rivers offer the only way forward. The Millennium Cave invites trekkers inside with cascading waterfalls painting its inner walls and then propels them with running waters to the exit and into the river beyond.

COLORFUL PAST, BRIGHT FUTURE

Prior to WWII, the island was a hub of activity as one of the South Pacific's largest producers of Copra, from the many plantations established in the late 1800's. In its plantation heyday, over 4000 expatriate farmers and their families, mostly of French descent, lived on the island.

Most of these plantations still operate and as you head out of the capital of Luganville, plantation staff can still be seen at the base of coconut trees, manually harvesting the coconut flesh. Old lorries stacked 3 meters high with bags of dried coconut, ply the coral roads as they transport their harvest to the processing plant. As a slow steady and steady rhythm of plantation life continues, the smell of coconut oil permeates the air and envelopes the senses.

Espiritu Santo is fast becoming Vanuatu's Mecca for nature adventurers with exploration of the island's jungles revealing many unique experiences. Paddling up the Riri River in local dugout canoes provides interaction with local communities and exposes the pristine river waters and their source, Santo's famous blue holes. These mini lakes are fed by underground rivers where water is filtered through coral and volcanic rock, deep below the earths crust.

DINING DIVERSIONS IN VANUATU

WITH its history shared equally between the British and the French, Vanuatu has made a name for itself throughout the Pacific for its superb cuisine and for its large variety of excellent restaurants. Whatever your tastes are they can be catered for.

Popular cuisines are French/European, Asian and custom South Pacific fare. Around Port Vila alone there are some 45 eateries. Try the local succulent tender beef which is recognised as not only the South Pacific's best beef, but also one of the worlds best. Also exceptional is the local seafood, such as the poulet fish (Long tailed deepsea snapper), named so because it was thought to be as tasty as chicken.

Other local specialties include ground pigeon, snails, flying fox, prawns or the famous Tahitian raw-fish salads.

A wide range of imported and local foods is available in the supermarkets as are wines, beers and spirits. Wines include selctions from Australia, New Zealand and France. Don't forget to visit the local markets for all your locally grown fresh fruit and vegetables.

VOLCANOES AND MAGIC

AMBRYM'S main features are its twin volcanoes, Mt Marum and Mt Benbow, and its seething lava lakes. As Ni-Vanuatu believe that magic is strongest on islands with active volcanoes, Ambrym is considered the country's most mystical. The Rom Dance, which occurs in August, is the island's most striking ceremony.

Ambae Island, the inspiration for South Pacific's Bali Hai, has a famous black sand beach called Vureas. The island's mountain, Lombenben, is often blanketed by mist and rain which has created a fine cloud forest. Lakes, jungle and craters make up this unusual area.

EXOTIC ISLAND EXPERIENCES

Epi is home to a school of dugong, which are friendly to tourists. It also offers many white or black sand beaches and inshore reefs. A well run guesthouse on the island provides a wonderful bases for exploration.

Malekula was the site of Vanuatu's last cannibal activity in 1969. The history of this area is fascinating to explore as is the diverse culture which includes monoliths up to 3 metres high at Vao.

Far north of the archipelago are the Banks and Torres Islands. The Torres Islands offers dazzling white sand beaches with local fishing practices said to be unique to the region. The Banks Islands are rich with stone relics and spectacular trekking.

LAND DIVING

LEAPS OF FAITH

PENTECOST Island is famous for its annual yam festival and 'bungee' jump. In April, as soon as the first yam crop appears, the villagers set to work building tall wooden towers at various sites in the far south of the island. These towers are usually 18-23 metres tall.

On chosen days, men and boys dive from these towers with only two long springy vines tied to their ankles to break their fall. Land-diving occurs in various places, including Lonorore Airfield. Two sites in the hills are set aside providing access to tourists and dives take place one day a week, generally Saturday during the season. The Pentecost visit is generally a day visit as accommodation opportunities on the island are limited.

Vanuatu
Another time, another pace

We Are Here To Help You!

Our friendly staff at the Vanuatu Tourism Office at Pilioko House are here to answer any questions or problems you have during your stay in Vanuatu. We offer advice, have a large range of leaflets, guides and maps and can help you find accommodation and contacts in most islands of Vanuatu.

Vanuatu Tourism Office

PO Box 209
Pilioko House
Lini Highway, Port Vila
Vanuatu
Tel: (678) 22 515/22 685/22 813
Fax: (678) 23 889
Email: tourism@vanuatu.com.vu
Internet: www.vanuatutourism.com

UNITED STATES
Sue Herrick
VTO Representative USA
245 Mt, Mt Hermon Road
PMB-B, Scotts Valley
CA, 95066 USA
Tel: (831) 335 5238 Fax: (831) 335 5239
Email: shenterprises2@aol.com

AUSTRALIA
Carol Gordon
VTO Representative Australia
4/14 Ewart Street, Dulwich Hill
NSW 2203
AUSTRALIA
Tel: (612) 9558 8011
Email: vtoaustralia@tourism.vu

NEW ZEALAND
Jacquie Carson
VTO Representative NZ
P O Box 17427, Greenlane
Auckland, NZ
Tel: (09) 277 6065
Fax: (09) 277 6065
Email: j.carson@xtra.co.nz

JAPAN
Hiroshi Tomita
South Pacific Tours Japan INC
NKK Building, 3F 2-18-2
Nishi-Shinbashi, Minatoku
Email: Hiroshi.Tmt@sptj.co.jp
Tel: 81(03) 5408 7471
Fax: 81(03) 5408 7472

NOUMEA/ EUROPE
Martine Lasnier
P O Box 1163
PORT VILA
VANUATU
Ph: (678) 22 515
Email: martine@vanuatu.com.vu

OTHER
ISLANDS

S OME of the best, most exciting, relaxed, friendly, romantic and culturally diverse
destinations may not necessarily be those whose names loom large in the tourism
brochures, and everything one imagines a tropical paradise should be Pitcairn Island,
traditional home of the Bounty mutineers. There's Nauru, whose fortunes were founded on
phosphate, the mysterious Easter Island, which is part of Chile yet lies 3600 kilometres from
the South American nation and Wallis and Futuna, the smallest of France's Pacific Ocean
territories.

Tuvalu is one of the smallest independent nations in the world. Tokelau revels in being a
haven of peace and tranquillity far from the hustle and bustle of the outside world.

DIFFICULT CHOICES

Although amazingly diverse, these islands provide something different. In some, tourism
facilities are limited and their isolation makes getting there a challenge. In others, greeting
visitors and making them feel at home are important aspects of their lifestyle.

The unifying link between all these islands is the sense of hospitality and range of
activities, some totally unique in terms of sights and sounds and experiences, that await the
visitor.

Turquoise waters, sheltered lagoons, long stretches of deserted beaches – these are the
stuff of tourist brochures. On closer examination, these islands provide much that is different
yet they remain resolutely Pacific in appeal.

Scuba diving, snorkelling, swimming, hiking long mountain trails through pristine
rainforest and sharing an amazing lifestyle that has changed little in hundreds of years – that's
the essence of the Pacific Islands. It's an appeal that draws visitors from around the world and
will continue to do so as long as adventure beats within visitors' souls.

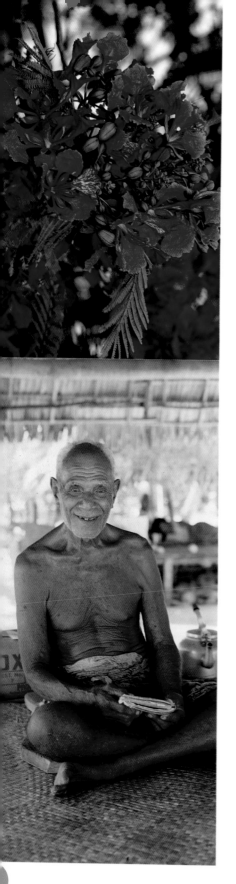

AMERICAN SAMOA

THE HEART OF POLYNESIA

THE only American territory south of the Equator, American Samoa presents something of a contrast to other Pacific islands. Although it has none of the high-rise resorts of Hawaii, the lifestyle still has much in common and it is light-years removed from neighbouring Samoa.

The seven (six of which are inhabited) islands of American Samoa present a never-ending series of delights and fascinating contrasts. Visitors will find that despite the often Americanised atmosphere, one thing remains constant – the warmth and friendliness of the Samoan people. Samoa is the heart of Polynesia.

With a land area of 197 square kilometres, American Samoa is bordered by Niue to the south, Tokelau to the north, Samoa and Tonga to the west and the Cook Islands to the east. The main islands include Tutuila, Aunu'u and the Manu'a Group of Ofu, Olosega and Ta'u. Hawaii lies 4000 kilometres to the north-east.

Tutuila is the largest island home to the magnificent Pago Pago Harbour, actually a submerged volcanic crater, immortalised by Somerset Maugham in Rain. Fagatogo is the largest town and overlooks the harbour with the administrative centre of Utulei just to the east. Tutuila is 32 kilometres long and has an area of 91 square kilometres.

STARS AND STRIPES

Just off the eastern extremity of Tutuila is Aunu'u Island. A natural wonderland, it boasts Red Lake, a lake jammed full of eels, and Pala Lake, a lake of red quicksand.

One hundred kilometres to the east is the Manu'a Group, which provides a more relaxed and traditional experience.

Polynesian Airlines and Samoa Air provide international services, while Hawaiian Air connects Samoa with Hawaii. All international arrivals disembark at Pago Pago International Airport.

American Samoa is three hours behind US Pacific Standard Time. English is the second language of a majority of the population. Most of the younger generation speak English, although Samoan is used in the home.

Linguistic and cultural evidence suggests that the first Samoan inhabitants migrated from the west about 3000 years ago, possibly by way of Indonesia, Vanuatu, Figi and Tonga to the eastern tip of Tutuila near the village of Tula.

Dutch explorer Jacob Roggeveen arrived in the Manu'a Group in 1722. By the 1860s, Pago Pago was a major refuelling point for shipping between San Francisco and Australia.

YAP

THE MYSTERIOUS ISLE OF STONE MONEY

KNOWN as the Mysterious Isle of Stone Money, Yap is a wonderful mix of past, present and future, where an ancient culture exists side by side with the 21st century. Located in the Western Caroline Islands, Yap is considered the most traditional corner of Micronesia. Opened for tourism in 1989, Yap offers a unique glimpse into Pacific Island culture. Centuries of old stone paths meander through lush tropical flora leading to thatched villages where traditional Men's Houses stand lined with huge disks of Stone Money.

More recently Yap has been recognised as a world-class dive destination where the magnificent Manta Rays of Yap appear daily. Skin Diver magazine calls Yap 'the most interesting island in Micronesia' and rates Yap as one of its top three dive sites!

Whether for business or pleasure, Yap has accommodations that will fit your needs. Choose from luxury resorts, full-service hotels, economical inns, home stay rooms and traditional faluw-style accommodations. All locations have up-to-date contact information for your reservation needs some of which offer online reservations for your convenience

PALAU

ENCHANTMENT AWAITS...

PALAU offers you the world's most beautiful tropical paradise. Famous for its diving, Palau rated as one of the world's best diving destinations by scuba aficionados. And why not...Palau has unspoiled reefs, caves and walls with the most amazing array of marine life you can ever imagine.

Palau beckons to you with some of the world's most awesome natural wonders. Imagine the whitest beaches you will ever see, gardens of coral just beneath the clearest waters, lakes filled to the brim with 'sting less' jellyfish. Forests, waterfalls and caves that have never been ravaged by man, and hundreds of islands of the purest beauty abound all along our pristine archipelago. Palau offers you the world's most beautiful tropical paradise.

Palau offers the traveller a wide variety of hotel accommodations, from full-service, luxury resorts and moderately priced bungalows, to economical motels and bungalows modeled on traditional architectural styles. While many of Palau's guests prefer to stay in the town of Koror, where most resorts and motels are located, some prefer the more private and secluded bungalows of the northern and southern islands. Whether price, comfort, or lifestyle is your considerations, Palau's natural beauty ensures a pleasant experience and memorable stay.

TUVALU

SMALL BUT PERFECTLY FORMED

THE seven atolls and two islands that make up Tuvalu also make up one of the smallest independent nations in the world. Tuvalu lies west of the International Date Line and 1000 kilometres north of Fiji just below the Equator.

There are no mountains, waterfalls or natural streams. The remoteness and relative isolation of Tuvalu appeal to many visitors. The islands are very small and separated by significant distances of nothing but water.

Tuvalu includes Vaitupu, Niulakita, Nukufetau Atoll, Nui Atoll, Niutao Atoll, Nanumea Atoll, Nukulaelae Atoll and Nanumaga Atoll. The capital is Funafuti Atoll, which has a vast lagoon measuring 24 kilometres in length by 18 kilometres.

Air Fiji has regular flights to Tuvalu. The legal currency is the Australian dollar. Tuvalu has a pleasant, tropical climate usually with little variation day or night of about 30° Celsius.

FAR FROM THE EVERYDAY

At their highest points, the islands are four metres above sea level and provide the classic image of blue sea and sky, white breakers along the fringing reefs, sand and swaying palms. Within the lagoons, the contrast between the colours of the deep and shallow water, the beach and vegetation is especially dramatic.

The smaller uninhabited atoll islets surrounding the lagoons are a unique attraction. The natural flora comprises only a restricted number of species. Pandanus and salt-tolerant ferns predominate. The few areas of atoll scrub are interesting and provide a valuable nesting habitat for birds. Other rare habitats include the uncommon but important mangrove areas.

Because of the remoteness of the islands and the present lack of speedy and regular transport, visitors usually only experience the immediate surrounds of Funafuti. The outer islands have attractions but are accessible only by boat. Only one hour from Funafuti lies Funafala, which is a true tropical experience.

The ancestors of Tuvalu's people are believed to have been Polynesians who arrived on the islands about 2000 years ago. Under the leadership of Chiefs known as "aliki" traditional Tuvaluan society continued for hundreds of years before it underwent significant changes with the arrival of European traders in the 1820s.

A DISTINCT HISTORY

Even greater changes took place when Samoan pastors of the London Missionary Society arrived in the 1860s. Tuvaluans soon embraced the new faith and virtually all the people are now Christians. Religion plays an important part in everyday life, although much of the previous culture and traditions are retained.

Tuvalu (then known as the Ellice Islands) first came under British jurisdiction in 1877. In 1892, Tuvalu became part of the British Protectorate of the Gilbert and Ellice Islands. Tuvalu was legally separated from the Gilbert Islands (now Kiribati) in October 1975, following overwhelming support for separation in a referendum held the previous year. The country became an independent constitutional monarchy and the 38th member of the Commonwealth in October 1978.

NAURU

FOUNDED ON INDUSTRY

IT was the phosphate industry that put Nauru on the map and it was the phosphate industry that forever altered the landscape. A small, oval-shaped island with a land area of just 21 square kilometres, it was first sighted by Europeans in 1798. A century of mining has stripped four-fifth of the land area, especially in the central plateau which now resembles a barren moonscape of jagged coral pinnacles up to 15 metres high. The Nauru Government is firmly committed to the rehabilitation of the mined areas

The Republic of Nauru lies 42 kilometres south of the Equator. Its nearest neighbour is Banaba, part of Kiribati, 305 kilometres to the east. Nauru lies 4000 kilometres from Sydney. Owing to its small size, Nauru has no capital. The island is surrounded by a coral reef, exposed at low tide and dotted with pinnacles. The island has a fertile coastal strip 150-300 metres wide. Coral cliffs surround the central plateau. The highest point of the plateau is 65 metres above sea level.

The only fertile areas are the narrow coastal belt, where there are coconut palms, pandanus trees and indigenous hardwoods such as the tomano, and the land surrounding the Buada Lagoon, where bananas, pineapples and some vegetables are grown. Some secondary vegetation grows over the coral pinnacles.

The population of Nauru is estimated at 9500 people. The majority are indigenous Micronesian-descended Nauruans with the remainder consisting of other Pacific islanders, Filipinos, Chinese, Indians and Europeans.

The climate is tropical with sea breezes. North-east trade winds blow from March to October. Daytime temperatures range from 24 degrees Celsius to 34 degrees Celsius. The monsoon season is November to February. During World War II, Nauru was subject to Allied bombing following its occupation by the Japanese. After the war, the island became a UN Trust Territory, administered by Australia in a similar partnership to the previous League of Nations mandate, and it remained a Trust territory until independence in 1968. Legislative and Executive Councils were established in 1966, giving the islanders a considerable measure of self-government.

In 1967, the Nauruans contracted to purchase the assets of the British Phosphate Commissioners and in June 1970 control passed to the Nauru Phosphate Company.

A road circles the island and hire and self-drive cars are available. Vehicles keep to the lefthand side of the road and the island speed limit is 60 kilometres per hour. Tours of Nauru's fascinating mining plateau are readily available. Other activities for visitors include deepsea fishing, snorkelling on the reef, golf and tennis. Numerous World War II military sites are spread throughout the island and such relics as pillboxes, bunkers and weaponry are easily seen.

WALLIS FUTUNA

SMALL & BEAUTIFUL

THE smallest Pacific territory administered by France, Wallis and Futuna comprise three major islands and 20 smaller ones. The Polynesian name for Wallis and Futuna is Uvea, meaning consolidation. In total, Uvea has a land area of 274 square kilometres. The islands are situated 340 kilometres east of Samoa and 3000 kilometres south-west of Tahiti. The territory is located midway between Fiji and Samoa. Air Caledonie makes regular stopovers on flights between Noumea and Tahiti. Wallis Island was uninhabited until the late 13th century when Tongan navigators landed. In 1942, Wallis and Futuna became a French colony. In 1959, 95 per cent of the people chose to have the status of T.O.M. (Overseas French Territory). The original population of Futuna came from Samoa.

EASTER ISLAND

THE LIVING MUSEUM

ONE of the most intriguing places on Earth. Known as Rapa Nui by its inhabitants, it has been declared a Cultural Patrimony of Humanity by UNESCO. It is a living museum of a civilisation that left no explanation for the strange stone statues that litter its landscape. The mysteries are numerous. The enigmatic stone faces, called moai, gaze out across the centuries.

Lan Chile makes regular flights from Santiago de Chile and Papeete, Tahiti. The island's airport is Mataveri. Spanish is the local language, with English, French, Italian and German spoken by those who serve the burgeoning tourist industry. The local currency is the Chilean peso. Easter Island is well served with transportation, especially during the tourist season. Explorations of the island should begin at the Rano Raraku volcano, where the moai and the platforms they stand on, called ahu, were originally crafted from the surrounding rock.

Come see the Marshall Islands in Beautiful Micronesia!!

"Pearl of the Pacific"

KIRIBATI VISITOR'S BUREAU

Ministry of Communication, Transport & Tourism Development
PO Box 487, Betio, Tarawa.
Phone: (686) 26003/04 Fax: (686) 26193
Email: tourism@mict.gov.ki

Another time, another pace

We Are Here To Help You!

Our friendly staff at the Vanuatu Tourism Office at Pilioko House are here to answer any questions or problems you have during your stay in Vanuatu. We offer advice, have a large range of leaflets, guides and maps and can help you find accommodation and contacts in most islands of Vanuatu.

Vanuatu Tourism Office

PO Box 209
Pilioko House
Lini Highway, Port Vila
Vanuatu
Tel: (678) 22 515/22 685/22 813
Fax: (678) 23 889
Email: tourism@vanuatu.com.vu
Internet: www.vanuatutourism.com

UNITED STATES
Sue Herrick
VTO Representative USA
245 Mt, Mt Hermon Road
PMB-B, Scotts Valley
CA, 95066 USA
Tel: (831) 335 5238 Fax: (831) 335 5239
Email: shenterprises2@aol.com

AUSTRALIA
Carol Gordon
VTO Representative Australia
4/14 Ewart Street, Dulwich Hill
NSW 2203
AUSTRALIA
Tel: (612) 9558 8011
Email: vtoaustralia@tourism.vu

NEW ZEALAND
Jacquie Carson
VTO Representative NZ
P O Box 17427, Greenlane
Auckland, NZ
Tel: (09) 277 6065
Fax: (09) 277 6065
Email: j.carson@xtra.co.nz

JAPAN
Hiroshi Tomita
South Pacific Tours Japan INC
NKK Building,3F 2-18-2
Nishi-Shinbashi, Minatoku
Email: Hiroshi.Tmt@sptj.co.jp
Tel: 81(03) 5408 7471
Fax: 81(03) 5408 7472

NOUMEA/ EUROPE
Martine Lasnier
P O Box 1163
PORT VILA
VANUATU
Ph: (678) 22 515
Email: martine@vanuatu.com.vu

www.airnewzealand.com

We fly to more Pacific Islands than anyone else.

You've got the pick of the bunch: the Cook Islands, Fiji, Samoa, Tonga, Norfolk Island, Tahiti, New Caledonia and Hawaii. Fly from Los Angeles, London, Australia or New Zealand. To book visit your Air New Zealand Travelcentre or your local travel agent.

AIR NEW ZEALAND

A STAR ALLIANCE MEMBER

Being there is everything.

Colenso0995